Gender, Genre, & Identity in Women's Travel Writing

PETER LANG
New York • Washington, D.C./Baltimore • Bern
Frankfurt am Main • Berlin • Brussels • Vienna • Oxford

Gender, Genre, & Identity in Women's Travel Writing

Kristi Siegel

EDITOR

PETER LANG
New York • Washington, D.C./Baltimore • Bern
Frankfurt am Main • Berlin • Brussels • Vienna • Oxford

Library of Congress Cataloging-in-Publication Data

Gender, genre, and identity in
women's travel writing / edited by Kristi Siegel.
p. cm.
Includes bibliographical references and index.
1. Travelers' writings, English—History and criticism.
2. Women travelers—Great Britain—Biography—History
and criticism. 3. Women travelers—United States—Biography—
History and criticism. 4. English prose literature—Women authors—
History and criticism. 5. American prose literature—Women authors—History
and criticism. 6. Travelers' writings, American—History and criticism.
7. Identity (Psychology) in literature. 8. Sex role in literature.
9. Travel in literature. 10. Literary form. I. Siegel, Kristi.
PR778.T72G46   820.9'32'082—dc22   2003025257
ISBN 0-8204-4905-9

Bibliographic information published by **Die Deutsche Bibliothek**.
Die Deutsche Bibliothek lists this publication in the "Deutsche
Nationalbibliografie"; detailed bibliographic data is available
on the Internet at http://dnb.ddb.de/.

Cover design by Sophie Boorsch Appel

Cover image (*Inscheping te Calais* by James Tissot) reprinted by permission
of Koninklijk Museum Voor Schone Kunsten Antwerpen

The paper in this book meets the guidelines for permanence and durability
of the Committee on Production Guidelines for Book Longevity
of the Council of Library Resources.

✑ Table of Contents

Acknowledgments ix

Introduction

INTERSECTIONS:
WOMEN'S TRAVEL AND THEORY
Kristi Siegel 1

Part One: Gender

Chapter One
THE GAZE OF THE VICTORIAN WOMAN TRAVELER:
SPECTACLES AND PHENOMENA
Ruth Y. Jenkins 15

Chapter Two
LADY MARY MONTAGU AND THE "BOUNDARIES" OF EUROPE
Sukanya Banerjee 31

Chapter Three
WOMEN'S TRAVEL AND THE RHETORIC OF PERIL:
IT IS SUICIDE TO BE ABROAD
Kristi Siegel 55

Chapter Four
THE DAUGHTERS OF THELMA AND LOUISE:
NEW? AESTHETICS OF THE ROAD
Jessica Enevold 73

Chapter Five
WOMEN WRITERS AND THE INTERNAL
COMBUSTION ENGINE: PASSING PENELOPE PITSTOP
Rachel A. Jennings 97

Part Two: Genre

Chapter Six
FRANCES TROLLOPE'S AMERICA AND ANNA
LEONOWENS'S SIAM: QUESTIONABLE TRAVEL AND
PROBLEMATIC WRITING
Chu-Chueh Cheng... 123

Chapter Seven
NANCY PRINCE AND HER GOTHIC ODYSSEY:
A VEILED LADY
Sarah Brusky... 167

Chapter Eight
ZILPHA ELAW'S SERIAL DOMESTICITY:
AN UNSENTIMENTAL JOURNEY
Rosetta R. Haynes... 181

Chapter Nine
WOMEN'S TRAVEL WRITING AND THE POLITICS OF LOCATION:
SOMEWHERE IN-BETWEEN
Heidi Slettedahl Macpherson 193

Chapter Ten
THE PROBLEM OF NARRATIVE AUTHORITY:
CATHERINE ODDIE AND KATE KARKO
Corinne Fowler 209

Part Three: Identity

Chapter Eleven
A PROTESTANT CRITIQUE OF CATHOLICISM: FRANCES CALDERÓN
DE LA BARCA IN NINETEENTH-CENTURY MEXICO
Linda Ledford-Miller.. 225

Chapter Twelve
IDENTITY IN ROSAMOND LAWRENCE'S *INDIAN EMBERS*:
"I CANNOT SOMEHOW FIND MYSELF"
Terri A. Hasseler 235

Chapter Thirteen
AMERICAN NATIONAL IDENTITY ABROAD:
THE TRAVELS OF NANCY PRINCE
Kristin Fitzpatrick 263

Chapter Fourteen
ALEXANDRA DAVID-NÉEL'S HOME IN THE HIMALAYAS:
WHERE THE HEART LIES
Margaret McColley 279

Chapter Fifteen
A FEMINIST LENS FOR BINX BOLLING'S JOURNEY IN
THE MOVIEGOER: TRAVELING TOWARD WHOLENESS
Kathleen Scullin 293

List of Contributors 309

Index.. 313

ℐ Acknowledgments

The issues surrounding women's travel writing are complex and multifaceted; fortunately, the contributors to this volume were more than up to the task. I would like to thank them for the rich and articulate perspectives they brought to this subject. In addition, they lightened this long editing process with their unflagging patience and good will; my gratitude seems inadequate.

The members of the Mount Mary College English department extended ongoing support and collegiality. Sylvia Linton located the book's cover design artwork as well as offering incisive wit and intelligent feedback. Throughout, Dr. Heidi Burns, the Senior Acquisitions' Editor at Peter Lang Publishing, provided excellent insight, advice, and friendship; my gratitude to her is profound. I would also like to thank Bernadette Shade, the Production Supervisor at Peter Lang Publishing, for her prompt and patient responses to my many questions. Finally, the only way I could have completed this book is with the support of my family; my love for my husband, Ron, and my four children, Aaron, Adam, Ross, and Elizabeth, is immeasurable.

In addition, grateful acknowledgments are made to the following for permission to include copyrighted selections:

Lil Red Riding Hood. Copyright 1966 Sony/ATV Songs LLC. All right administered by Sony/ATV Music Publishing 8 Music Sq. W., Nashville, TN 37203. All rights reserved. Used by permission.

For the material from the manuscript letters of Mary Kingsley to Violet Roy, permission is granted by RGS Archives, LBR. MSS., Kingsley, Mary.

Permission is granted by the rights-holder, Trackless Sands Press, for using quotations in excess of 500 words from *Indian Embers*, as indicated in the attached article by Terri Hasseler.

Non-exclusive auotisons à reprodire, à titre gracieux, une citation de 329 mots tirée du livre *Correspondance avec Son Mari* d'Alexandra David-Néel (Plon, 2000), dan votre article intitulé "Alexandra David-Néel's Home in the Himalayas: Where The Heart Lies."

✑ Introduction

Intersections
Women's Travel and Theory

Kristi Siegel

...that feeling comes over me again, the feeling of being too recent and flimsy for the landscape I am in. I try to imagine who I would be if I had lived all my life here at this temple by the river. I wonder what I would want if I had grown up without ads telling me my heart's desires: to be thinner, richer, sexier, look better, smell better, be all that I can be, have a fast car, a brighter smile, lighter hair, whiter whites, hurry now, don't miss out, take advantage of this special offer.
　　　—Jamie Zeppa, *Beyond the Sky and the Earth: A Journey into Bhutan*

Gendered Journeys and Gender Trouble

In the above passage, the imprint of gender is unmistakable. Many women could identify with the list of cultural expectations and sense of frenzy that Jamie Zeppa contrasts to her experience in Bhutan, and many women would not. Gender matters, but it matters in a way that is irreducibly complex. As merely one illustration, gender's imprint is much harder to discern within the lean prose of Beryl Markham's *West with the Night* where she recounts her travel to Africa; in fact, the reader has no clear indication that the author is a woman until page nine, when Markham writes simply, "So far as I know I was the only professional woman pilot in Africa at that time," and then resumes writing about her activities in a nearly genderless fashion.

The essays collected here examine women's travel in terms of the overlapping categories of gender, genre, and identity, but also strive, as Sara Mills might advise, to situate a woman's experience within a specific context (36). Without sufficient attention to determinants such as race, class, location, historical circumstance, and power—to name just a few—any conclusions drawn about women's travel become meaningless. Both Jamie Zeppa and Beryl Markham had the means to travel and to write about it. Like most women travel writers, these women were relatively privileged, and their journeys were voluntary. Consider, then, the vast number of women's journeys that have never been written—journeys of flight, exile, expatriation, homelessness; journeys by women without the means to document their travel; and journeys whose records have been lost or ignored. Boxcar Bertha, who was a hobo in the 1930s, serves as an example of a woman whose travels might never have been noticed. Mary Morris, in *Maiden Voyages: Writings of Women Travelers,* includes an excerpt from Boxcar Bertha's account, but she does not mention the story's background. Bertha describes the "hundreds" of hobo women who flocked to Chicago during the Great Depression: Many of them were "bedraggled, dirty, and hungry. Half of them were ill" (161). However, it is unlikely Boxcar Bertha's narrative—so different from those of most women travel writers—would exist if it had not been "told to" and written down by Ben Reitman, a physician who treated the hobo men and women and frequently traveled with them (Long 80, 149). Bertha's narrative exists not only because Reitman wrote it, but also because Bertha did not. Who would have published Bertha's travel writing? Ben Reitman's name and position legitimized the story and guaranteed its audience.

Clearly, then, in contrast to the many women unable to write or publish their journeys, women travel writers constitute a select group. Similarly, Mary Morris notes that "early women travel writers were women of the upper classes in European society, invariably white and privileged. This trend has not shifted greatly in the past two hundred years....Travel literature by both men and women awaits its full range of multicultural voices and perspectives" (xxi). Given the number of unrecorded journeys, overlooked journeys, as well as the diversity within even an historically "select" group like that of women travel writers, it is not only important to recognize gender's imprint, but also to avoid positing generalizations that serve to erase women's difference.

Gender

Early women travel writers skirted a delicate course. To get an audience, a woman needed to provide material that was reasonably exciting; to keep an audience, she needed to remain a lady. Given that travel—and particularly unescorted travel—was deemed inappropriate for a lady, women often employed a narrative stance that could be described as the decorum of indecorum, a fine balance in which they strained the conventions of femininity, but did not break them. Most early travel writing began with an apology (e.g., for writing in the first person, for engaging in such inappropriate activity, for bothering the reader with their trivial endeavors, and so forth) that, again, affirmed their status as ladies and also served to reassure readers they would not be competing with men.

It would be pleasant to think that western women, often dominated themselves, would bond in sisterhood with women of other cultures, but that was not always the case. As discussed, early women travelers had a lot at stake; they needed to establish some narrative credibility while, at the same time, countering attacks against their femininity prompted by their so-called unnatural and inappropriate behavior. Ruth Y. Jenkins provides a nuanced reading of the tensions and desires contact with non-British women produced in three Victorian women travelers: Amelia Edwards, Lady Florence Dixie, and Lady Lucie Austin Duff Gordon. Jenkins uses cultural criticism, informed by feminist and colonial/postcolonial theories, to tease out the inherent contradictions and ironies produced when the three women travelers train a typically androcentric gaze at non-British women, whom they view as spectacles and phenomena. To establish their difference (and their superiority) from non-British women, Edwards, Dixie, and Gordon work to repress any similarities they see between themselves and these "other" women as well as the discomfort and desires the women's customs—and often greater freedom—elicit.

Lady Mary Montagu, like the three women travelers Jenkins presents, also negotiates a delicate path; although Montagu does find similarities between the women of her culture and some of the non-British women she meets, she packages her findings carefully in order to keep her ladylike status intact. Sukanya Banerjee offers a complex reading of the letters of Lady Mary Montagu, who travels to the Ottoman Empire in the early eighteenth century. As Banerjee notes, Montagu's early writings on the Ottomans provide an alternate view to previous male-authored accounts, and have elicited recent critical attention as a "key text" in discussions of travel and gender, the politics of cross-cultural encounters, women's roles and implication in colonial discourse, and the Orientalist ideologies underlying European narratives of the East. However, Banerjee argues that attention has focused almost exclusively on the "Turkish component" of Lady

Mary's letters rather than viewing them in the larger context of her journeys to Europe, Asia, and Africa. Read against this larger context, Banerjee presents a subtle analysis of Lady Mary's letters, demonstrating how they highlight the porous nature of Europe's real and imagined boundaries.

Although contemporary women may not be burdened with the intricate narrative stance required of early women travel writers, some sense of lingering uniqueness vis-à-vis women's travel remains. In contemporary travel writing, titles such as *The Lonely Other: A Woman Watching America* (Diana Hume George); *Solo: On Her Own Adventures* (Susan Fox Rogers); *Wild Writing Women: Stories of World Travel* (Lisa Alpine, et al.); *A Journey North: One Woman's Story of Hiking the Appalachian Trail* (Adrienne Hall); *Without Reservations: The Travels of an Independent Woman* (Alice Steinbach); and *Without a Guide: Contemporary Women's Travel Adventures* (Katherine Govier) suggest that unescorted travel by women is still considered risky and less common. Kristi Siegel contests some of travels' most basic assumptions, in particular, the recurrent warnings—the "rhetoric of peril"—leveled at women travelers, and particularly women who travel alone. Among the various subtexts embedded in these travel warnings is the long-held fear of women "on the loose," a fear that is apparent in the frequent confusion between issues of mobility and issues of morality. More importantly, Siegel deconstructs the rhetoric embedded in social history, medicine, media, and fairy tales such as "Little Red Riding Hood," to determine precisely *what* travel and *what* women are being addressed and thus culturally valued.

Had a woman succeeded in publishing a road trip narrative at the same time Jack Kerouac did in 1957, it would be hard to envision the book provoking the same response: Kerouac's novel, *On the Road,* quickly became a cult classic and a seminal text in the Beat Movement. Not surprisingly, in Kerouac's road novel, women function as objects of conquest, rather than as mobile subjects. Jessica Enevold demonstrates how *Thelma & Louise* (1991) serves to "re-script" the implicit man/woman binaries in male road buddy narratives. However, as Enevold provocatively asserts, *Thelma & Louise* accomplished more than simply reversing the gender binary. In addition, following—and clearly influenced by—that groundbreaking film, a new generation of women writers emerged who "de-script" road narratives in a way that opens up, renews, and regenders the genre.

Focusing on even more recent women travel writers, Rachel A.

Jennings explores how women have represented themselves in relation to automobiles and the ways women "traveler-writers" negotiate the dominant role of automobile as metal girlfriend/phallic symbol on wheels and the road trip as rite of passage for the adolescent American male. Jennings first discusses the character, Penelope Pitstop (from the Hanna Barbera cartoon, *The Wacky Races*), and then concentrates on "roadlogue" writer Lesley Hazleton as well as other recent writers such as Cameron Tuttle, Jean Lindamood Jennings, and Melanie McGrath.

Genre

Following a course similar to theorizations on women's life writing, some critics have posited that women's travel writing demonstrates unique characteristics: Compared to travel writing by men, it is less directed, less goal-oriented, less imperialistic, and more concerned with people than place.[1] Such sweeping statements, however, are hard to defend. Though gender inevitably affects genre, it is nearly impossible to construct a set of commonalities that would cut across lines of race and class. Nevertheless, like autobiography, women's travel writing might be characterized by its textual turbulence. Undeniably, women, throughout history, often have been relegated to the private sphere. A woman writing an autobiography necessarily occupies the subject position and puts her life on display. Arguably, women travel writers had to be even bolder. In addition to presenting themselves as subjects, in traveling, women literally had to inhabit and negotiate the public sphere.

Despite its challenges, travel writing has proved to be an especially attractive genre for women. The cultural taboos surrounding women's travel frequently ensured their writings would garner an audience and, often, a needed income. For many women, comparisons of home and abroad provided a subtle method of critiquing their own culture. Further, while some women travel writers managed to elude the imperialist tone that so often characterized earlier travel literature; many did not. Whether or not a woman adopted imperialist practices, her role differed from that of a man's. Clearly, the tension between the constraints travel writing posed and the benefits that it promised surface as one of the genre's distinguishing characteristics.

Chu-Chueh Cheng focuses on Frances Trollope and Anna Leonowens, two Victorian travel writers who actively used the genre to gain fame and fortune by writing about their adventures abroad.

Cheng provides a close reading of Trollope's *Domestic Manners of the Americans* and Leonowens's *The English Governess at the Siamese Court* and *The Romance of the Harem*. In reading these three books "against the grain," to use Cheng's expression, Trollope and Leonowens emerge as savvy writers whose distorted depictions of America and Siam (Thailand) help reinforce the Victorian popular imagination of other lands.

In Sarah Brusky's analysis of Nancy Prince, genre is used far differently. Nancy Prince, an African American travel writer, published her book, *Narrative of the Life and Travels, of Mrs. Nancy Prince. In A Black Woman's Odyssey through Russia and Jamaica,* in 1850. As Brusky comments, critics have often argued that Prince's identity never emerges in her work. In contrast, Brusky's insightful analysis uncovers how Prince strategically uses gothic elements throughout her writing to veil and reveal her character.

Women's sentimental writing, like gothic fiction, was another genre popular in the nineteenth century. Rosetta R. Haynes shows how Zilpha Elaw, a nineteenth-century African American itinerant preacher who, in writing her spiritual autobiography, draws upon and revises two strands of women's sentimental writing—the privileging of maternity and the assertion of home as women's proper sphere. Perceptively, Haynes demonstrates how Elaw uses these aspects of women's sentimental writing to empower herself as well as to challenge a public sphere hostile to blacks and a society insistent that women were the property of men.

The terms *fiction* and *nonfiction* imply a clear divide. However, as Heidi Slettedahl Macpherson's lucid argument reveals, in practice these generic distinctions begin to unravel. Fictional travel narratives emulate "reality," and nonfictional travel writing entails a considerable amount of construction and performance. Concentrating on three contemporary writers—Bharati Mukherjee, Marilynne Robinson, and Paule Marshall—Macpherson contends that fictional travel narratives cannot be neatly categorized, but rather fit somewhere "in between" the concept of nonfiction as a mirror of reality and the poststructuralist stance that meaning, in either a fictional or nonfictional context, is endlessly deferred.

Corinne Fowler also focuses on contemporary writers, but shifts the focus back to nonfiction travel narratives. In a tightly argued analysis, Fowler contests a common theorization made about women's travel women: the idea that women's narratives are somehow less imperialistic than their male contemporaries. Using Kate Karko's *Namma: A Tibetan Love Story* (2000) and Catherine Oddie's *Enkop Ai: (My Country) My Life with the Maasai* (1994) as her primary texts, Fowler demonstrates how these travel narratives—as contemporary anthropologists have found with ethnography—remain subject to the genre's colonial undertow.

Identity

In her book, *Repossessing the World: Reading Memoirs by Contemporary Women*, Helen M. Buss draws a distinction between memoir and autobiography that is often true of travel writing as well. As opposed to autobiography, which often encompasses the span of an entire life, Buss contends that memoir typically records the experiences of a limited period of time and thus has a more intense focus (2). Similarly, travel writing generally treats a finite period of time—a few days, a few weeks, a few years—rather than an entire lifetime. Also, possibly prompted by memoir's concentrated focus, the writer often delves through layers of self, and, in a performative way, constructs and reconstructs his/her identity (19–23). Travel writing elicits a similar identity upheaval. Arguably, whether travel writers record the collision of their identity with a new culture or not, travel necessarily brings about change. Travelers might lose their sense of identity altogether or, conversely, find their sense of self sharpened by the journey.

Although travel writers, to some degree, construct their own persona, the process of travel constructs them in return. This interplay is evident in Linda Ledford-Miller's insightful discussion of Frances Calderón de la Barca, a Scottish-born American who accompanied her husband, a Spanish ambassador on a diplomatic mission, to Mexico from 1839 to 1842. In the series of letters that Calderón published upon returning home, she reveals her distaste, and even horror, at the Catholic religious practices she observes in Mexico. In Ledford-Miller's analysis, Calderón's perspective is colored by her Protestant background, her sense of what would constitute social justice for Mexican women, and her own family history. Interestingly, despite the consistently harsh criticism evident in her published letters, five years after returning from Mexico, Calderón converted to Catholicism.

For Rosamond Lawrence, writing in the early twentieth century, travel's impact on identity is pronounced. As Terri A. Hasseler explains, upon arriving in British colonial India in 1914, Lawrence faces a number of daunting roles: wife and "helpmate" to a man who was previously married to her sister; supporter of imperialism; and "burra-memsahib"; a position laden with expectations and intricate codes of conduct. Hasseler describes her reaction as one of estrangement and offers a quote from Lawrence's journal that captures her sense of dissociation nicely: "I cannot somehow find myself." In Hasseler's thoughtful study, the journal serves to document Lawrence's many aborted attempts to find herself and to furnish a vivid record of the social elite that governed India for centuries.

The process of identity construction was undoubtedly even more challenging for Nancy Prince, an early nineteenth-century travel writer. Kristin Fitzpatrick argues that Americans traveling abroad needed to "anchor" their narrative with a clear sense of their identity as Americans. However, if a woman travel writer has a difficult time constructing an authentic self, a black woman faced even greater challenges, for she, as Fitzpatrick notes astutely, must negotiate an allegiance to her oppressors as well as forge an identity in relation to a nation predicated on whiteness. Fitzpatrick traces Prince's path through Russia, Jamaica, and back to the United States and adeptly situates Prince's "identities" historically and politically to reveal how gender, ethnicity, and national identity mesh to form an American national identity.

For many travelers, a sense of identity and place can be achieved only by finding connections between their new surroundings and their memory of home. In contrast, Alexandra David-Néel, an early twentieth-century travel writer, remembers her childhood home as suffocating, inert, and bourgeois. Margaret McColley notes the many times David-Néel, who lives alone in Tibet, punctuates the letters she writes to her husband with the word "home." However, rather than looking for connections to her childhood home, David-Néel seeks precisely the opposite. McColley sums up David Néel's sense of home adroitly: "Home was a place she carried inside of herself, a spiritual place that called for few material accoutrements." In breaking away from the widely accepted nineteenth-century construction of home and domestic life, David-Néel invites her husband to meet her on a purely intellectual level and ultimately achieves the life of peace and simplicity she desired.

Kathleen Scullin's philosophical discussion of a metaphoric journey toward wholeness in the face of a culture determined to privilege the mind over body, serves as an especially appropriate final essay.

There are numerous discussions of the lack of embodiment in women's autobiographies,[2] and the same often applies to women's travel writing. However, without integration of mind and body, whatever journey a person undertakes—literal or metaphoric—will be incomplete. Scullin's intelligent discussion of Binx Bolling's journey in Walker Percy's *The Moviegoer* traces a path toward wholeness mirroring the contention of many feminists that western culture, still permeated by Cartesian principles, distorts our understanding of human existence and sabotages the journey toward human wholeness.

***

A twentieth-century, self-declared "biker babe"; an early nineteenth-century black woman whose travels take her to countries of relative freedom and back again to areas of intense bigotry; an eighteenth-century noblewoman who, in the midst of traveling to other parts of Europe and Asia, writes one of the first accounts of the Ottoman Empire. What do these women and their travels have in common? On the surface, not much. However, each journey bears the unmistakable imprint of gender. On a specific level, the ways that gender affects each of these travels may be examined and theorized; on a broader level, it may be less productive. In a similar manner, gender also shapes genre and identity; the slight contortions, the slight negotiations that women travel writers evinced, and perhaps still demonstrate, are noticeable in distinct, specific ways. The writers here pay careful attention to the intertwining strands of gender, genre, and identity, but give equal accord to the many factors that make each journey unique. A collection—such as this one—that foregrounds women's travel writing, begs the question: Does women's travel (and its writing) fundamentally differ from that of men's? The contributors in this collection answer the question in the only sound way possible—specifically, and at the level of production.

Notes

1   See, for example, Susan Blake's "A Woman's Trek: What Difference Does Gender Make?" *Western Women and Imperialism*, edited by Nupur Chaudhuri and Margaret Strobel, for a discussion of women travel writers' "anti-imperial relationship" (31); Karen R. Lawrence's contention that "women, in general, have tended to mistrust the rhetoric of mastery, conquest, and quest that has funded

a good deal of male fictional and nonfictional travel" (20) in *Penelope Voyages: Women and Travel in the British Literary Tradition*; Mary Morris's discussion of the connectedness and focus on body for female versus male travelers in *Maiden Voyages*, xvii–xviii; or Jane Robinson's comments on the inward focus especially common in women travel writers (xvi–xvii) in the introduction to her book, *Unsuitable for Ladies: An Anthology of Women Travellers*.

2   See, as examples, of the mind/body split evident in women's autobiographical writing, "A Body Among Minds" from *Women's Autobiographies, Culture, Feminism* by Kristi Siegel (37–62); "Autobiography and the Construction of the Feminine Body" by Shirley Neuman; "Mother-Daughter Relationships: Psychodynamics, Politics, and Philosophy" by Jane Flax; or *The Female Body in Western Culture: Contemporary Perspectives*, edited by Susan Rubin Suleiman.

Works Cited

Alpine, Lisa, et al. *Wild Writing Women: Stories of World Travel*. Guilford, CT: Globe Pequot P, 2002.

Blake, Susan. "A Woman's Trek: What Difference Does Gender Make?" *Western Women and Imperialism*. Eds. Nupur Chaudhuri and Margaret Strobel. Bloomington: Indiana UP, 1992. 20–34.

Buss, Helen M. *Repossessing the World: Reading Memoirs by Contemporary Women*. Waterloo, Ontario: Wilfrid Laurier P, 2002.

Flax, Jane. "Mother-Daughter Relationships: Psychodynamics, Politics, and Philosophy." *The Future of Difference*. Eds. Hester Eisenstein and Alice Jardine. Boston: G. K. Hall, 1980. 20–40.

George, Diana Hume. *The Lonely Other: A Woman Watching America*. Urbana: U of Chicago P, 1996.

Govier, Katherine, ed. *Without a Guide: Contemporary Women's Travel Adventures*. St. Paul: Ruminator Books, 1996.

Hall, Adrienne. *A Journey North: One Woman's Story of Hiking the Appalachian Trail*. Boston: Appalachian Mountain Books, 2001.

Karko, Kate. *Namma: A Tibetan Love Story*. London: Hodder and Stoughton, 2000.

Kerouac, Jack. *On the Road*. 1957. New York: Penguin Books, 1999.

Lawrence, Karen R. *Penelope Voyages: Women and Travel in the British Literary Tradition*. Ithaca: Cornell UP, 1994.

Leonowens, Anna. *The English Governess at the Siamese Court*. London: Arthur Barker, 1870.

———. *The Romance of the Harem*. 1873. Ed. Susan Morgan. Charlottesville: UP of Virginia, 1991.

Long, Judy. *Telling Women's Lives: Subject/Narrator/Reader/Text*. New York: New York UP, 1999.

Markham, Beryl. *West with the Night*. 1942. San Francisco: North Point Press, 1983.

Mills, Sara. "Knowledge, Gender, and Empire." *Writing Women and Space: Colonial and Postcolonial Geographies*. Ed. Alison Blunt and Gillian Rose. New York: Guilford P, 1994. 29–50.

Morris, Mary, ed. *Maiden Voyages: Writings of Women Travelers.* New York: Vintage Books, 1993.

Neuman, Shirley. "Autobiography and the Construction of the Feminine Body." *Signature* 2 (Winter 1989): 1–26.

Oddie, Catherine. *Enkop Ai (My Country). My Life with the Maasai.* East Roseville: Simon and Schuster, 1994.

Percy, Walker. *The Moviegoer.* New York: Alfred A. Knopf, 1980.

Prince, Nancy Gardner. *Narrative of the Life and Travels, of Mrs. Nancy Prince. In A Black Woman's Odyssey through Russia and Jamaica.* Ed. Ronald G. Walters. 1850. New York: Markus Wiener Publishing, 1990.

Robinson, Jane. *Unsuitable for Ladies: An Anthology of Women Travellers.* Oxford: Oxford UP, 1994.

Rogers, Susan Fox. *Solo: On Her Own Adventures.* Seattle: Seal P Feminist Publishers, 1996.

Siegel, Kristi. *Women's Autobiographies, Culture, Feminism.* New York: Peter Lang, 1999, 2001.

Steinbach, Alice. *Without Reservations: The Travels of an Independent Woman.* New York: Random House, 2002.

Suleiman, Susan Rubin, ed. *The Female Body in Western Culture: Contemporary Perspectives.* Cambridge and London: Harvard UP, 1986.

Thelma & Louise. Dir. Ridley Scott. Perf. Susan Sarandon and Geena Davis. MGM/UA Studios, 1991.

Trollope, Frances. *Domestic Manners of the Americans.* London: Whittaker, Treacher, 1832.

Zeppa, Jamie. *Beyond the Sky and the Earth: A Journey into Bhutan.* New York: Riverhead Books, 1997.

Part One

Gender

Chapter One

The Gaze of the Victorian Woman Traveler
Spectacles and Phenomena

Ruth Y. Jenkins

The "other" is never outside or beyond us; it emerges forcefully, within cultural discourse, when we think we speak most intimately and indigenously between ourselves.

—Homi Bhabha, *Nation and Narration*

For the Victorian woman traveler, questing for self meant traversing boundaries of cultural propriety as well as negotiating definitions of cultural identity. In their efforts to construct alternative definitions of the Victorian female, many women—traveler or colonial resident—found resources in the land and people that the British Empire defined as "other." The discourses of such women—letters, journals, travelogues, and essays—articulate autobiographical quests and definitions of selves less possible in England. Although limited by cultural constraints, women found participation in sociological expeditions a primary venue to explore the intricate boundaries of culture and self, whether they located their journey in England or abroad, whether they participated in a literal expedition or, as Alison Blunt describes, a "psychological" one (21).

Although traveling had been an integral part of the social agenda for wealthy English society since the mid-eighteenth century, the "Grand European tour" considered essential for a gentleman's education, the phenomenon of the "lady traveler" did not emerge until the nineteenth century. By the end of the century, however, the independent woman traveler was a "more commonplace if eccentric feature of the English bourgeoisie" (Levine xvii). Predominantly middle-class and middle-aged, independent female travelers, Dorothy Middleton writes, claimed "undeniable bravery" from "the hierarchi-

cal assurances lent them by age, social class and a modicum of traditional English superiority" (quoted in Levine 6), as well as the "vantage point of moral high ground" that Annie E. Coombes notes was
implicit in the "colonial gaze" (97). This superiority, supporting and
supported by empire, contributed significantly to women's definitions of self, whether through complicity with the imperial ideals or
through the opportunity found in the distant spaces that such policies
appropriated for British subjects.[1]

Much has been written about colonial discourse—from earlier
studies that problematize Occidental perceptions of the East (Said,
Orientalism) to more recent ones that link constructions of nations and
national identities to narrative productions (Bhabha, *Nation*). In her
groundbreaking *Imperial Eyes*, Mary Louise Pratt specifically analyzes
Victorian discovery rhetoric, arguing that the "male" discourses associated with this rhetoric were not readily available for women writers
(213). Rather, as Sara Mills asserts, women adopted the "imperialist
voice" less easily, tending to "concentrate on descriptions of people as
individuals, rather than on statements about the race as a whole" (3).
Thus, exploring not just geographical boundaries but also territories
of human experience, many women travelers located their "discoveries" in sociological enterprises.

The focus in this essay is on the ironies and tensions that result
when British women encounter other women, regardless of race. In
their travels, Amelia Edwards, Lady Florence Dixie, and Lady Lucie
Austin Duff Gordon all enacted their "inappropriate" desires by appropriating the critical imperial gaze of British culture toward "inexplicable women," toward what Edwards called the "phenomenon"
(*Untrodden* 333). In each of their encounters with female Phenomena—
in Europe, South Africa, and Egypt—these British women faced a mirror of their own desires. Each had distinct parallels with the women
who captured their rapt gaze. All of these phenomena began, from the
British women's perceptions, as desexed objects, unknowable outside
a clearly demarcated understanding of gender and culture; each
displayed a degree of gender transvestism as well as a degree of self-
reliance and self-sufficiency; each existed on the margins of masculine
control; and each enacted some aspect of the British female traveler's
desire for freedom of movement—not just across geographical
domains but also across those of gender. Moreover, most significantly
for the purposes of this essay, each one produced discomfort or
disbelief in the British woman traveler. Specifically, the "spectacles"

of Edwards, Dixie, and Gordon and their spectatorship of their respective phenomena will be explored. In their own quests for self, these women found a connection to another woman, ironically by voicing androcentric interpretations of the eccentric female.

All of the women considered in this article felt the need to present their exploits within socially acceptable patterns of behavior, and many found themselves confronted by the very gender-based issues, such as marriage and decorum, that they sought to escape. With the cultural interdictions against female prodigality, the challenges to social propriety that travel and exploration evoked proved to be significant for definitions and redefinitions of self for women. The "British imperial project," Laura Ciolkowski writes, "pulled together the increasingly divergent interest of women and Nation" at an historical moment when the "ideology of Victorian womanhood was under assault by the 'new Women' who not only were seen as unwomanly but whose professional rather than domestic aspirations also made them seem distinctly un-English" (349). Many women were faced with the twin desires to remain "appropriate" and still enact their "inappropriate" desires. Many felt compelled to masquerade their intentions or deflect criticism by maintaining a rigorous code of propriety. Their quests were routinely couched within socially appropriate behavior—traveling as a colonial wife, recovering from illness, or completing work left unfinished by a man, especially a father. Their journeys were often named "excursions," rather than expeditions, their pilgrimages "endured" for the apparent needs of others, rather than their own.

As women, most female travelers met with resistance in a variety of ways, especially if they ventured forth unchaperoned by a husband or another appropriate male companion. Furthermore, in contrast to their male counterparts, the female travelers evoked a range of pejorative responses to their endeavors: pity, paternalism, even horror—the very responses that Edwards, Dixie, and Gordon would later direct toward other women.

Although not considered at length here, the experiences of Mary Kingsley, possibly the most renowned Victorian women traveler, may serve as a touchstone for the androcentric responses to nontraditional women. Having traveled down the Rembwé to Gaboon, Kingsley recounts being chided by Mr. Hudson, who "did not approve. He had heard of most of my goings on…[and] persisted in his opinion that my intentions and ambitions were suicidal, and took me down the

Woermann Road, the ensuing Sunday, as it were on a string" (*Travels* 351–52). Earlier, Kingsley, as an independent woman traveler, met with not just paternalism but also apprehension. Off the coast of Liberia, Kingsley reported that the ship's "Captain said the truth was he had looked forward with *horror* to having a single lady passenger to take down the Coast," but that after traveling with her, "he did not mind me somehow and was liable to forget my existence" (letter to Violet Roy, emphasis added). The progression of the Captain's response from horror to a virtual *non*response, seen in his ability to "forget [her] existence," reveals not just the cultural assessment of the female traveler but also the difficulty and complexity for that female to define the self. To enact her desires, possibly through unfeminine or culturally inappropriate behavior, is to be named monstrous, horrific, and unnatural as well as to risk the potential elimination of self, to be written out of existence.

Amelia Edwards—suffragette, novelist, journalist, and renowned Egyptologist—evoked similar judgmental responses, even in her travels through the Dolomites of Northern Italy. When their guide took Edwards and her female companion, L, to see the villagers of Caprile, their presence created something of a scene: women "stopped in their work to stare in speechless wonder. The children shouted and ran indoors, as if [the travelers] were goblins" (*Untrodden* 187). Their intentions were questioned, and when the residents learned that Edwards and her companion had come to sketch, the local response to them was that they must be "quite demented" (*Untrodden* 187). As often happened for female travelers, their marital status was also questioned. When Edwards responded that she and her companion were neither sisters nor married, the initial reaction of "surprise" by the residents evolved into "consternation," and the two women were labeled "poverine," poor little things (*Untrodden* 321, 322).

Such experiences suggest that authoring oneself outside of the cultural definitions of appropriate female behavior could prove debilitating. Kingsley insisted that she was a "perfectly ordinary Victorian woman who happened to have traveled to West Africa" (quoted in Frank 219). For her part, Edwards journeyed down the Nile "by accident." "For in simple truth," she maintained, she "had drifted hither...with no excuse of health, or business, or any serious object whatever; and had just taken refuge in Egypt as one might turn aside into the Burlington Arcade or the Passage des Panoramas—to get out of the rain" (*Thousand Miles* 14). Despite their decidedly "unfeminine" exploits, both women contextualized their actions with culturally appropriate explanations and, in this way, demonstrate the manner by which the "ideal" of Victorian womanhood was, as Ciolkowski notes, "most efficiently created" outside of England (338). To distance themselves from the "horror" they in fact embodied, Edwards, Dixie, and Gordon all adopted an androcentric gaze toward women remarkably like themselves; consequently their discourse reveals the complex and complicated space available for women to author themselves, especially for public consumption.

Travel writing, whether formalized travelogues or letters home, proves a particularly rich source by which readers can examine such constructions of both individual and cultural representatives of "self." As a genre, travel writing translates the "other" into "bodyscapes" for consumption (Pratt 64). The "contact zones" that Pratt identifies represent the geographic spaces in which ongoing colonial encounters supply the resources for these translations (6). Rather than consider the panoramic or aestheticized visions that some travel writers create from their experiences in contact zones, I want to analyze internalized contact zones—the subjective frontier in which the encounter is between a potentially authentic self and that constructed within the context of cultural expectation. When another woman mirrors the spectator, the gaze of the spectator is problematic. In the space and articulation of their gazes, these women do more than simply articulate cultural judgments of "inexplicable" women; they interpret and repudiate *both* themselves and the other for public consumption. For Edwards, Dixie, and Gordon, no apparent sororial sympathy with these women is acknowledged; instead, these reflective moments suggest repressed desires, even self-denial—a response that strikingly reenacts that of Kingsley's ship captain, who essentially "eliminates" her.[2] Even if the appropriated androcentric gaze, with its associated judgment of female Phenomena, represents a fabricated subject position to assuage a Victorian reading public suspicious of any "odd" woman, it nonetheless represents a distorted construction of self.

Films, similarly to travelogues, make the absent present, and consequently cinematic theories of the "gaze" may prove useful in understanding Edwards's, Dixie's, and Gordon's responses to other women. To gaze, as opposed to look, exposes a spectator's pleasure derived from a (possibly subconscious) narcissistic identification with the on-screen image and not only provides the spectator (traditionally presumed male) an illusion of control through interpretive agency but also reveals a potential fear of castration that either fetishizes the threatening, dangerous woman or seeks to punish the perceived source of the fear (Hayward 4, 105, 334). Scopophilia, then, results from a "wish to intermingle with likeness and recognition," recalling the mirror stage and the moment of self-recognition that Lacan considers "crucial for the constitution of the ego"; such recognition is implicitly "overlaid with misrecognition" where the image is superior to the self (Mulvey 17–18). The gaze, however, is more complicated for the female spectator because she is conventionally, as Laura Mulvey has argued, the "bearer, not maker of meaning" (15) and therefore "must either identify with the passive, fetishized position of the female character...or if she is to derive pleasure must assume a male position" since only subjects can gaze (Hayward 335).[3]

By definition, travel produces looking-relations with those different from oneself, and such alterity is essential for the construction of subjectivity. The resulting tensions between self and other are necessary, Hennessy and Mohan suggest, to establish the "limits of acceptability—even intelligibility" upon which cultural identities of race, gender, and class depend (466). However, the subject position of the female spectator is especially complicated when she adopts not just the male but also the imperial gaze. In *Looking for the Other*, E. Ann Kaplan explores this intersection of the male and imperial gazes, which she suggests are inseparable in western patriarchal cultures (xi), arguing that in the imperial gaze, anxiety results in a "condescending paternalism" (79). If, as Bhabha has argued, the "construction of the colonial subject in discourse...demands articulation of forms of difference" ("The Other Question" 313), then the female spectator, to be a spectator and not "inexplicable" herself, must differentiate herself from another woman to establish her subject position. Identity is most secure for the traveler or colonizer by establishing and maintaining difference. Although referring to a traveler's desire to distance himself from other travelers, Trinh T. Minh-ha notes that he "maintains his difference by despising others like himself" (quoted in Dubinsky 251). Such "despising others like himself" is central to understanding the complicated constructions of self revealed through the gaze Edwards, Dixie, and Gordon direct toward other women. To gain a voice, to claim agency, women like Dixie, Gordon, and Edwards repress any connection between themselves and similar women because only subjects can speak; that is, one can only know the other as a *subject,* and as a subject one constructs oneself "differently because in relation to this Other" (E. Ann Kaplan 155).

Although such foregrounded difference is evident in much discourse by Victorian women travelers or colonial subjects, their subject positions complicate the articulation of that difference. Writing on British autobiographies produced during the Raj in India, Nancy L. Paxton analyzes how colonial confrontations with colonized people affected the colonizers' "understanding of their own position and agency as speaking subjects" (388). Mervat Hatem provides instances of "how" such encounters affected women's position: she concludes that European women, in their perceptions of Egyptian women, "'project' onto the other what is feared the most in oneself" and thus evade any acknowledgment of their own "powerlessness and gender oppression at home" (37). Kaplan points to the "contradictory position" of white women travelers, "whose subjectivities are caught between objectification in white patriarchy and white privilege in colonialism—between, that is, the male and imperial gazes" (E. Ann Kaplan 15). In her important article "The Other Woman and the Racial Politics of Gender," Sidonie Smith also addresses this contradictory position of white women travelers in colonial space, arguing that this translocation "stimulates and confounds identification, crystallizes and obscures differences, subverts and conserves prevailing ideologies" (431). In short, these women may achieve the agency of the gaze only in the context of the other (E. Ann Kaplan, 81). Consequently, the space of their internalized contact zones, Edwards's, Dixie's, and Gordon's gazes at the other women—gazes that simultaneously and ironically establish their own presence by transforming women similar to themselves into spectacles—reveal the tensions of being subject and object, imperial agent and androcentric horror.

Perhaps the most intriguing examples of this are the references to "inexplicable" women found in the discourse of Edwards, Dixie, and Gordon. Edwards names her inexplicable woman the phenomenon, and she and her party met their phenomenon in Corfara (*Untrodden* 333). Her initial descriptions of this woman desex and dehumanize her, using the third-person pronoun "it" and its derivatives to identify her: "Its hair is sandy; its complexion crimson; its age anything between forty-five and sixty. It carries a knapsack on its back, and an alpenstock in its hand" (334). When any kind of sex or gender distinction is made, the first designation makes her decidedly unfeminine, describing her as having "the voice of a man" (334); her face, "tanned and travel-stained," however, "is the face of a woman" (334). The woman's ability to communicate, to participate in symbolic discourse, is questioned: "She is babbling German—apparently describing her day's tramp across the mountains—and seems highly gratified by the peals of laughter which occasionally interrupt her narrative" (*Untrodden* 334). This disruption of narrative, the eruption of what Kristeva names the semiotic into the symbolic, places this woman on the margins of culture, locating her as hysteric (*Desire* 6). Because the semiotic must be suppressed to realize symbolic conventions, it becomes, by definition, marginal to the dominant language system, so any discourse that allows the semiotic to erupt, then, defies the conventional rules that would suppress it. This suppression of the semiotic becomes particularly significant in understanding Edwards's gaze at her inexplicable woman. By locating this other woman outside symbolic discourse, Edwards distances herself and her actions from those of this eccentric other and positions herself in the symbolic; that is, Edwards authors herself as subject, ironically, by judging female behavior (in which she also participates) as unconventional.

Distinctly echoing the earlier experiences of Edwards and her traveling companion identified only as L, this phenomenon, this similar female traveler, balks at the question of her needing a male guide:

> "A guide?" she exclaims, replying to an observation of some by-stander. "Not I! What do I want with a guide? I have carried my own knapsack and found my own way through France, through England, through Italy, through Palestine. I have never taken a guide, and I have never wanted one. You are all lazy fellows, and I will have nothing to do with you. Fatigue is nothing to me—distance is nothing to me—danger is nothing to me. I have been taken by brigands before now. What of that? If I had had a guide with me, would he have fought them? Not a bit of it! He would have run away. Well, I neither fought nor ran away. I made friends of my brigands—I painted all their portraits—I spent a month with them; and we parted, the best comrades in the world. Ugh! guide, indeed! All very well for incapables, but not for me. I am afraid of nothing—neither of the Pope nor the Devil!" (*Untrodden* 334)

Defying expected masculine (to fight) or feminine (to flee) responses to her encounter with the brigands, this phenomenon chooses to create an alternative model of human interaction. Rather than enact the gender-specific responses, she "made friends" and "painted their portraits," redefining them from threat to companions. Similarly to Edwards, this phenomenon travels, sketches, and wants to be free of the fetters of social propriety.

Despite these affinities, Edwards and her companion are "Somewhat startled by this tremendous peroration" and report to the reader their relief that this woman can be contained, labeled, explained: "I had never experienced a more lively sense of gratification and relief than when I presently learn that this lady is a German. She is no stranger, it seems at Corfara, but appears every now and then in this *mad* fashion, sometimes putting up at the Rottenaras for several weeks together. *She paints, she botanises, and I think they said she writes*" (*Untrodden* 335, emphasis added). In short, although more extreme, she is a mirror of Edwards, but Edwards finds that reflection startling, even disturbing. Edwards's perception of herself differs distinctly from how she perceives the phenomenon, despite the unequivocal similarities. Confronted by a glimpse of how others might read her own behavior, Edwards, ironically, mirrors the response of her dominant culture. Although the natives had found Edwards and L also "quite demented," Edwards either fails to see the parallel or chooses not to record that recognition in this public record. What does this blind spot mean about Edwards's perceptions of self? How much does it reveal a conflict between enacting her desires and maintaining a modicum of respectability and British gender roles? Was it simply too frightening to recognize the cost of such choices, either to risk horrific disdain or, as Kingsley experienced, to face the possibility of "nonexistence?" Alternatively, might it simply be too frightening to sever one's ties to culture when female definitions of self traditionally develop from connections with others? Reexamining patterns of male and female moral development in *In a Different Voice*, Carol Gilligan describes distinct developmental paradigms that result from either a perspective of separate (male) or connected (female) object relations (167). In this paradigm, separation proves threatening for women, so, possibly, it is less psychologically disruptive to mimic the cultural response to the nontraditional woman than to identify oneself with this female Phenomenon—even with the resulting subjective dissonance. The connection to culture appears to be more significant for the construction of Edwards's identity than any connection that might be established through identification with another, non-British woman with whom she might have much in common. However, where Gilligan's study reveals a triangularization of doubled identity and connection that results for the young female with both her mother and father, with both another who is similar (as female) and another who is dissimilar (as male), Edwards resists such a double-consciousness by denying a connection with the "similar" (as inexplicable woman herself) and instead identifying with the position of the "dissimilar" (as female appropriating a male gaze). Ironically, then, Edwards shapes a discourse of her experiences by denying who she is; she constructs her story by adopting a "self-destructive" subject position.

Similarly, Florence Dixie—journalist and activist for the Irish, animals, and women (Blake 19)—met with her phenomenon in South Africa. Dixie and her husband journeyed to South Africa, in part, to help alleviate the suffering of soldiers wounded in the recent Boer War and, in part, to substitute for their postponed excursion across the Bering Straits (Dixie 1–2). During their journey from Bethlehem to Windbur, Dixie and her husband stop at a house to rest their horses and observe a woman sprawled across a sofa "rolling about and groaning in the most distressing manner" (226). Although they try to sneak back out of the home, the woman calls, stopping them, and

> for the next hour or so she raved and talked away about deeds she had done, how she had shot Zulus down during the Zulu War, and Kaffirs down during the Kaffir War, and how she would do it again if she only got the chance. Then she began to cry, and to complain of fearful pains in the head, which last statement made me fairly believe that we had got into the abode of a raving maniac. (Dixie 266)

Here again is a woman unrestrained by gender expectations: She has fought Zulus and Kaffirs; she groans and cries. Her behavior, like that of Edwards's phenomenon, locates her at the margins of her culture. Furthermore, comparable to the phenomenon, this marginal position—contained by neither traditionally masculine nor traditionally feminine behavior, voiced both in symbolic and semiotic utterances—foregrounds that marginality. Later in their excursion, when Dixie and her husband temporarily suspend their traveling to allow a sick horse to die, the Boer family at whose farm they wait witnesses Dixie's unrestrained reaction to watching her husband forced to drink tea: She "fairly laughed outright, which at once drew upon me the astonished glances of Frau and family, who doubtless thought that they had unwittingly admitted a raving lunatic into their house" (Dixie 298). Dixie perceives her behavior through the eyes of the Boer family, specifically the mother, as that of a "raving lunatic," an appellation that distinctly echoes her own judgment of the earlier woman. Whether consciously or not, Dixie suggests parallels between herself and a woman who defies cultural definitions for women.

Raised in English intellectual and literary circles, Lucie Gordon traveled to Egypt in 1862 after contracting tuberculosis and there meets her inexplicable women.[4] For Gordon, an encounter with "an eccentric Bedawee young lady...eighteen or twenty at most," functions like Edwards's and Dixie's Phenomena and provides an opportunity for cultural comparison (110). Like Edwards's example, she is "dressed like a young man," but this young Bedawee is also "feminine and rather pretty, except that one eye was blind" (110). Gordon continues that her "dress was handsome, and she had women's jewels, diamonds...a European watch and chain" (110). After considering her appearance, Gordon considers her "manner," which she describes as "excellent, quite *ungenirt* (sic) [unabashed], and not the least impudent or swaggering, and I was told—indeed, I could hear—that her language was beautiful, a thing much esteemed among Arabs" (110). In lieu of her appearance or emotional state, it is this woman's unchaperoned freedom of movement that causes the surprise and doubt as to her propriety. The young woman's behavior is soon explained to Gordon, who, in turn, tells her reader:

> She is a virgin and fond of travelling and of men's society, being very clever, so she has her dromedary and goes about quite alone. No one seemed surprised, no one stared, and when I asked if it was *proper*, our captain was surprised. "Why not? If she does not wish to marry, she can go alone; if she does, she can marry—what harm? She is a virgin and free."
> (110)

Rather than have her virginal state be the reason for her to be chaperoned, to restrict her movement, it is a license for freedom. In contrast to Gordon's (and Edwards's and Dixie's) culture, this Arab community understands the young woman outside of androcentric boundaries. For Gordon, once a woman in an Arab culture connects herself with a man, defines herself against him, she becomes his possession—literally or metaphorically—and, consequently, there would then exist a reason to sequester or protect her. Gordon's concern with the propriety of this young woman may in fact betray her own conflict with propriety; as Hatem notes, Gordon lived in "considerable anxiety and fear of being discovered in an illicit affair [with a younger Egyptian man] by both European and Egyptian patriarchies" (54).

Each of these encounters by Edwards, Dixie, and Gordon with female Phenomena—in Europe, South Africa, and Egypt—reflects women faced with a mirror to their own desires through their rapt gaze. The internalized contact zone that results reveals conflicts within these British women about their own identity and place in their culture. The exploits and accomplishments of these Phenomena represented a degree of self-reliance and self-sufficiency worthy of note, if not respect: defending oneself from roving bandits, fighting Zulus and Kaffirs, or merely commanding admiration as a solitary traveler. Each one existed on the margins of masculine control—whether because they were simply "eccentric" or virginal—and remained unmarked by that control. Each one enacted some aspect of the British female's desire for freedom of movement or lifestyle—not just across geographical domains but also across those of gender. Moreover, each one produced a reaction of discomfort or disbelief from Edwards, Dixie, or Gordon, suggesting a problem with such potential recognitions of self as well as with their own responses to these women.

Desexed, at times dehumanized, and apparently unknowable outside a clearly demarcated understanding of gender and culture, these "other" women represented the potential horror and inexplicability of the experiences of Edwards, Dixie, and Gordon. Dressed male, each phenomenon, when recognized as female, produced a visual conflict as well as tension of identity in the British women. In "Film and the Masquerade," Mary Ann Doane analyzes the oscillation between masculine and feminine perspectives, noting that for the female spectator, the self (as another female) is also the image of the gaze; for the female gazing at another woman, to look "demands a becoming" and risks the collapse of spatial (or even subjective) distance (231). In the context of their gaze at the other women (and the spectator's pleasure from narcissistic identification) and their inability to recognize themselves in their human mirrors, the transvestism of the spectacles was particularly significant in understanding the British women's responses. The British women, adopting the male and imperial gazes, neither recognized themselves nor gained pleasure from these similarly transformed women.[5] Edwards, Dixie, and Gordon neither essentialized the other women into sexual or childish objects nor elevated them for sororial association. Instead, their descriptions sound strikingly like self-portraits informed by culturally complicit constructions of themselves and suggest the "double-voiced" (if not double-consciousness) quality found in much nineteenth-century women's travel writing, which both reinforces androcentric definitions of the feminine and undermines such definitions (Mills 44). Although writing specifically about Mary Kingsley,

Stevenson explains that such "conflicting voices express not only...complex, conflicting personal needs but also [a] sense of the punitive expectations of the readers of travel books" (142). Caren Kaplan describes such texts as "outlaw genres" that represent not just "individual authorship" but also a "discourse of situation" and "location" (119). Primarily by "rewriting the Other" in the trope of travel, imperial travelers can, Simon Gikandi writes, "understand themselves and their condition of possibility" (51).

For Edwards, Dixie, and Gordon, the simultaneous attraction and aversion to the "Phenomena" revealed not just the extent to which cultural values of women and non-Anglos saturated their perceptions of others but also the conflicts within their own perceptions of self. Kristeva writes that "only a thorough investigation of our remarkable relationship with both the *other* and *strangeness within ourselves* can lead people to give up hunting for the scapegoat outside their group" (*Nations* 50–51). It is possible that within this context these British women travelers see, if only subconsciously, the phenomenon as themselves, their scopophilia revealing some degree of narcissistic identification even if unacknowledged. In their own quests for self, these women established their own agency, ironically, by voicing the androcentric interpretations of the eccentric female. To acknowledge the inexplicable woman as odd, even hysterical, may have nonetheless transformed their own potential "nonexistence" into existence, to make what their culture had made absent, present. Female Victorian travel writers should not be essentialized by suggesting a uniform response to their experiences. In fact, these women travelers did more than simply embark upon geographical treks; they journeyed on sociological expeditions—to see the self in the other, to see the other in themselves—both located on the margins of cultural borders.

Notes

1   Such complicity, Antoinette M. Burton argues, should not be surprising, given the number of premises that "liberal, bourgeois feminism in Britain" shared with imperialism: ideas of moral superiority and responsibility as well as racial purity and motherhood (138–39).

2   This elimination of self has distinct echoes to the anxiety of authorship that Sandra M. Gilbert and Susan Gubar have identified for many nineteenth-century female authors, but I would suggest that this threat transcends literary productions to also include constructions of self.

3   Laura Mulvey's ideas in *Visual and Other Pleasures*, although eliciting extensive

debate, have been crucial for subsequent scholarship that problematizes and complicates the subjectivity of the female spectator.

4   See Mervat Hatem's essay "Through Each Other's Eyes" for an expanded analysis of Gordon's response to Egyptian women, especially 47.

5   In "The Other Woman and the Racial Politics of Gender," Sidonie Smith provides an important analysis of Beryl Markham's and Isak Dinesen's varying responses to African women, differentiating their respective distancing (414) and identification (426). Analyzing Beryl Markham's tendency to marginalize African women in her narratives, Smith suggests that such

> autobiographical transvestism...reaffirm[s] a colonizing poetics, that romanticized troping of the mythic adventure story that promotes generic stability, dependent upon the literal and discursive marginalization of the African other, particularly the other woman. To acknowledge the other (woman, African) would be to contaminate "the white continent" of Western subjectivity and its autobiographical practices. (421–22)

Works Cited

Bhabha, Homi. "The Other Question: The Stereotype and Colonial Discourse." *The Sexual Subject: A "Screen" Reader in Sexuality*. London: Routledge, 1992. 312–31.

————. ed. *Nation and Narration*. London: Routledge, 1993.

Blake, Susan L. "A Woman's Trek: What Difference Does Gender Make?" *Western Women and Imperialism: Complicity and Resistance*. Ed. Nupur Chaudhuri and Margaret Strobel. Bloomington: Indiana UP, 1992. 19–34.

Blunt, Alison. *Travel, Gender, and Imperialism: Mary Kingsley and West Africa*. New York: The Guilford Press, 1994.

Burton, Antoinette M. "The White Woman's Burden: British Feminists and the Indian Woman, 1865–1915." *Western Women and Imperialism: Complicity and Resistance*. Ed. Nupur Chaudhuri and Margaret Strobel. Bloomington: Indiana UP, 1992. 137–57.

Ciolkowski, Laura E. "Travelers' Tales, Empire, Victorian Travel, and the Spectacle of English Womanhood in Mary Kingsley's *Travels in West Africa*." *Victorian Literature and Culture* 26.2 (1998): 337–66.

Coombes, Annie E. "The Recalcitrant Object: Culture, Contact and the Question of Hybridity." *Colonial Discourse/Postcolonial Theory*. Ed. Francis Barker, Peter Hulme, and Margaret Iversen. Manchester: Manchester UP, 1994. 89–114.

Dixie, Lady Florence. *In the Land of Misfortune*. London: Richard Bentley and Son, 1882.

Doane, Mary Ann. "Film and the Masquerade: Theorizing the Female Spectator." *The Sexual Subject: A "Screen" Reader in Sexuality*. London: Routledge, 1992. 227–43.

Dubinsky, Karen. "Vacations in the 'Contact Zone': Race, Gender, and the Traveler at Niagara Falls." *Nation, Empire, Colony: Historicizing Gender and Race*. Ed. Ruth Roach Pierson and Nupur Chaudhuri. Bloomington: Indiana UP, 1998. 251–69.

Edwards, Amelia. *A Thousand Miles Up the Nile*. New York: H. M. Caldwell Co., 1877.

————. *Untrodden Peaks and Unfrequented Valleys: A Midsummer Ramble in the Dolomites*. 1873. "Introduction" by Philippa Levine. Boston: Beacon Press, 1987.

Frank, Katherine. *A Voyager Out: The Life of Mary Kingsley*. Boston: Houghton Mifflin Company, 1986.

Gikandi, Simon. "Englishness, Travel, and Theory: Writing and the West Indies in the Nineteenth Century." *Nineteenth-Century Contexts: An Interdisciplinary Journal*. (Special Issue: Colonialisms) 18.1 (1994): 49–70.

Gilbert, Sandra M., and Susan Gubar. *The Madwoman in the Attic: The Woman Writer and the Nineteenth-Century Literary Imagination*. New Haven: Yale UP, 1979.

Gilligan, Carol. *In a Different Voice: Psychological Theory and Women's Development*. Cambridge: Harvard UP, 1982.

Gordon, Lady Lucie Austin Duff. *Letters From Egypt (1862–1869)*. London: Routledge and Kegan Paul, 1969.

Hatem, Mervat. "Through Each Other's Eyes: The Impact on the Colonial Encounter of the Images of Egyptian, Levantine-Egyptian, and European Women, 1862–1920." *Western Women and Imperialism: Complicity and Resistance*. Ed. Nupur Chaudhuri and Margaret Strobel. Bloomington: Indiana UP, 1992. 35–58.

Hayward, Susan. *Key Concepts in Cinema Studies*. London: Routledge, 1996.

Hennessy, Rosemary, and Rajeswari Mohan. "The Construction of Woman in Three Popular Texts of Empire: Towards a Critique of Materialist Feminism." *Colonial Discourse and Post-Colonial Theory*. Ed. Patrick Williams and Laura Chrisman. New York: Columbia UP, 1994. 462–79.

Kaplan, Caren. "Resisting Autobiography: Out-Law Genres and Transnational Feminist Subjects." *De/Colonizing the Subject: The Politics of Gender in Women's Autobiography*. Ed. Sidonie Smith and Julia Watson. Minneapolis: U of Minnesota P, 1992. 115–38.

Kaplan, E. Ann. *Looking for the Other: Feminism, Film, and the Imperial Gaze*. New York: Routledge, 1997.

Kingsley, Mary. *Travels in West Africa*. 1897. 3rd ed. London: Frank Cass & Co. Ltd., 1965.

————. Letter to Violet Roy (17-8-[18]93). Royal Geographical Society ms. London.

Kristeva, Julia. *Desire in Language: A Semiotic Approach to Literature and Art*. Trans. Thomas Gora, Alice Jardine, and Leon Roudiez. Ed. Leon S. Roudiez. New York: Columbia UP, 1980.

————. *Nations without Nationalisms*. Trans. Leon Roudiez. New York: Columbia UP, 1993.

Levine, Philippa. "Introduction." *Untrodden Peaks and Unfrequented Valleys: A Midsummer Ramble in the Dolomites*. By Amelia Edwards. Boston: Beacon Press, 1987.

Mills, Sara. *Discourses of Difference: An Analysis of Women's Travel Writing and Colonialism*. London and New York: Routledge, 1991.

Mulvey, Laura. *Visual and Other Pleasures*. Bloomington: Indiana UP, 1989.

Paxton, Nancy L. "Disembodied Subjects: English Women's Autobiography under the Raj." *De/Colonizing the Subject: The Politics of Gender in Women's Autobiography*. Ed. Sidonie Smith and Julia Watson. Minneapolis: U of Minnesota P, 1992. 387–409.

Pratt, Mary Louise. *Imperial Eyes: Travel Writing and Transculturation*. London: Routledge, 1992.

Said, Edward. *Orientalism*. New York: Vintage Books, 1979.

Smith, Sidonie. "The Other Woman and the Racial Politics of Gender: Isak Dinesen and Beryl Markham in Kenya." *De/Colonizing the Subject: The Politics of Gender in Women's Autobiography*. Ed. Sidonie Smith and Julia Watson. Minneapolis: U of Minnesota P, 1992. 410–35.

Stevenson, Catherine Barnes. *Victorian Women Travel Writers in Africa*. Boston: Twayne Publishers, 1982.

Lady Mary Montagu and the "Boundaries" of Europe

Sukanya Banerjee

The letters written by Lady Mary Montagu during her sojourn in the Ottoman Empire (1716–1718) mark a critical turning point in the genre of female travel writing. As Billie Melman contends, they not only present the "first example of a secular account, by a woman, on the Muslim Orient," but by challenging previous male-authored narratives on the Ottomans, they constitute "the cornerstone in the new, alternative discourse that developed in the West on the Middle East" (78). Accompanying her husband, Edward Wortley, who had been appointed ambassador to the Ottoman Porte, Lady Mary traveled across Europe to Turkey, where, privileged on account of both her class and gender, she enjoyed access to women's quarters forbidden to male travelers. Such an opportunity not only allowed her to question previous male accounts of the Ottoman Empire, but also helped reformulate the underlying precepts of travel discourse: As she wrote from Adrianople to her sister, Lady Mar, "Thus you see dear Sister, the manners of Mankind doe not differ so widely as our voyage Writers would make us believe [sic]" (April 1, 1717; Montagu 329–30). If Montagu's letters created a stir during the time of their posthumous publication in 1763, they have emerged, not surprisingly, as a key text in our own present moment in discussions of issues relating, among other things, to the gendering of travel narratives, the implication of women's roles in colonial discourse, and the Orientalist ideologies underlying European narratives of the East.

Read in these contexts, Lady Mary's letters have been hailed for their remarkable undermining of the paradigmatic and evaluative differences between Europe and the Orient. While Mary Jo Kietzman suggests that Lady Mary's *Letters* narrate a radically "decentring experience" (537) that overturns seemingly settled distinctions between

"colonizing subject and objectified Other" to "foster a productive relativism" (538), Lisa Lowe perceptively points out how "the competing
narratives of culture, class, and gender in Montagu's *Turkish Embassy
Letters* serve as one example of the variety of representational forces
that may complicate a particular orientalist situation" (34). Indeed,
Lady Mary's descriptions of the lives of upper-class Turkish women,
detailing their relative economic and sexual independence as well as
the opportunities provided to them for establishing bonds of female
solidarity, not only subvert received notions of the subjugation of Ottoman women, but also question the supposed superior status of
women in eighteenth-century England. However, while Lady Mary's
narrative has been read as marking an ethnographic shift in narrating
the cultural encounter between Europe and the Orient, it is interesting
that the critical commentary on her letters has not sufficiently examined the reference points of this encounter: Turkey's emblematization
as "Oriental" seems to have been taken for granted. This is, of course,
not to engage in any "Orientalist gate-keeping" by suggesting that
any particular site is innately more "Oriental" than the other. In fact,
Edward Said's premise in *Orientalism* famously foregrounds precisely
the "imaginative geography" (55) that "Orientalize[s]" the Orient (67).
However, if the contouring of the Orient (or Turkey as "Oriental") is
more a matter of discursive construction, then it is worthwhile to reflect upon how Turkey, occupying an intermediary position between
Europe and Asia, between Christianity and Islam, has been "Orientalized" in the critical imaginary. Contrary to much of the commentary
on Lady Mary's letters that seem to accept the geopolitical paradigms
of Europe and its "other" (in this case, Turkey), even as they seek to
prove how the letters destabilize them, this essay presents a reading
of Lady Mary's *Letters* that emphasizes the cultural and gender politics complicating the implicit assumptions of such a framework. Arguing not so much for the letters' disruption of the East/West divide
as for their contesting of the very terms of that divide, the essay suggests that Lady Mary's letters exceed the epistemological logic distinguishing Europe from its "other" by their foregrounding of the
contingent nature of Europe's boundaries, as well as its highly contiguous (and hence ambiguous) relationship with Turkey.[1]

While the collection of fifty-two letters written during the tenure
of the embassy at Constantinople comprises an autonomous set published on its own, it is significant that the published letters appeared
originally under the following title:

Letters of the Right Honourable Lady M___ y W_____y M_____e:
Written during her Travels in Europe, Asia and Africa, To Persons of Dis-
tinction, Men of Letters, & c. in different Parts of Europe. Which Contain,
Among other Curious Relations, Accounts of the Policy and Manners of
the Turks; Drawn from Sources that have been inaccessible to other
Travellers.

While the original title draws attention to the novelty of the "Turkish
component" of her letters, it also situates it within the expanded scope
of Lady Mary's travels in Europe, Asia, and Africa, rather than com-
pressing it into the singularly polarized cultural interchange as suggested by the abbreviated, though more manageable, title, "Turkish
Embassy Letters." Although this shortened title, one preferred by recent commentators for obvious reasons,[2] is accurate inasmuch as it
refers to the letters penned during Wortley's assignment as ambassador to Turkey, it also seems to have directed critical focus to primarily
those letters written from within the Ottoman Empire. Relatively little
attention has been paid to Lady Mary's letters written while traveling
through the Continent, though they comprise the same collection; the
references to these letters seem incidental and are treated as but a
prelude to the "Turkish" letters, which are generally read in isolation
from their "European" counterparts. The surprising imbalance in the
reading of the letters proves counterproductive, for it repudiates what
critics have found most notable about the content of the letters,
namely their undermining of an apparently self-evident demarcation
between a Christianized Europe and the Ottoman Empire. As Lowe
notes, for instance, "[Montagu's] rhetoric of similitude directly con-
tradicts the logic of difference that characterizes the observations of
the male travel writers," who foregrounded a "construction of the
Orient as 'different'" (45).[3] To concentrate on the "Turkish" letters too
exclusively, then, runs the risk of implicitly redrawing those boundaries that Montagu's letters have been lauded for dismantling.

Redirecting attention to the letters in their entirety, though, actually raises
the question of boundaries, but from a more reflexive angle. At what point
do the letters register, if at all, a "crossing over" to the supposedly strange
and unfamiliar world of the Ottomans? Upon arriving at Adrianople, "the
first European seat of the Turkish empire" (353–54) Lady Mary remarks, "I
am now got into a new World where every thing I see appears to me a
change of Scene" (to Lady ___, April 1, 1717; 312). However, the narration
of her experiences on the fringes of Eastern Europe belies the novelty and
distinctiveness of the Ottoman Empire, as implied by the above statement.
Her letters from Hungary, in fact, highlight the porousness of Europe's

borders, detailing its continual engagement with the Turks, an encounter which had left its imprint on the landscape. "Nothing can be more melancholy," she writes, "than travelling through Hungary, refflecting [sic] on the former flourishing state of that Kingdom and seeing such a noble spot of Earth allmost [sic] uninhabited" (to Lady Mar, January 30, 1717; 298). In describing the desolate landscape, however, Lady Mary refrains from invoking familiar images of Christian lands being attacked by Turkish invaders; in fact, she counteracts such notions by explaining how the land had been impoverished not only "by the long war between the Turks and Emperour," but by the "more cruel civil War occasion'd by the barbarous persecution of the Protestant Religion by the Emperour Leopold," whom she describes as being "more cruel and treacherous to his poor Hungarian subjects than ever the Turk has been to the Christians" (299).

In narrating the alternating custodianship of the Hungarian provinces that had long witnessed ongoing skirmishes between Turkish power and German, Austrian, and Hungarian forces, Lady Mary describes Hungary more in terms of its liminality and unfamiliarity. Describing the towns which "look very odd," the peasants, whose dress is "very primitive, being only a plain sheep's skin without other dressing," and the terrain they passed through that was "very dangerous from the vast quantity of wolves that herd in them" (301–02), she experiences a breakdown of referential frameworks when describing the Emperor's troops accompanying them on their way to Belgrade. The German and "Rascian" soldiers, "who are very numerous all over Hungary," seem alien to her, appearing more as "Vagabond Gypsies or stout beggars than regular Troops" (to Alexander Pope, February 12, 1717; 304). Puzzled by "this race of Creatures," who have a "Patriarch of their own at Grand Cairo" but are "realy [sic] of the Greek Church," Lady Mary is intrigued by the fact that they "let their Hair and beards grow inviolate," and can best describe their appearance as those of "Indian Bramins [sic]" (304). Her sense of wonder is so piqued in Hungary that she almost seems to be addressing herself when she writes to her sister, "Hungary being a part of the World that I beleive [sic] quite new to you, I thought you might read with some pleasure an Account of it" (303). In light of Lady Mary's descriptions of Hungary, and the fact that during her journey to Turkey she traverses across Austro-Hungarian provinces which still bore the remnants of Turkish sieges (Hungary in fact was still fortified by Turkish garrisons), one could very well ask, at what point can "Europe" be even seen to end, and Turkey, emblematized as the signifier of "Oriental difference," begin?

The thrust of such a question lies in foregrounding the historical contingencies of a geography of difference. If Eastern Europe is represented through a lens of unfamiliarity, then it is important not only to question the implications of that particular lens, but also to question how in the critical commentary of Lady Mary's letters, the idea of "difference" gets transposed more onto Turkey instead. Such a transposition overlooks the anxieties undergirding the construction of "Europe," one that was by no means settled or unitary. In fact, as Larry Wolff remarks, the intellectual processes of the Enlightenment had "invented" an "Eastern Europe" in terms of its remoteness and anteriority such that "Western Europe and Eastern Europe together, as complementary concepts defin[ed] each other by opposition and adjacency" (5). If the "invention of Eastern Europe" was an "intellectual project of demi-Orientalization" (Wolff 7), then a reading of Lady Mary's letters should be accompanied by a reflexive consciousness about the discursive nature of "Europe" itself. Such a consciousness not only foregrounds Turkey's uncertain relationship with(in) Europe, but helps understand better Lady Mary's nuanced depiction of it.

Lady Mary constitutes Turkey through a remapping of Europe that exceeds the logic of similitude (or difference). Such an imaginative remapping assumes significance, for it runs contrary to the hegemonic influence of eighteenth-century principles of Enlightenment cartography, whose depiction of the Ottoman Empire was informed by a "specific political agenda of driving the Turks out of Europe" (Wolff 149). Lady Mary's innovative cultural cartography, one foregrounding Turkey's more nuanced (and continuous) relationship with Europe, is impelled by her position as a female English subject. While it has been pointed out that her encounters with Turkey mark a cultural decentering in which she runs the risk of forfeiting her "Englishness," the opposite rings true as well: Lady Mary's letters offer her an opportunity to refashion both an "Englishness," as well her own identification with it.[4] Both these processes are marked by her gendered position and perspective that render a reconstellated Europe (and "Englishness"), thus yielding therefore a "feminized geography" that Gillian Rose describes as one "acknowledg[ing] women as social subjects" (3). Such a geography, however, is not isolated from the implicit claims and presumptions of a masculinist cartographic imaginary; rather, it is situated in constant negotiation with its implications.

That she very self-consciously presents herself as a female traveler, one perhaps more suited to the rigors of journeying than her male counterparts, is evident from the very first letter Lady Mary writes from Rotterdam describing the crossing of the Channel: "I never saw a Man more frighted than the Captain. For my part I have been so lucky neither to suffer from Fear or sea sickness" (to Lady Mar, August 3, 1716; 249). Writing to a friend a few days later, she begins the letter by noting, "I make haste to tell you, dear Madam, that after all the dreadfull fatigues you threaten'd me with, I am hitherto very well pleas'd with my journey" (to Jane Smith, August 5, 1716; 250). Her self-fashioning as a somewhat intrepid traveler signals an anxiety to eliminate doubts regarding her capability to undertake a challenging endeavor marked, thus far, primarily as masculine. After all, her sister and friends had tried to dissuade her from embarking on this particular venture, and while departing England, Lady Mary is reported to have been attired, interestingly enough, in a masculine riding habit and a "black full-bottomed wig: a huge, elaborate, expensive, and exclusively male item of dress" (Grundy 117). However, if in England Lady Mary can assume the role of a traveler only by obfuscating her gender identity, the narrative space of her letters written away from England explicitly allows her to draw attention to herself as a female traveler. Furthermore, in etching her identity as a female traveler, Lady Mary is also careful to avoid what she perceives to be the common foibles of the genre of travel writing: a lack of credibility. Her letters, in fact, are replete with oblique references to the narrative liberties exercised by male travel writers, and very early on she proclaims, "but upon my word I have not yet made use of the privilege of a Traveller, and my whole account is writ with the same plain Sincerity of Heart" (to Lady Bristol, August 22, 1716; 256). Although she protests her veracity, Lady Mary's earnestness in carving a niche for herself in contradistinction to male writers alerts one to the ideological imperatives underlying her rendition of the journey, determined as she was to render an "alternative" account of it.

Despite her stated claims to distinguish herself from the ordinary band of male travel writers, Lady Mary's initial letters from Europe reproduce a familiar trope of contemporary travel writing to the Continent, that of castigating Catholicism. As Jeremy Black points out in his survey of English travelers' accounts of Catholicism in the Continent, "credulity and superstition" were widely seen to characterize Catholic culture (238). Almost as if on cue, Lady Mary is at once impressed by the magnificence of the Catholic churches, but also equally skeptical of the rituals and superstitions enshrined by them: "I could not enough admire the magnificence of the altars, the rich Images of the Saints (all massy silver) and the enchasures of the Relicks, tho I could not help murmuring in my heart at that profusion of pearls, Diamonds and Rubys bestow'd on the adornment of rotten teeth, dirty rags, etc" (to Lady __, August 16, 1716; 253). Not only do Montagu's derisive comments reproduce an existing trope of travel writing, but they closely replicate the prose style of *Some letters containing an account of what seem'd most remarkable in traveling thro' Switzerland, Italy, and some parts of Germany* (1688), written by Bishop Gilbert Burnet, a Protestant cleric, Whig politician, and one of Lady Mary's mentors (Chung 119).

An adherence to recognizably Protestant-English descriptions of Catholicism allows Lady Mary to balance her role as a "female traveler," while at the same time constituting herself as an "English subject," an otherwise difficult conjunction of roles, given the prescriptive ideals of English domesticity that would perhaps have marked female travel literature as "un-English": "travel literature by women, indeed the very experience of travel *ipso facto*," as Melman points out, "subvert[s] gender ideology and the ethoses of domesticity" (17). While fashioning herself as an English female traveler, it is almost as if Lady Mary compensates for her transgression of an ideology of separate, gendered spheres by emphasizing an "Englishness" distilled through an anti-Catholic rhetoric. That such a rhetoric played a crucial role in consolidating an otherwise disparate and loosely woven British identity over the eighteenth and nineteenth centuries is evident from the fact that it was a "commitment to Protestantism," one inscribed most conspicuously through diatribes against Catholicism, which proved that "the English, the Welsh and the Scots could be drawn together— and made to feel separate from much of the rest of Europe" (Colley 18). Lady Mary's denigration of Catholic Europe provides her, then, with an opportunity to consolidate her position as an "English" traveler, though female. In doing so, it also marks an inroad into the visibly male enterprise of carving a national identity that by denying women political rights had otherwise contracted the role of female citizenship but to a "cult of prolific maternity" (Colley 240).

A critique of Catholic idolatry also emphasizes her own rational judgment, a quality that would have helped consolidate her credibility as a female narrator, a position whose perceived shortcomings she recognized only too well. Writing to Alexander Pope, for instance, she confesses that "I find that I have (as well as the rest of my sex), whatever face I set on't, a strong disposition to beleive [sic] in miracles"; however, she is quick to reassure him with the statement, "Don't fancy, however, that I am infected by the air of these popish Countrys" (September 14, 1716; 262). Her deliberate references to the debased forms of Christianity prevalent in the Continent, then, are critical not only in establishing her reliability as a narrator in an age privileging reason and rationality, but also in containing English anxiety about female susceptibility to the enticements of Catholicism in the Continent. Her marking of "these popish Countrys (262)," however, also situates England in contradistinction to a "Catholic other." Thus, when upon having arrived in Adrianople Lady Mary writes to the Princess of Wales, "I have now Madame, past a Journey that has not been undertaken by any Christian since the Time of the Greek Emperours" (April 1, 1717; 310), the obvious exaggeration of the claim[5] reflects, in fact, the exaggerated nature of implied distinctions between Christian Europe and the Islamic Ottoman Empire (ironically, Adrianople was still technically within Europe).

> In contrast to her ridiculing of the "popish Countrys," Lady Mary presents a radically different picture of Islam, as evinced from the description of her conversations in Adrianople with the Effendi, Achmet Beg, a scholar learned in Arabic and Persian. During her involved conversations with Achmet Beg, whom she describes as "more polite than many Christian men of Quality" (to Alexander Pope, February 12, 1716; 308), Lady Mary is struck by the Effendi's amenability to the tenets of English Protestantism. "I explain'd to him," she points out, "the difference between the Religion of England and Rome, and he was pleas'd to hear there were Christians that did not worship images or adore the Virgin Mary" (to Abbe Conti, April 1, 1717; 317). In fact, the course of the conversation convinces her of the parallels between Islam and English Protestantism to the extent that she remarks upon how even the more controversial and unorthodox members of the Anglican Church would find easy acceptance in Turkey: "Upon comparing our Creeds together," she notes, "I am convinc'd that if our friend Dr. [Clarke] had free Liberty of preaching here, it would be very easy to perswade the Generallity to Christianity, whose notions are already little different from his" (317).

Her conversation with the Effendi not only enlightens her about specific aspects of Islam, which had been misrepresented by an earlier writer such as Paul Rycaut, whose text, *The Present State of the Ottoman Empire* (1668), Lady Mary refers to, but she also departs from the general characteristics Rycaut had imparted to Islam. Rycaut had apparently followed the Alcoran in tracing the movement from an earlier ethos of tolerance to a credo of persecution that, he felt, presently informed the religious disposition of the Turks:

> [The Turks] know they cannot force mens Wills, nor captivate their Consciences, as well as their bodies; but what means they may be used to render them contemptible, to make them poor, their lives uncomfortable, and the interest of their Religion weak and despicable, are practised with divers Arts and Tyranny, that their toleration of Christianity is ratherto to afflict and persecute it, then grant any favour or dispensation. (Rycaut 103)

Lady Mary, on the other hand, not only emphasizes the corrupted versions of the Alcoran presented to Christians by Greek priests, "who would not fail to falsify it with the extremity of Malice" (318), but she also goes on to substantiate her tirade against the Greek Orthodox priests by aligning them with the persecutory practices of the Roman Catholic Church. Stating that "No body of Men ever were more ignorant and more corrupt" than the Greek priests, she overturns the referents of Rycaut's argument by stating "yet [the Greek priests] differ so little from the Romish Church, I confess there is nothing [that] gives me a greater abhorrence of the cruelty of your Clergy than the barbarous persecutions of 'em whenever they have been their masters, for no other reason than not acknowledging the Pope" (319). Interestingly, this particular letter is addressed to the Abbe Conti, a cosmopolitan scholar of Italian origin, whom Lady Mary had met in London in 1715. Conti, though ordained as a Catholic priest, had left his religious order in 1708, thereafter distancing himself from Catholicism (Grundy 89).

In directing her letter to a "lapsed Catholic," Lady Mary not only assures herself of a sympathetic hearing, but also makes it rather evident that her elucidation of Islamic principles needs to be read within a framework of anti-Catholicism. To be sure, her valorization of Islam followed, as Melman points out, a familiar logic wherein "the tolerance of the Turks was a stick which Protestants...used to beat with Catholic intolerance" (94). However, by specifically deploying that rhetoric within the framework of a travel narrative across Europe and Asia that, in its depiction of Islam, goes against the grain of contemporary travel accounts, Lady Mary questions the ideological bases of their cartographic imaginary. Commenting upon Lady Mary's radical representation of a "rational Islam," Teresa Heffernan points out that she "resist[ed] the East/West divide of modernity" (213), which portrayed Islam as "arrested, irrational, and backward, still enslaved by despots" (205). This acknowledgment of Lady Mary's resistance to the East/West divide still maintains, however, the structuring principle of such a demarcation. Belying the assumptive logic of mapping the cultural encounter between "East" and "West" along easy (and settled) binaries, Lady Mary presents, instead, a more complicated geography, one that not only questions the representation of a secular or progressive Europe, but also of a unified West.

The single feature of Lady Mary's letters that has attracted most attention is perhaps her description of Turkish women. Although previous male travelers had never been allowed access into the women's quarters, they presented, as a token of Oriental degeneracy, exotic accounts of Turkish women's sensuality, sexual avariciousness, and virtual enslavement at the hands of despotic males.[6] Lady Mary, though, not only attests to the women's moral comportment—"As to their Morality or good Conduct, I can say like Arlequin, 'tis just as 'tis with you" (327)—but also proclaims them to be "the only free people in the Empire" (to Lady Mar, April 1, 1717; 329).[7] Writing to her sister, she emphasizes the privileges enjoyed by Turkish women, pointing out how though polygamy was permissible, it was rarely followed in practice (329). Moreover, the practice of veiling, she notes, rather than encumbering female liberty, actually enhances women's mobility, for not only could women from the upper classes venture outdoors without being recognized, but they could also negotiate romances, even extramarital, without fear of being discovered (328). Interestingly, even as Lady Mary concludes the letter to her sister with the observation, "Thus you see, dear Sister, the manners of Mankind doe not differ so widely as our voyage Writers would make us believe [sic]" (330), the letter actually does not do much to substantiate such a claim. Lady Mary attempts to translate Turkish marital practices in terms of a regularized English context. However, there is little she can find to establish a similitude between England and Turkey, other than the fact that because marriages were mostly monogamous in Turkey, when a husband "happens to be inconstant (as such things will happen)," he "keeps his mistrisse in a House apart and visits her as privately as he can," which, as Lady Mary points out to her sister in England, is "just as 'tis with you" (329). In fact, the purported novelty of the letter lies in its presenting a picture of Turkish womanhood that holds up the position of Turkish women as a possible ideal for their counterparts in England. Further, even as Lady Mary uses frameworks of reference familiar to an English audience, these frameworks had not yet been actualized within a female context in England. Thus, when visiting the women's bath house in Sophia, she describes the exclusively female space of the baths by concluding "in short, tis the Women's coffee house, where all the news of the Town is told, Scandal invented, etc" (to Lady __, April 1, 1717; 314), it is significant to note that while coffeehouses were emerging as key sites for fraternal bonding in eighteenth-century England, women's coffeehouses were nonexistent at the time (Aravamudan 175; Bohls 192; Lew 441). Lady Mary's comment that "Tis very easy to see [the Turkish women] have more Liberty than we have" (328), tellingly alludes, in fact, to the marked difference between English women and their Turkish counterparts, and as Lowe suggests, Lady Mary "appropriates Turkish female experience for the purpose of defending English feminism" (44).

Even so, in fashioning a certain English female identity, however utopian, Lady Mary provides a narrative framework that counters the political equation between Europe and the Ottoman Empire. Her husband had been deputed to persuade the Austrian Emperor to desist from engaging in further warfare with Ottoman forces. While from an English point of view such a move was intended to secure Austrian resources against Spain, the situation also reveals a conjoining of European powers vis-à-vis Turkey. Interestingly, in face of the ongoing hostility between Austria and Turkey, Lady Mary draws both of them together through a common framework of gendered interests: Her account of the Turkish women's independence is refracted through the narrative of her encounter with the women in Austria. Such an account not only provides her with a vocabulary with which to critique the workings of English patriarchy, but also places the women of Austria and Turkey along a coterminous plane that provides an unlikely configuration disrupting the assumptions of a masculinist geopolitics.

Lady Mary's perceptions of women in Turkey are distilled through her experiences in Vienna. Her description of the Empress's palace in Vienna, for instance, seems to provide a narrative framework for her description of her visits to the Turkish harems. When in Vienna, she is impressed by the fact that the Empress's drawing room is "very different from that of England," for "No man enters it but the old Grand Master, who comes in to advertise the Empress of the Approach of the Emperor" (to Lady Mar, September 14, 1716; 266). In imparting a sense of a female community, Lady Mary pays special attention to how "The Table is entirely serv'd and all the dishes set on by the Empresse's Maids of honnour," who have "no salary but their chambers at Court where they live in a sort of confinement" (267). The notion of a well-defined female community is explicitly foregrounded when she visits the Empress Amalia, wife of the late Emperor. Lady Mary describes an exclusively female shooting competition that the Empress presides over, where "All the men of Quality at Vienna were [but] Spectators, [and] only the Ladys had permission to shoot" (268). Noting how the regularity of occasions such as these "make the young Ladys skilfull enough to defend a fort," she also describes how the women "laugh'd very much to see me afraid to handle a Gun" (269). That the shooting competition makes Lady Mary acutely aware of the impingements upon her own position as an English woman is evident from her almost compensatory attempt to remind the reader of her role as author and the extent of her learning: "I was very well pleas'd with having seen this Entertainment, and I don't know but it might make as good a figure as the prize shooting in the Aenid if I could write as well as Virgil" (268).

Interestingly, Lady Mary's encounters with Turkish women are marked by surprisingly similar details. On visiting the women's baths in Sophia, she points out that "tis no less than Death for a Man to be found in one of these places," (315) and the seemingly autonomous space of the baths reminds her, as in the shooting competition at Vienna, of the limitations of her own position as an English woman. When the women invite her to undress for a bath, she reveals her sartorial inability to do so by showing them her "Stays," which convince the women that she was "so lock'd up in that machine that it was not in [her] own power to open it, which contrivance they attributed to [her] Husband" (314). Importantly, as Srinivas Aravamudan points out, even as the Turkish women mistakenly perceive her stays as a limitation imposed by her husband, Lady Mary "does not dispute the perception of this theatricalized cruelty, and accepts the commiseration she receives from her hosts" (178). Aravamudan suggests that by banking on Turkish cultural misapprehension," Lady Mary "narrowly escapes the sacrifice of her English virtue" (178). The fact that she felt compelled to adhere to the norms of virtue and decency expected by her English readers indicates the larger and more prohibitive "cultural stays" she was operating under, in contrast to the Turkish and Viennese women. Moreover, as in Vienna, when visiting the women's apartments in Turkey, she is similarly impressed by the self-sustaining female community that she encounters, taking care to mention the everyday tasks performed by the slave girls inhabiting the harem, whose confinement to their duty does not seem very dissimilar to that of maids of honor in Vienna. The narrative follows a very structured pattern, which is evident from the fact that Lady Mary pays attention even to similar details in both Austria and Turkey. Her awe at the devout acts of penance and mourning undertaken by the Empress's mother in Vienna (267) is matched, if not surpassed, by her amazement at the Sultana in Constantinople, whose "uninterrupted Mourning" for her husband, Lady Mary pronounces, is undertaken with a "constancy very little known in Christendom" (381).

Kietzman perceptively notes that "Montagu's first experience of gender-segregated space in Vienna liberates her" and "prefigures the way she will construct gender-segregated Turkish society as a genuine alternative to the West's strictly hierarchical organization of social space" (542). Kietzman's comment seems also paradoxical, for while it usefully points out the relevance of Lady Mary's encounters with women in Vienna, it seems reluctant to place it along a continuum with her Turkish experience. By suggesting that Lady Mary's depictions of gender segregation in Turkey offer a "genuine alternative to the West's strictly hierarchical organization of social space," Kietzman acknowledges how Montagu's descriptions of Turkish female society function as exemplary models for an undifferentiated West. Such an observation, however, accords a curious no-place to the relevance of the comparable female space that Montagu encounters in Vienna and the particular relation she forges *between* Austria and Turkey. Montagu's experience in Vienna, a place she describes as "paradise for old Women" (to Lady Rich, September 20, 1716; 270) not only prefigures, but also provides a lens with which to view Turkey. It is in Vienna that she notes the sexual liberties enjoyed by married women, for whom it is more the norm than the exception to boast of a lover.[8] "That perplexing word Reputation," Montagu remarks, "has quite another meaning here than what you give it at London, and getting a Lover is so far from loseing [sic], that 'tis properly geting [sic] reputation" (270). It is precisely this sexual freedom that Lady Mary locates in Turkey, where she interprets the benefits of veiling as a "perpetual Masquerade [that] gives [Turkish women] entire Liberty of following their Inclinations without danger of Discovery" (to Lady Mar, April 1, 1717; 328). Of course, Lady Mary's particular reading of the practice of veiling as a form of masquerade hearkens to the subversive potential ascribed to forms of masquerade in eighteenth-century England, where masquerade "was all the rage, and the occasion for transgressions of gender boundaries as well as of station and rank" (Garber 313). However, it is not only the transgressive aspects of masquerade that impel Lady Mary to opine that Turkish women have more liberty than English women, but also the fact that she is able to locate its liberating prospects within a more sustained framework of economic independence guaranteed to Turkish women, one whose importance she was alerted to in Vienna itself. Observing that Austrian laws of matrimony make "many Ladys much richer than their Husbands," she explains how she "attribute[s] to this considerable branch of prerogative the Liberty that they take upon other Occasions" (to Mrs. T___l, September 26, 1716; 272). Similarly, she is able to make a case for the sexual freedom enjoyed by Turkish women precisely by attributing it to their relative economic independence: "Neither have they much to apprehend from the resentment of their Husbands, those Ladys that are rich having all their money in their own hands" (329). For Lady Mary, whose own life had been plagued by the financial vulnerabilities occasioned by her gendered status (Grundy xxi; Melman 88), the value of such an economic self-sufficiency would surely not have been lost.

It is important to highlight the continuity between Lady Mary's observations of Austria and Turkey, for they reveal the extent to which her experience in Austria mediates her reading of Turkish women. Jill Campbell suggests that "it is her own culture's vocabulary of sexual roles that Lady Mary draws upon as she translates her experience in Turkey into English" (78). However, as I have tried to point out, while Lady Mary's awareness and critique of an increasingly prescriptive English bourgeois sexuality impels her to locate and laud alternate models of sexual morality, it is her exposure to and appreciation of the cultural mores in Vienna through which she filters her observations in Turkey. Ironically, when she visits the harem of the Kahya's wife in Adrianople, her first visit to a harem, she goes attired in "the Court habit of Vienna," which she declares to her sister to be "much more magnificent than ours" (to Lady Mar, April 18, 1717; 347). By visiting the Turkish harem in Viennese finery, Lady Mary does not necessarily forgo her "Englishness," but brackets it off as discontinuous to the Austro-Turkish framework of her gendered critique. Lady Mary's letters construct, as Felicity Nussbaum suggests, a "feminotopia," a term Nussbaum borrows from Mary Louise Pratt, who coined it to denote "idealized worlds of female autonomy, empowerment, and pleasure" (qtd. in Nussbaum 135). However, it is interesting to note that Lady Mary's "feminotopia" provides a gendered re-reading of Orientalist topography not simply by undermining notions of an enslaved Oriental womanhood signifying eastern male tyranny, or by likening Turkish practices to English customs. Rather, Lady Mary views the lives of Turkish and Austrian women through a similar optic that not only "others" English women, but by doing so situates England in contradistinction to an Austro-Turkish imaginary that questions both Europe's internal and external "boundaries." Not surprisingly, Lady Mary's first letter from Vienna literally bears testimony to the "shrinking nature" or permeability of Europe's borders, for she concludes the introductory paragraph with the passing reminder, "I saw the great Towns of Passaw [sic] and Lintz, famous for the retreat of the Imperial Court when Vienna was beseig'd" (to Lady Mar, September 8, 1716; 259). However, while she blurs the boundaries between Austria and Turkey in her imagining of a feminotopia, it becomes evident that Turkey has to be "regularized" in order to be presented as a cultural ideal. Thus, even as her observations in Austria enable her to frame Turkish society along lines of a certain congruency, it also imposes a certain rhetoric of class and race through which to view Turkey.

Despite her many observations that question self-evident assumptions about the "difference" that Turkey emblematizes, Lady Mary is also acutely conscious of the sense of novelty that Turkey seems to conjure. In contrast to her earlier letters in which she refrains from delving into tedious details about her places of visit for fear that she might write a "whole Quire of the dullest stuff that ever was read" (to Lady X__, October 1, 1716; 275), she realizes, upon arriving in Adrianople, that a "Letter out of Turkey that has nothing extraordinary in it would be as great a Disapointment [sic] as my visitors will receive at London if I return thither without any raritys to shew them" (to Anne Thistlethwayte, April 1, 1717; 340). It is not without a certain self-congratulatory glee that she provides effusive accounts of the rich splendor she encounters, "But what would you say," she writes to her sister, "if I told you that I have been in a Haram [sic] where the winter Apartment was wainscoted with inlaid work of Mother of Pearl, Ivory of different Colours and olive wood" (March 10, 1718; 385). However, even as she seeks to meet her readers' expectations of the extraordinary, her sensuous descriptions are also careful to counteract residual images of eroticism or hypersexuality.

She is able to attain this balance through clever use of what Elizabeth Bohls describes as a "contemporary discourse of aesthetics" that Lady Mary "pit[s] against the offensive idiom of early Orientalism" (181). Interestingly, by taking recourse to an aesthetic discourse, Lady Mary is able to mark her own entry into the male bastion of English aesthetic judgment (Bohls 183), but the specifically upper-class lineament of this discourse also informs and influences her specific domains of representation. When she arrives at the baths, she points out how the surrounding women were all in "the state of nature, that is, in plain English, stark naked" (Montagu 313); however, she is careful to emphasize not only that "there was not the least wanton smile or immodest Gesture amongst 'em," but also that they were as "exactly proportion'd as ever any Goddess was drawn by the pencil of Guido or Titian," "perfectly representing the figures of the Graces" (to Lady __, April 1, 1717; 314). As Bohls notes, "[the bathing women] are recast from oversexed houris," which is how they were conventionally portrayed, "into Venus, Eve, and the Graces, bringing them closer to upper-class European sensibilities" (188). Not coincidentally, Lady Mary had used much the same rhetoric while describing the Empress in Vienna: "all that the Poets have said of the mien of Juno, the air of Venus come not upto the truth. The Graces move with her; the famous statue of Medicis was not form'd with more delicate proportions" (Montagu 266).

Lady Mary's narrative strategy, borne from a certain class specific aesthetic discourse, not only constructs a "feminotopia" within an exclusive upper-class purview, both in terms of rhetoric and subjects of representation, but also impels her to frame the Turkish ladies in as much the same way as the women of the Austrian court. By doing so, however, Lady Mary locates the Turkish women beyond the realms of their own cultural history. With reference to the scene at the baths, in fact, Campbell points out that Lady Mary "begins by projecting the Muslim women...back into Judaeo-Christian prehistory," and then "she relocates the women within the distant past, placing them within the world of classical mythology" (79). In describing the women in the harems, too, Lady Mary presents a largely depoliticized and ahistorical picture, abstracting the women from the materiality of their cultural roles. She describes the ladies, somewhat enviably, as living a life of "unintterupted pleasure, exempt from cares, their whole time being spent in visiting, bathing, or the agreeable Amusement of spending Money and inventing new fashions" (to Countess __, May

1718; 406). Though it can be argued that she only mingled with the upper echelons of Turkish society, hence her upper-class referents, it is significant to note that by aestheticizing the women, she largely ignores the considerable political or social influence wielded by them. While in her historical study of the Ottoman harem, Leslie Peirce has broadly argued for Ottoman female authority in the public sphere (8), it is noteworthy that Lady Mary gauges the privileges of the harem only through idealized descriptions that overlook its political centrality by ignoring that with the Ottomans, "conventional Western notions of public and private were not congruent with gender" (Peirce 8). Such a framing presents a skewed picture of the women's actual lives, enabling Lady Mary to narrate them through what Cynthia Lowenthal describes as a "veil of romance" (112).

Interestingly, the idealized description of Turkish women is also transposed onto Turkey as a whole, which she often describes in terms of an idyllic pastoral retreat. "Must not you confess to my praise," she asks in a letter to Pope, "that tis more than an ordinary Discretion that can resist the wicked Suggestions of Poetry in a place where Truth for once furnishes all the ideas of Pastorall?" (April 1, 1717; 331). Morever, in contrast to her earlier letters from Austria and Hungary, wherein she attends to specificities of dates and historical events, Turkey is often narrated through a timelessness that hearkens insistently to a classical past. In the same letter to Pope she recounts how she had read over his recent translation of the *Iliad* and was able to understand several passages that she "did not before entirely comprehend the Beauty of many of the customs and much of the dress then in fashion being yet retain'd" (332). The extensive use of neoclassical imagery certainly enables Montagu to further secure her credentials as a female wit (the letter after all was addressed to Pope); such a rhetoric also presents, in its familiar imagery, a more "stable antiquarian 'Levant'" (Aravamudan 187). Interestingly, even as Lady Mary situates Turkey in the distant past, the sense of an eternal past is instrumental in rendering present-day Turkey more "acceptable." Said points out that when the "Orient was re-discovered by Europe" from the late eighteenth century onward, "its history had been a paradigm of antiquity and originality, functions that drew Europe's interest in acts of recognition or acknowledgement but *from* which Europe moved" ("Orientalism Reconsidered" 95; original emphasis). In contrast, Lady Mary's emphasis on Turkey's antiquity provides her an opportunity to embellish and familiarize it as a site whose present ordering of social gender relations should be admired, and perhaps aspired toward, not disavowed on account of its alienness.

However, in making present-day Turkey more "familiar" by viewing it through a lens of European antiquity, she establishes a genealogy between the practices of the inhabitants of Ottoman territory and Europe's classical legacy, thus invoking "a cultural continuity which dissolves national boundaries" (Turner 123) and befuddles the sociopolitical divide between Europe and "the East."[9] Intrinsic to this rendition, though, is a curious evacuation of Turkey: If Turkey is "reclaimed" through its European antecedents, then it is oftentimes also presented as *not* being inhabited by Turks. In the same letter to Pope, Lady Mary writes, "I don't wonder to find more remains here of an Age so distant than is to be found in any other Country, the Turks not takeing that pains to introduce their own Manners as has been generally practis'd by other nations" (332). It is almost as if she can foreground Turkey's classical heritage only by erasing the imprint of present-day Turks. The erasure had been made possible, however, by the tolerance practiced by the Ottoman Turks that facilitated the co-existence of several religious, ethnic, and linguistic identities under the aegis of Ottoman rule without imposing a particular "Turkish" cultural identity (McCarthy 9). In fact, as David Kushner notes, while the Europeans "had long used the term "Turks" or "Turkey" with reference to the Ottomans and the Ottoman empire...the Turks themselves allowed the term to be almost forgotten" (8). It is precisely this lack of a core identity that Lady Mary highlights in deflecting any notion of a stable, definable Turkish culture. In describing the idyllic landscape of Turkey, she pronounces that "gardiners [sic] are the only happy race of Country people in Turkey," adding that "they are most of 'em Greeks" (332). Fatima, one of the upper-class Turkish women whom Lady Mary is enraptured with, is, after all, born of a Polish mother, and, while describing her own household in Pera, Constantinople, Lady Mary enumerates its hybrid nature: "My Grooms are Arabs; my footmen French, English and German; my Nurse an Armenian; my Housemaids Russians; halfe a dozen other servants Greeks; my steward an Italian; my Janizarys Turks" (to Lady __, March 16, 1718; 390). If this cosmopolitanism evacuates Turkey of an identifiably "Turkish" culture, it also establishes its contiguity with Europe. Thus, when visiting an old town, even an incidental remark made by Montagu noting that "The Christians still call it Calcedonia, and the Turks give it a name I forgot, but which is only a corruption of the same word" (413) introduces a rhetoric of continuity in describing Turkey, rather than one merely of similitude.

However, even as Lady Mary situates Turkey on a plane of continuity with Europe, it becomes evident that such a logic is facilitated by a particular grammar of race and class. Significantly, she lives mostly in European-dominated Pera, and while those whom she writes about in Turkey can be accommodated within a classical-pastoral setting on account of their racialized identification with Europe, or within a familiar aesthetic and intellectual discourse on account of their class privilege, her letters while traveling through Tunis, "the Africk shore," register a very different rendition. Even when describing a scene very similar to ones she had described while in Turkey, she offers a strikingly different reading:

> It now being the season of the Turkish Ramadan (or Lent) and all here professing, at least, the Mahometan Religion, they fast till the going down of the Sun and spend the night in feasting. We saw under the trees in many places Companys of the country people, eating singing, and dancing to their wild music. They are not quite black, but all mulattos, and the most frightfull Creatures that can appear in a Human figure. They are almost naked, only wearing a piece of coarse serge wrap'd about them, but the women have theie Arms to their very shoulders and their Necks and faces adorn'd with Flowers, Stars and various sort of figures impress'd by Gunpowder; a considerable addition to their natural Deformity, which is, however, esteem'd very ornamental amongst them, and I believe they suffer a good deal of pain by it. (to Abbé Conti, July 31, 1718; 425)

Such a description departs, of course, from her aestheticized account of the bathing women who could be likened to classical figures of European art, or the "country people," mostly of European descent, whom she had described as perfectly mingling in with their sylvan setting. The incongruity of the peasants she sees in Tunis, an incongruity emphasized in terms of their "wild music," "natural deformity," and "frightfull appearance," discloses the extent to which the informing influences of race and class had enabled Lady Mary to reconstitute Turkey within the imaginative spaces of Europe. Thus upon visiting "one of the finest" bagnios in Constantinople, she could remark not only on how the Turkish ladies "have at least as much wit and Civillity, nay Liberty, as Ladys Amongst us (407)," but also comment upon how the wedding festivity she witnessed there "made me recollect the Epithalamium of Helen by Theocritus, and it seems to me that the same customs have continu'd ever since" (406). Conversely, when visiting the ruins of Carthage in North Africa, she is unable to establish a similar line of continuity or congruity, almost lamenting, instead, that the ruins of what she perceives to have been splendid summer apartments were now used as granaries by the local populace, whom she describes as "differ[ing] so little from their own country people, the Baboons, tis hard to fancy them a distinct race" (427).

In light of Lady Mary's inability to accommodate the natives of northern Africa even within the realm of humanity, it would be worthwhile to remind ourselves that contrary to critical opinion which suggests that she dispels the logic of difference while describing Europe's encounter with the "Orient," Lady Mary, rather than subverting the logic of the equation between Europe and its "other," reformulates the terms of that equation by questioning Turkey's status as "other." By arguing for her inclusion of Turkey within a "European imaginary," I do not intend the inclusion to be read as a badge of redemption; rather, Lady Mary's representation of Turkey provides a history of the political geography of Orientalism, highlighting Turkey's ambiguous relationship with Europe, as well as the ambiguities of Orientalist discourse itself. Çaglar Keyder notes that "The West has, of course, been identified with Europe, and Turkey's intimate relations with this entity have made for an almost pathological definition of its most fundamental cultural questions in the optics of the relationship with Europe" (32). Lady Mary's account, by foregrounding Turkey's continuity with Europe, probes precisely the pathologies of this relationship; her letters also allude to the importance of introspecting Europe's own monolithic status, an introspection prompted in no uncertain measure by her gendered imperatives and anxieties. Moreover, if, as Katherine Turner points out, the "attractive vision" of Turkey, as presented by Lady Mary, was transformed over the course of the eighteenth century into one emphasizing its degeneracy and barbarism, a transformation coinciding with England's imperial ascendancy (127–28),[10] then Lady Mary's letters are significant in reminding us not only of the genealogy of that transformation of Turkey, but also of the logic of race and class underlying the possibilities and limits of its representation. Such a reminder is perhaps not entirely irrelevant in our present time as Turkey's bedeviled attempts to enter the European Union have continued to perplex other members of the European community.

Notes

I am thankful to George Haggerty and Parama Roy for their helpful feedback on earlier versions of this project. My thanks, also, to Mark Netzloff and Kristi Siegel for their useful suggestions, and I am grateful for a timely fellowship from the Center for Women's Studies, University of Wisconsin-Milwaukee.

1   Turkey, in fact, would occupy a particularly interesting position within the Orientalist framework, for it reveals the ruptures and uncertainties of the discourse. According to Said, the Orient can be classified into the "Near Orient" (covering the areas of the Levant contiguous to Europe) and the "Far Orient." It is the "Near Orient," in particular, that on account of its "familiarity" induces what Said describes as a compensatory dynamic of "vacillation" between "West's contempt for what is familiar and its shivers of delight in—or fear of—novelty" (*Orientalism* 59), thus foregrounding the obvious processes wherein a site like Turkey is Orientalized.

2   Srinivas Aravamudan is among the few exceptions. Though he understandably does not use the original title in full, he cites one of its shortened incarnations (used by J. A. St. John in 1838), *Letters from the Levant, During the Embassy to Constantinople, 1716–1718*, pointing specifically to its more expansive scope, as compared to "Turkish Embassy Letters" (159).

3   In contrast to Lowe, Meyda Yegenoglu argues that a rhetoric of similitude does not necessarily counteract the implications of an Orientalist discourse. See Meyda Yegenoglu. *Colonial Fantasies: Towards a Feminist Reading of Orientalism* (Cambridge: Cambridge University Press, 1998).

4   In describing Lady Mary's encounters with the Turkish women, Aravamudan outlines a process wherein Lady Mary's cultural identity, though unsettled, is not reversed. Aravamudan in fact describes how Lady Mary moves from a pluralistic position of "eclectic relativism" to a "cultural liminality," which threatens to absorb her into Turkish culture. Such an assimilation, Aravamudan suggests, is counteracted by a "banal return home rather than romance metamorphosis" (161–62). My reading does not foreground Lady Mary's "cultural liminality" as much as it highlights what Aravamudan describes as a "reaggregation" of Lady Mary's cultural identity. While Aravamudan views this "reaggregation" more through Lady Mary's "return" to an "antiquarian classicism," I view the "reaggregation" as one that determines her reading of the cross-cultural encounter itself, helping her reformulate (and locate herself more definitely within) the spaces of a contemporary "Englishness."

5   Robert Halsband records that "Christians [in fact] had made the journey by land—as early as the sixteenth century, when the Imperial Ambassador, Ogier de Busbeq, had traveled by land from Belgrade to Adrianople" (310).

6   Previous male accounts of the harem include that of Robert Withers, *A Description of the Grand Signor's Seraglio, or Turkish Emperours Court* (1650). The authorship of Withers's text, however, is contested. See Godfrey Goodwin's introduction to *The Sultan's Seraglio: An Intimate Portrait of Life at the Ottoman Court* (London: Saqi Books, 1996). Other narratives include *Sir Paul Rycaut, The Present State of the Ottoman Empire* (1668); Jean Dumont, *A New Voyage to the Le-*

vant (1696); and Aaron Hill, *A Full and Just Account of the Present State of the Ottoman Empire* (1709).

7   Even though Lady Mary's statement that Turkish women are the "only free women in the Empire" is often quoted as proof of her observation of their unmitigated independence, it is worthwhile to keep in mind that Lady Mary frequently resorts to such superlative expressions. While describing the gardens of Adrianople to Alexander Pope, she exclaims that "These gardeners are the only happy race of country people in Turkey" (April 1, 1717; 332) and writing to Mrs. Thistlethwayte on the same day, she remarks that the birds in Turkey are "the happiest subjects under the Turkish government" (341). This frequent narrative move, though lessening the impact of her observations of Turkish women, does not, of course, undermine the fact that Lady Mary was convinced of the liberty enjoyed by them. However, its obvious rhetoricity points to the ways in which she was more invested in presenting a particular, though not necessarily accurate, portrayal of the lives of Turkish ladies in order to critique the status of contemporary English women.

8   Montagu's specific use of the term *Liberty* is noteworthy, for eighteenth-century ideas of liberty were chauvinistic as they referred only to men. Lady Mary, though, refers to the idea of *Liberty* as a "moral-free and natural sexual conduct [as] applicable to both sexes" (Melman 86).

9   See Martin Bernal's *Black Athena: The Afroasiatic Roots of Classical Civilization*. Vol. 1. *The Fabrication of Ancient Greece 1785–1985* (New Brunswick: Rutgers UP, 1987) for an account of the ways in which the legacy of classicism was wrested and claimed by a "European" rather than "Eastern" tradition.

10   For an account of the changing impressions of Turkey over the course of the eighteenth century, see also Asli Çirakman, *From the "Terror of the World" to the "Sick Man of Europe": European Images of Ottoman Empire and Society from the Sixteenth Century to the Nineteenth Century* (New York: Peter Lang, 2002).

Works Cited

Aravamudan, Srinivas. *Tropicopolitans: Colonialism and Agency, 1688–1804*. Durham and London: Duke UP, 1999.

Bernal, Martin. *Black Athena: The Afroasiatic Roots of Classical Civilization*. Volume I. *The Fabrication of Ancient Greece 1785–1985*. New Brunswick: Rutgers UP, 1987.

Black, Jeremy. *The British Abroad: The Grand Tour in the Eighteenth Century*. Stroud: Alan Suton, 1992.

Bohls, Elizabeth. "Aesthetics and Orientalism in Lady Mary Wortley Montagu's Letters." *Studies in Eighteenth Century Culture* 23 (1994): 179–205.

Campbell, Jill. "Lady Mary Wortley Montagu and the Historical Machinery of Female Identity." *History, Gender, & Eighteenth–Century Literature*. Ed. Beth Fowkes Tobin. Athens and London: U of Georgia P, 1994.

Chung, Rebecca. "Travellers into the Levant." *Travel Knowledge: European "Discoveries" in the Early Modern Period*. Eds. Ivo Kamps and Jyotsna Singh. New York: Palgrave, 2001.

Çirakman, Asli. *From the "Terror of the World" to the "Sick Man of Europe": European Images of Ottoman Empire and Society from the Sixteenth Century to the Nineteenth Century.* New York: Peter Lang, 2002.

Colley, Linda. *Britons: Forging the Nation: 1707–1837.* New Haven and London: Yale UP, 1992.

Dumont, Jean. *A New Voyage to the Levant containing an account of the most remarkable curiousities in Germany, France, Italy, Malta, and Turkey: with historical observations relating to the present and ancient state of those countries.* London, 1696.

Garber, Marjorie. *Vested Interests: Cross-Dressing and Cultural Identity.* New York and London: Routledge, 1992.

Goodwin, Godfrey. Introd. *The Sultan's Seraglio: An Intimate Portrait of Life at the Ottoman Court.* By Ottaviano Bon. Annotated and Introduced by Godfrey Goodwin. London: Saqi Books, 1996.

Grundy, Isobel. *Lady Mary Wortley Montagu.* Oxford: Oxford UP, 1999.

Halsband, Robert, ed. *Complete Letters of Lady Mary Wortley Montagu.* By Lady Mary Montagu. 3 vols. Oxford: Clarendon Press, 1965.

Heffernan, Teresa. "Feminism Against the East/West Divide: Lady Mary's *Turkish Embassy Letters.*" *Eighteenth–Century Studies* 33. 2 (1999–2000): 201–15.

Hill, Aaron. *A full and just account of the present state of the Ottoman Empire in all its branches: with the government, and policy, religion, customs, and way of living of the Turks, in general/faithfully related from serious observations taken in many years travels thr' those countries by Aaron Hill.* London, 1709.

Keyder, Çaglar. "The Dilemma of Cultural Identity on the Margin of Europe." *Review* 16.1 (1993): 19–33.

Kietzman, Mary Jo. "Montagu's *Turkish Embassy Letters* and Cultural Dislocation." *Studies in English Literature* 38.3 (1998): 537–51.

Kushner, David. *The Rise of Turkish Nationalism 1876–1908.* London: Frank Cass, 1977.

Lew, Joseph W. "Lady Mary's Portable Seraglio." *Eighteenth-Century Studies* 24.4 (1991): 432–50.

Lowe, Lisa. *Critical Terrains: French and British Orientalisms.* Ithaca and London: Cornell UP, 1991.

Lowenthal, Cynthia. *Lady Mary Montagu and the Eighteenth Century Familiar Letter.* Athens and London: U of Georgia P, 1994.

McCarthy, Justin. *The Ottoman Peoples and the End of Empire.* London: Arnold, 2001.

Melman, Billie. *Women's Orients: English Women and the Middle East Sexuality, Religion and Work 1718–1918.* Ann Arbor: U of Michigan P, 1992.

Montagu, Lady Mary Wortley. *Complete Letters of Lady Mary Wortley Montagu.* Ed. Robert Halsband, Vol. 1. Oxford Clarendon Press, 1965.

Nussbaum, Felicity. *Torrid Zones: Maternity, Sexuality, and Empire in Eighteenth-Century English Narratives.* Baltimore and London: Johns Hopkins UP, 1995.

Peirce, Leslie P. *The Imperial Harem: Women and Sovereignty in the Ottoman Empire.* New York and Oxford: Oxford UP, 1993.

Pratt, Mary Louise. *Imperial Eyes: Travel Writing and Transculturation.* London: Routledge, 1992.

Rose, Gillian. *Feminism and Geography: The Limits of Geographical Knowledge.* Cambridge: Polity Press, 1993.

Rycaut, Paul. *The Present State of the Ottoman Empire.* 1668. New York: Arno Press & the *New York Times*, 1971.

Said, Edward. *Orientalism*. New York: Vintage Books, 1978.

———. "Orientalism Reconsidered." *Cultural Critique 1* (Fall 1985): 89–107.

St. John, J. A., ed. *Letters from the Levant during the Embassy to Constantinople, 1716–1718*. By Lady Mary Montagu. 1838. New York: Arno Press, 1971.

Turner, Katherine H. "From Classical to Imperial: Changing Visions of Turkey in the Eighteenth Century." *Travel Writing and Empire: Postcolonial Theory in Transit*. Ed. Steve Clark. London and New York: Zed Books, 1999.

Withers, Robert. *A Description of the Grand Signor's Seraglio, or Turkish Emperours Court*. London: Printed for Jo. Martin and Jo. Ridley, 1650.

Wolff, Larry. *Inventing Eastern Europe: The Map of Civilization on the Mind of the Enlightenment*. Stanford: Stanford UP, 1994.

Yegenoglu, Meyda. *Colonial Fantasies: Towards a Feminist Reading of Orientalism*. Cambridge: Cambridge University Press, 1998.

Women's Travel and the Rhetoric of Peril
It Is Suicide to Be Abroad

Kristi Siegel

> Hey there Little Red Riding Hood,
> You sure are looking good.
> You're everything a big bad wolf could want.
> Listen to me...
> I don't think little big girls should
> Go walking in these spooky old woods alone.
>   —*Sam the Sham and the Pharaohs*, 1962

The Myth

A ngela Carter's provocative short story, "The Company of Wolves," provides a point-by-point rebuttal of the myths embedded in the more modern versions of "Little Red Riding Hood." Interestingly, the earliest versions of the fairy tale were primarily oral and far more risqué. These versions included sexual elements such as the wolf (actually a "werewolf" in the oldest versions) telling Red Riding Hood to throw her clothes, one by one, into a fire (Leeming and Sader 391). Further—in these early versions—Red Riding Hood tricks the wolf by pretending that she needs to go outside to relieve herself. Once outside, Red Riding Hood quickly removes the rope attached to her, ties it to a tree, and escapes (Bushi). In these original versions, Red Riding Hood outwits the fox, and the sexual overtones are explicit. By the time Charles Perrault wrote his version in 1697, the story had been sanitized into a lesson on young girls' morality. In Perrault's version, the story serves to warn young girls about the threat men pose to their sexual innocence, but does not include the mother's warning to "stay on the path," that appears in most later versions (such as that of Jacob and Wilhelm Grimm in 1812). Instead,

Perrault ends his tale with an overt moral warning: Young ladies—in particular, well-bred and attractive young ladies—should not be beguiled by men's wolfish charm (3). Jacob and Wilhelm Grimms' version [originally called "Little Red-Cap"], far more familiar to American and English audiences than that of Perrault's, casts Little Red Riding Hood as a younger girl (i.e., even more vulnerable) and begins with the famous warning: "[W]alk nicely and quietly and do not run off the path" (Jacob and Wilhelm Grimm 110). Predictably, Little Red Riding Hood forgets her mother's warning, strays off the path, and gets "deeper and deeper into the wood" (Jacob and Wilhelm Grimm 111). Once in the woods, Little Red Riding Hood's troubles begin. Ultimately, a hunter, who just happens to be passing by, saves her.

Of most significance is the decided shift the fairy tale has undergone through time. In the original versions, Little Red Riding Hood saves herself and is never gulled by the wolf. In versions dating from the seventeenth century onward, the girl strays from the path, actually believes the wolf might really be granny, and is saved by a huntsman. Further, in the Grimms' version and its modern variations, Red Riding Hood's comment at the end of the story demonstrates that she has learned her lesson: "As long as I live, I will never by myself leave the path, to run into the wood, when my mother has forbidden me to do so" (Jacob and Wilhelm Grimm 113). However, the fairy tale's other messages to young women are more embedded and more destructive: We are easily distracted and disobedient; we are not safe alone in the woods (traveling off the beaten path); we are fairly stupid; we get ourselves in trouble; and we need to be rescued by a man.

In contrast, Angela Carter's short story, "The Company of Wolves," restores the tale's original elements—such as the overt sexuality and a heroine who is resourceful rather than helpless—but adds a decidedly feminist slant. Carter's heroine is "strong-minded," packs a carving knife in her basket of goodies, and is powerful because of her virginity: "She stands and moves within the invisible pentacle of her own virginity. She is an unbroken egg; she is a sealed vessel; she has inside her a magic space...she is a closed system; she does not know how to shiver. She has her knife and she is afraid of nothing" (2234). Further, in Carter's version, Red Riding Hood does not just protect herself, but controls the "game." The seduction scene plays out like a modern slasher movie; as the girl—at the wolf's bidding— removes each item of clothing and ostensibly becomes more and more vulnerable, we begin to see her as a victim. Just as we become lulled by the predictable script in motion, the girl, now completely naked, responds to the wolf's threat, "All the better to eat you with," by bursting into laughter: "[S]he knew she was nobody's meat" (2238). Even given the background Carter provides in the story's beginning, the scene startles. We knew the girl was strong, independent, and armed. However, the pattern of woman-alone-traveling-alone-helpless-alone-victim is so embedded in our consciousness that we are caught off-guard.

Further, the difference between Perrault's version and that of the Grimms enacts a gesture repeated through time. In the earlier story, Perrault concerns himself with a young girl's sexual purity; his focus is primarily moral. In the Grimms' story, the girl's need to stay on the path is couched in terms of safety. Of most interest is the slippage between the rhetoric of safety and morality. In the Grimms' version little girls (or women) traveling alone risk their safety; the sexual overtones are more covert. In Perrault's version a woman traveling alone risks losing her virginity (and thus her value) while safety appears to be of secondary concern. At heart, though, the two versions of "Little Red Riding Hood" issue the same message: A woman traveling alone is vulnerable, disobedient, and quite possibly, immoral. At this point, though, some clarification needs to be made. What is the definition of "travel" being used, and—precisely—what women are being warned?

What Travel and What Women

Prior to the enlightenment, the meaning of the word *travel* was closer to its Old French root *traveiller*, which meant "to labor," and this original sense of the word reflected the arduous nature early journeys often entailed. For the most part, people traveled out of necessity. Travel was a means to get from one spot to another, rather than a pursuit in itself. Throughout and postenlightenment, as Inderpal Grewal points out, travel took on new meaning: "The rhetoric and discourse of European travel was an eighteenth century construct that began with the Grand Tour that young men of the English aristocracy undertook as part of their education" (1). Caren Kaplan similarly identifies travel—in its voluntary sense—as being "very much a modern concept, signifying both commercial and leisure movement in an era of Western capitalism" (3). Travel must be defined because the word itself is a generalization that has been used imprecisely to refer to any kind of mobility, a gesture "that erases or conflates those mobilities, that are not part of this Eurocentric, imperialist formation..." (Grewal 2). Clearly, travel in its Eurocentric form is marked by privilege, rank, class, and motive and represents an activity far different from the categories of travel Kaplan identifies such as "expatriation, exile, homelessness, and immigration, to name a few" (3). Further, this travel served to educate young men; women, apparently, could be educated at home. Specifically, then, travel, as the word is used here, focuses on mobility in its privileged, white male/occasionally privileged, white female, Eurocentric mode.

Before pursuing the attitudes regarding solitary women travelers (or women traveling at all) any further, it is critical to identify what women are being warned. All women traveling alone may or may not be safe. Additionally, women traveling with other women could be included in this group as it is only by the presence of a male escort that women can remain safe and unsullied. However, though all "un-escorted" women could conceivably be at risk, it is doubtful that all women are being addressed. Jane Robinson makes it clear who she is addressing when she writes (somewhat ironically), "And where should a lady go on her travels?" in the introduction to her large book, *Unsuitable for Ladies: An Anthology of Women Travellers* (2). The word *lady* immediately implies privilege, and its various definitions support this inference, e.g., a lady is "a woman having proprietary rights or authority...a woman of superior social position...a woman of refinement and gentle manners" and so forth. Robinson's stance here is somewhat disingenuous; though she warns against "lumping together...women-in-general," she admits she will be guilty of the same crime. Her candor serves to suggest that just the opposite will take place. However, Robinson's introduction repeatedly refers to women (or ladies) in generalized terms, and her anthology, ostensibly comprehensive due to the vast period of time and areas of the world depicted, overwhelmingly presents the travelogues of eighteenth- and nineteenth-century upper-class English women.

In addition, although it is clear from accounts of lady travelers that an entourage often accompanies them, sometimes including other women, these women are their maids or servants, and, as such, are rendered invisible.[1] Generally, the "lower-class" women who were, of course, enduring the same hardships are not mentioned at all or are mentioned in a manner that implies *their* suffering would not be the same as that of a lady. In an excerpt from Lady Shell's travels in Persia, for example, she first explains the relative discomfort of her trip, even though she is riding in a carriage. Lady Shell comments that—though the carriage was not ideal—it was far preferable to the "large box, called a takhterewan" suspended between two mules that was generally reserved for the "ladies." In contrast to both the carriage in which she is riding and the "large box" suspended more safely *between* two mules, Lady Shell comments matter-of-factly on the travel arrangements for the two English maids accompanying her. Given that their route included narrow mountainous roads, the maids' situation is dangerous as well as uncomfortable. However, there is no sense in Lady Shell's comments that she intends to do anything to improve their circumstances: "The two English maids were mounted one on each side of a mule in two small boxes...where, compressed into the minutest dimensions, they balanced each other and sought consolation in their mutual fate..." (Robinson 174).

In a different context, Margaret Fuller underscores the invisibility of lower-class or non-white women when she comments, sardonically, on the notion that women are too feeble to be involved in politics (or to do much at all). Although the women likely to engage in politics—if they were allowed—would be women of privilege, Fuller cites the drudgery of working-class women to drive her point home:

> If kept from "excitement," she is not from drudgery. Not only the Indian squaw carries the burdens of the camp, but the favorites of Louis XIV accompany him in his journeys, and the washerwoman stands at her tub, and carries home her work at all seasons, and in all states of health. Those who think the physical circumstances of Woman would make a part in the affairs of national government unsuitable, are by no means those who think it impossible for negresses to endure field-work, even during pregnancy, or for sempstresses to go through their killing labors. (296)

In 1844, when Fuller wrote this article ("Woman in the Nineteenth Century") it is unlikely the men banning women (i.e., ladies) from politics had ever contemplated or noticed the work of lower-class or nonwhite women at all. In 1851, Sojourner Truth reiterates this point emphatically and repeatedly in her famous speech:

> That man over there says that women need to be helped into carriages and lifted over ditches, and to have the best place everywhere. Nobody ever helps me into carriages, or over mud-puddles, or gives me any best place! And ain't I a woman? Look at me! Look at my arm! I could have ploughed and planted, and gathered into barns, and no man could head me! And ain't I a woman? I could work as much and eat as much as a man—when I could get it—and bear the lash as well! And ain't I a woman? I have borne

thirteen children, and seen them most all sold off to slavery, and when I cried out with my mother's grief, none but Jesus heard me! And ain't I a woman? (253)

To return to the subject of women's travel, although upper-class women were clearly those being addressed in most of the dire warnings about women traveling alone, paradoxically, these women were often the ones at least risk. Patricia Cline Cohen explains that "not all women abroad were equally at risk to the depredations of all men. Class and race status generally protected many traveling women from uncomfortable assertions of male sexual privilege" (5). Further, with the advent of public transport in early nineteenth-century America more working-class women were traveling (often by necessity rather than as a leisure pursuit) and—as opposed to many of the upper-class women travelers—they "were younger, inexperienced, and unprotected by class status" (5). As a case in point, Cohen tells of a woman traveling on a railway car in 1819 who protected herself by inventing a story "that at once established her class position" (7). When the woman pretends that her brother, whose name is instantly recognized as a "leading merchant," has promised to send her an escort, her "ruse worked to establish her own privileged position, on which none of these men would dare to presume" (7). The point here is not to argue that upper-class women travelers never suffered hardships or that they were uniformly insensitive to the plight of women less powerful. Rather, society considered upper-class women a more valuable commodity, which, in turn, made their safety and purity of critical concern. In nineteenth-century western ideology, the gap between a "woman" and a "lady" remained vast: "[T]he working-class woman could never be a lady—and indeed the verbal distinction between 'woman' and 'lady' was a crucial one" (Gilbert and Gubar 290). Furthermore, because of her precarious economic circumstances, any working-class woman was viewed as a potential prostitute. Rather than fretting about the purity or safety of working-class women, nineteenth-century society worried that these women could be a corrupt, contagious influence on other women (i.e., "ladies"). Sandra Gilbert and Susan Gubar sum up this divided viewpoint nicely: "In particular, an anxiety about the female body led, on the one hand, to fantasies about the upper-class woman's rare spirituality and, on the other hand, to imaginings of working-class women's corrosive sexuality" (296).

Additionally, there was a prevailing sense that lower-class women were somehow sturdier and able to withstand hardships more easily. Women of more "refined sensibilities," just as the genuine princess in the "Princess and the Pea" fairy tale, would perceive even minor discomforts immediately. By this logic, less privileged women could withstand the risks of travel more easily and their virginity (that is, their marketability as a sexual commodity) was of less value.

Although middle- and upper-class women were precisely the women being addressed in warnings about traveling alone, these women were the ones with the means to travel extensively, the women with the time or financial resources to write about their experiences, and the women whose travel narratives excited the most public interest. Consequently, the "rhetoric of peril" being discussed does focus primarily on white, western, privileged women. However, by drawing this distinction, western attitudes about the women not included (e.g., working-class women, women from other races or cultures) become patently obvious.

Nevertheless, whether the rhetoric of peril—and, again, the interplay between concepts of safety and morality may be observed— applied to all women who traveled, or just middle- and upper-class women, a question arises: How did women come to be viewed as so inherently frail and weak? In terms of women's travel, the question becomes significant. Is the belief that women are too weak to travel alone (or unescorted) socially constructed or biologically determined?

Medicine and the Rhetoric of Peril

Medical viewpoints and terminology may be used as an index to gauge the way society views a woman's body. As various critics have noted, the language of women's health care—particularly concerning reproduction and sexual practice—could be described as the "rhetoric of peril." Ever since male physicians began to take charge of childbirth and women's health care in the eighteenth and nineteenth centuries, a woman has been seen as innately weak, a frail vessel whose well-being is closely tied to her hormones, ovaries, and womb. Emily Martin, in her excellent study, *The Woman in the Body: A Cultural Analysis of Reproduction,* explains that prior to the eighteenth century, men and women's bodies were considered "structurally similar"; women's genitals were simply inside the body, while men's were outside (27). By the early eighteenth century, these views began to change. As Martin points out, the scientific "proof" that men and women were fundamentally and biologically different served to solidify and define their social roles because these differences "were grounded in nature, by virtue of the dictates of their bodies" (32). The ideological shift in medical rhetoric becomes critically important as it served to keep women in their place; a woman who rejected being relegated to the domestic sphere not only waged a war against "Nature" itself, but also could be labeled unnatural (32). When men's and women's bodies were considered roughly analogous, a woman's bodily functions were explained in relation to those of a man's and thus were considered normal. Once men and women were deemed fundamentally different, a woman's bodily functions provoked more scrutiny. As Martin explains, menstruation, ovulation, menopause, and birth—formerly considered normal processes of a woman's body—were now viewed as pathological states (32–67). Consequently, it was not only morally proper for a woman to stick to home and hearth but also a matter of safety: A woman's inherently diseased body required the care of her husband and the constant surveillance of (male) physicians. Here again, the slippage between morality and safety may be observed.

In the twentieth century, *Williams Obstetrics* (Pritchard and Macdonald), arguably the "bible" of obstetrics, continues to shift the attitude toward pregnancy (in particular) from a natural state to one that without constant surveillance and control will easily become a pathological one. The dynamics of medical rhetoric serves not only to control women's behavior but also to suggest a moral code as well. Good women, those who obey their doctors' orders docilely, will have relatively easy labors. Women who rebel—by questioning medical protocol, by using alternate methods of childbirth, or by taking unnecessary risks (such as a trip "abroad")—may, by this line of reasoning, suffer consequences that are their own fault. In the ideal or normal model of reproduction, the doctors function as knowing overseers, while the women's body—since there is no sense of the woman herself in this discourse—functions with complete docility. Repeatedly, the rhetoric in *Williams Obstetrics* emphasizes the inherent dangers of pregnancy; a philosophy Dr. Perri Klass similarly noted during her obstetrical training at Harvard Medical School (1982–1986). Ironically, Klass studies obstetrics at the same time she herself is pregnant. Klass quickly notes the rhetoric of peril embedded in women's health care and comments—rather nervously—that "most of us, including me, came away from the course with a sense that in fact pregnancy is a deeply dangerous medical condition, that one walks a fine line, avoiding one serious problem after another, to reach the statistically unlikely outcome of a healthy baby and a healthy mother" (49).

Similarly, the language of *Williams Obstetrics* concentrates on the dangers—rather than the normalcy—of pregnancy and thus the need for constant monitoring. The text also implies that the ideal patient, that is, one who trusts her doctor completely, will deliver her baby painlessly and easily. The text bases the conclusion—that a woman's emotional status directly affects her pain in labor—on a 1950 study done by a British obstetrician, Grantly Dick-Read. Although women could simply tell doctors that labor is rarely painless and more often ranges from pretty uncomfortable to downright excruciating, the text relies instead on the secondhand observations of a male obstetrician to determine the nature of a woman's pain. Read's contention that fear may be the "chief pain-producing agent" serves to emphasize the need for a woman's docility and trust. In fact, the text adds that fear (and thus pain) "may exert a deleterious effect on the quality of uterine contractions and on cervical dilatation" (Pritchard and Macdonald 405). The domino effect of this argument may now be observed. The nervous woman—a woman not responding appropriately to her doctor's calming presence—will experience fear. The fear will cause pain and the pain "may" inhibit normal uterine contractions and cervical dilatation. In short, this argument suggests that a woman is responsible for both her painful labor and the resultant complications her inappropriate behavior may incur.[2]

To summarize, the "rhetoric of peril" embedded in medical language dating from the eighteenth century explained how women's bodily processes, once considered normal, were now viewed as innately pathological. Menstruation, ovulation, pregnancy, and menopause all served to weaken women's clearly inferior bodies. It was natural, then, that women should stay at home, safely protected in the domestic sphere. By the twentieth century, the rhetoric became subtler but presented a variation on the same theme. Medically and morally, a woman needed to stay "on the path." A woman who deviated from the path—by not trusting her doctor or by using alternative forms of medicine—would be punished. A good woman, who obeyed her doctor, would have an easy labor, deliver a healthy baby, and would, of course, stay at home.

The Peril Continues: It Is Suicide to Be Abroad

Just as medical rhetoric—as demonstrated by the short history of obstetrics presented—became more subtle, by the twentieth century,
and especially in America, warnings about women traveling alone
were delivered largely by exempla, i.e., in the plots of popular novels
and—most markedly—by the movies. Movies and other forms of
mass media do not replicate a society exactly but do provide, as Susan
J. Douglas explains, a rough approximation:

> These stories and images [from mass media] don't come from Pluto: our
> deepest aspirations and anxieties are carefully, relentlessly re-
> searched...Despite what TV executives like to say, the mass media are not
> simple mirrors, reflecting "reality." To borrow Todd Gitlin's metaphor,
> they are more like fun-house mirrors that distort and warp "reality" by ex-
> aggerating and magnifying some features of American life and values
> while collapsing, ignoring, and demonizing others. (16)

For the most part, then, Hollywood delivered what "we" wanted to
see and, in the process, often echoed current cultural mores. One index regarding social attitudes about women traveling alone—or traveling at all—may be inferred by the sheer paucity of movies treating
that topic. Prior to *Thelma & Louise* (1991), arguably women's first
road trip movie, few models exist. When women traveled at all, in
Hollywood's mainstream movies dating from the 1930s to as late as
the 1980s, the subtext was nearly always a man. Women traveled to
find a man, get away from a man, or both. The few women that traveled for nonman-related reasons could be characterized as exempt
from the sexual marketplace, because they were impossibly good or
"othered" by reasons of age or eccentricity. Those in the saintly category include characters like Sister Luke (played by Audrey Hepburn)
who travels to the Belgium Congo in *The Nun's Story* (1959), or Gladys
Alyward (played by Ingrid Bergman) who works as a quasi-
missionary and travels to China in *Inn of the Sixth Happiness* (1958).
The "othered" include older women and/or eccentrics such as the
flamboyant Mame Dennis (played by Rosalind Russell) who travels to
show the world to her nephew in *Auntie Mame* (1958), or maternal
figures with magical powers such as Eglantine Price (played by Angela Lansbury) who travels with three orphans while honing her
skills as a witch in *Bedknobs and Broomsticks* (1971) or Mary Poppins
(played by Julie Andrews), a "practically perfect" nanny who whisks
about putting British households in order (*Mary Poppins* 1964).

Like "Little Red Riding Hood" and other fairy tales, movies send powerful messages. Many American baby boomers grew up on the movies of the 1950s and 1960s. In this period, movies featuring younger, sexually attractive, generally white, middle- to upperclass women traveling alone were usually comedies. Often these movies focused obsessively on the woman's ability to maintain her chastity despite being placed in a Hollywood-constructed sexual minefield of wolfish men and delicate situations. The "Tammy" movies, e.g., *Tammy and the Bachelor* (1957), *Tammy Tell Me True* (1961), *Tammy and the Doctor* (1963), starring first Debbie Reynolds, and then Sandra Dee in the leading role, follow this general plot pattern. The "Gidget" movies also depict the pattern of a young girl remaining chaste despite being away from home and subject to temptation: *Gidget* (1959), *Gidget Goes Hawaiian* (1961), and *Gidget Goes to Rome* (1963). Similarly, *Take Her, She's Mine* (1963), portrays Sandra Dee traveling away to college and then to Europe, although here the focus is less on her role than that of her overprotective father (played by James Stewart) who follows her from place to place in a determined effort to safeguard her virginity. Conversely, movies such as *Three Coins in a Fountain* (1954), *How to Marry a Millionaire* (1953), or *The Pleasure Seekers* (1964), feature women who relocate or travel to find romance (preferably in the form of a rich man); however, even in these movies, the women generally remain chaste and choose love over money. Doris Day's characters were known for adroitly eluding one mantrap after another, but her role as Ellen Wagstaff in *Move Over, Darling* (1963) provides a nice contrast to its modern male counterpart, Chuck Nolan (played by Tom Hanks) in *Cast Away* (2000). Ostensibly, the plots of these two movies are very similar; the main character in each survives a plane crash and becomes stranded on a desert island for a number of years. However, in *Cast Away*, more of a modern *Robinson Crusoe*, the movie's drama (and most of its time) pivots on watching Tom Hanks learn how to survive and finally "master"-mind a grueling escape back to civilization. In *Cast Away*, the story before and after the plane crash serves as a frame; the main action takes place on the island. In *Move Over, Darling*, Doris Day's five years on a desert island are referred to but never shown. "We" (Hollywood's target audience) were apparently just not interested in how a woman might survive. Instead, the movie treats what happens (after the adventure, after the action) when she returns home to find her husband newly married and her children unable to recognize her.

In a sense, many mainstream movies about women traveling worked so hard at keeping these women protected and passive that the women might as well have stayed at home. This recurrent impression of a woman's stasis even when she is supposed to be in motion (traveling) parallels Laura Mulvey's Freudian film analysis of male/female dynamics. Mulvey contends that the feminine cannot be constructed as *"different* [from the masculine], but rather only as *opposition* (passivity)...or similarity (the phallic phase)" (31, original emphasis). Femininity, then, can only be defined in relation to masculinity, leaving a woman "shifting between the metaphoric opposition 'active' and 'passive'"; it comes as no surprise, then, that the "correct road, *femininity*, leads to increasing repression of 'the active'" (31, original emphasis). To summarize, a woman may travel, but her activity is continuously undercut to maintain her femininity; the tension stems from Hollywood's schizoid determination to portray a woman simultaneously "off the path," and thus experiencing some adventure by traveling alone, and "on the path," and thus remaining chaste and properly feminine.

Perhaps no movie depicts this tension better than *Where the Boys Are* (1960). Susan J. Douglas cites this movie's contradictions and tensions as well in her book, aptly titled, *Where the Girls Are: Growing Up Female with the Mass Media*. As Douglas points out, the four girls in *Where the Boys Are* operate as "female archetypes" (79). Arguably, this movie not only presents female archetypes but is also an implicit morality play, like an updated version of *Everyman* that provides—by example—the proper code of conduct for young women. *Where the Boys Are* warrants further discussion because it plays out the central ideas presented in this chapter: The rhetoric of peril, the social constructions of women traveling alone, the slippage between concepts of safety and concepts of morality, the importance of a woman's virginity in the sexual marketplace, the physical and emotional weakness of women, and the way a woman's perceived class and status determine how much concern society accords her.

The plot line of *Where the Boys Are* is straightforward: Four young women travel from a Midwestern college to Fort Lauderdale, Florida—a popular spring break location that promises fun, sun, and, of course, is *where the boys are*. Little emphasis is placed on the trip itself—the movie poses no threat to men's road movies. Rather, once again, women travel, but the emphasis is on a woman traveling without really moving (i.e., the girls[3] talk about leaving and are seen arriving; the journey itself is hardly shown). Once the four women arrive in Fort Lauderdale, there is a sense of stasis; the women may "catch" a man, but should not engage in active pursuit. In addition, the four women represent a clear hierarchy. Merritt ("merit") Anderson [Delores Hart], the lead character, is cast as highly intelligent and possessing a cool, chaste beauty similar to other Grace Kelly–Hollywood types who drip with class. Tuggle [Paula Prentiss], though closest in character to Merritt, ensures her secondary status by being portrayed as somewhat gauche and gawky, i.e., possessing less intelligence, less beauty, and less class. Angie [Connie Francis] talks too loudly and is supposed to be viewed as less attractive; these liabilities, in addition to her love of sports (which apparently makes her a "tomboy"), place her slightly below Tuggle. Angie, like Tuggle, is cast as a comic character; however, in relation to class, Angie is aligned more closely to Melanie Coleman [Yvette Mimieux]. In the film's promotional materials, all four girls are shown traveling in a convertible, despite the fact so little time is accorded to their journey in the actual movie. Tellingly, Melanie and Angie occupy the back seat. Tuggle, more assertive than Merritt, is shown driving the car, and though all four girls are smiling, Merritt's contemplative smile and downward glance make her look almost prim in comparison to the others. Melanie, who is clearly the lowest character in this hierarchy, corresponds to Merritt in terms of her beauty, but it is beauty of a certain sort. In the movie's implicit code, Melanie's beauty is cheap—she dresses provocatively and offers herself too readily. Her beauty—like that of Marilyn Monroe's—is to be read as fragile and fey, a fault line applying to her character as well as her appearance. All four girls are "after" boys; Melanie just errs by making her desires explicit.

Although all three girls act as foils, Melanie is most clearly Merritt's opposite. Merritt is pursued by Ryder Smith, a sophisticated Ivy Leaguer; their courtship consists largely of witty banter and—at one point—Ryder inquires about Merritt's IQ. When Merritt answers "138," we are supposed to laugh at Ryder's response: He whistles and quips, "This is going to be a long siege." What is funny, however, is the fact that we then learn that Ryder's IQ is 140—a small, but critical difference. The IQ scene serves as both verbal striptease and sexual foreplay; Ryder's additional two "points" ensure that his masculinity will remain intact.

In contrast, Melanie has relationships, rather than a relationship, and, quite clearly, strays off the path. Ultimately, Melanie is date raped and wanders off, drunkenly, until she is hit by a car. Melanie lives, but as Susan J. Douglas also notes—ironically—this is "supposed to be a comedy" (79), a point borne out by the movie's classification as a comedy and its original trailer, "So for an entertaining look at co-ed fun, go where the sun is hot and the mood is romantic...go *Where the Boys Are.*"

However, how can this movie be a comedy? The answer hearkens back to the original questions. When we consider the "rhetoric of peril" in relation to women traveling alone, it is important to ask, "What women?" The movie, at least in 1960, could retain its comedic status, because Melanie's relative value had already been established; in Hollywood terms, she has been a "bad girl," and the consequences—which are brushed aside rather readily—should be read as her due.[4] Had Merritt been raped, however, the movie would have been classified as a drama. The difference pivots entirely on class; just as lower-class women were often excluded from travel warnings—or, as in the examples presented from the nineteenth century earlier in the chapter—not even mentioned, Melanie is more expendable than Merritt: what happens to Melanie simply is not as important.

Twenty years later, little seems to have changed. Though Robyn Davidson's tone is wry, self-deprecating, and honest throughout, the marketing of her 1980 book, *Tracks,* serves to illustrate some of the central issues raised in this chapter. In large lettering, on the front cover, the book is described as "A Woman's Solo Trek Across 1,700 Miles of Australian Outback," a description designed to promote the key elements of the book's likely market appeal: a woman, traveling alone, in a remote area. Clearly, Davidson is a woman who has decided to stray from the path. Predictably, the people of Alice Springs, Australia—where Davidson prepares for her journey—think she is crazy and launch repeated warnings. However, the warnings all focus on the same topic: If Davidson ventures out alone into the desert she will be raped, but not by just any man; only the Aboriginal men were viewed as dangerous. Davidson characterizes the townspeople's bigoted warnings astutely:

> Everyone...warned me against it [the journey]. The blacks were clearly the enemy. Dirty, lazy, dangerous animals. Stories of young white lasses who innocently strayed down the Todd at night, there to meet their fate worse than death. It was the only subject anyone had gotten fired up about. (22)

It would be interesting to know what the townspeople's reaction would have been if an Aboriginal woman had proposed the same journey. Would she have received the same warnings? Any warnings? Most importantly, would her trek have even attracted attention?

Now, early in the twenty-first century, it is clear that travel is still viewed as far more hazardous for women than for men. An Internet hunt using the search string "women's safety + travel" yields nearly twice as many suggested sites as a parallel search (men's safety + travel), and most of the men's sites have nothing to do with travel risks at all, but rather concern travel kits and "safety" razor blades. Further, most of the sites target a specific group of women: businesswomen or women interested in leisure travel—in short, women of means. Helen Gibson, a professor in tourism at the University of Florida, and Fiona Jordan, a senior lecturer in the School of Leisure, Tourism and Hospitality Management at Cheltenham and Gloucester College of Higher Education in Cheltenham, the United Kingdom, conducted a study that challenges the rhetoric of peril associated with women's travel. Gibson commented, "Guide books, travel magazines and the travel sections of newspapers are filled with caution, sending the message that women are crazy to embark on such journeys because they make themselves vulnerable to harassment and other attacks" (Keen quoting Gibson). In contrast to these dire warnings, Gibson and Jordan's study (based on interviews of fifty women between the ages of 20 and 63) revealed that the fifty women "unanimously reported they found solo leisure travel to be empowering rather than frightening" (Keen, Internet). Certainly, travel incurs distinct risks for women, and I have no desire to dilute that reality, but studies like that of Gibson and Jordan strive to separate fact from fiction.

Ultimately, it is impossible to determine what degree of danger travel poses for a woman; however, the question needs to be framed far more complexly. *What* is at risk—a woman's safety or her morality? Is the amount of risk entirely real or, in part, magnified by its long social and medical history? Most importantly, *what* women are being warned and *what* kind of travel is being addressed? In privileging only certain women and certain travel experiences, the rhetoric of peril leveled at women journeying alone proves myopic in scope and riddled with issues of race and class.

Notes

1   As Mary Suzanne Schriber points out in *Telling Travels,* even when women travelers portrayed themselves as being alone, they were often in the company of other women (xxix). See Sarah Brusky, "Nancy Prince and her Gothic Odyssey," in this book (chapter 7).

2   Portions of the discussion on *Williams Obstetrics* are adapted from Kristi Siegel's *Women's Autobiographies, Culture, Feminism* (New York: Peter Lang) 114–15.

3   Though I would normally use the term *women* rather than *girls,* in the boys/girls culture of the movie, *Where the Boys Are, girls* seems more appropriate.

4   Susan J. Douglas comments on the "subtext" of Melanie's punishment as well (80) in her excellent analysis of the movie.

Works Cited

Auntie Mame. Dir. Morton DaCosta. Perf. Rosalind Russell, Forrest Tucker, and Coral Browne. Warner Bros., 1958.

Bedknobs and Broomsticks. Dir. Robert Stevenson. Perf. Angela Lansbury, David Tomlinson, and Roddy McDowall. Walt Disney, 1971.

Bushi, R. "RedGhost. Introduction: Circles of Resolution: from 'Little Red Riding Hood' to *The Bloody Chamber.* Accessed May 25, 2002. http//www.members.lycos.co.uk/thaz/RedGhost/intro.htm.

Carter, Angela. "The Company of Wolves." *The Norton Anthology of Literature by Women.* Ed. Sandra M. Gilbert and Susan Gubar. New York: W. W. Norton, 1985. 2326–34.

Cast Away. Dir. Robert Zemeckis. Perf. Tom Hanks, Helen Hunt, and Nick Searcy. Fox, 2000.

Cohen, Patricia Cline. "Women at Large: Travel in Antebellum America." *History Today.* December 1994: 1–12.

Davidson, Robyn. *Tracks.* 1980. New York: Vintage, 1995.

Douglas, Susan J. *Where the Girls Are: Growing Up Female with the Mass Media.* New York: Times Books, 1995.

Fuller, Margaret. "Woman in the Nineteenth Century." *The Norton Anthology of Literature by Women.* Ed. Sandra M. Gilbert and Susan Gubar. New York: W. W. Norton, 1985. 293–309.

Gidget. Dir. Paul Wendkos. Perf. Sandra Dee, James Darren, and Cliff Robertson. Columbia Pictures, 1959.

Gidget Goes Hawaiian. Dir. Paul Wendkos. Perf. James Darren, Michael Callan, and Deborah Walley. Columbia Pictures, 1961.

Gidget Goes to Rome. Dir. Paul Wendkos. Perf. James Darren, Jessie Royce Landis, and Cindy Carol. Columbia Pictures, 1963.

Gilbert, Sandra M., and Susan Gubar. *The Norton Anthology of Literature by Women: The Tradition in English.* New York: W. W. Norton, 1985.

Grewal, Inderpal. *Home and Harem: Nation, Gender, Empire, and the Cultures of Travel.* Durham and London: Duke UP, 1996.

Grimm, Jacob, and Wilhelm Grimm. "Little Red-Cap." *Household Tales*. Trans. Margaret Hunt. London: George Bell, 1884. Vol. I:110–14.

How to Marry a Millionaire. Dir. Jean Negulesco. Perf. Betty Grable, Marilyn Monroe, and Lauren Bacall. Fox, 1953.

Inn of the Sixth Happiness. Dir. Mark Robson. Perf. Ingrid Bergman, Curt Jürgens, and Robert Donat. Fox, 1958.

Kaplan, Caren. *Questions of Travel: Postmodern Discourses of Displacement*. Durham and London: Duke UP, 1996.

Keen, Cathy. "Study Shows Women Find Solo Travel Liberating Rather Than Dangerous." *UF News* (11 March 2002). Gainesville: U of Florida. Accessed April 19, 2003. http://www.napa.ufl.edu/2002news/solowomen.htm.

Klass, Perri. *A Not Entirely Benign Procedure: Four Years as a Medical Student*. New York: Plume Press, 1994.

Leeming, David Adams, and Marian Sader, eds. *Storytelling Encyclopedia: Historical, Cultural, and Multiethnic Approaches to Oral Traditions around the World*. Phoenix: Oryx Press, 1997.

Martin, Emily. *The Woman in the Body: A Cultural Analysis of Reproduction*. Boston: Beacon Press, 1992.

Mary Poppins. Dir. Robert Stevenson. Perf. Julie Andrews, Dick Van Dyke, David Tomlinson, and Glynis Johns. Walt Disney, 1964.

Move Over, Darling. Dir. Michael Gordon. Perf. Doris Day, James Garner, and Polly Bergen. Fox, 1963.

Mulvey, Laura. *Visual and Other Pleasures*. Bloomington and Indianapolis: Indiana UP, 1989.

The Nun's Story. Dir. Fred Zinnemann. Perf. Audrey Hepburn, Peter Finch, Edith Evans, and Peggy Ashcroft. Warner Bros., 1959.

Perrault, Charles. "Little Red Riding Hood." *Folklore and Mythology: Electronic Texts*. Ed. and/or Trans. D. L. Ashliman. University of Pittsburgh. Accessed July 15, 2002. http://www.pitt.edu/~dash/type0333.html, 1–9.

The Pleasure Seekers. Dir. Jean Negulesco. Perf. Ann-Margaret, Tony Franciosa, and Carol Lynley. Fox, 1964.

Pritchard, Jack A., and Paul C. Macdonald. *Williams Obstetrics*. 16th ed. New York: Appleton-Century-Crofts, 1980.

Robinson, Jane. *Unsuitable for Ladies: An Anthology of Women Travellers*. Oxford: Oxford UP, 1994.

Schriber, Mary Suzanne. *Telling Travels: Selected Writings by Nineteenth-Century American Women Abroad*. DeKalb: Northern Illinois UP, 1995.

Siegel, Kristi. *Women's Autobiographies, Culture, Feminism*. New York: Peter Lang, 1999, 2001.

Take Her, She's Mine. Dir. Henry Koster. Perf. James Stewart, Sandra Dee, and Audrey Meadows. Fox, 1963.

Tammy and the Bachelor. Dir. Joseph Pevney. Perf. Debbie Reynolds, Leslie Nielsen, and Walter Brennan. Universal, 1957.

Tammy and the Doctor. Dir. Harry Keller. Perf. Sandra Dee, Peter Fonda, and Macdonald Carey. Universal, 1963.

Tammy Tell Me True. Dir. Harry Keller. Perf. Sandra Dee, John Gavin, and Charles Drake. Universal, 1961.

72   *Kristi Siegel*

Thelma & Louise. Dir. Ridley Scott. Perf. Susan Sarandon, Geena Davis, and Harvey Keitel. MGM, 1991.

Three Coins in a Fountain. Dir. Jean Negulesco. Perf. Clifton Web, Dorothy McGuire, Jean Peter, Louis Jourdan. Fox, 1954.

Truth, Sojourner. "Ain't I a Woman?" *The Norton Anthology of Literature by Women.* Ed. Sandra M. Gilbert and Susan Gubar. New York: W. W. Norton, 1985. 252–53.

Where the Boys Are. Dir. Henry Levin. Perf. Delores Hart, George Hamilton, Yvette Mimieux, and Jim Hutton. MGM, 1960.

✍ Chapter Four

The Daughters of Thelma and Louise
New? Aesthetics of the Road

Jessica Enevold

Introduction

In their critical analysis of twentieth-century travel narratives, *Tourists with Typewriters* (1999), Patrick Holland and Graham Huggan ask if it is "possible in a genre [travel writing] much given to repetition, to come up with something new?" (x). I agree with Holland and Huggan that in travel writing there exists a repetition of clichés, which cannot be overlooked. Nevertheless, I want to stress the importance of looking upon both travel writing and its clichés again from a slightly different, strategically important, perspective—that of gender.

Gender and genre are in this study thrust into a tight embrace. I see *genre* as constituted by a number of linguistic elements, constructed bodies of style, settings, ideologies, characters, and plots, and so forth. Its sibling word *gender* can be accounted for in much the same way. Their etymological kinship demonstrates an axiomatic association between the two: They are separated only by the "d," as Jacques Derrida writes in "The Law of Genre," where he also goes on to question the opposition between the two. Lidia Curti, taking the cue, states that "genre is traversed by the discourse of sexual difference as if the vicinity of the two English words—genre and gender, divided by 'd' (for difference?)—recalled coincidence and dislocation, obedience and transgression at one and the same time" (53). Considering their intimate and long-standing relationship, can these familiar associates breed into something unfamiliar, that is, new?

Attempting to answer this question, in what follows I focus on a certain subgenre of contemporary travel writing, which I refer to as the *road genre*. What I mean by the road genre is roughly what Ronald Primeau (*Romance of the Road* 1996) calls "The Literature of the American Highway," and Kris Lackey (*RoadFrames* 1997) "The American Highway Narrative."

The critics referred to above discuss travel writing under the auspices of genre, while—and here lies an important difference between their studies and my own project—the aegis of my investigation is gender. Gender is thus the basis for my analysis rather than another element hybridizing with another royal genre; gender becomes the cardinal critical category and diagnostic criterion rather than another chapter in another survey of travel literature.[1]

To pay primary attention to gender entails considering the questions of gendered authorship. The last thirty years of critical activity have been favorable to a literary climate in which the significance of the author has been undermined and the text privileged. A simultaneous movement to resurrect the rejected writer has, however, existed. It has been sustained by feminist and postcolonial critics protesting against, for example, the "neutralization" of the author, that is, the implicit whitening, masculinizing, or even erasure of the author. As far as travel writing is concerned, the author should be raised from the dead for good. An author's role becomes particularly urgent to consider as he or she, as writer and sometimes narrative subject, can be understood both metaphorically and literally as the navigator of the ship. Helmsmanship has been the key to journey narratives from the *Odyssey* to *On the Road*. Holland and Huggan implicitly draw the issue of helmsmanship (that is, subjectivity) into their analysis by singling out as a trademark of contemporary travel writing a feature that they label "specialization." One of their examples is "women's travel." In their example, "woman" becomes the determining agent for the definition of the travel narrative. They have thus focused on the agent of travel—the one who travels and who presents/writes the subsequent travel narrative. Their focus on the agent is nevertheless vague. Another example of specialization is "ecological tourism," in the account of which the traveler loses its specific gender, that is, "reverts" to a supposedly neutral status, and in which the analytical focus is redirected to observe instead the narrative determinants of, for example, "new" ideological (in this case ecological) elements of travel. I would like to advocate an even closer pursuit of the traveler-navigator subjectivity, stalking in this process the implications of genre analysis as gender governs its perspective.

Where Do We Find Ourselves?

In 1947, Simone de Beauvoir traveled across the United States from New York on the East Coast to Los Angeles on the West Coast, and back. She kept a detailed diary, which was published in French in 1948 as *L'Amerique au jour le jour*, and in English in 1952 as *America Day by Day*. In 1996, a new translation with a foreword by Douglas Brinkley was published. Brinkley concluded his praise of the book with the words: "For women, and men, who want to experience vicariously Jack Kerouac's open road with less macho romanticism and more existential savvy, *America Day by Day*, hidden from us for nearly fifty years, comes to the reader like a dusty bottle of vintage French cognac, asking only to be uncorked" (Brinkley xvi). Brinkley also noted that in 1952 the book...

> generated few sales and little notice. But with the passage of time, *America Day by Day* emerges as a supremely erudite American road book—that distinctive subgenre based on flight of fancy rather than flights from economic hardship, as in John Steinbeck's *Grapes of Wrath*. In broader sociological terms, her critique outpaces William Least Heat-Moon's *Blue Highways: A Journey into America*. (xi–xii)

Brinkley's statement resonates with my triad of concepts: genre, gender, and "the new." First of all, Brinkley places de Beauvoir, the traveler/writer, in the "road book" genre.[2] He compares her account with Kerouac's *On the Road* and William Least Heat-Moon's *Blue Highways*. Both *On the Road* and *Blue Highways* have become road classics; both were published after *America Day by Day* by ten and forty years, respectively. Interestingly enough, Brinkley canonizes, in 1997, a work written in 1948, into a road genre which can be said to have been defined as such first in 1958.[3] In other words: Brinkley has articulated "something new" by inserting something "old" into something else which is also "old." He has revised a very "male buddy genre"[4] by bringing a woman straight into the core of its canon. Gender and genre are here brought into a productive crisis, as it were, although in his review Brinkley does not reflect on this, and definitely not in these terms. In his short introduction to the book, the genre reveals no sign of being gendered, but is presented as an all-inclusive, all-neutral vehicle of story and history telling.[5] He thus follows the traditional story (and theory)[6] that reserves no place for non-WASP travelers who are not male. One could conclude, then, that de Beauvoir must be a man, because the prototypical American storyteller was always a man, and the prototypical traveler was always a man, and has remained so until the present. Something must have happened. The essence of Brinkley's review, as I read it, is that it divulges that now even a *French woman's diary entries* may pass for customized Xeroxes of American (male) culture in the making, and remaking.[7] This, indeed, is one way of making the travel genre "new." I find it, however, an extremely problematic and unproblematized one.

I wonder whether Brinkley is conscious of his "revision" of the road genre, or if his recommendation to infuse the road genre with Beauvoir's "savvy existentialism" is actually gender blind or ignorant of the gender-dependence[8] of the genre history.[9] Even so, this gender-dependence is evident since the very literary "inception" of the road genre. In a Judeo-Christian tradition, this inception can be placed as far back as in the biblical "Exodus."[10] Gender is ubiquitous in the genres of travel writing and must not be neglected, or cursorily treated by the cultural critic.

New Stories of Women on the Road

In 1998, the editors of the collection *Wild Ways: New Stories about Women on the Road*, Margo Daly and Jill Dawson, announced a change in what I want to call the traditionally gendered pattern of mobility. "Women these days are big on adventures," they wrote, "Thelma and Louise captured the Zeitgeist....Finally gals got a look in on the road trip" (x). As Daly and Dawson imply, the entrance of the traveling woman had been long in the making. Compensating for her extended absence, she crossed the threshold quite powerfully in the shape of *Thelma & Louise* in 1991. The movie's role as an efficient promoter of feminist values has been discussed.[11] Its impact on the road genre is nevertheless unquestionable. *Thelma & Louise* broke into a road narrative, which ever since the 1950s had been *the* masculine "buddy-genre," gendered as such by Jack Kerouac's novel *On the Road*, and later reinscribed as such by Peter Fonda and Dennis Hopper's road movie, *Easy Rider*.

By what could be called a simple reversal, *Thelma & Louise* laid bare the stereotypical gender-dependence of the road genre and exposed a vulnerability of women on the road, particularly when they are without guns or money. The mere substitution of two females for the customary male buddy protagonists, the appropriation of the road for two women, radically altered the genre's premises. These premises include male escape from societal constraints represented by women and what they stand for: domesticity, commitment, wed*lock*, in other words, immobilizing obligations. *Thelma & Louise* exposes the traditional stereotyping of male-female relationships where men "are" spermatic mobile men, and women waiting egg-bearing to-be-mothers in fixed locations, whose deviation from the stove seems automatically to translate them into "women on the loose" whose mere presence in public space announces that sex is up for grabs.[12]

In *Thelma & Louise*, the escape was transformed into an escape from patriarchal values and boundaries. Some critics emphasize the escape from heterosexuality; that is, they stress the friendship between Thelma and Louise as an evolving lesbian relationship.[13] According to Barbara Johnson, though, the film "failed to deliver...a lesbian plot" ("Lesbian Spectacles" 161). Thus, *Thelma & Louise* performs, within a long-established heterosexual institution, an attack on conventional patterns of chauvinist male behavior toward females. Women strike back on sexual harassers and patriarchal guardians of law and marriage. The rapist is shot, Thelma's husband is cheated on and abandoned, the highway patrol officer is bereft of his gun and locked into the trunk of his car, and the truck driver is confronted, his cap confiscated, and his truck blown up. To put it tersely, there are several assaults on men and their machines.

Perhaps it is due to its violence that many reviews of *Thelma & Louise* have reported puzzled reception; the film has been surrounded by "furor" (Rapping 33) and said to be "phony feminism [that] fails on the silver screen" (Sharrett 57). It has been presented as an "acting out [of] a male fantasy of life on the road" that "can hardly be called a woman's movie or one with a feminist sensibility" (Carlson 57). The critic John Leo remarks on its "repeated paean to transformative violence" not to be found in any male-buddy movies, and with which, he claims, we leave "Dworkin [only to enter] a Mussolini speech. Here we have an explicit fascist theme, wedded to the bleakest form of feminism" (20). Leo criticizes the movie reviewers for their generally, in his mind, excessively positive reception, and goes on to refute the affirmative "pleasingly subversive" (Leo quoting reviewer Kennet Turan 20) and "big-hearted movie" (Leo quoting reviewer Jack Knoll 20). In point of fact, Leo claims, this is a "morally and intellectually screwed up...small-hearted, toxic film." With what can be interpreted as disgust, he notes that several of the female spectators appeared "to leave the theater in something of a daze" (20).

Violent feminism, some say; no feminism, say others. "Women

cheer the movie," yet others say (Carlson 57). The connections made by the critics between the film and women, and between the film and feminism are noteworthy. The list of films starring violent or forceful males is endless, but whenever does male audience reception get reported in a similar manner? Not very often—one reason is that those movies pass by the critical eye of the general observer because a man in a role is, as always, not considered as a male, but as a protagonist.

The action of/in *Thelma & Louise*—as is implied by some reviewers—needs to be defended, or "protected" against certain viewers (or "viewings"). "I enjoyed this movie," Rapping writes, "so did my male companions" (31). She adds: "[A]nyone daring to go on the Oprah Winfrey show to defend the creep who attacked Thelma and was shot down by Louise had better be prepared to be yelled down by audience, crew members, and the loudmouthed hostess herself" (31). My personal experience confirms this Thelma and Louise–effect. Wherever (on the screen, as a home video, in the classroom) and whenever (in 1992, 1996, or now), I have seen the movie or taught it, the women's violent performances have been received by the audience with elated sanction. There is something about the movie that rouses its audiences. As Sarandon put it in an interview, "'[W]e all underestimated *Thelma & Louise*. I thought it was a Western, with two women, and you know, trucks. But the fact is, there was such a…she pauses in a rare, rare loss of words, '…just a fanatic, deeply difficult something in that movie'" (DiClementi 31).

With *Thelma & Louise,* we seem to reach a disjunction between political correctness and feminist/emotional investment. A similar disjunction appears toward the end of the 1990s when Girl Power is, by some, experienced as a major backlash on 1970's feminism and as solidifying traditional gender stereotypes into a feminist impasse, rather than as empowering female tactics.[14] However, when at these kinds of critical disjunction, it is crucial not to envision women as merely "fronting for Hugh Hefner," as one critic of *Thelma & Louise* wrote (Carlson 57). Each and every time feminism, or rather, representations of women (that invoke discourses of feminism), are perceived as facing a major crisis, feminism is forced into dialogue with its past, and our sociocultural framework of understanding is challenged. We must try to understand the responses that *Thelma & Louise* elicits, but how can we do that? Which discourses does the film violate or infringe upon to cause such reactions? To clarify the confusion and "mess" *Thelma & Louise* creates, the film is subsequently discussed as an example of a regendering of a genre through rescripting. Implementing this regendering through rescripting, *Thelma & Louise* represents what I have termed an appropriative turn in the evolution of the road narrative.

Rescripting the Road Narrative: The Appropriative Turn

The regendering of a genre can be understood in other ways than as a mere substitution of women for men in the lead roles.[15] This substitution in *Thelma & Louise* could at first glance be called a simple reversal; it is in fact much more complex. *Thelma & Louise* unmistakably excites and upsets the professional critics as well as the general audience because, in this movie, gender and genre are intersecting at a major cusp, intruding on each other's paths—rescripting one another, and in the process crossing culturally scripted, binary boundaries. What then is *scripting*, and what binary boundaries are crossed?

I use the term *scripting* loosely after Derek Gregory. Gregory understands scripting as "a developing series of steps and signals, part structured and part improvised, that produces a narrativized sequence of interactions through which roles are made and remade by soliciting responses and responding to cues" (116). Gregory admits that describing the "cultural practices involved in travel and tourism" in the terms of scripting is not original. James Buzard, for example, has written on "'the scripted continent,' but he [has done so] in ways that constantly folds travel back into the text"; that is, Buzard (as does Gregory) relates to a tradition of "guiding texts," which have influenced nineteenth-century travel writing. However, Gregory claims, whereas Buzard maintains a predominantly "textual" perspective on the territories and "boundaries mapped out by those prior texts," Gregory wishes to accentuate the "production (and consumption) of spaces that reach beyond the narrowly textual" and to "bring into view practices that take place on the ground" (116).[16] Then how is scripting important to travel writing? This is what Gregory says:

> In the first place, it directs our attention to the ways in which travel writing is intimately involved in the 'staging' of particular places: in the simultaneous production of 'sites' that are linked in a time-space itinerary and 'sights' that are organized into a hierarchy of cultural significance. Travel scripting produces a serialized space of constructed visibility that allows and sometimes even requires specific objects to be seen in specific ways by a specific audience. (116)

Not only Egypt that Gregory investigates, but also "the road" in general has been written down, mapped, and charted for its subsequent travelers. That is why road narratives (films and books) that have become "road classics" predispose authors and readers to stage and identify their stories in certain prefigured ways. In *Thelma & Louise* we find residues of the traditional road script concurrent with a violation of its "sites" and "sights" in terms of gender. *Thelma & Louise* wreaks havoc on the road genre's long-standing gender polarization, or in the familiar feminist terminology—on the hierarchy of binaries.

In her essay "What Is a Woman?" Toril Moi does a "critical analysis of some of the presuppositions of poststructuralist thinking about sex, gender, and the body" (118). She exemplifies her analysis with a number of cases, one of which is treated in Mary Anne Case's essay "Disaggregating Gender from Sex and Sexual Orientation: The Effeminate Man in the Law and Feminist Jurisprudence." To illustrate her argument, Moi reproduces the list Case uses of attributes regularly categorized as either "masculine" or "feminine."[17] The qualities of the different genders (or, more correctly, sex-based stereotypes, as Moi points out) are grouped as follows:

MASCULINE	FEMININE
aggressive	affectionate
ambitious	cheerful
analytical	childlike
assertive	compassionate
athletic	flatterable
competitive	gentle
dominant	gullible
forceful	loyal
independent	sensitive
individualistic	shy
self-reliant	soft-spoken
self-sufficient	sympathetic
strong	tender
	understanding
	warm
	yielding

Moi critiques "the theoreticism of poststructuralist feminist theory," with the intention of freeing us "from a theoretical picture that tells us how things must be, and so blinds us to alternative ways of thinking" (118). She wants to show "that in the case of a question that truly matters to [her], namely 'What is a woman?' there are good reasons to consider alternatives to the sex/gender distinction." Still, she finds that the distinction may be useful, for example, "when it comes to opposing biological determinism à la Geddes and Thomson" (119).

Thelma & Louise provides no neat distinctions between the two columns of binaries; it does not stay safely on the female/femininity side of the binary division of qualities. Nor are the characters a simple reversal of the masculine/feminine polarization. Things are much more "untidy" than that. *Thelma & Louise* guides its audiences into a fog[19] of binaries, a haze of notions of sex-based stereotypes. It argues that there is not *one* thing a woman is—which is one of the points Moi wants to make with her Beauvoirean approach to working out "a theory of the sexually different body," a theory, which, in her view, gains nothing from a "rethinking of the concepts of sex and gender," as it will not yield a "good theory of the body or subjectivity" (4).[20]

Thelma & Louise is not only a conquest of a male buddy genre, but also an appropriation of a set of qualities traditionally viewed as traits of masculinity characterizing male human beings (here: inhabiting the road) while, at the same time, retaining traditional qualities of femininity. Thelma and Louise are yielding and assertive, affectionate and aggressive; they are loyal and independent; they are tender and forceful; they are gentle and strong, and so on.

Describing the Road Narrative: The Metafictional Turn

Thelma and Louise constituted a renewal of the road genre. However, as has been noted, they do die in the end—a rather bleak result that makes it tempting to say that the movie failed, rather than succeeded, when it comes to the question of liberating women.[21] Although the film did liberate the road genre script, Thelma and Louise were never able to sit down comfortably in the director's chair; this is, however, what the "daughters" of Thelma and Louise do.

Although Thelma and Louise died, it is obvious from the narratives discussed below that a new generation of women has survived and grown up with Thelma and Louise's revolutionary adventure vividly in their minds. These women (or female characters) seem to thrive on what Thelma and Louise did, and they refuse to drive off the cliff; they want to resolve the road differently. Presented here are a few examples from *Wild Ways: New Stories of Women on the Road,* and *Flaming Iguanas: An All-Girl Road Novel Thing.*

The *Wild Ways* collection shows that *Thelma & Louise* has had an undeniable and impregnating impact on many of its (writing) descendants. The movie did indeed accomplish an appropriation of territory. Not only did it appropriate the road as a generic space, but judging by the "acts" of its daughters, it also opened up a space for road mothers, who thus appropriated the important role of road models.

Such female role models are invoked repeatedly in *Wild Ways*. Sometimes the role models are juxtaposed to the road fathers who previously reigned supreme, sometimes they quietly supersede them, sometimes they explicitly reject them. Although in *Flaming Iguanas* role models assume different shapes, the rejection of road fathers is nonetheless up-front. The following examples from three different stories from *Wild Ways* indicate which female forerunners the women of these "new" (to quote the collection title) road stories relate. The first example, from Bidisha's story "Leaving," shows an interesting combination of influences: "And here I am, an ordinary writer writing ordinary things…thinking about a story I have to write. Travelling, journeys, feminism—I arrange my hat and think of lipstick, Thelma and Louise—Cindy and Barbie" (Bidisha, "Leaving" 109). Does this combination of names imply an analogy (between the two pairs Thelma and Louise and Cindy and Barbie), or is it the contrasting effect Bidisha is after when she lists images coming to her protagonist's mind when she thinks of "travelling, journeys, feminism"? Rather, the reference is a reflection on the images of women brought to the narrator since adolescence (or childhood). These act as scripts which develop, to repeat Gregory's words again, a "series of steps and signals, part structured and part improvised, that produces a narrativized sequence of interactions through which roles are made and remade by soliciting responses and responding to cues" (116). However, the point here is that the response solicited is "Thelma and Louise—Cindy and Barbie," not "Kerouac and Cassady—Ken and Action Man."

"Tofino" by Jill Dawson is a story about two women, Nickie and Ann, and Nickie's teenage daughter (who is the narrator of the story), traveling down the British Columbia Coast into Washington state and then back to Canada. The party set out four weeks earlier, initiating their journey by renting a car:

> They were disappointed initially when the guy at Budget Rentals produced a Chevy that was so unlike their dreams. Brand spanking new for a

start…This Chevrolet, this white Chevy Cavalier, with its *Beautiful British Columbia* is a bit too much like a Nissan Micra for Mum's taste. But hell, what does she know about cars anyway? They decide that Thelma and Louise would still have driven it if it was all the rental company had on offer, and that, after a short giggle at their own silliness with this Thelma and Louise thing, seems to do the trick. (Dawson 55)

They have had "a fantastic trip. Fantastic scenery, fantastic motels, fantastic food. The only thing missing has been fantastic sex, and you can't have everything….Perhaps we should pick up a hitch-hiker, like Thelma and Louise, what about it Nickie?" (57). The repeated reference to Thelma and Louise as road models, however facetious, is thought-provoking. The reference recurs in Emily Perkins's "Can't Beat It." Here the characters Cecilia and Marcie (as the narrating character has chosen to call herself during the stay in America), two Australian women on a road trip in the United States, financed by a grant from the Australian Arts Council, stage themselves as Thelma and Louise. As we can see, Thelma and Louise again surface in the narrative, enabling a rescripting of the road. In another scene, the narrative playfully issues a territorial claim on the road by moving beyond its male road predecessors and their scripts. "Can't Beat It" literally stages and rescripts the road:

> In a way, we're paying homage to Kerouac and to Cassady—they refused to accept a strict, narrow time structure…they also colluded with phallocentrism—look at the benefits they reaped, the fame, the 'freedom', the access to naïve—I don't say stupid—women. So we must look further than these men. We look to the road itself and pay homage to that, to the passive, 'female' land that must bear the scar of the road that man has carved through it, the burdened road, burdened land that carries its traffic in much the same way the female carries the male … (Perkins 6–7).

Marcie, obviously bored, leaves the camera running and goes for a little walk.

In "Men and Women" I claimed that in the various travel genres women were traditionally "walk-ons," not heroes. In "Can't Beat It," the female characters are not only protagonists, they also take on the role of film director. To use another cinematic metaphor, women can be said to have promoted themselves from the relatively hidden position of assisting script-girl to that of woman-director. Cecilia and Marcie (by way of Perkins's narrative scheme) are toying with the founding text, the textual directors, the "original script" of the road, the traditional gendering of landscape as female or feminine, and with their own "artistic" situation. By way of metafictional commentary these "new" women on the road shed light on the genre's burdened past and its conservative constructions of female subjectivity. They are addressing belatedness with a self-conscious and ironic vengeance—without a trace of anxiety.

"Can't Beat It" refers extensively not only to the road genre but also to America in a way that makes their road trip a model example of what Eco would call travel in hyperreality[21]: Perkins's Cecilia and Marcie exemplify the mind-boggling experience of the traveler who, for the first time, encounters the material/spatially tangible phenomenon of the "real" United States, heretofore the make-believe (and, it should be added, the stereotypical and genre-typical) America mediated through films and commercial icons. They exclaim: "Here we are in the United States of America. We are *so* excited! It is like a dream. It's like the movies. It's *just* like the movies" (3, original emphasis). The hyperreality of silverscreen-America is projected onto "reality," making it real and true. There are several references to American cultural/movie and media icons. Cecilia "smokes Kent, because Audrey Hepburn used to smoke them" (4). It is a big event coming across "Our first drugstore! Cecilia bought 'a pack a Trojans.' They were the most American things we could think of. I recorded the event on our Super 8 camera. The guy asked what kind, and Cecilia said Ribbed, buddy—for her pleasure" (5). In the car "we play Bruce Springsteen exclusively. I thought some of the lyrics would go against Cecilia's feminist stance, but she sings along regardless" (9). This pattern of metafictional and postmodernist self-conscious rhetoric justifies, I would argue, another modification of the scripting term; "Can't Beat It" comes closer to a de-scripting, that is, a deconstructive re-scripting of the road narrative.

Whereas the patriarchal yoke in *Thelma & Louise* seemed to require an engagement of violence to be lifted off women's shoulders, in "Can't Beat It" the yoke of forefathers, patriarchs, and contemporary males seems easily cast off. For example, the references to other "big" male names, more loosely associated to the road in terms of its wider meaning of Western, are given with humorous zest: Cecilia "sprays herself with Evian three times a day 'toning and moisturising in one'" and comments, "I am surprised to find that I like not washing. Did Martin Sheen wash in *Badlands*? Did Billy the Kid wash? Did Jim? No way" (8).

Apart from deflating potential patriarchal pressure, the sentence harbors self-conscious play; the stereotypical qualities associated with women—the pampering of the skin, the paying attention to beauty and maintenance of outer signs of femininity are juxtaposed with the delight in not washing. Marcie may, of course, also have referred to *Thelma & Louise,* in which there is a gradual shift in appearance of the two women as their journey progresses, from a very neatly clad and well-groomed exterior, from skirt and lace frills to dirty faces without make-up, suntans and hair let loose, jeans, T-shirts, and bandanas. The "appropriation" of "both/and"-binaries in *Thelma & Louise* is also taking place in "Can't Beat It," but it is enacted in a self-conscious manner, the women constantly observing their own activities, their own de-scripting.

The reviewers of *Thelma & Louise* were the ones articulating feminist interpretations of the film and filmic interpretations of feminism. The authors and characters of the three quoted stories from *Wild Ways* explicitly deal with the stakes of feminism; feminism is, in fact, ubiquitous in the three quoted narratives. Even so, its status is always hemmed in, made ambivalent. In Erika Lopez's novel *Flaming Iguanas,* this ambivalence becomes acute and is to a high degree connected to the "issue" of road models, and to the long-standing questions in the debates on feminism, that is, "what feminism," and "whose feminism"? The main character of *Flaming Iguanas,* Jolene alias Tomato, whose intention it is to cross the United States on a motorcycle, never mentions Thelma and Louise, although one of its reviewer's does: "Lopez gives Tomato an outlaw integrity that Thelma and Louise only hinted at" (Patricia Holt, *San Francisco Chronicle*—reprinted on the book's back cover). The publisher's blurb on the back cover of *Flaming Iguanas* also wants to connect Lopez's narrative to that of male road ancestors: "Tomato Rodriguez hops on her motorcycle and embarks on the ultimate sea-to-shining-sea all-girl adventure—a story that combines all the best parts of *Alice in Wonderland* and *Easy Rider.*" However, it should be noted that Lopez/Tomato never mentions *Easy Rider.* The divergence between the two narratives becomes particularly conspicuous if one considers the fact that *Easy Rider* does not contain one grain of comedy and takes itself very seriously, whereas *Flaming Iguanas* is extraordinarily funny and self-ironic. The similarities between Tomato, a Latina lesbian-biker-bitch-to-be, and Captain America, a snow-white heterosexual dead-to-be drug smuggler, begin and end with their preferred choice of transportation. If there are any undertones of the *Easy Rider*–narrative, they could possibly be found in Lopez's "Before"-statement. However, she advertises the pre–road trip state of affairs in a tone of voice very far from a venerable homage to Billy and Captain America. She can be said to venerate the road, but it is a road that changes with the eye of its beholder, and in Lopez's view nothing is too sacred to be made fun of—including herself and her highway project. *She* is the director of this adventure. Her "statement of purpose" is well worth quoting:

> Magdalena and I are gonna cross America on two motorcycles. We're gonna be so fucking cool, mirrors and windows will break when we pass by. We'll have our own hardcore theme music that makes our heads bend back and bite the sky, and women wearing pink foam curlers in passing RVs will desire us and we'll slowly turn to them at seventy-five miles an hour and mouth "hello" back....We'll be riding the cheapest motorcycles we can find/stopping every forty-five minutes for gas. And we'll be spitting our mango pits like fucking bullets if anyone says anything about our huge Latin American Breasts. (1–2, slash in original)

The quote adamantly states that we are women, and we like other women, thus bringing out explicitly the theme of homosexuality. It also asserts that women on motorcycles are women without the need to pretend to be men and that women have an equal right to the road. It also says that if anyone objects to the fact that we are women on the road we will launch a counterattack, and it will be violent. Of course, the tone is self-consciously jocose, but given the gendered legacy of the genre, the underlying assumption of what *must* be de-scripted is extremely serious.

Although there is no direct reference to *Easy Rider* or *Thelma & Louise,* there is, nevertheless, a straightforward rejection of other (genre-important) road fathers:

> Ever since I was a kid, I'd tried to live vicariously through the hocker-in-the-wind adventures of Kerouac, Hunter Thompson and Henry Miller. But I could never finish any of the books. Maybe I just couldn't identify with the fact that they were guys who had women around to make the coffee and wash the skid marks out of their shorts while they complained, called themselves angry young men, and screwed each other with their existential penises. (Lopez 27)

In conjunction with this "counterattack" on men's and women's traditional roles, I want to recall Brinkley's review of de Beauvoir's *America Day by Day,* and agree with him that de Beauvoir does indeed

imbue the road genre with "savvy existentialism," although in a completely different sense than he had in mind. In addition to the "existential penises," the following certainly supports the claim:

> Erica Jong was there for me in my mother's bookshelf between *Vaginal
> Politics* and *The Second Sex*, unapologetically running around the world in
> heat with her panties stretched taut around her ankles. But I never identi-
> fied with her being tied to relationships like a dog to a tree/like a tongue
> to its mouth. (Lopez 27)

It is very interesting to note what can either be a reference to
Ellen Frankfort's 1972 book, *Vaginal Politics*, or a mischievous allusion
to Kate Millet's *Sexual Politics*. Such a comment would, in combination
with the unquestioned influence of de Beauvoir's *The Second Sex*, signal a certain ambivalence to feminism, as does the dismissal of Erica
Jong's *Fear of Flying*. The indirect mention of *Fear of Flying* demonstrates an ambiguous relationship to a potential female predecessor.
Fear of Flying is often mentioned among the works of "liberating"
feminist fiction, and also given as an example of modern picaresque.[22]
However, there is no such generic association anywhere in Tomato's
account.[23] Lopez has called her book a "road novel thing." She has
chosen a genre (which she uses whichever way she pleases) and acknowledges the fact that there is a generic past while simultaneously
throwing it out. Road fathers are ousted with suggestive determination. This is an "*All-Girl* kind of road novel thing."

Tomato's choice of role model, then, falls only partly on a French
feminist philosopher. Xena, Warrior Princess, is mentioned as another
("Xena must live forever" 163), and others are "wanted"; when Tomato reaches her final destination, San Francisco, she finds herself in
the arms of a lover who "was like a queen lesbian going 120 miles an
hour down hill without an iota of hesitation about turning on a
somewhat straight girl" (248). Tomato's reflection on the experience
brings the burning question of role models and feminism to a high-
point:

> To my relief, the next morning I didn't feel like a member of a lesbian
> gang. I didn't feel the urge to subscribe to lesbian magazines, wear flannel
> shirts, wave DOWN WITH PATRIARCHY signs in the air, or watch bad
> lesbian movies to see myself represented. No. I wanted a Bisexual Female
> Ejaculating Quaker role model. And where was she dammit? From now on
> I would demand to be represented. (251)

As shown by the previous quote, Tomato de-scripts all potential male residues latent in the genre. As one reviewer expressed it: "Lopez isn't your father's road warrior. She's way too passionate to be beatnik cool" (Stovall 17). However, in addition to expelling male road models, she calls for a new one: She demands "to be represented." Her search for a representative after which to model herself sexually and racially is expressed throughout the narrative. Tomato keeps commenting on her own constitution as ethnic and sexual being. Thus, *Flaming Iguanas* will not content itself with merely a regendering of the road persona, but wants a further expansion of the territory of subjectivity to include other races, other ethnicities, and other sexualities than white, North-American heterosexuality. Thus, regendering is only one aspect of this narrative, which demands more and more room for the female mobile subject.

Thelma & Louise takes one step away from the gender of the scripts of *On the Road* and *Easy Rider* by way of re-scripting. With *Wild Ways,* the regendering escalates from re-scripting to *de-scripting.* This de-scripting consists of metafictional commentary, as well as a postmodernist self-conscious rhetoric. In the first case, an appropriative turn takes place, in the second, a metafictional one. In both these "turns" the *regendering* of the road narrative is crucial. But, to return to the title of this essay—how new is this "new" aesthetic?

New? Aesthetics of the Road

Holland and Huggan claim that "postmodern devices have not so consistently infiltrated the travel book as they have the contemporary novel" (158). It is nevertheless true that there are a number of postmodernist literary devices, which are present in the new aesthetics of the new women's road narratives analyzed here: extreme self-consciousness, self-theorizing, parody, irony, and playfulness. Holland and Huggan also point out that when "postmodernism impinges on travel writing, then, it usually does so obliquely, under the sign of 'meta': metatravel, metahistory, invariably metanarratives, reflecting on their own status as texts—as theoretical texts—on travel" (158). This can also be said, to a certain extent, about women's recent road narratives. However, which travel narratives do Holland and Huggan analyze as postmodern? They analyze the "metanarratives" by Italo Calvino, Roland Barthes, Umberto Eco, Jean Baudrillard, Bruce Chatwin, Robert Dessaix, and Paul Theroux (158). None of these narratives is written by a woman, or is about a woman traveler. Holland and Huggan touch very superficially upon gender in their analysis of these so-called postmodern itineraries. In their analysis they ask, for example: "Is there a space for the individual traveler within the over-arching system?" (159). They answer with Calvino's words by point-ing to the "indeterminate and evanescent movement of subjectivity" (159). Holland and Huggan thus speak of "the traveler" of metanarra-tives as a gender-neutral entity, and of "travel" in a very general sense. Having moved through the terminology of migrancy and no-madism (174), and Jonathan Raban's and Paul Theroux's "increasing tendencies toward metafictionality" (176), Holland and Huggan con-clude that "while the various techniques of metafiction provide scope for injecting a sense of play into travel narrative, by definition they also detract from the travel book as a more or less 'authentic' autobio-graphical account" (178).

Holland and Huggan insist on rejecting the "new" in travel writ-ing and stubbornly emphasize its repetitions, despite their identifica-tion of various "countertravelers" as including "women travelers, subverting the male traveler's traditional values and privileges; gay male travelers, either seeking liberatory spaces or flouting heterosex-ual travel codes; and ecological travelers, reacting against the envi-ronmental damage they most frequently associate with tourists" (198). Although they observe that these countertravelers "generally locate themselves in opposition to 'conventional' modes of travel," they in-terpret this oppositional stance as providing "a further alibi for travel writing while still depending on its traditions" (198). They insist on the repetitiveness of the genre, although at certain points they hint at the possibility of something new transpiring in the genre, for instance by mentioning that "counter travel, of one sort or another, has cer-tainly energized travel writing...in the decades since the war" (198). Despite this, and despite their investigations under the rubrics "Women's travel writing and/as feminist critique," and "Transgres-sion, performativity, and the gay male traveling subject," and their brilliant introduction of the narratives investigated in these sections as interrogations of male clichés, phallic myths, and male tropologies "clearing a space in the process for the subjectivities of women travel-ers, and for the exploratory journeys and performances of gay men" (110), they disconnect genre from gender. They make gendered sub-jectivity secondary to a higher generic order governed by repetition. Thus, they observe that "oppositional narratives cannot escape but being haunted by an array of hoary tropes and clichés (originary, primitivist, exotic, and so forth) any more than they can hope to distill 'authentic' encounters from their commodified sources" (198).

In their final words, Holland and Huggan invite the travel book to "reexamine its biases" as the genre, despite its involvement in the processes of commodification, has the capacity to "engage large numbers and several different kinds of readers," and as such merits its existence. In other words, the final statement of the investigation turns into an attempt at "rescuing" the travel book from its death, rather than declaring what in it is new (217).

Holland and Huggan thus end up where they begin, despite all their excellent examples of "new" subjectivities on the road. Because they are caught up in the theories and vocabularies of postmodernism and postmodernity and because of their intensive focus on genre, they fail to see the new, which becomes visible only when gender governs the perspective of the analysis. Consequently, the narratives analyzed in my article are not "new" by virtue of being metafictional accounts, or postmodern picaresques, but rather, due to the simple—yet complicating—fact that the mobile subjects are women. Thus the genre is vitally and fundamentally regendered. As *Flaming Iguanas* shows, the genre calls for additional reorganization—"resubjectivization." What I have done is to describe two phases of the development of the road genre in terms of its employment of certain narrative devices, here conceptualized as re-scripting and de-scripting. The regendering of the genre is "something new" and something too significant to be set adrift among the strong undercurrents of postmodernism, eventually to be submerged by its greater literary paradigm.

Notes

1   Opacki has proposed a theory of genre evolution that emphasizes hybridization, that is, the cross-fertilization of a "royal" (or "dominant" in Russian Formalist terms) genre over time by other genres. "A literary genre entering, in the course of evolution, the field of a particular literary trend, will enter into a very close 'blood relationship' with the form of the royal genre that is particular to that current" (121). A royal genre attracts basically all other genres at a certain time but without fusing them all into one single genre. While the literary trend lasts, a new form of the genre emerges. It could be argued, for example, that "metafiction" is now a literary current become royal genre that draws into it several other genres that nevertheless keep their distinguishing features. Metafiction may earlier have been a "feature" of another genre. As it is "promoted" to a

royal genre, its features become "characteristic of the entire literary trend thereby ceasing to be something distinctive for that genre, becoming non-distinguishing features. They become features that make it similar to other genres" (123).

2   He prefers to distinguish the "American road book" from Steinbeck's *The Grapes of Wrath,* but to me, this too is a road narrative.

3   Of course he is not the first one to make this kind of anachronistic move. Placing *Tristram Shandy* among the postmodern works of fiction is one of the better known examples of retrospective genre categorization.

4   See Jessica Enevold Madesdotter, "Men and Women on the Move: Three Dramas of the Road."

5   At the same time he seems to make an ad hoc differentiation between the road book and the road story of *The Grapes of Wrath,* which to me becomes very paradoxical. I am somewhat surprised that Brinkley chooses to skip *The Grapes of Wrath* to go straight to *On the Road.* His move to make *America Day by Day* into "an erudite American Road book" would have been slightly less anachronistic had he chosen to define *The Grapes of Wrath,* from the 1930s, as an embryo of the road narrative of the 1950s.

6   Nina Baym, "Dramas of Beset Manhood: How Theories of American Fiction Exclude Women," *American Quarterly* 33 (1981): 123–39.

7   By "pass for," I am of course sarcastically referring to what I deem to be a belated, avaricious transfer of what could be called symbolic cultural capital accumulated by de Beauvoir for more than half a century, by way of a gesture of charitable inclusion into the American genre of literature.

8   See Enevold Madesdotter "Men and Women on the Move" for a detailed discussion of the issue of gender-dependences.

9   It is essential to note that Brinkley is an accomplished historian who has written his own book on the road (*The Majic Bus: An American Odyssey*) as well as edited/written forewords to editions of the road books of others, for example, Hunter S. Thompson's *Fear and Loathing in Las Vegas,* and *The Proud Highway,* Theodore Dreiser's *A Hoosier Holiday,* and Carl Thomas Rowan's *South of Freedom.* I expect that he is well aware of the genre history. Nevertheless, acknowledging simultaneously the affirmative character of the genre of forewords and back-cover blurbs, I would advocate caution when speaking of the road book in order not to neglect its "genderedness."

10 See, for example, Enevold "The Motherhood of the Road."

11 See Rapping 1991, Sharrett 1991, Morf and Andrew 1991, Carlson 1991, Leo 1991, Pochada 1992, and Cooper 2000.

12 See Enevold Madesdotter, "Men and Women," and Enevold, "Motherhood."

13 For example Cathy Griggers who writes about the "lesbian body [that] appeared masquerading as the latest American outlaw hero in *Thelma & Louise*" ("Lesbian Bodies in the Age of (Post)Mechanical Reproduction" 1992), and Lynda Hart, who in *Fatal Women: Lesbian Sexuality and the Mark of Aggression* (1994) treat the "Female Buddy Film" (qt. in Roach 1996). It is very interesting to note that *Lesbian News* downplays the lesbian theme in *Thelma & Louise.*

14 For a discussion of Girl Power, see Enevold "Girl Powers and Power Girls."

15   Another possibility is the substitution of men for women or any other sex /gender-related alteration/replacement of the traditional main character/s.

16   Gregory's essay "Scripting Egypt" is published in an anthology that builds upon "Edward Said's oft-cited claim that Orientalists past and present have spun imaginative geographies where they sought ground truth [which] has launched a plethora of studies of fictive geographies" (Duncan and Gregory i). Gregory forwards an argument "triangulated by three ideas: the construction of the Orient as *theatre*; the representation of other places and landscapes as text; and the production of travel and tourism as a scripting" (115). Please consult the anthology for a more exhaustive and just account of Gregory's presentation of travel as "an intrinsically hermeneutical project" (115).

17   Case draws on "the so-called Bem Sex-Role inventory (BSRI). [She] lists a number of adjectives that psychologists and other researchers regularly consider coded masculine and feminine in contemporary American culture" (Moi 103).

18   In her afterword, in which she explains "The Point of Theory," Moi refers the reader to Wittgenstein's standpoint that "the role of philosophy is to be therapeutic, to produce a diagnosis of the theoretical pictures that hold us captive, not in order to refute them, but in order to make us aware of other options: 'A picture held us captive. And we could not get outside of it, for it lay in our language and language seemed to repeat it inexorably' (PI §5)" (qt. in Moi 119). Moi reminds us of Wittgenstein's thought that a philosophical problem is a "question that arises when we are lost in a kind of linguistic fog" (119). Moi understands Wittgenstein's view of the "clearing of the fog as an intellectual liberation" as a never-ending task which, she hopes, will be a "philosophical therapy [that] would help feminist critics and theorists not to get lost in meaningless questions and pointless arguments, and enable us instead to raise genuine questions about things that really matter" (120). And by things that really matter she means "the sphere of the ordinary...in which our political and personal struggles actually take place" (120).

19   See Moi, *What Is a Woman? And Other Essays*.

20   From here on, *Thelma & Louise*, the road movie, more or less "fuses" with Thelma and Louise, the characters, and vice versa. One reason for this is the fact that the narratives that I analyze in the following sections regularly allude to the road movie through its characters, who thus come to symbolize both female subjects and the road genre.

21   See Umberto Eco's travel narrative "Travels in Hyperreality" from *Faith in Fakes*. See also Baudrillard's travel narrative *America* for an interesting analysis of America in this vein, and see Holland and Huggan for a specific analysis of Eco's and Baudrillard's travel narratives.

22   See Robert J. Butler, "The Woman Writer as American Picaro: Journeying in Erica Jong's *Fear of Flying*," and Maria Lauret, *Liberating Literature*.

23   Jong could possibly stand for the picaresque novel *Fanny* (1980), but that is less likely, particularly since makes no specific connection with this older type of travel genre.

Works Cited

Baudrillard, Jean. *America*. 1986. Trans Chris Turner. London & New York: Verso, 1996.

Baym, Nina. "Dramas of Beset Manhood: How Theories of American Fiction Exclude Women." *American Quarterly* 33 (1981): 123–39.

Beauvoir de, Simone. *America Day by Day*. 1952. Trans. Carol Cosman. Foreword by Douglas Brinkley. Berkeley: U of California P, 1999.

———. *Le Deuxième Sexe*. Paris: Gallimard, 1949.

Bidisha. "Leaving." *Wild Ways: New Stories about Women on the Road*. Eds. Margo Daly and Jill Dawson. London: Hodder and Stoughton, 1998. 100–12.

Brinkley, Douglas. "Foreword." *America Day by Day*. Simone de Beauvoir. Berkeley: U of California P, 1999. i–xviii.

———. *The Majic Bus: An American Odyssey*. New York: Harcourt Brace, 1993.

Butler, Robert J. "The Woman Writer as American Picaro: Journeying in Erica Jong's *Fear of Flying*." *Centennial Review* 31 (1987): 308–29.

Buzard, James. *The Beaten Track: European Tourism, and the Ways to Culture, 1800–1918*. Oxford: Clarendon, 1993.

Carlson, Margaret. "Is This What Feminism Is All About?" *Time* June 24, 1991: 57.

Case, Mary Anne C. "Disaggregating Gender from Sex and Sexual Orientation: The Effeminate Man in the Law and Feminist Jurisprudence." *Yale Law Journal* 1.205 (1995): 1–105.

Cooper, Brenda. "Chick Flicks' as Feminist Texts: The Appropriation of the Male Gaze in *Thelma & Louise*." *Women's Studies in Communication* 3.23. (2000): 277–306.

Curti, Lidia. *Female Stories, Female Bodies: Narrative, Identity, and Representation*. Washington Square: New York UP, 1998.

Daly, Margo, and Jill Dawson, eds. *Wild Ways: New Stories about Women on the Road*. London: Hodder and Stoughton.

Dawson, Jill. "Tofino." *Wild Ways: New Stories about Women on the Road*. Eds. Margo Daly and Jill Dawson. London: Hodder and Stoughton, 1998. 51–62.

Derrida, Jacques. "The Law of Genre." *Glyph* 7 (1980): 202–13.

DiClementi, Deborah. "Feminist, Sex Symbol and Mom." *Lesbian News* 1.25 (1999): 30–32.

Dreiser, Theodore. *A Hoosier Holiday*. New York: Lane, 1916.

Duncan, James, and Derek Gregory, eds. *Writes of Passage*. London: Routledge, 1999.

Easy Rider. Dir. Dennis Hopper. Perf. Peter Fonda. Columbia Pictures, 1969.

Eco, Umberto. "Travels in Hyperreality." *Faith in Fakes: Essays*. 1973. Trans. William Weaver. London: Secker and Warburg, 1986.

Enevold Madesdotter, Jessica. "Men and Women on the Move: Three Dramas of the Road." *European Journal of Cultural Studies* 3.3 (2000): 403–20.

Enevold, Jessica. "Girl Powers and Power Girls: New Feminisms, New Women, and the Use of Contradictions at the Turn of the Millennium." Paper presented at Women's Worlds: The Seventh International Congress on Women, Tromsö, Norway, June 26 to July 2, 1998.

———. "The Motherhood of the Road: From *Paradise Lost* to *Paradise*." *Interpreting the Maternal Organisation*. Eds. Heather Hoepfl and Monika Kostera. London: Routledge, 2002. 79–103.

Frankfort, Ellen. *Vaginal Politics*. New York: Quandrangle, 1972.

94   *Jessica Enevold*

Gregory, Derek. "Scripting Egypt." *Writes of Passage*. Eds. James Duncan and Derek Gregory. London: Routledge, 1999.

Griggers, Cathy. "Lesbian Bodies in the Age Of (Post)Mechanical Reproduction." *Postmodern Culture* 3.2 (1992): 1–6. .http://muse.jhu.edu/journals/post-modern __ culture/v200/2.3griggers.html.

Hart, Lynda. *Fatal Women: Lesbian Sexuality, and the Mark of Aggression*. Princeton: Princeton UP, 1994.

Heat-Moon, William Least (William Trogdon). *Blue Highways: A Journey into America*. Boston: Little, Brown, 1982.

Holland, Patrick, and Graham Huggan. *Tourists with Typewriters: Critical Reflections on Contemporary Travel Writing*. Ann Arbor: U of Michigan P, 1998.

Johnson, Barbara. "Lesbian Spectacles." *The Feminist Difference. Literature, Psychoanalysis, Race, and Gender*. Cambridge, MA: Harvard UP, 1998. 157–64.

Jong, Erica. *Fanny: Being the True History of the Adventures of Fanny Hackabout-Jones*. New York: New American Library, 1980.

———. *Fear of Flying*. New York: Holt, Rinehart and Winston, 1973.

Kerouac, Jack. *On the Road*. New York: Viking Press, 1957.

Lackey, Kris. *RoadFrames: The American Highway Narrative*. Lincoln and London: U of Nebraska P, 1997.

Lauret, Maria. *Liberating Literature: Feminist Fiction in America*. London & New York: Routledge, 1994.

Leo, John. "Toxic Feminism on the Big Screen." *U.S. News & World Report*. June 10, 1991: 20.

Lopez, Erika. *Flaming Iguanas: An All-Girl Road Novel Thing*. New York: Simon & Schuster, 1997.

Millet, Kate. *Sexual Politics*. Garden City, NY: Doubleday, 1970.

Moi, Toril. *What Is a Woman? And Other Essays*. Oxford: Oxford UP, 1999.

Morf, Isabel, and Stephen Andrew. "Tales of Angry Women." *World Press Review* 38.9 (1991): 51.

Opacki, Ireneusz. "Royal Genres." *Modern Genre Theory*. Ed. David Duff. Trans. David Malcolm. Essex, UK: Longman, 2000. 118–26.

Perkins, Emily. "Can't Beat It." *Wild Ways: New Stories about Women on the Road*. Eds. Margo Daly and Jill Dawson. London: Hodder and Stoughton, 1998. 3–14.

Pochada, Elizabeth. "*Thelma & Louise*, Us & Them." *Nation* March 16, 1992: 344–49.

Primeau, Ronald. *Romance of the Road: The Literature of the American Highway*. Bowling Green: Bowling Green State U Popular P, 1996.

Rapping, Elayne. "Feminism Gets the Hollywood Treatment." *Cineaste* 4.18 (1991): 30–33.

Roach, Joseph. "Fatal Women: Lesbian Sexuality and the Mark of Aggression." Book Review. *Theatre Journal* 1.48 (1996): 111–12.

Rowan, Carl Thomas. *South of Freedom*. New York: Knopf, 1952.

Sharrett, Christopher. "Phony Feminism on the Silver Screen." *USA Today Magazine* November (1991): 57.

Steinbeck, John. *The Grapes of Wrath*. New York: Collier, 1939.

Stovall, Natasha. "Penis Frenzy." *Village Voice* 37.42 (1997): 17.

Thelma & Louise. Dir. Ridley Scott. Perf. Susan Sarandon, Geena Davis, and Harvey Keitel. MGM, 1991.

Thompson, Hunter S. *Fear and Loathing in Las Vegas: A Savage Journey to the Heart of the American Dream.* New York: Random House, 1971.
———. *The Proud Highway: Saga of a Desperate Southern Gentleman, 1955–1967.* Ed. Douglas Brinkley. New York: Villard, 1997.

℘ Chapter Five

Women Writers and the Internal Combustion Engine
Passing Penelope Pitstop

Rachel A. Jennings

> The cars are approaching the starting line. First is the Turbo Terrific driven by Peter Perfect....Right behind is the Anthill Mob in their Bulletproof Bomb. Then there's ingenious inventor Pat Pending in his Convert-a-Car. Oh! Here's the lovely Penelope Pitstop, the glamour gal of the gas pedal.
> —From the opening narration of *The Wacky Races*

In *Penelope Voyages*, Karen Lawrence illustrates the traditional western restriction on women's travel with the figure of Penelope who waits faithfully at home for Odysseus (ix). Though Penelope Pitstop (a character in the popular 1968–1970 Hanna Barbera cartoon *The Wacky Races*) has more agency than her mythical namesake, her characterization as an airhead blonde who needs Peter Perfect to rescue her when in peril on the racetrack leaves much to be desired. Post *Thelma & Louise* (1991), the "glamour gal of the gas pedal" may appear somewhat outdated. However, *The Wacky Races* is still aired on the Cartoon Network, and related representations of women drivers are alive (if not perfectly well) now. As the lone female in a race of eleven vehicles, Penelope is indicative of the minority status of women road trip writers in the latter half of the twentieth century and provides some clues as to their cultural coding. The aim of this chapter is to use a survey of contemporary representations of women and cars as a means to explore women's positioning within the male-dominated road trip narrative. Analysis of how femininity is constructed and questioned by women's interactions with automobiles will be used to measure how far women writers can enter male road trip territory and how free they are to open up new female spaces on the road.

According to Kris Lackey in *RoadFrames: The American Highway Narrative,* one quarter of all U.S. road narratives before World War II were written by women, though few of these were lone motorists and most traveled with husbands or female companions (28). Following a paradigm shift marked by Kerouac's *On the Road* (1957), postwar women road writers are proportionately more scarce, due to the diminishing visibility of kin and heterosexual couple trips in both road literature and road movies (Lackey 28; Cohan and Hark 2–3). Dominant representations favor male writers by maintaining that lone travel makes the best travel writing, yet is too dangerous and/or socially unacceptable for women. Contemporary women writers (such as Marilyn Abraham), who publish accounts of heterosexual couple or kin trips, do not challenge norms of femininity like those who drive alone. The latter draw attention to themselves by claiming the masculine rights to anonymity and freedom from domesticity afforded by the road.

The novelty status of lone women road trippers can be turned to advantage, replenish a traditionally male-dominated genre with new voices and open up "liberated spaces through which women's travel writing can emerge as an exploration of female desire" (Holland and Huggan 112). This potential, however, is tempered by cultural and textual constraints. As Sara Mills notes in *Discourses of Difference: An Analysis of Women's Travel Writing and Colonialism,* writing is a negotiation rather than simply self-expression (9). The fact that lone women road writers are spectacles as well as spectators has implications for how they construct their narrating personae and are in turn constructed by publishers and readers. The foregrounding of the role of storyteller makes narration in nonfiction travel narratives a conscious performance for the writer. Acting the role of road trip storyteller is complicated for women by a doubly heightened awareness (both for writer and reader) of performance of gender, because they cross borders into two areas of masculine territory: that of the automobile, and that of the road trip.[1] These writers, whose negotiations with cars and the road have developed alongside such products of the heyday of the male road trip as Penelope Pitstop, are limited as to how far they can pull out and pass her.

This chapter outlines the gender codings of women and cars negotiated by contemporary women writers of nonfiction American road trip narratives (or roadlogues) with primary reference to a case study by Lesley Hazleton, a British-born automotive journalist. Published in 1998, *Driving to Detroit: An Automotive Odyssey* is a pilgrimage to the holy places for cars; it is both an outward investigation of the American fascination with the automobile and an inward rite of passage for the writer in U.S. citizenship.[2] By locating Hazleton's narrative in relation to other texts from various road genres, the following discussion marks out postwar road trip territory in order to address such questions as: How much control do women writers have over their narrative vehicles? How far are they constrained by dominant representations, marketing, and reception? How far do and/or can women's roadlogues make inroads into a masculine genre and how far is this desirable? What strategies can women writers adopt to open up new female territory?

Women and Cars

In her study, *In the Driver's Seat: The Automobile in American Literature and Popular Culture*, Cynthia Dettelbach claims that, "Little boys who play with little cars grow up to be big boys who play with big cars, often without much change in attitude" (92–93).[3] This begs the questions: If little girls play less with cars, how does this affect how big girls play with them? Do they try to emulate big boys? What implications does this have for female road narrator construction?

A scene introducing the narrator's vehicle is common to the opening sections of many roadlogues. By describing how a vehicle is purchased or outfitted, narrators set up relationships with their machines that construct the parameters of their journeys. Factors such as the type of vehicle, its pet name, and whether it is old or new, introduce the machine as an important character, while simultaneously setting up the stance of the narrator's relationship to the landscape. For instance, Simon Mayle signifies his daredevil comedic stance and willingness to cross social boundaries in *The Burial Brothers* with his choice of a 1973 Cadillac Hearse. In *Blue Highways,* William Least Heat-Moon connotes a longing for a simplified and uncluttered lifestyle by listing the modest contents of his camper van, and sets up his nostalgic attitude by naming it *Ghost Dancing* (8). The Ford Expedition, which Lesley Hazleton describes as her "narrative vehicle" (using Jonathan Raban's term) (11), is somewhat distanced from her persona because it is borrowed, rather than personally selected, and is a boy's toy intended to show onlookers that she is "going the distance" (12).

Although Hazleton's stated preoccupation concerns automobiles and national identity, questions of gender inevitably arise when considering human interaction with cars, perhaps most obviously because women have traditionally been denied the driver's seat. The label "women drivers" (which excludes women from the privileged term "drivers") derives from notions that women are largely intimidated and/or bored by technology. Gender also plays a part in the complex sexualization of cars, which are often referred to as "she" while simultaneously representing their male drivers' penises. Car coding does not stop here. As P. J. O'Rourke puts it: "The automobile bears a symbolic weight that fridge and toaster never can" (1). The following discussion will begin to unpack this layered coding by considering four functions assumed by cars related to gender construction: clothing, prosthesis, companion, and fetish. These functions, apparent in road literature, movies, and advertising, are by no means discrete; one particular car can inhabit several categories simultaneously.[4] In fact, it is the car's capacity for multiple signification which makes it such a potent symbol.

Cultural codes are in constant flux. Many are contradictory, such as the fact that cars are used to flaunt heterosexuality while being hermaphroditic. Despite the multiple and changing signals, there is only an extent to which a writer can do exactly what she wants with a narrative vehicle; how it is interpreted by writers and readers is influenced by a plethora of past and coexistent representations.

Car as Clothing and Prosthesis

The metaphor of car as clothing is used in the 1999 television commercial aired in the United Kingdom in which supermodel Claudia Schiffer strips naked to drive her Citroen Xsara. Such examples make it clear that cars can be used to mark boundaries of gender and sexuality. In "Not from the Back Seat," Lydia Simmons goes so far as to claim that the car, "like a designer's dress...is one of the primary means of setting female off from male" (188).

Penelope Pitstop, reminiscent of a blonde ponytailed Barbie Doll, wears a pink minidress with a heart-shaped belt buckle positioned tantalizingly close to crotch level. Penelope's car equals her own outfit in feminine allure. The Compact Pussycat is deep pink and yellow, its headlights are big eyes with long lashes, its front bumper is a pair of pouting lips, and its chassis is distinguished by curvy lines. Instead of a roof, this glamorous convertible sports a frilly parasol to protect

Penelope from the elements. Peter Perfect and his vehicle provide a stark contrast. The handsome, strong-jawed Peter drives The Turbo Terrific, which bears a striking resemblance to male genitalia. Consisting of a long, sausage-shaped body, with two giant testicular wheels at the rear, Peter's vehicle emphasizes the phallic qualities of the typically male-driven race car.[5]

The Wacky Races illustrates that "car-clothes" can make both sexes attractive by representing a driver's idealized physical and personal qualities. Other examples include the film version of Stephen King's novel *Christine* (1983), in which teenager Arnie Cunningham loses the hallmarks of his "geek" image as he works on restoring his demon-possessed 1958 Plymouth Fury (aptly named after a spiteful woman), and consequently gets the prettiest girl in school. When visiting a junkyard in Houston, Lesley Hazleton articulates the more sordid side of cars endowing sexiness by comparing an abandoned car to "a Lurex dress taken off after a hard night on the town and left discarded on the floor, having done its job, perhaps too well" (202). Hazleton herself prefers practical car clothes and describes the Expedition as too new and shiny for her purpose (11).

The wrong car on the wrong person stands out like inappropriate clothing, illustrated effectively by imagining Penelope and Peter swapping cars. The Compact Pussycat is far too effeminate for Peter Perfect's macho image. Similarly, when shopping in Los Angeles for his narrative vehicle, Scottish actor Robbie Coltrane (in *Coltrane in a Cadillac*) rejects anything too fancy that would be a suitable ornament for a hairdresser or rock star, painted the color of a "tart's handbag" (18). His response to cars that resemble Penelope's is, "If I wanted to look like Jayne Mansfield I would have the operation, thank you" (18). Hazleton uses the same rhetoric when she reminisces about army vehicles she rode while a journalist in Israel, describing them as "testosterone proof: no frills, no padding" (69). She investigates the macho aspect of cars as armor by visiting an armoring company and draws an amusing comparison between her hyper-masculine lunch party and a Mary Kay Cosmetics group in the same restaurant (269–70). Car as protective shell is linked to the concept of car as extension of the self and thus raises the issue of power. The Compact Pussycat is hopelessly inadequate for Peter, while Penelope seems incapable of controlling what could be described as his "power tie" on wheels. This marks an important area of gender inequality: Though Penelope is in the driver's seat, she lacks equal potency. Her car has no balls.

Lackey likens the automobile to a prosthesis because it responds so effectively to the desires of individual drivers that it appears to be an extension of the body (4). With the exception of the Arkansas Chugabug (which, with its rickety stovepipe and barefoot Southern driver, shows that class and regionalism are issues here in addition to gender), the prostheses of the male drivers in *The Wacky Races* appear more powerful than Penelope's. The Pussycat's gadgets are designed to make Penelope attractive, rather than a serious contender in a race. The controls on her dashboard are "Hair Spray, Hair Dryer, Make Up." In contrast, the Creepy Coupe boasts "Dragon Power, Monster Power, Bat Power, Horror Power," while Professor Pat Pending's Convert-a-Car has "Sails, Giant Spring, Submarine, Balloon" and can morph into a boat or plane. There are several variations of the Convert-a-Car in popular culture with rather more sinister powers: James Bond's cars; *Kitt* in the 1982 television series *Knight Rider*; and the movie *Christine*. Although Hazleton compares a customized car to Boadicea's chariot (127), it seems that post Boadicea's revolt, the power-giving gadget car is largely the province of the male. The Pussycat's attributes hark back to the 1920's assumption of automobile manufacturers, noted by Virginia Scharff in *Taking the Wheel: Women and the Coming of the Motor Age*, that women prefer frills over power (111–33).

Hazleton investigates the lust for power by entering, like Penelope, the masculine territory of the racetrack where "The car is on the outer limits of control...." (146). She confesses a perverse love for the skid pad (146). However, the opening of her roadlogue, which describes an accident at the end of her journey where she nearly dies, takes this feeling of being on the edge too far for her liking (1–7).

For a car to be an effective prosthesis, the driver must have total control. Penelope needs to be rescued when she has car trouble, making her a less independent and less powerful agent, despite the fact that she wins as many races as her rivals. That feminine women are not meant to be mechanics is illustrated by *The Adventures of Priscilla, Queen of the Desert*, a 1994 movie about three drag queens on an Australian road trip. When their bus breaks down in the middle of the desert, the queens are unable to repair it and have to wait for a "real man" to come along to fix it for them. Drag queens perform the extremes of socially constructed femininity, which, in this case, includes vulnerability. Another illustration of the above is *The Perils of Penelope Pitstop*, a 1969 spin-off show from *The Wacky Races*. Inspired by the silent movie series *The Perils of Pauline,* this cartoon gives Penelope a 1930's makeover (Schmidt, *Perils*). Penelope spends each episode tied in melodramatic fashion by Sylvester Sneakly (alias the Hooded Claw) to a hi-tech killing contraption until her wealthy Southern Belle's cries of "hayulp hayulp" summon the Anthill Mob (a team from *The Wacky Races*) to her rescue. The Compact Pussycat is taken away from Penelope in this show in which she becomes a victim of technology. Women continue to be at the mercy of "technovillains" in many postwar movies, such as the James Bond series.

It would be an oversimplification to suggest that all passengers are powerless, and all drivers have power. Issues of power cannot be reduced to gender and who holds the steering wheel alone, but these points are complicated by other factors such as class and race. For instance, famous etiquette advisor Emily Post has control over her son "chauffeur" from her cross-country seat in the tonneau in *By Motor to the Golden Gate* (1916). Another example exploring passenger-driver power relations is the 1989 movie *Driving Miss Daisy,* in which a rich Jewish woman and her black chauffeur play out an intricate power struggle-*cum*-friendship. However, keeping these qualifications in mind, by and large the traditional categorization of women as passengers or inadequate drivers, denies them equal access to an American dream based on individualism and control of one's future.[6]

Though Hazleton's accident demonstrates that even experts are vulnerable in cars at times, if women road writers want power equal to men's, they might feel it necessary to perform as transvestite driver-mechanics. In the preface to her edited anthology, *Road Trips, Head Trips, and Other Car-Crazed Writings,* automotive journalist Jean Lindamood Jennings describes how she changed her clothes in the past to coordinate with the male territory of her career (vii–xii). Her attire, when a cab driver, consisted of "bib overalls and a ski hat, or skirts down to the ground with army boots" (viii). She completed the role by smoking cigars and not shaving her legs (viii). Similarly, her feminine long hair was a hindrance when working as a mechanic, because it became caught in some machinery, causing amusement for the boys (ix).

Cross-dressing is a strategy found in women's travel writing outside the U.S. road trip.[7] However, though one might expect western women to feel that donning masculine attire in eastern countries will aid ease of travel in this or previous centuries, it might be somewhat surprising to realize that western women in the contemporary

United States face a similar metaphorical choice. It is indicative of the masculine bias of Americanness that American women feel the need to cross-dress in their own nation if they want to participate in the American passion for the automobile (or at least the non–powder puff automobile).

Typical representations show males to be more desirous of a relationship with the machine (along the lines of Robert Pirsig's close identity with his motorcycle in the canonical *Zen and the Art of Motorcycle Maintenance*). Despite their relative scarcity, however, transvestite women driver-mechanics are nothing new. Lackey distinguishes prewar women who travel without men, such as Winifred Dixon (author of *Westward Hoboes: Ups and Downs of Frontier Motoring*), from "their finicky white-gloved cousins like Emily Post," who travel with men (29). Lackey notes that writers like Dixon, as a "result of necessity rather than overt rebellion against sex roles" slowly change into "sturdy vagabonds" who "boast of their trousers, their dirty bodies, and their growing mechanical savvy" (29). Advertisers, meanwhile, decided ladies could be enticed to buy gasoline cars once the latter became clean and easy to operate, based on the assumption that women are not interested in mechanics and do not like to get dirty (Dettelbach 59; Scharff 51–66). Postwar, as a result of advanced car design and a developed infrastructure, the practical need for both female and male motorists to become mechanics has lessened. However, women road writers may choose to learn the workings of cars in order to regain the agency of their prewar dirty-gloved sisters.

Car maintenance can be equated with hospital care, thus endowing the automobile with animate qualities (Dettelbach 95). Animate cars are no longer tools but companions, illustrated by the clichéd cry of men starting up a powerful car uttered by Tim Cahill's co-driver Gary Sowerby in *Road Fever*: "Let's see what this baby'll do!" (Cahill 125).

Car as Companion and Fetish

Dastardly and Muttley, the scheming melodrama villain throwback and his mischievous dog sidekick in *The Wacky Races*, fit the popular category of male buddy road trippers. Where a lone driver such as Penelope is concerned, the car can become principal companion (illustrated by the Compact Pussycat's personification), and can be a primary means for constructing its driver's character. When this relationship becomes obsessive or mystical, the line is crossed from companion to fetish.

Among the most common companion roles taken on by cars are horse, friend, baby, and lover. These functions inevitably slide into each other. Steinbeck's camper van Rocinante is named after Don Quixote's mount (6). Hazleton refers to her truck as a "magnificent steed" (11), and its manufacturer's name of Expedition portrays her companion as one that allows her to venture into the wilds. Car as horse indicates the obvious fact that the automobile has replaced this animal as the most popular personal conveyance, and also points to the status of the road trip as successor of the western. The latter can result in women identifying with male western heroes and thus initiate self-conscious gender performance. Hazleton herself uses the Lone Ranger as her road persona (132), though she does not problematize her gendered role-play.

Although she neglects to name her truck, Hazleton becomes very attached to it. She feels insulted on its behalf (67), is saddened when leaving it at the Los Angeles airport (128), and pats its hood (292). The extent of her attachment is demonstrated when she decides that, instead of taking the easy option and flying home to Seattle from Detroit at the end of her pilgrimage, she must drive the Expedition full circle (290).

Similarly, in Melanie McGrath's roadlogue, *Motel Nirvana: Dreaming of the New Age in the American Desert*, the car is an unsexed friend that she names after the railroad carriage in the country and western song "Don't Fence Me In." Though she says she "avoids sentimentality" (4), McGrath connects with Caboose and gives it animate qualities (16). Prewar, Winifred Dixon's car seems characterized as a female guardian or chaperone: "a Cadillac Eight, with a rakish hood and matronly tonneau; its front was intimidating, its rear reassuring" (2).

"Friend" appears to be the category into which most women's car-companions fit. Where car is baby and/or lover, a border may be crossed into the territory of fetish in three senses: something drivers are obsessed with, an object that endows sexual satisfaction, or the embodiment/abode of a spirit or magical powers. For example, old cars (or those in a prewar context) need to be regularly tended like infants. Modern cars are babies if they have proud parent/partner owners, illustrated by a 1999 U.S. billboard advertising Mercedes Benz service which reads: "Who's going to look after your baby?"

Lydia Simmons's description of her old car constructs it as a substitute for human companionship: "It became my baby, and I was able to lavish upon it the care and love I felt no human would accept from me" (190). Her car relationship is unusual when compared to typical coding in which dominant representations play on the idea of men (only) being in love with their cars. It is difficult to imagine women being featured in two 1999 Continental Tyres commercials aired in the United Kingdom which portray fetishizing men. The first shows a topless man standing up in his convertible with outstretched arms with the voiceover: "Take care of the one you love." The second implies that men gain sexual satisfaction as they fondle their cars' contours to the strains of a love song.

Rather than being represented as car fetishizers, women are more often shown to be replaced by, and therefore jealous of, automobiles. The lack of images of women fetishizers partially derives from the dominant representation of car as wife/possession, which Dettelbach links to the male's traditional ownership of the female in certain societies (97). Though Dettelbach risks essentializing male drivers, it is reasonable to suggest that those contemporary men who desire a beautiful, idealized 1950's-type trophy-wife requiring care and protection might look for a car to fill the void.

Coltrane compares his 1951 Cadillac to Rita Hayworth as "built in Detroit" (22). Despite the long road trip ahead, he considers the fact that the car has some technical problems an advantage, saying: "What the hell, it would be a pleasure handling any hiccups from this baby. Besides, I had my toolbox with me" (22). Fixing the Cadillac is a way to prove his manhood and distinguishes him from "nancy boys" (presumably with smaller toolboxes) who buy modern cars that require little maintenance (22). Hazleton shows her awareness of this type of gender coding when she compares jeeps to difficult females: "And what young man, in uniform or out, wouldn't want to tame such a creature, each one Petruchio wrestling with his own private shrew?" (70). Such representations derive from gender assumptions made in the first two decades of the twentieth century when, often contrary to the reality, men were perceived to prefer cranks and manual gears over conveniences like electric starters and automatic transmissions; the latter, though they benefited all drivers, were purportedly designed specifically for women so that men could save face (Scharff 65).

It is a short step from car maintenance to the male territory of customizing in which Hazleton meets Big Daddy Roth, who believes that men who treat their cars as wives have a spiritual relationship with them (225–26). Customizers are like modern-day Pygmalions who sculpt cars into ideal lovers and objects of worship; their cars connote sex, death, and spirituality. Dettelbach describes the interiors of many customized cars as boudoirs, which indicates why women might have ambivalent relationships with cars and be less likely to fetishize what they view as scenes of rape or exploitation (87). Dettelbach notes that, "When the male does the driving (car as vehicle, car as penis), the more passive female is usually exploited," citing as an example Kienholz's lurid sculpture *Back Seat Dodge—'38* (66). Hazleton, although she celebrates her first car as the place of sexual initiation (44), compares customized car interiors to coffins (221).

Coltrane combines spirituality and/or mysticism with sex when he describes the garage from which he purchases his Cadillac as comparable to Tutankhamen's tomb, going on to say...

> If someone had told me that I had died and gone to heaven, I would not have argued. Everywhere I looked there was a Cadillac, each one sweeter than the last. It was like a dream I used to have, but in that I always used to wake up just as my hand touched the first car. Now I was caressing, even climbing into, magnificent Cadillacs and nobody was waking me up. (18)

The tomb here seems very much like a womb and is reminiscent of Hazleton's description of Craig Breedlove's relationship with his land speed vehicle, the Spirit of America, designed to fit his body perfectly. He sees his car as a sanctuary and likes to sit inside "her" to think (20).

Although Hazleton does not use the term "fetishism," a large proportion of her journey is devoted to investigating this subject. For example, she falls into a trance-like state when sitting in a classic car at a show (49); she describes car auctioneers as selling sex (55); she looks into the "beating heart" of a combustion engine at a laboratory and feels tender toward it (63); she describes her horrid fascination for J. G. Ballard's *Crash* and claims Indy spectators are there for the accidents only (104–08; 149); and she crushes a car at a junkyard, perhaps resulting from a desire to combat her obsession with automobiles (207). It is her possession by the Expedition and the road, described by Hazleton as a "road warrior" state (302), which leads to the near-fatal accident at the end of her journey.

Similar states of consciousness are described by other road writers. In *Storm Country,* Pete Davies uses the term "road addiction" (32), metaphorically linking cars and road trips with drugs. Hazleton investigates the addictive quality of speed when interviewing a race driver who talks of the all-consuming nature of the race (156–57). Her analysis of intoxication by speed brings to mind the road movie *Vanishing Point* (1971), in which an ex–race driver takes the drug speed during a breakneck run from Colorado to California. When driving becomes a drug, drivers can become possessed by their car fetishes.

Guys Versus Girls

From the (mostly) postwar American and European examples given above, it is apparent that representations of people's relationships with cars and road trips in all genres play on guy/girl dichotomies. Though the foregrounding of the human-car relationship in most of these examples is by no means typical of all road narratives, they provide vivid means to expose gender codings that underlie roadlogues where the relationship is backgrounded. The dominant characteristics of each pole in the west during the postwar period might be roughly outlined as follows: First, men are in the driver's seat; they are victors; they fetishize cars (perceiving them to be traditional wives/ possessions/trophies); and they are capable car mechanics. Second, women should be passengers or drive only powder puff cars; they are victims; they do not fetishize cars and are jealous of them (perceiving them as rivals); and they are incapable mechanics. Though guy/girl definitions differ among texts at any one moment and change over time, these poles seem remarkably stable when compared with Scharff's description of gender coding in relation to automobiles through the 1920s. This is all the more surprising when it is considered that, as Marilyn Root notes in *Women at the Wheel,* women currently buy almost half of the cars sold in the United States (2). Though there are practically as many women motorists, their relationships with cars are not represented as equal to men's.

Savvy road writers can exploit dominant representations for effect. A male might put himself in the "girl" category by describing himself as a nondriver or poor driver to establish a vulnerable or impotent persona. Writers (such as Andrei Codrescu in *Road Scholar*) can use this stance for comic effect, to gain the sympathy of a particular readership, or possibly to connote un-Americanness. However, these reversals confirm, rather than deconstruct, the gender polarization.

Women road writers need to negotiate their entrance into guy territory. Do they want to become guys (or bad girls, or tough girls), or try to break down the distinction? Marilyn Root's collection of forty-two interviews represents (in prose and photographs) women from a variety of states, age groups, and ethnic backgrounds who are passionate about their cars. Her book functions as a consciousness-raising exercise, giving voices to women who are mechanics, customizers, and lovers of power and technology. However, although the label sheds its negative connotations in this context, this book affirms the term *women drivers* by virtue of its overall conceit. In contrast, Jean Lindamood Jennings's *Road Trips, Head Trips,* is a collection of essays, poems, and stories by men and women, the cover of which says that it "explores our love affair with the automobile." Though she highlights gender in her introduction, the practice of bringing men's and women's texts together under one cover and one theme goes some way toward breaking down distinctions and including women road writers in the mainstream.

In evaluating her past, Lindamood Jennings notes that she was always "trying to be a guy" (vii). After years of role-play, she has a revelation and notes: "As it turns out, my life has not really been about being a guy or being a woman. All along I have simply been trying to do the things I love to do" (xi). She declares the guy/girl dichotomy a farce here, pronouncing the struggle to perform as a "car guy" a waste of time. Like Scharff, she shows that representations based on an apparent need to differentiate masculine from feminine, rather than to reflect actuality, constrain both men and women (Scharff 165–75).

Lesley Hazleton, although she professes at one point not to love cars (160), fetishizes automobiles with the very design of her journey: a pilgrimage to their holy places. She has very different relationships with automobiles from that of Penelope to the Compact Pussycat. Unlike Penelope, Hazleton is knowledgeable about all aspects of mechanics and all methods of driving, and her borrowed Ford Expedition is more traditionally masculine than feminine. However, she denies that she is a "car guy," defining this species as one who celebrates cars with a "torrent of clichés," whereas she wants to "reach deeper," to "journey into the heart, soul, and wallet of the enduring American obsession with the car" (8). Hazleton suggests "car guys" are superficial, engage in tedious technospeak, i.e., "the usual litany of male automotive appreciation, recited entirely in numbers" (220), and want to complete pointless hypermasculine tasks like driving slower than walking pace off-road on the Rubicon Trail (82). She describes her companions on this trail as "'car guys' in a way [she] would never be nor want to be, however deep [her] involvement with cars" (71). Hazleton goes some way toward deconstructing the guy/girl dichotomy by moving "car guys" to the underprivileged side. She mixes masculine and feminine characteristics by describing "car guys" as superficial, a trait traditionally associated with girls, according to Scharff (119).

Cameron Tuttle provides a more extreme challenge to gender coding of human-car relationships in *The Bad Girl's Guide to the Open Road*. In addition to giving car maintenance tips to empower women drivers and promoting female love of cars (142), she goes so far as to describe the automobile as "a huge vibrator on wheels" (59). Her fetishizing "road sisters" reverse the norm by threatening to replace men with cars. The hot pink vinyl cover of the *Guide* reverses the usual good-girl signification of Penelope Pitstop/Barbie/Mary Kay-pink. The term *Bad*, for girls with guy characteristics, does not conform to the dominant coding in this case, because Tuttle uses it to signify "empowered" as well as "naughty."

Although women road writers perform extreme guy roles, either for novelty or to open up new liberating spaces, some aspects of guy-hood are neither positive nor liberating. While Penelope would benefit from being a mechanic, becoming a fetishizer is constraining. A woman motorist may benefit from the artistic expression customizing offers (as illustrated by many of the stories in Root's book), but she may well wish to avoid the dehumanizing effect of being possessed by a car. Christine's driver is a fictional warning: Arnie as ultimate fetishizer becomes dehumanized, drops everyone who loves him for his car, and finally becomes a psychotic killer at her wheel.

A driver who does not fetishize automobiles is freer to point out their faults, including detrimental effects on the environment. Lackey notes that the vast majority of road writers, in thrall to the romance of the car, fail to point out its environmental consequences (40–41). Contemporary women road writers are better positioned to problematize the freedom promised by the car than men. This is not a result of any biological determinacy, but first, because of the history outlined above which has made them less likely to fetishize cars, and second, because they began to gain access to the driver's seat just as environmental issues started to gain ground. I wish to avoid essentializing, however, by noting that late-century male writers such as James Morgan (author of *The Distance to the Moon*) address environmental issues, and it is not too late for some women to be fetishizing "car guys," judging by Tuttle and examples in Root's book. Hazleton is conscious of the contradiction in her love of the automobile and desire for a sustainable environment (e.g., 35, 60, 72). She also highlights the fact that her freedom is dependent on mind-numbing labor by joining the production line at a Saturn plant (249–56). In this way, although she problematizes the freedom offered by the automobile, Hazleton collapses the dichotomy further than women writers who seriously represent car guydom as one hundred percent desirable.

Marketing and Reception

That women writers are not in full control of their narrative vehicles is illustrated by the examples of past and present representations of women and cars given above. With knowledge of their histories, women road writers can exploit or deconstruct dominant representations to an extent. However, their ability to create new female spaces or enter male spaces with their narrative vehicles is also constrained by issues of how publishers and readers place women and cars within travel writing and literature in general.

The increased visibility of travel books over the last twenty years has led to marketing strategies that either seek to align texts with influential predecessors or to foreground the difference of a new book from its contemporaries. For instance, the cover of Martin Fletcher's roadlogue, *Almost Heaven: Travels through the Backwoods of America*, reads: "An enthralling, addictive book to compare with John Steinbeck's *Travels with Charley* or Bill Bryson's *The Lost Continent*." This analysis aligns Fletcher's book with the classic roadlogue on the United States and with a contemporary bestseller. The first two references authenticate it; the third is designed to attract the myriads that enjoy Bill Bryson. Both illustrate the fact that the genre is male dominated.

The opposing strategy is to emphasize a book's uniqueness by focusing on, e.g., unusual vehicle, route, or quest choice. Lawrence notes that travel writers were pressured to find new angles in the eighteenth century due to a saturated market (24). Presumably the situation is much exacerbated by now. The female sex of a roadlogue's writer can be a marketing opportunity; it is a way to promote the difference (albeit often a superficial or problematic difference) of one road trip book from the majority of others. Due to the history of representations of women and cars, a lone woman motorist is bound to arouse curiosity and certain reader expectations, especially in a genre in which the narrating persona plays such a prominent role. Thus, through a combination of marketing and reader expectations, writers such as Hazleton can become as interesting as specimens/ spectacles as the places/people they visit.

Construction of narrating personae is, therefore, partially out of the hands of the writer. Although this discussion up to now has assumed that *Driving to Detroit* is one text with one narrating persona, the reality is more complex, as revealed by an analysis of marketing in two separate editions. The inside cover of The Free Press edition, first published in the United States in 1998, shows a small headshot of Hazleton dressed in nostalgic male driver fashion. She wears a leather jacket with upturned collar. Her short, straight hair is tucked under a flat tweed cap. Her eyes look straight at the viewer, and she does not smile, seeming to mean business. This edition is shelved with Travel Narratives and/or General Automobiles in large U.S. chain bookstores.

In stark contrast, the Scribner edition, first printed in the United Kingdom in 1999, positions its larger black-and-white headshot in the center of a bright red, glossy page inserted next to the back cover. In this picture, slightly more of Hazleton's upper body is shown. She has no hat and her hair is longer and softly curled. A flowery blouse contrasts with the leather jacket of the previous picture. A slight smile softens her eyes and makes them less staring and businesslike. In short, this picture emphasizes her femininity and aligns her more with romance writers than automotive journalists. Her relationship with cars has not changed her feminine clothing. One message this headshot constructs is, "Women who love cars don't have to be butch." It allays readers' and/or publishers' fears of the "ghost in the closet" of lesbianism which Sherrie A. Inness (*Tough Girls: Women Warriors and Wonder Women in Popular Culture*) describes as lurking whenever women are represented as performing masculine roles (23).

The front covers of these editions of Hazleton's book converse with the photographs inside. On the cover of the Free Press edition the title is given as, *Driving to Detroit: An Automotive Odyssey*. In contrast, the cover of the Scribner edition foregrounds the sex of the writer. Here, the title on the front cover is, *Driving to Detroit: Memoirs of a Fast Woman*, below which is a quotation from feminist critic

Naomi Wolf: "A writer who has always been ahead of the curve in illuminating women's unique relationship to speed, power and discovery." (Although this quotation appears in the other edition, it is given less prominence by being positioned on the back cover.) The Scribner edition appears to be marketed to attract a mainstream female readership.[8]

Marketing women's travel texts based on their difference from men's can lead to pitfalls. Melanie McGrath downplays her sex throughout her text and objects when a man she meets on the road groups her with "indomitable British traveller women" (45). Some women object to being identified as "women writers," because of the label's potential connotations of second-class status and threat to individuality.

The recent spate of anthologies and other books on women and cars and/or motorcycles is linked to the increased visibility of women's travel writing anthologies in general at the turn of the century. It is part of the larger move to commodify women's literature.[9] Though this creates increased publishing opportunities for women road writers, it has drawbacks. Focus on a writer's female sex can lead to women's travel writing being valued for extraordinariness, rather than for literary merit, as Sara Mills has noted (*Discourses* 110–12). It can also lead to pigeonholing and essentialism. For instance, if a bookstore were to shelve Erika Lopez's motorcycle trip *Flaming Iguanas: An Illustrated Motorcycle All-Girl Road Novel Thing* under lesbian literature alone, it would likely reduce its circulation and diminish its chances to join or replace canonical male road novels. Hazleton's *Driving to Detroit*, whether by design or accident, has the best of several worlds by appearing under Women's Studies, Travel Writing, and General Automobile in U.S. chain bookstores. Her articles appear in automotive magazines with predominantly male readers and Elinor Nauen's edited anthology, *Ladies, Start Your Engines: Women Writers on Cars and the Open Road*, presumably directed at a female readership. She is able to escape confinement to the category of "extraordinary" or "eccentric woman."

Road Sisters

Although other areas could be investigated (such as literary influence), clearly, representations of women and cars provide a useful barometer to measure the relationship of women to the male-dominated U.S. roadlogue in the postwar period.

Of those current car commercials aimed at the female market, a large proportion uses promises of freedom to attract buyers. In one example, the car enables a woman to leave her boyfriend (Renault Clio); in another it recaptures a rebellious childhood (Fiat Seicento); and in still another it is a means for female companions to have humorous (legal, socially acceptable) adventures together in a much toned down version of *Thelma & Louise* (Peugeot 106). These examples, aired on television in the United Kingdom in 1999, give much more agency to women drivers than that enjoyed by Penelope Pitstop. They are more empowering to women than 1920's advertising, which mostly marketed cars to housewives to help them fulfill their family duties, rather than to single, employed women to give them freedom from domesticity (Scharff 118). First, these examples illustrate that cars marketed to women remain smaller and less powerful than those marketed to men. *Thelma & Louise* would have caused much less controversy if its protagonists had driven a diminutive Peugeot 106 rather than a 1966 Ford Thunderbird. Second, it is difficult to imagine a commercial showing a woman taking to the road in order to become sexually promiscuous or to leave her children. By their construction of women's relationships with cars, these commercials illustrate that the anonymity and escape from domesticity afforded to males by the road trip remains less than fully accessible to females if they are unwilling to challenge gender boundaries.[10]

As pointed out earlier, women narrators taking on "car guy" roles can serve to reinforce guy/girl dichotomies. A common criticism of women's travel writing is that it largely conforms to masculine paradigms and is insufficiently disruptive; that it enters male territory without opening up new female spaces.[11] However, discussing dominant representations and issues of marketing and reception, women writers have limited control over their narrative vehicles, making any unqualified criticism of their shortcomings unfair.

Despite the limits imposed by certain textual constraints, when compared with the commercials mentioned above, it is apparent that contemporary women road writers do more to disrupt and resist constraints than dominant media representations, though their texts reach a much narrower audience. There are various strategies open to women road writers who wish to pass Penelope Pitstop, as outlined by this discussion. To summarize, they can downplay gender construction and cars (McGrath), explore it with a serious inquiry (Hazleton), or expose it with extreme role reversal and shock tactics (Tuttle).

Women can seek to appropriate all aspects of being a "car guy" (Root, Tuttle), or take on the positive, while rejecting the negative, traits (Hazleton). Women can redress the sex imbalance in representation of people-car relationships by anthologizing women's stories (Nauen, Root), or bring women writers in from the margins by grouping their car narratives with men's (Lindamood Jennings).

It is difficult to gauge which strategies are most disruptive. Women-only anthologies are hampered in that they do not entirely escape the "glamour gal of the gas pedal" image and are largely marketed to only female readers. However, their contribution to the increased visibility of women and cars in road literature at the turn of the century is significant. Marked (or prompted) by *Thelma & Louise*, a late-century cross-generic challenge to the postwar male-dominated road trip suggests that women road writers are beginning to lose their novelty status. This rise in representations of (more empowered) women and cars is part of what Inness identifies as a significant increase in the last thirty years (from Penelope Pitstop's era onwards) in "tough girls" in popular culture who challenge traditional gender roles by adoption of masculine traits (178). Although she does not analyze travel writing, Inness's criteria for measuring "toughness" are useful to evaluate how much Lesley Hazleton's narrating persona in *Driving to Detroit* exceeds gender norms. Inness claims that tough girls are compromised when they become passive sex objects for men, are not as tough as tough men, or have maternal instincts (161–68). For the purposes of this discussion, maternal instincts will be replaced by how far women escape domesticity.

Penelope Pitstop is compromised, because her primary function is to be a spectacle for the male gaze. Despite featuring in a cartoon principally for children, the sexual allure of her outfit (both regular clothes and car clothes) is obvious. Her status as "lovely glamour gal" differentiates her from her male competitors who are, in the description of the *Wacky Races* line up (partially quoted at the opening of this chapter), largely introduced by name and car alone rather than attributes like attractiveness. Penelope is also compromised because, embodying feminine vulnerability, she needs to be rescued. In contrast, Lesley Hazleton is a subject, rather than an object, and is to be taken seriously as a professional automotive journalist who is equal to men in knowledge and control of cars. She describes the state of "semi-domesticity," which allows her to roam in response to schoolchildren who ask her if she has a husband to travel with, illustrating that norms of propriety in women's travel are established at an early age (217). Hazleton both challenges social norms and is indicative that they are slowly changing.

Cameron Tuttle pushes boundaries further than Hazleton. Though there is some ambiguity in this book due to its spoof-guide status (one is not always sure what is serious and what is tongue-in-cheek), it largely urges women to abandon conventional feminine beauty and exploit men for casual sex (16–17). Road sisters (who travel alone or with each other) are certainly not glamour gals. Once they see the car as a "freedom fighter," rather than the socially conditioned view of it as a "motorized shopping cart" (48), road sisters are free to shun makeup and have bad hair (16–17), chew tobacco (54), and relish urinating at the side of the road (123). Tuttle's guide encourages road sisters to perceive breakdowns as opportunities to exercise their creativity, rather than times to wait to be rescued (e.g., 145). Tuttle pushes the envelope further by suggesting to the female reader about to take a road trip: "Remove your wedding ring: Why risk losing it—or all those free drink opportunities—along the way?" (46). Perhaps her most controversial tip is, "If you have children, don't ever bring them with you. It's so easy to lose small things on the road" (31). These suggestions are made partially in jest (perhaps to make them more easily digestible). However, the fact that they jar reveals the bias that naturalizes, and makes acceptable, the urge of men (such as Steinbeck, Fletcher, and Morgan) to leave spouses and children for lone road trips, but constructs as uncaring or unnatural those women who do likewise.

Obviously, becoming a fully fledged road sister would not be an empowering experience for all women if it meant abandoning their families. Neither should lone women's road trips necessarily be privileged over couple trips or kin trips. As previously noted, taking on all aspects of "car guyness" is not necessarily desirable. However, writers like Tuttle and Hazleton clearly identify those biases that limit women's road freedom. They challenge the naturalness of men's close relationships with cars and the road by revealing their underpinning cultural construction, thus showing women that they have a choice as to how they perform gender. Tuttle's road sisters (though often humorously unrealistic) have total control over their cars and bodies, providing a welcome shift toward the representation of women drivers who pass Penelope Pitstop.

Notes

1   The notion of gender as performed, rather than biologically determined, is based on Judith Butler's model in *Gender Trouble,* which has been used productively in other studies on travel writing such as Lisle's. My approach owes much to Sara Mills's *Discourses,* a study of personal voice in relation to textual and societal constraints in British women's travel narratives from the mid-nineteenth to the early twentieth centuries.

2   The Works Cited list includes two editions of Hazleton's book with two different subtitles. Both are published by divisions of Simon and Schuster, and both adopt identical page numbering. The two versions are listed because their different book covers are discussed later in this chapter.

3   For a shorter, but more recent survey than Dettelbach's, see Zurbrugg.

4   These functions are also apparent in music about cars. See Heining for examples.

5   Graphics of all *Wacky Races* participants and their cars can be found in the following Web sites: Schmidt, Wingnut Productions, and The Wacky Races. These include links to *The Perils of Penelope Pitstop.* In their history of cars as costume, Marsh and Collett compare car engines to codpieces (27–44).

6   For a full discussion of women and chauffeurs see Scharff 23. For discussions of American dreams of possession and control see Roberts 60; Dettelbach 119.

7   For examples see Holland and Huggan 117.

8   For a thorough discussion on how marketing affects authorial persona and genre see Horner and Zlosnik.

9   See Holland and Huggan 113; Hanson, regarding the commodification of women's literature.

10   For further discussion of car commercials, see Rice and Saunders.

11   For example, see Holland and Huggan 132.

Works Cited

Abraham, Marilyn J. *First We Quit Our Jobs: How One Work Driven Couple Got on the Road to a New Life.* New York: Dell, 1997.

The Adventures of Priscilla, Queen of the Desert. Dir. Stephan Elliott. Perf. Hugo Weaving, Guy Pearce, and Terence Stamp. Polygram Video, 1994.

Ballard, J. G. *Crash.* New York: Farrar, Straus and Giroux, 1973.

Bryson, Bill. *The Lost Continent: Travels in Small Town America.* London: Little, Brown, 1989.

Butler, Judith. *Gender Trouble: Feminism and the Subversion of Identity.* New York and London: Routledge, 1990.

Cahill, Tim. *Road Fever: A High Speed Travelogue.* 1991. London: Fourth Estate, 1995.

Christine. Dir. John Carpenter. Perf. Keith Gordon, John Stockwell, and Alexandra Paul. Columbia Tristar Home Video, 1983.

Citroen Xsara. TV Advertisement. July 1999.

Codrescu, Andrei. *Road Scholar: Coast to Coast Late in the Century.* New York: Hyperion, 1993.

Cohan, Steven, and Ina Rae Hark. Introduction. Cohan and Hark 1–16.

———. eds. *The Road Movie Book*. London and New York: Routledge, 1997.

Coltrane, Robbie, and Graham Stuart. *Coltrane in a Cadillac*. London: Fourth Estate, 1993.

Continental Tyres. TV Advertisements. August 1999.

Davies, Pete. *Storm Country: A Journey to the Heart of America*. London: Heinemann, 1992.

Dettelbach, Cynthia. *In the Driver's Seat: The Automobile in American Literature and Popular Culture*. Westport, CT and London: Greenwood Press, 1976.

Dixon, Winifred Hawkridge. *Westward Hoboes: Ups and Downs of Frontier Motoring*. New York: Scribner, 1928.

Driving Miss Daisy. Dir. Bruce Beresford. Perf. Morgan Freeman and Jessica Tandy. Warner Home Video, 1989.

Fiat Seicento. TV Advertisement. August 1999.

Fletcher, Martin. *Almost Heaven: Travels through the Backwoods of America*. London: Abacus, 1999.

Hanson, Clare. "Marketing the 'Woman Writer.'" Simons and Fullbrook 66–80.

Hazleton, Lesley. *Driving to Detroit: An Automotive Odyssey*. New York: The Free Press, 1998.

———. *Driving to Detroit: Memoirs of a Fast Woman*. London: Scribner, 1999.

Heat-Moon, William Least. *Blue Highways: A Journey into America*. Boston: Houghton Mifflin, 1982.

Heining, Duncan. *Cars and Cars—The Car, Masculinity and Pop Culture*. Ed. David Thoms, Tim Claydon, and Len Holden. Aldershot: Ashgate, 1998. 96–119.

Holland, Patrick, and Graham Huggan. *Tourists with Typewriters: Critical Reflections on Contemporary Travel Writing*. Ann Arbor: U of Michigan P, 1998.

Horner, Avril, and Sue Zlosnik. "'Extremely Valuable Property': the Marketing of *Rebecca*." Simons and Fullbrook 48–65.

Inness, Sherrie A. *Tough Girls: Women Warriors and Wonder Women in Popular Culture*. Philadelphia: U of Pennsylvania P, 1999.

Kerouac, Jack. *On the Road*. 1957. London: Penguin, 1991.

King, Stephen. *Christine*. New York: Viking, 1983.

Knight Rider. Universal TV. 1982.

Lackey, Kris. *RoadFrames: The American Highway Narrative*. Lincoln, Nebraska: U of Nebraska P, 1997.

Lawrence, Karen. *Penelope Voyages: Women and Travel in the British Literary Tradition*. Ithaca and London: Cornell UP, 1994.

Lindamood Jennings, Jean. Preface. *Road Trips, Head Trips, and Other Car-Crazed Writings*. Ed. Lindamood Jennings. New York: Atlantic Monthly Press, 1996. vii-xii.

Lisle, Debbie. "Gender at a Distance: Identity, Performance and Contemporary Travel Writing." *International Feminist Journal of Politics* 1.1 (June 1999): 66–88.

Lopez, Erika. *Flaming Iguanas: An Illustrated Motorcycle All-Girl Road Novel Thing*. New York: Simon and Schuster, 1997.

Marsh, Peter, and Peter Collett. *Driving Passion: The Psychology of the Car*. London and New York: Routledge, 1991.

Mayle, Simon. *The Burial Brothers: From New York to Rio in a '73 Cadillac Hearse*. New York: Ballantine, 1996.

McGrath, Melanie. *Motel Nirvana: Dreaming of the New Age in the American Desert*. New York: Picador USA, 1995.

Mercedes Benz. Advertisement. Billboard, United Kingdom. August 1999.

Mills, Sara. *Discourses of Difference: An Analysis of Women's Travel Writing and Colonialism*. London and New York: Routledge, 1991.

Morgan, James. *The Distance to the Moon: A Road Trip in the American Dream*. New York: Penguin Putnam, 1999.

Nauen, Elinor, ed. *Ladies, Start Your Engines: Women Writers on Cars and the Open Road*. Boston: Faber and Faber, 1996.

O'Rourke, P. J. Introduction. Lindamood Jennings 1–8.

The Perils of Penelope Pitstop. Hanna Barbera, 1969–1971.

Peugeot 106. TV Advertisement. August 1999.

Pirsig, Robert M. *Zen and the Art of Motorcycle Maintenance: An Inquiry into Values*. Vintage, London, 1974.

Post, Emily. *By Motor to the Golden Gate*. New York and London: D. Appleton, 1916.

Renault Clio. TV Advertisement. July 1999.

Rice, Jenny, and Carol Saunders. "'Mini Loves Dressing Up': Selling Cars to Women." *The Motor Car and Popular Culture*. Ed. David Thoms, Tim Claydon, and Len Holden. Aldershot: Ashgate, 1998. 276–86.

Roberts, Shari. "Western Meets Eastwood: Genre and Gender on the Road." Cohan and Hark 45–69.

Root, Marilyn. *Women at the Wheel: 42 Stories of Freedom, Fanbelts and the Lure of the Open Road*. Naperville, IL: Sourcebooks, 1999.

Scharff, Virginia. *Taking the Wheel: Women and the Coming of the Motor Age*. Albuquerque: U of New Mexico P, 1991.

Schmidt, John V. *The Perils of Penelope Pitstop*. 2 Sept. 1999. http://www.hotlink.com/wacky/pitstop/.

———. *The Wacky Races*. Sept. 2, 1999. http://www.hotlink.com/wacky.

Simmons, Lydia. "Not from the Back Seat." Lindamood Jennings 187–92.

Simons, Judy, and Kate Fullbrook, eds. *Writing: A Woman's Business*. Manchester: Manchester UP, 1998.

Steinbeck, John. *Travels with Charley in Search of America*. London: Heinemann, 1962.

Thelma & Louise. Dir. Ridley Scott. Perf. Susan Sarandon and Geena Davis. MGM/UA Studios, 1991.

Tuttle, Cameron. *The Bad Girl's Guide to the Open Road*. San Francisco: Chronicle, 1999.

Vanishing Point. Dir. Richard C. Sarafian. Perf. Barry Newman and Cleavon Little. Twentieth Century Fox, 1971.

Wacky Races. Cartoon Network: Dept. of Cartoons. Sept. 2, 1999. http://www.cartoon-network.com/doc/wackyraces/index.html.

The Wacky Races. Hanna Barbera, 1968–1970.

Wingnut Productions. *Wacky Races*. Sept. 2, 1999. http://w3.nai.net/~wingnut/Wacky_Races.html/.

Zurbrugg, Nicholas. "Oh What a Feeling!—The Literatures of the Car." *The Motor Car and Popular Culture*. Ed. David Thoms, Tim Claydon, and Len Holden. Aldershot: Ashgate, 1998. 9–27.

Part Two

Genre

Chapter Six

Frances Trollope's America and Anna Leonowens's Siam
Questionable Travel and Problematic Writing

Chu-Chueh Cheng

Metageographical discourse reminds us that all geographical boundaries are imposed on the earth and that a map is always encoded with its maker's (or patron's) interests. The metacognition that enables geographers to redefine their discipline is equally applicable to our remarking of the generic terrain of travel writing. The contingency of boundaries means that, while one draws borderlines according to one's perceived relation to others, these lines are constantly trespassed. Travel—with its association with transience, movement, and displacement—dissolves boundaries in the act of crossing. Travel writing likewise cannot be contained within the parameters of a certain genre; it encompasses genres beyond its allotted borders.

Travel writing's generic multiplicity sets the established literary conventions and classifications in motion, for it shares certain literary features with some seemingly irrelevant (or antithetical) genres. First, travel literature is generally considered journalistic and autobiographical. Nearly all travel writing is narrated in the first person and the narrator is usually the author-traveler who presents empirical evidence of another culture. Isabella Bird's travel accounts in Northeast Asia, for example, are a variation on (or segments of) her autobiography.

In addition to its affinity to autobiography and social critique, some Victorian travel writing resembles adventure stories and domestic novels in its exaltation of Britain and vilification of racial others. It features the traveler's vigor, legendary (if not entirely unprecedented) experiences, and exotic spectacles. Sir Richard Burton, for instance, is a historical figure who traveled incognito to Mecca. Burton is just as legendary as Kim, Kipling's fictional character who works for British intelligence while accompanying a Tibetan lama to search for a sacred destination. The theatricality of Burton's travels makes us wonder which story is more fictional—Burton's *Pilgrimage to El-Medinah and Meccah,* or Kipling's *Kim.* In addition to its intrinsic rhetoric of exploration, travel writing also contains the rhetoric of investigation. For travel writers, accounts of foreign countries provide a forum for addressing domestic issues of the traveled regions, those of their homeland, or a combination of both. Jonathan Swift's *Gulliver's Travels* (1726), for instance, illuminates the social ills of England through its protagonist's metaphorical journey to others' lands. A Victorian example would be Captain Basil Hall's *Travels in North America* (1829), one of the best-known British versions of American domestic novels attacking Americans' continuing practice of slavery.

Perhaps most important yet least recognizable is travel writing's strong affinity to diaspora (migration) literature. The correlation and sometimes conflation of these two genres triggers questions. What is travel? How does travel differentiate itself from migration? Do we really need such a distinction? If travel remains historically contingent, should we rechart the generic terrain for travel literature from time to time? None of these questions has an easy answer. This chapter does not attempt one. Rather, it intends to render visible the multiplicity of travel, the problematic of writing, and the treacherousness of travel writing as a literary genre.

Travel is commonly defined as a movement from place to place. According to *The Random House College Dictionary,* travel as a verb means "to go from one place to another or from place to place." The *Collins Cobuild English Dictionary* gives a similar definition: "If you *travel,* you go from one place to another, often a place that is far away." Though the definition of travel seems straightforward, a rigorous interpretation of *place* is overdetermined. As a noun, *place* contains more than twenty meanings—chiefly evolving from *space, location, position, job, function, duty, rank,* and *identity. Place*-related idioms also abound: *give place, go places, in place, know* or *keep one's place, out of place, put someone in his place, take place,* and so forth. The complexity of travel, therefore, derives less from the simple act of movement than from the plural connotations of *place.*

The multiple meanings that *place* connotes derive from its association with boundaries—spatial, cultural, national, social, geographical, gendered, and so on. Of the correlation of place and propriety, Tim Cresswell asserts that

> place plays a significant role in the creation of norms of behavior and thus in the creation of deviance...*Outsider* is commonly the term used to describe people new to a place or people who do not know the ways of a place. The use of the term *outsider* indicates that a person does not properly understand the behavior expected of people in town, region, or nation. Outsiders are often despised and suspected of being trouble-makers. They are people "out of place." (25–26, original emphasis)

Cresswell's observation applies equally well to the theorization of travel. More than just an act of physical movement, travel also implies transience, transgression, and deviance. As travel often inscribes in the popular imagination the defiance of boundaries, travel literature translates that transience into literary classification: It defies the containment and confinement of a fixed category. Travel writing intrinsically trespasses on other literary genres and subsequently appropriates them into its own terrain.

There are several ways to look at travel literature's generic encroachment. Historically, travel writing has been deployed as an author's strategy of validating his or her viewpoint. Like their literary predecessors, many Victorian writers used distant and exotic travels to authenticate their experiences, which in turn ascertained the authority of their writing. Socially, travel writing relocates ideological transgressions to a distant land and thereby allows the author greater freedom to address controversial issues. Keenly aware of the empowerment of travel, Victorian women writers used travel literature effectively to win recognition for themselves. Of foreign travel's impact on Victorian feminine discourse, Maria H. Frawley astutely observes:

> Travel enabled many Victorian women to create a connection to and establish authority with a part of English culture that hitherto had evaded them because they lacked the education that decreed cultural authority...In essence, travel conferred on many Victorian women a measure of cultural competence that derived not from education but from experience. (24)

Victorian women writers also used travel writing as a transitional genre to mediate the conflicting roles they played in the private sphere and the public arena. Travel literature allowed them to voice their views in an acceptable form that veiled their participation in public forums through seemingly personal accounts. Thus, it should not come as a surprise that a significant number of Victorian women writers wrote as travelers when they were actually investigating the social, political, or religious components both at home and abroad.

Frances Trollope: The Returned Emigrant

Like many of her contemporaries, Frances Trollope perceived the United States as a site of new discursive possibilities as well as a land of professional opportunities. Some critics may readily dismiss her as a typical British bourgeois traveler, and there are indeed causes for such an easy dismissal.

Accompanied by an entourage of family members, servants, and a friend, Trollope indeed embarked on a seemingly formulaic journey that carried the comfort of home among strange places, an experience widely duplicated among Victorian bourgeoisie and aristocrats. Some critics also regard her travel account of America as nothing more than a replica or rearrangement of preceding America-bashing books. Critics of her time and ours note that Trollope's *Domestic Manners of the Americans* (1832) reproduces or rearranges the commonplace notions of America that appear in Captain Hall's *Travels in North America* (1829). An unidentified American editor claims "either that Captain Basil All [sic] is Mrs. Trollope in breeches, or that Mrs. Trollope is Captain Basil All in petticoats."[1]

Captain Basil All is a (possibly deliberate) mistake for Captain Basil Hall. Hall traveled extensively during his lifetime and recorded his journeys in several volumes of work. *Travels in North America in the Years 1827 and 1828* (1829) recounted his trip to the United States and Canada in the late 1820s. The book infuriated American readers because it attacked the practice of slavery at a time when the newly invented cotton gin had created a greater need for slaves. Americans accused Hall of being unfair to their society—a charge that they also leveled against Frances Trollope. However, Trollope was not merely incidentally related to Hall on account of their common prejudice against America. There was a professional connection between the two authors: Hall was Trollope's literary predecessor and mentor; he proofread her manuscript and recommended it for publication.[2]

In addition to her intellectual link to Hall, the theme and style of *Domestic Manners* were greatly determined by the political dynamics of travel discourse, in particular that of British travelers. Of the intertextuality among British accounts of North America, Percy G. Adams notices that "[b]efore the Revolution they were normally favorable, very often propaganda," and that after the Revolution, British traveler-writers were "openly antipathetic to the vulgar new society that had disgraced the mother country by attaining its freedom" (189–90). This national prejudice not only ingrains itself in most travel accounts of America but also cultivates literary conventions and political convictions for subsequent travel books on the United States. This prejudice evidently shapes the style of Trollope's representation of America, the former colony of Britain.

Aside from her seemingly formulaic experience and banal comments, the site of Trollope's travel does not impress, much less captivate, us. For Victorians, America was not exactly an exotic locale in comparison with Fiji, Japan, or West Africa. By all standards, Trollope's travel in America cannot match the scale of audacity of either Isabella Bird's exploration in Northeast Asia or Mary Kingsley's adventures in West Africa,[3] nor can *Domestic Manners* match the intellectual profundity of Alexis de Tocqueville's *Democracy in America* (1835). A Frenchman delegated to study American institutions, Tocqueville documented his observation in *Democracy*, which European scholars generally regarded as a fair representation of the States. So what is the point of citing Trollope—a stereotypical British traveler—if this essay is to invigorate and complicate the discourse of travel and travel literature? Trollope's attraction is partially grounded in the alleged banality of her observations and the notorious popularity of *Domestic Manners*, but mostly it is invoked by the trans-Atlantic controversy that the book ignited and by the author—"so much read, so much admired, and so much abused."[4]

As stated above, Trollope may appear to be a typical Victorian bourgeois traveler. Biographical information, however, indicates that at the age of forty-seven, Trollope saw America as a land of opportunities where she could re-establish the family, in particular her youngest son, Henry. While she traveled with three of her five children, two servants and a tutor, her husband and two older sons remained in England.[6] It is rather obvious that Trollope's travel veiled her real intention: to work and support the family. Her journey across the Atlantic thus signified a social and gender transgression. Away from the homeland, where her role was categorically defined and her family finances were in crisis, she was free—or at least felt free—to start anew and reinvent new gender and social roles.

To start a new life, Trollope could not altogether forsake old roles. She needed the excuse of a vacation to serve as a transition between her role as a member of the leisure class and that of the working (or professional) class. Little is explicitly mentioned in her account about the family's seeking economic opportunities in America, but the implied worries exemplify how often the desperation for work is eclipsed or obscured by our customary glorification of travel. In November of 1827, the Trollope entourage sailed from London in the hope that some of them would teach at Nashoba, a school founded by Frances Wright to educate liberated slaves. To their great dismay, Nashoba was more a concept than a reality. As Trollope recalls, when they arrived...

> no school had been established. Books and other materials for the great experiment had been collected, and one or two professors engaged, but nothing was yet organized...All I know farther of Nashoba is, that Miss Wright having found (from some cause or other) that it was impossible to pursue her object, herself accompanied her slaves to Hayti, and left them there, free, and under the protection of the president. (45)

In this excerpt, the traveler's rhetoric of objective observation may intend to contain or suppress the job seeker's disappointment. The frustration, though concealed in words, distorts her view of the landscape, for she later notes: "I found no beauty in the scenery round Nashoba, nor can I conceive that it would possess any even in the summer" (45).

After the Nashoba fiasco, the Trollope family ventured to Cincinnati, where Trollope tried a wide range of projects, but most of them seemed to fail. The Bazaar, her grandest scheme, was a combination of mall, theater, amusement park, and museum. However, miscalculations and misfortune turned the Bazaar into another fiasco, one that eventually drained the Trollopes' wealth and shattered the author's last hope of settling the family in America.

For the Trollope family, the joy of travel had to be predicated on the certainty of their future. However, a series of failed ventures seemed to deprive them of the leisurely pleasure of sightseeing, and a tone of resignation prevails:

> We quitted Cincinnati [at] the beginning of March, 1830, and I believe there was not one of our party who did not experience a sensation of pleasure in leaving it. We had seen again and again all the queer varieties of its little world...[so] we left nought to regret at Cincinnati. The only regret was that we had ever entered it; for we had wasted health, time, and money there. (150)

The ultimate objective of Trollope's travel apparently complicated her role as a visitor and thereby dictated (or distorted) her view of the country: With one failed venture after another, she was so mired in her misery that she saw only destitution and hostility in the New World.

Several biographers and critics of Frances Trollope speculate that earning some income was the key factor in determining the nature of *Domestic Manners*. Teresa Ransom cites a number of personal letters to validate such a speculation. In a letter dated November 25, 1831 to Julia Pertz, Trollope wrote: "[M]y only anxiety is, what will be paid for it? This same poverty has a mighty lowering effect on ones [sic] sublimities" (qtd. in Ransom 74). This letter confirms the speculation that the publication of Trollope's first book was indeed driven by an urgent need for money.

Her account of America not only marks vocation in vacation but also epitomizes this inevitable correlation of work and travel. Read in the context of its author's financial despair, *Domestic Manners* epitomizes the paradox of travel writing. Whereas travel is generally associated with leisure, writing is by all means an intense labor. It is reported that both Frances Trollope and her son, Anthony, wrote while traveling on the train; they were literally writing during traveling. Travel writing hinges on the threshold of job and joy, and travel writers such as Trollope are writers donning the guise of travelers.

As Trollope's pretense of travel obscures her intention for work, her account of America vacillates between the Old World and the New World. This vacillation parallels her adjustment to life in America and observation of its customs and institutions. Arriving in the States with a sizable entourage, Trollope literally travels with and in her home. Though she declares an intention to stay only temporarily until her youngest son, Henry, establishes himself, details about family matters seem to suggest a stronger intent for permanent residence. The author notes: "Cincinnati was the most favorable for a young man to settle in; and I only awaited the arrival of Mr. T. to fix our son there, intending to continue with him till he should feel himself sufficiently established" (58). Tentative (and ironic) as it is, this passage suggests the author's longing for a home and her awareness of social propriety. Though abroad without her husband, Trollope manages to retain a façade of proper womanhood. She waits for her husband's arrival to tend to matters that have long been in her charge. In the meantime, she also endeavors to duplicate English domesticity in

America, which, though not quite a home, is a place she does tarry in to restore her family fortune.

To make herself *at home* and *a home* in the New World, Trollope insists on maintaining an English bourgeois household, complete with a couple of servants to wait on her. Servants or maids, to her dismay, are hard to find in America:

> The greatest difficulty in organizing a family establishment in Ohio, is getting servants, or, as it is there called, "getting help," for it is more than petty treason to the public to call a free citizen a *servant*. The whole class of young women, whose bread depends upon their labor, are taught to believe that the most abject poverty is preferable to domestic service... (61, original emphasis)

The author's search for servants exemplifies how differently Britons and Americans viewed domestic service. Class division existed in both countries but varied in the form of its presence: In the States it was manifested (and still is) in a contingent economic hierarchy, while in England it remained an inherent social hierarchy.

Though social hierarchy may seem a cumbersome cultural baggage to carry abroad, it served to reaffirm Trollope's social status as a bourgeois Englishwoman. Knowing that the Trollope family stayed abroad chiefly because they could not afford a decent lifestyle at home, one might think that Trollope's frustration over maid-searching sounds ironic and her assertion of social superiority absurd.[6] The episode of an English traveler seeking American housemaids discloses some of the entanglement of adventure and domesticity. The presence of housemaids enabled Trollope to duplicate an English household in America; it also reaffirmed her gender propriety as "an angel in the house" while she was actually defying Victorian womanhood by working and living apart from her husband.

The eternal return to home also sets the parameters of each adventure and accordingly determines the scope of that experience. Just as the episode of servant-searching criticizes the American other to assert the English self's righteousness, Trollope's documentation of America constitutes a rhetoric of departure and return; her writing exemplifies a dual odyssey which consists of a geographically centrifugal journey to the States and an ideologically centripetal quest in Britain.

Targeting her compatriots as the primary audience, she writes as if she were gossiping to "you," the Britons, about "them," the Americans. The customary superiority of the traveler's country to the traveled region prevails in her account. Of the Americans' religion, she notes that "both Protestant England and Catholic France show an infinitely superior religious and moral aspect to moral observation, both as to reverend decency of external observance, and as to the inward fruit of honest dealing between man and man" (243).

About the Americans' transport vehicles, she continues: "[t]heir carriages of every kind are very unlike ours," and to the stagecoaches of England "they can bear no comparison" (243–44). However, Trollope's cultural superiority is most ostentatious when she comments on American literature:

> The immense exhalation of periodical trash, which penetrates into every cot and corner of the country, and which is greedily sucked in by all ranks, is unquestionably one great cause of its inferiority…Another obvious cause of inferiority in the national literature is the very slight acquaintance with the best models of composition which is thought necessary for persons called well-educated. (249–50)

To ensure (or rather to improve) the quality of American literature, the author cannot help but digress to the cause of English literature's superiority; she cites Chaucer and Spenser as if they could function as antidotes to American literary deficiency (250–51).

The ambiguity of Trollope's intention to move homeward and simultaneous pretension to travel outward noticeably contributes to the fluid generic boundaries between a travel account and a domestic novel. As a visitor in America, Trollope presents herself as a home-*bound* figure residing in shifting settings—a paradox obscuring conventional boundaries between home and abroad. Hence, America is more than the site of Trollope's sightseeing. Metaphorically, the New World serves as a locus of cultural intersection at which the author inscribes English values and through which Britain reinforces its received notion of America.

Perhaps an overlooked biographical detail will shed some new light on our conceptualization of Trollope's "home." After returning to England, the author continued to write—over thirty novels and four other travel books. Plagued by financial worries, she resided for much of the time in Italy, where she remained a central figure among expatriates such as the Brownings. Though she eventually moved back to England and passed away there, it is difficult to determine whether she was a traveler or an expatriate. The same difficulty occurs when one has to judge where Trollope's home was and yet cannot decide whether England was her site of departure, her point of arrival, or both. As a perennial traveler-writer, she exemplified the transient who resides in multiple locations, and her travel accounts of these foreign countries defeat our attempt at distinguishing travel writing from domestic novels. When a traveler becomes an expatriate, and when the boundaries between homeland and foreign land blur, the genre of his/her travel account suggests plural possibilities: It can be a domestic novel or a social critique of the traveled region.

This generic multiplicity is further enhanced when a travel account is distributed in both the traveler's homeland and the traveled region. On the reciprocity between Trollope's home audience and her observation abroad, Linda Abess Ellis remarks: "Many of these commonplace notions of America appear in Mrs. Trollope's novels, partly in response to the demands of the marketplace. Her readers, most of whom believed in the stereotypes portrayed, expected to find confirmation of their prejudices" (21). A comparative study of Trollope and other writers also leads Ellis to detect a psychological factor in the production of travel literature, in particular the reproduction of a certain homebound ideology: "The traveler's abuse, however, has a more complex motivation than concern for sales; it is closely connected to the writer's position as an outsider and his need to validate his own culture. The conventional portrayal of Americans violating accepted British social norms has roots in this feeling of foreignness" (22). Ellis insightfully unravels the complex nexus of cultural presuppositions, readers' receptions, and writers' positions: Her observation well articulates Trollope's position as the mediator between the home culture and the alien culture.

Readers on either side of the Atlantic Ocean reacted to the book according to their individual political, religious, and ideological standpoints. Some readers may have considered the book a travel account, a journalistic report of a Victorian woman's encounter with Americans. Others (many of them Americans) may have regarded the book as a (pre)fabrication of America's domestic issues, a fictional construct by an outsider.

Genre and Authorship

Like the clearly marked, sometimes colorfully drawn, borderlines that structure the world in a map, generic classification imposes an order on the world of literary texts. However, there do not always exist, and perhaps have never existed, clearly demarcated territories among literary genres because different genres do merge with one another, as national territories often overlap. As M. M. Bakhtin points out, "the boundaries between fiction and nonfiction...are not laid up in heaven" and "the growth of literature is not merely development and change within the fixed boundaries of any given definition; the boundaries themselves are constantly changing" (33). The intrinsically contingent boundaries among genres are further problematized when a text itself functions as a meeting place between different cultures. Moreover, a travel account best illustrates how the author's (self-claimed or perceived) position interacts with the generic borderline of her text.

To better understand the intricacy of Trollope's travel, few analyses are as illuminating as James Clifford's observation of the multifariousness of travel. Clifford quests for the true nature of travel and wonders what distinguishes a traveler from a migrant worker. He notes:

> The political disciplines and economic pressures that control migrant labor regimes pull very strongly against any overtly sanguine view of the mobility of poor, usually non-white, people who *must* leave home in order to survive. The traveler, by definition, is someone who has the security and privilege to move about in relatively unconstrained ways. (107, original emphasis)

Trollope in America fits both the description of bourgeois travelers and that of migrant workers. Modern readers may no longer equate travel with vacation, but in the Victorian era travel connoted privilege and leisure—only upper and middle classes could afford the luxury of mobility for pleasure.

Trollope's conflicting roles in the New World unsettle the received distinction between leisure-class travelers and working-class migrants. In comparison with the working class of her time, Trollope did "have the security and privilege to move about in relatively unconstrained ways," but biographical information also assures us that she "*must* leave home in order to survive." The inconsistency of her intention to work and her pretension to travel accordingly hinders us from fixing her in a definite social position—she traverses multiple social places.

On the structural inconsistency of the account, Helen Heineman contends that "*Domestic Manners* is really two books, with two distinct kinds of styles and material" (*Mrs. Trollope* 83). While the first section of the book primarily features narratives of her everyday life in Cincinnati, the second section mostly presents a general review of American society:

> When she headed East, Mrs. Trollope became an ordinary traveler...Instead of the intimate revelations of the well-informed English homemaker and businesswoman in painful confrontations with American egalitarian society, the book becomes a conventional account, dedicated to the inspection and description of famous scenes. (*Trollope* 83)

Heineman's analysis explains how Trollope's dual role in the States shapes her account of the host country. From chapter 18 onward, the author starts visiting tourist spots, such as Maryland, Virginia, Philadelphia, New York, Niagara, and so on. After Cincinnati, her view of America also gradually shifts from a microcosmic to a macrocosmic one: Topics significantly change from the category of quotidian activities—such as "servants," "lecture," "private amusement," and "sickness"—to the category of institutional philosophy such as "slavery," the "influence of females," "literature," and "election."

Trollope's eventual return to England dictates how we have classified her observation of America because we consider it a fragment of her autobiography. The author intends *Domestic Manners* to be a travelogue by reminding us that her writing is synchronous with her travel experience: "And here I beg to assure the reader, that whenever I give conversations they were not made *à loisir*; but were written down immediately after they occurred, with all the verbal fidelity my memory permitted" (62). She deliberately highlights the simultaneity of her travel and writing because she believes that her readers desire a sense of empirical immediacy.

To further convince her readers of the authenticity of her observation, Trollope details her persistent pursuit of documentary accuracy. Of the revision she did while staying in Maryland, she says:

> While reading and transcribing my notes, I underwent a strict self-examination. I passed in review all I had seen, all I had felt, and scrupulously challenged every expression of disapprobation; the result was, that I omitted in transcription much that I had written, as containing unnecessary details of things which had displeased me; yet, as I did so, I felt strongly that there was no exaggeration in them; but such details, though true, might be ill-natured, and I retained no more than were necessary to convey the general impressions I received... (237–38)

This metacompositional discourse—though intended to assert documentary objectivity—reveals the author's posttravel revision (recollection or reconfiguration) of that authentic experience.

The fact that Trollope revised (or even restructured) her notes seems to validate Heineman's argument that the author adopts a very different attitude after her departure from Cincinnati. As Trollope the tourist eventually supersedes Trollope the would-be immigrant, so does the rhetoric of sightseeing succeed that of adjusting. The genre of *Domestic Manners* is thereby determined by its author's teleological redefinition of that American experience: The result of Trollope's residence in America, in retrospect, determines how the experience should be narrated. A failed emigrant, one might suppose, is very likely to claim herself a returned native and expect others to view her likewise.

Genre and Readership

Most travel accounts are published in the writer's respective home country for they often target the home audience only. At the time of its first publication, *Domestic Manners* was one of the very few travel accounts that was published and marketed in both the traveler's homeland and the traveled land. This rarity, in conjunction with the banality of Trollope's observations and the popularity of her work, generated a reciprocating process of cultural inscription across the Atlantic.

To fully understand general readers' reception of Trollope's account of America, we must look closely at its market reality. The book achieved an unprecedented popularity for an unknown author's first attempt, and at the age of fifty-two. *Domestic Manners* quickly exhausted its first edition and subsequently ran through many printings, translations, and pirated editions. In London, the first edition of *Domestic Manners* was printed by Whittaker, Treacher, & Co. The same edition was simultaneously circulated in America. In 1832 alone the book went through four English and American editions.

In 1838 a fifth American edition was released, and in 1839 Bentley's Standard Library of Popular Modern Literature issued a fifth English edition. A few years later, the popularity of *Domestic Manners* swept through the European continent; it was translated and published in Spain, Germany, France, and the Netherlands.[7] This smashing success ensured Trollope's status as a professional writer, for she subsequently wrote similarly successful books about Belgium, Paris, Vienna, and Italy.

Analyses of the author's instant success generally overlook the fact that, as a language shared by Americans and Britons, English enables parallel publication in both countries. A shared language is a pivotal (and unusual) element that generates the immediate dynamic between the observing country and the observed region. Because most travel writers represent a foreign culture in a language that is alien to the native, responses from the traveled country always come much later than those from the traveler's country. The customary belatedness of the native's comments or criticisms hence hampers an immediate determination of the generic classification of a text that is about them. Translation from the traveler's language to the native's often takes time, and the consumption of a translated book requires money that the native may not have. The inequality of economic power between the traveler's country (often the West) and the traveled region (in general, the non-West) was even more drastic in the Victorian era than now. *Domestic Manners* is an unusual case in travel literature because Trollope's authority to represent America was immediately under the scrutiny of her American readers. The publication of *Domestic Manners* instantly inaugurated an intense debate, across the Atlantic, over the authority and authenticity of Trollope's representation.

Reinventing herself as a traveler, Trollope intends her narrative to convince her readers to see her as such. According to the preface, the author encourages her compatriots to "hold fast by the constitution that ensures all the blessings which flow from established habits and solid principles" (iii). She also warns them: "If they forego these, they will incur the fearful risk of breaking up their repose by introducing the jarring tumult and universal degradation which invariably follow the wild scheme of placing all the power of the state in the hands of the populace" (iii). Deploying the conventional rhetoric of a returned traveler, Trollope concludes the book with an affirmation that we (the Britons) are superior to them (the Americans). In the conclusion, she predicts that the current political climate may change Americans' beloved government: "If this ever happens, if refinement once creeps in among them, if they once learn to cling to the graces, the honors, the chivalry of life, then we shall say farewell to American equality, and welcome to European fellowship one of the finest countries on the earth" (325). The wording in both the preface and the conclusion undoubtedly complies with some conventions of travel discourse, in particular British visitors' views of America.

A superimposed framework for Trollope's travel notes, the preface and the conclusion also suggest that *Domestic Manners* indirectly addresses the issue of the Reform Bill (1832) in Britain by attacking democracy in the United States. Trollope's book was published at a time when a good number of Victorians associated democracy with "some wild outbreak of the masses that would overthrow the established order and confiscate private property" (Houghton 55). During their struggle with reform, Britons took great interest in American politics, hoping to learn a few things about their own. Hence, a great number of Victorian travelers' accounts of America blended Britons' fear of democracy abroad with their anxiety about reform at home. Readers on either side of the Atlantic Ocean responded to the book in a wide range of ways, but chiefly their political standpoints determined how it was categorized. Not only did Americans differ from Britons in their reception of *Domestic Manners*, but Britons (as well as Americans) themselves also disagreed with one another.

Trollope rode the trend, and her popularity (or notoriety) proved that her themes were public concerns on either side of the Atlantic. Compliments came from her like-minded readers in both countries. In an unsigned review from the *Quarterly Review*, Captain Basil Hall praised the book for its author's insightful view on topics that "only a female eye could correctly appreciate, or a female pen do justice to in description" (qtd. in Heineman *Mrs. Trollope* 99). Another unsigned review in *Fraser's Magazine* considered Trollope's account "acute and amusing," while denouncing the United States as "a transition country for a lady to travel in" (qtd. in Heineman *Mrs. Trollope* 99). Across the Atlantic, Samuel Clemens (Mark Twain) echoed these compliments. "Dame Trollope," he notes, "lived three years in this civilization of ours; in the body of it—not on the surface of it, as was the case with most of the foreign tourists of her day. She knew her subject well, and she set it forth fairly and squarely, without any weak ifs and ands and buts" (392). Twain is not the only American literary figure who spotted the value in Trollope's trenchant candor. At the turn of the twentieth century, in *As Others See Us*, John Graham Brooks joined Twain in acclaiming Trollope as "one of the foreign visitors whose criticisms have had a salutary effect on the States" (qtd. in Cunliffe 40).

Not all of Trollope's contemporary reviewers favored her account of America. In England alone, opinions were divided. Because the work was published in the same year the Reform Bill was passed, the domestic reception of *Domestic Manners* was greatly affected by the immediate political turmoil. Of his mother's book and its political aftermath, Thomas Trollope remarks: "It was emphatically the book of the season, was talked of everywhere, and read by all sorts and conditions of men and women. It was highly praised by all the conservative organs of the press, and vehemently abused by all those of the opposite party" (161). Indeed, as he observes, both liberal and conservative critics, when judging books on America, were influenced by their conceptualization of democracy. Suspicious of democracy, the Tories praised Trollope's book as a warning of the pitfalls of equality. Conversely, the Whigs and Radicals denounced the book as a pack of lies; sympathetic to America and democracy, they tended to question the accuracy of Trollope's negative account.

Harsh criticisms of the author were clearly proportionate to the book's popularity. While many negative comments addressed her religious and political views, some of the most scathing remarks went so far as to denigrate her moral character. The *New Monthly Magazine*, for instance, responded with a malicious attack on the author's religious views: "Mrs. Trollope's facts are exceedingly suspicious; her *comments* absolutely indecent and revolting...she gives way to a pert, coarse, and prurient style of innuendo and description, which is as inconsistent with delicacy as it is with fairness and candor" (qtd. in Heineman *Mrs. Trollope* 95, original emphasis). Personal attacks against Trollope in the name of literary criticism were (and still are) widely practiced in the States (and elsewhere).

Anti-Trollope sentiment was so intense among Americans that many magazines considered bashing her a journalistic obligation. The *Illinois Monthly Magazine* claimed that Trollope's book was a dangerous attempt to remove from women the "restraints of religion and morality," and it accused Trollope, Frances Wright, and Robert Owen of having attempted "to convert 'the natives to atheism'" (qtd. in Heineman *Mrs. Trollope* 97). The *American Quarterly Review* considered her complaints about American women's gossip tedious:

> They are mostly evils of the tea-table and the toilet—subjects, we grant, of infinite importance among the young and budding of her sex, but, we should think, not exactly such as should very greatly provoke the anger, or occasion, the severe censure of an ancient and intelligent personage of Mrs. Trollope's dimensions. (qtd. in Heineman *Mrs. Trollope* 97–98)

Whether the criticism was of the seditiousness of the book, the triviality of her observation, or the irregularity of her womanhood, it seemed to address *Domestic Manners* just as much as a social forum or a travel account as an autobiography.

The multitude of responses that American and British readers had to the work explains why generic categorization has never been able to accommodate the complex interaction among a text, its readers, its author, and their context(s). What *Domestic Manners* exemplifies is the shifting borderline among travel writing, journalistic writing, autobiography, social critique, and (im)migrant literature: The generic classification of a text is not only determined by literary conventions (which are historically contingent) but is also subject to the sociopolitical context(s) in which the text is produced and circulated.

Anna Leonowens: The Siamese King's English Governess

Perhaps the name of Anna Leonowens does not sound so familiar to us now as it did to western readers in the Victorian era, although most of us have heard of, if not seen, the movie *The King and I* (1956). A classic of American musical cinema, the film adapts Margaret Landon's *Anna and the King of Siam* (New York, 1943), a work based on Leonowens's *The English Governess at the Siamese Court* (London, 1870) and *The Romance of the Harem* (Boston, 1873). In these book titles, "Siam" is a former name for Thailand between 1856 and 1939. Upon their publication, the two books captured the imagination of Victorian readers and consequently drew attention to Siam. Not a colony of any western power, Siam was located in a geographical vacuum, a territory unmarked by contending empires.[8] What Leonowens unintentionally achieved, then, was to mark noncolonial Siam in the imaginary map of western readers and help them conceptualize the Southeast Asian nation in relation to European powers.

Leonowens's inadvertent achievement, however, conflicted with King Mongkut's efforts to modernize his country and consequently bring it into the international arena. Though both the Siamese monarch and the English governess contributed significantly to the West's growing recognition of Siam, they differed drastically in presenting the Southeast Asian country. Unlike Mongkut, who endeavored to cultivate a progressive image of Siam, Leonowens reinforced in her readers the West's stereotypical conception of Oriental despotism. It is precisely the drastic disparity between Leonowens's delineation of Siam and the actuality of the country that has sparked fierce accusations against the author.

Written at a time when the West knew almost nothing about Siam, Leonowens's experience was unprecedented and therefore unduly trusted. With very few contending versions available, her travel accounts about this Southeast Asian country nearly monopolized Victorian readers' understanding of Siam.[9] However, a number of Thai experts from both Thailand and the West consider Leonowens's travel account fictional, and some even accuse her of distorting the image of King Mongkut. In general, historians credit King Mongkut with taking major steps to modernize Thailand while maintaining its independence from western control. For this very reason, they find Leonowens's quasi-documentary narrative infuriating.

Dramatizing incidents in the harem, Leonowens still claims that "[m]ost of the stories, incidents, and characters are known to me personally to be real" and purports to retell these stories as they were narrated to her (*Romance*, preface). What most enrages historians derives from her overt fictionalizing of a historical figure, King Mongkut. Though praising the monarch's role in the public sphere, Leonowens portrays him in private as a man of cruelty, rages, and lust. The stark contrast between Mongkut's public and private character, as the author presents it, has generated a heated debate over the reliability of Leonowens's narrative.

D. G. E. Hall, for instance, writes that the author "was gifted with more imagination than insight" and that her travel accounts give "some idea of the contradictions." Of King Mongkut, Hall continues:

> The Siamese memory of him today is certainly not of a revengeful or cruel man, nor of one needlessly suspicious. Judged against the background of his own people, he emerged both morally and intellectually head and shoulders above the level of Siamese aristocracy of his day. It is not too much to claim that among the benevolent despots of the world he ranks high. (579)

Alexander B. Griswold shares Hall's suspicion. Noting the anachronism of characters and events in Leonowens's accounts of Siam, Griswold accuses her of

> glancing through some earlier writer on Siam, or even on neighboring countries...[and seizing] on a lurid story that appealed to her; she would remove it from its context and transpose it to Bangkok in the 1860's; and then, after a moment's reflection, she would re-write it with a wealth of circumstantial detail, and with contemporary men and women as the protagonists. (*King* 46)

Both Griswold and Hall pinpoint the fictitiousness in the governess's representation of Siam. To them and many other Thai scholars from the West and Thailand, *The English Governess at the Siamese Court* and *The Romance of the Harem* do not present historical accounts of Siam but constitute romances with Siam as a historical setting.

Echoing Hall and Griswold, Abbot Low Moffat continues the historians' disparaging of Leonowens's authority. Moffat asserts that several episodes in her books "can be brought to justice by detective work" because she "carelessly leaves proof of her transposed plagiarism" (224). This anti-Leonowens contention has dictated, or smothered, the academic reception of the author's writing until recent feminist studies provided an alternative approach. Giving the tarnished *Governess* and *Romance* some polish, feminist scholars have recently rekindled scholarly interest in Leonowens and her books on Siam.

The Romance of the Harem, edited and with an introduction by Susan Morgan, was released in 1991. In response to decades of accusations that Leonowens reconstructed historical facts, Morgan argues: "The more extreme specifics of Leonowens's tales are melodramatic and surely false. But the more substantive question is whether the spirit of her stories is to some degree true" (xxxiv). Morgan's defense undoubtedly provides an alternative reading, but in doing so, she is openly accepting, if not inviting, romances and adventure stories into the generic terrain of travel writing.[10] Granted the right to rearrange facts to pursue a greater truth, does the travel writer become a romance writer, twisting details to seduce a readership?If so, then what distinguishes Leonowens's travel accounts from Ballantyne's or Kipling's adventure stories? In her defense of the author, Morgan seems to suggest the generic fluidity of fiction and non-fiction. *The Romance of the Harem*, she claims,

> in all its excess, uncovers that consistently hidden, politically inconvenient truth. It also offers another, that the women in Nang Harm [royal women's quarter] are not mere victims, any more than they are less fully human than men or that their lives and personal suffering are less important than the greater good of a unified Thailand…It does not do so through an objective or sociological account of the facts, any more than Dickens presented mid-century London through detached eyes. (xxxvi)

Morgan is correct that rearranging facts to tell a greater truth is a common practice among authors. However, the analogy of Dickens's London and Leonowens's Siam seems to result in further confusion: Whereas Dickens portrays London in novels, Leonowens presents Siam in travel writing—a genre she claims to be truthful.

If, as Morgan asserts, *Romance* tells a greater truth, where does the truth lie: Is it in or behind Leonowens's fabrication? In the one-page preface to *Romance*, Leonowens writes:

> "Truth is often stranger than fiction," but so strange will some of these occurrences related in the following pages appear to Western readers, that I deem it necessary to state that they are also true. Most of the stories, incidents, and characters are known to me personally to be real, while of such narratives as I received from others I can say that "I tell the tale as it was told to me," and written down by me at the time...

Evidently the author intends her writing to be taken as a documentary, for she consciously builds that intent into her ethos. Even so, does she "tell the tale as it was told"? The greater truth of Leonowens's travel accounts has just as much to do with the context that necessitates her fabrication. Beyond Siam as the site of her travel, we need to look at Leonowens the author and Britain the context.[11] The context for Leonowens's travel writing chiefly consists of her double-layered interaction with Siam; that is, the personal dynamic of Leonowens and King Mongkut and the cultural interaction of the West and Siam. Both individually and communally, the author's relation with Siam is fully intertwined with race, class, and gender.

A practical question arises when we think of the incentive(s) of Leonowens's writing. Who needed her travel accounts of Siam? Definitely not the Siamese. Just as Trollope wrote *Domestic Manners* to redeem her financial ruin, Leonowens published *The English Governess at the Siamese Court* and *The Romance of the Harem* for pecuniary reasons. After leaving Siam, Leonowens stayed in the United States for ten years and then settled in Canada. Her writing about Siam, later marketed in book form, was first published in the *Atlantic Monthly*, a magazine featuring abolitionist writing. To supplement her income from writing, she also lectured on Siam to North American audiences. The need to make a living and the awareness of her target readers' preference help explain why she displayed Siam as a spectacle for western audiences to gaze at.

The exoticizing (and eroticizing) of Siam served not only to meet the author's financial need but also to satisfy the reader's voyeuristic curiosity. Victorian readers' hunger for exotic stories and their fascination with Oriental mystery were strong incentives for contemporary travel writers to stage authenticity and unprecedented authority in their representations of Oriental others. Travel proved to travel writers not only that seeing is believing but also that seeing is possessing and consequently selling. Leonowens's accounts of Siam in particular exemplified the principle that the more unprecedentedly exotic the traveled region is, the more enticing an account of it becomes. Working as a governess in Siam, Leonowens claimed to have authentic encounters with the natives and thus assumed an ethos of authority in representing them. Her authorial position dictated how Siam is presented in her work, for this representation is complicated by her racial superiority, social inferiority, and gender propriety.

Leonowens feels compelled to differentiate herself from the women in the harem, for whom she constantly claims to have compassion. Her rhetoric reveals a sense of superiority in being English and Christian. When some women in the harem suggest that she might marry either the Siamese king or the prince, she immediately responds: "An English, that is a Christian, woman would rather be put to the torture, chained and dungeoned for life, or suffer a death the slowest and most painful you Siamese know, than be the wife of either" (*Governess* 16–17). The English governess makes it very clear to her home audience that even the Siamese king or the prince is beneath her, and that to marry either of them is worse than to die of torture.

Leonowens's role at the Siamese court is ambiguous because she works not only as an English governess but also as a royal secretary. This double office further complicates how she is positioned in relation to the Siamese king. Sometimes the governess-secretary describes England as Siam's protector and portrays herself as the monarch's equal. In one passage of *Governess*, she writes:

> His Majesty, though secretly longing for the intervention and protection of England, was deterred by his almost superstitious fear of the French from complaining openly. But whenever he was more than commonly annoyed by the pretensions and aggressive epistles of his Imperial Majesty's consul he sent for me—thinking, like all Orientals, that, being English, my sympathy for him, and my hatred of the French, were jointly a foregone conclusion. (221)

What the double office of tutor and scribe grants to Leonowens is a culturally and socially intermediary position. She is both "the disciplinary governess" who educates the Siamese royalty (including the monarch) and "the disciplined governess" who has been inculcated and disciplined by British imperialism.[12] Leonowens is simultaneously a receiver and promulgator of imperial pedagogy, transplanting into the Siamese court the culture with which she has been implanted. The double office also constitutes a gender transgression on her part:

As a royal secretary, she literally takes a man's place[14] and trespasses on the masculine world of domestic affairs and international policies.

Leonowens is thus a double informant who, in writing, domesticates the exoticism of Siam for Britons and, in teaching, translates and transplants English values to the indigenous ruler and his royal family. This unique position enables the travel writer to monopolize or manipulate how the Siamese and the British conceptualize each other; doing so has triggered scholarly distrust of her work. Aside from the accusation that she rearranged facts, Leonowens also stirred up class and gender issues. The dynamic of the governess' racial superiority and social inferiority accentuates the theatrical effect of her stories. She is at the same time a working woman and a traveling European in Asia: a social inferior and racial superior.[14]

Evidently, the peculiarity (or charm) of Leonowens's travel accounts derives from the fact that what was then considered her "racial superiority" and the King's social supremacy turn her disadvantaged position into a privileged and extremely self-righteous one. Assuming the voice of authority, she represented Siam to her readers in the West. Her texts are about Siam, but the context is the West (chiefly Britain and America) at a crucial historical juncture when the abolitionist and women's suffrage movements emerged and prevailed in the public discourse of Britons. Though abroad, Leonowens incorporated this discourse of women's suffrage and abolitionism into her travel accounts.

In 1807, before other European countries did, Britain abolished its slave trade, and in 1833 it decreed slavery abolished throughout the British Empire, again before others did so. Ever since, Britain has reinvented itself as the savior of slaves and often justified its invasion of African territory as an act of humanitarian intervention to eradicate the practice of slavery. Mary Kingsley, for instance, in her travel account of West Africa, addresses the issue of slavery; likewise, Frances Trollope attacks Americans' practice of slavery in *Domestic Manners*. Like Trollope, Leonowens blends antislavery contention into her travel accounts so as to court her readership on both sides of the Atlantic.

The first edition of *Romance* was published by James R. Osgood[15] in Boston in late 1872; Trubner and Company published its English edition in early 1873; and then during the spring of 1873, Porter and Coates in Philadelphia published the second American edition. Leonowens's years in Siam (1862–1867) coincided with the American

Civil War (1861–1865), and slavery was an issue that she addressed to woo her readership in the West, particularly in America. Though Siam is in neither Africa nor America, Leonowens transplanted anti-slavery rhetoric into her representation of the Southeast Asian country. This antislavery rhetoric pervades both of her books, but it is far more emphasized in *Romance*, which primarily concerns itself with the condition of women in Nang Harm.

The English governess groups nearly all the women in the harem as slaves, although many of them are actually concubines or servants.[16] Is she truly confused by them or does she deliberately conflate one with the other? Should we take her misrepresentation of Nang Harm as an unintentional or a strategic misreading of Siam? While no single answer can fully explain the complexity of her applying western abolitionism to the Oriental harem, it is certain that Leonowens presents Siamese women as victims of both despotism and slavery. She uses the Siamese harem as a synecdoche for Oriental (sex) slavery. For instance, of one of the many custodians of the harem, she remarks:

> The repulsive uncomeliness of this woman had been wrought by oppression out of that which must have been beautiful once...In the brutal tragedy of a slave's experience—a female slave in the harem of an Asian despot—the native angel in her had been bruised, mutilated, defaced, deformed, but not quite obliterated. (*Governess* 16)

Despite the fact that the woman custodian considers it her privilege "to watch and guard these favored ones," Leonowens is determined to portray her as a pitiful prisoner (15–16). So is she determined to present the Siamese harem as a royal prison:

> How I have pitied these ill-fated sisters of mine, imprisoned without a crime...they who with a gasp of despair and moral death first entered those royal dungeons, never again to come forth alive...The misery which checks the pulse and thrills the heart with pity in one's common walks about the great cities of Europe is hardly so saddening as the nameless, mocking wretchedness of these women, to whom poverty were a luxury, and houselessness as a draught of pure, free air. (*Governess* 83–84)

Feminist critics tend to regard such a portrait as the author's humanitarian attempt to liberate Siamese women. Leonowens's accounts of Siam, however, cannot and should not be thus simplified because the feminist contention is intertwined with racial issues. Although she claims that both accounts are dedicated to her "ill-fated sisters" in Siam, she does not consider them to be her equals.

Leonowens's travel accounts function not only as a forum for political discussion but also as a bridge to ideological coalition. As Mary Louise Pratt points out, "travel books by Europeans about non-European parts of the world went (and still go) about creating the 'domestic subject" of Euroimperialism" (4). To emulate Victorian women in England, she fabricates a powerful sense of mission to rescue the Siamese women, a mission that allows her to "share, if unequally, the white man's burden" (Zltonick 49). In her rhetoric of emancipation, Leonowens deploys Nang Harm as a foreign locale to address Britain's domestic issues: It projects Englishwomen's struggle with patriarchal power and social inequality. Though she implies an international sisterhood between the East and the West, the female bonding is chiefly for and among western women.[17] As Caren Kaplan notices: "In a critical alliance between abolitionist and feminist rhetoric and ideology, Leonowens fashioned a portrait of British womanhood in marked contrast to Asian women's lives, thereby transforming the conditions and possibilities of western women's lives and illustrating the helpless dependency of non-Western women" ("Getting" 36). Kaplan perceptively identifies the entanglement of race, gender, and class in the author's simplistic rhetoric of abolitionism.

Leonowens simultaneously allies herself with Siamese women and distances herself from them. While her gender may allow her to see from these women's perspective, it is her race that empowers her to speak for them (women, native, and other).[18] The author's double gesture works on two levels. In the Dedication of *Romance*, Leonowens writes: "To the noble and devoted women whom I learned to know, to esteem, and to love in the city of the Nang Harm, I dedicate the following pages, containing a record of some of the events connected with their lives and sufferings." Instead of liberating the Siamese women from the royal dungeon, the rhetoric of feminist abolitionism serves far more effectively to cement the author's connection with the West and (most likely) to secure a good reception among the target readers in America.

The European Traveler Working for/on the Indigenous King

Transforming her travel accounts into a social forum, Leonowens emerges as a metonymic figure of Englishness rivaling the Siamese monarch; rearranging historical facts into an historical romance, she represents Mongkut as a spectacle of essential Orientalness. To communicate with western readers, the author utilizes common ground, the West's essentializing of the Oriental world, of which despotism and the harem are the most fascinating elements. Constructed to reinforce such a cultural stereotype, Mongkut is portrayed as a phenomenon—both a spectacle of Oriental tyranny and a site of cultural reinscription.

His Majesty, Leonowens recalls in *Governess*, was "the most capricious of kings as to his working moods":

> Before my arrival in Bangkok, it had been his not uncommon practice to send for a missionary at midnight...to inquire if it would not be more elegant to write *murky* instead of *obscure*, or *gloomy dark* rather than *not clearly apparent*. And if the wretched man should venture to declare his honest preference for the ordinary form of expression, he was forthwith dismissed with irony, arrogance, or even insult, and without a word of apology for the rude invasion of his rest. (211, original emphasis)

Leonowens continues to recall what happened after she took the double office of governess and private secretary to the king: "His moods were so fickle and unjust, his temper so tyrannical, that it seemed impossible to please him; from one hour to another I never knew what to expect" (232). After she left her office in the Siamese court, the author notes, Mongkut was "fast failing in body and mind," and "the whole nation [was] given up to gambling" (*Governess* 238). In a most earnest tone, she concludes *Governess* with a return to the issue of slavery and an emphasis on western supremacy: "What may be the ultimate fate of Siam under this accursed system, whether she will ever emancipate herself while the world lasts, there is no guessing. The happy examples free intercourse affords, the influence of European ideas, and the compulsion of public opinion, may yet work wonders" (238). With both exaggeration and fabrication, Leonowens reproduces the western stereotypical notion of the Oriental despot. She has deliberately characterized Mongkut's irrationality and barbarity counterpointed by her own sagaciousness and civility.

Contrary to Leonowens's portrayal, the Siamese king was neither a self-isolated despot nor a cultural innocent. Not only did he have frequent contacts with foreigners, such as envoys, missionaries, traders, and professionals, but he also pursued western knowledge with great enthusiasm. Conscious of Siam's precarious position among western powers, he took major steps to modernize his country in the hope that it would retain its independence. According to Moffat, the king "was interested in the scientific knowledge of the west and in its mechanical application. From the American missionaries he also learned much about the major western countries, their histories...He began to read English books and newspapers and to acquire western devices and machines" (21). What Mongkut accomplished before and in his reign was unusual among despots, let alone oriental tyrants. Having interacted with international figures and deliberately ushered in western influences, the Siamese king exemplified a cross-cultural figure more than a metonymic figure of Orientalness.

On occasion, even Leonowens has to contradict herself and admit the king's impressive enthusiasm for learning about the West: "Before the arrival of the Protestant missionaries, in 1820, he had acquired some knowledge of Latin and the sciences from the Jesuits; but when the Protestants came he manifested a positive preference for their methods of instruction, inviting one or another of them daily to his temple, to aid him in the study of English" (*Governess* 202).

The author also recognizes, although with some reservation, the monarch's achievements during his reign[19]:

> [H]e appeared, to those who observed him only on the public stage of af-
> fairs, to rule with wisdom, to consult the welfare of his subjects, to be con-
> cerned for the integrity of justice and the purity of manners and
> conversation in his own court, and careful, by a prudent administration, to
> confirm his power at home and his prestige abroad. Considered apart from
> his domestic relations, he was, in many respects, an able and virtuous
> ruler. His foreign policy was liberal; he extended tolerance to all religious
> sects; he expended a generous portion of his revenues in public improve-
> ments...though he felt short of his early promise, he did much to improve
> the condition of his subjects. (205)

Leonowens's portrayal of King Mongkut features a contradictory merging of primitive despotism and liberal humanitarianism.

Her conflicted delineation of Mongkut suggests the textual incon-sistency of the governess' travel writing and the cultural hybridity of Mongkut. *Governess*, for instance, is a (post)travel account which vac-illates between a journalistic report of indigenous customs and a sen-timental narrative with personal prejudices. It is not unjust to say that the author shifts between the decentered English traveler-observer and the recentered resident-participant of Siam. The equivocation of Leonowens's self-positioning is inscribed onto Mongkut's position as an Oriental monarch negotiating among western powers. An avid cultural absorber and determined reformer, Mongkut poses an insurmountable challenge to rigid and simplistic stereotyping.

The centrality of the English governess is consequently in question. In many respects, the Siamese king is just as multicultural as the governess, if not more so. Though the monarch did not travel as extensively in foreign lands as the governess did, during his twenty-seven years of exile in a monastery, "[H]e made long pilgrimages on foot to different parts of the country...His travels gave him a knowledge of geography that was rare in those days of poor communications, while his friendly talks with the people gave him an insight into their minds and needs such as few rulers ever attain" (Griswold, "Perspective" 13). Mongkut not only deeply cared about his subjects but also worked diligently to broaden his knowledge of the outside world.

Before employing Leonowens in 1862, the king had known at least two European languages. His letter of employment addressed to Leonowens illustrates a mind widely open to western knowledge and a head clearly aware of Siam's position in relation to foreign influences. To "Mrs. A. H. Leonowens," he writes:

> Madam: We are in good pleasure, and satisfaction in heart, that you are in willingness to undertake the education of our beloved royal children. And we hope that in doing your education on us and on our children...you will do your best endeavour for knowledge of English language, science, and literature, and not for conversion to Christianity; as the followers of Buddha are mostly aware of the powerfulness of truth and virtue, as well as the followers of Christ, and are desirous to have facility of English language and literature, more than new religions... (*Governess* vii)

Native speakers of English may easily spot the idiomatic awkwardness of Mongkut's wording, but the letter is in general eloquent and elegant. Most important of all, it conveys a clear and firm message that he expects Leonowens to serve as a tutor rather than to subvert the court as a reformer, and that English is to be used as a medium for daily conversation rather than as a tool for religious conversion.[20]

While the Siamese monarch understood English reasonably well, Leonowens relied heavily on interpreters to communicate with the natives. Siamese is not an easy language to learn, and textual evidence seems to suggest that the English governess never mastered the native tongue. Though in *Governess* and *Romance* she occasionally inserts some Siamese words, such as *kha, sunnoh* or *my di,*[21] these words are more a display of accentuated exoticism than indispensable or untranslatable phrases. She never attempts longer or more complex sentences than "*Mash-Allah! A Tala-yea kia hai?*"[22] As Griswold points out, *Governess* (as well as *Romance*) "contains numerous words and sentences purported to be Siamese; but they are jabberwocky, and with the best will in the world it is often impossible to discover what she intends" (*King* 46). It remains questionable how "full" and "faithful" Leonowens's accounts of Siam could be when she claims that the scenes and characters "were gradually unfolded to me as I began to understand the language" (*Governess* viii).

Did the English governess understand the language as well as she wanted us to believe? Perhaps at a level of simple and fragmented conversation, she could manage to grasp some ideas. As to what degree she understood what the palace ladies or their slaves told her, that is in great doubt. Did they tell her the truth? Even if they did, how much of the truth did she understand and how well did she remember the truth years later when she attempted to recall and record it in detail? A far more crucial question arises when we approach Leonowens's representation of Siam in the context of the language barrier: How can she be granted the authority to represent Siam, a society about which she learned merely through fragmented phrases? [23]

Along with the language barrier, the uncertainty of her ancestry problematizes the binary oppositions of the West and East that she emphasizes so much in her accounts. Not only does the cultural diversity that Mongkut embraced defeat a stereotype of the oriental despot, but Leonowens's alleged Eurasian upbringing also contests her claim to authentic Englishness. Among scholars who compete for a truer version of Leonowens's life story, W. S. Bristowe presents a very compelling argument. Piecing together bits from birth certificate, marriage records, army lists, and burial records in England, India, Wales, Singapore, and Penang, Bristowe discovered that Leonowens was born in India, probably to a "Eurasian" mother and a Welsh father (23–31). No biographical information validates her claim that she was educated in Wales; in fact, documents tend to suggest that she may have attended garrison schools in India. At the age of fourteen, she traveled to the Middle East before returning to India and marrying Major Thomas Leon Owens (an Englishman). The Owens (or Leonowens) family moved several times among India, Australia, and Malaya; after the death of Major Leonowens in 1862, Anna

Leonowens left Singapore to take the position of governess at the Siamese court (Bristowe 23–31).

Not until after leaving Siam did Leonowens set foot in England for the first time, and in 1868 (or early 1869) she settled in the United States. Later, in the 1880s, she moved to Canada to live with her daughter. Another equally interesting yet often overlooked fact is this: Both *Governess* and *Romance* were first published in America before being released in England. Biographical information thus illustrates an amusing contradiction between Leonowens's self-proclaimed "Englishness" and the virtual absence of her firsthand living experiences in England. What amuses even more is that while she represented herself as an Englishwoman, her travel accounts of Siam targeted American readers.

The English governess spent nearly her entire life residing at the periphery of the British Empire, traveling from one colony to another. Her geographical and genealogical "ex-centricity," as Susan Brown astutely observes, was further accentuated by the fact that "she had been hired by an oriental monarch to teach inside a harem. Her employment at the major site of centuries-old Orientalist constructions of a simultaneous fascinating and repellent Eastern sensuality represented a serious threat to the already dubious propriety, controversial and precarious in the 1860s, of her position as a middle-class working woman" (592). The eccentricity of King Mongkut delineated in *Governess* and *Harem* hence mirrors the governess's marginality rather than reflecting the monarch's peculiarity. She transcribes her own dis-*place*-ment onto the characterization of Mongkut, which serves as a rhetorical vehicle for her to re-*place* herself at the ideological center of Englishness.

She exoticizes Mongkut to familiarize Victorian readers with herself. Perhaps Edward Said best captures the nature of the colonial discourse when he notes that "the Orient has helped to define Europe (or the West) as its contrasting image, idea, personality, experience" (*Orientalism* 1–2). Indeed, one of the striking features in Leonowens's accounts of Siam, in particular the monarch, rests on the drastic differences between Britain and Siam, herself and Mongkut. While Siam, a noncolony of Britain, sits at the periphery of the empire, the dramatized Orientalness of the Siamese monarch affirms the English governess' affinity with the West.

The process of Leononwens's dis-*place*-ment and re-*place*-ment goes far beyond her self-centering in cultural geography; it actually extends to her position and profession.[24] She is simultaneously *in place* and *out of place*; though she does not always know her *place*, she evidently *goes places*. As a governess and secretary, Leonowens does not always observe social decorum: She frequently intervenes in both domestic and foreign affairs when assisting the king. Though geographically displaced in Siam, Leonowens is professionally rewarded with a distinguished office; and her experiences at the Siamese court later ensure her a successful career as a writer and lecturer. Leonowens's experience as the Siamese King's governess interestingly inverts the recurrent characterization of the native servant, the European's wishful projection of the indigenous. Literary examples of the native servant abound. H. Rider Haggard, for instance, imposes an Anglocentric wishfulness upon Umbopa, the Zulu king, who willingly submits himself to the European adventurers. Mongkut, in the case of Leonowens, is the master and also the native's servant. Reversed in the relation of master and servant may seem in her case, the author is by no means the willing servant of the native king. *Governess* and *Harem* portray an English governess exerting her influence upon nearly every matter and a Siamese king benefiting from her sagacious advice.

To transcend her social inferiority, Leonowens never fails to remind the reader of her supposed "racial superiority" and intellectual influence upon the Siamese. The rhetoric of self-exaltation continues throughout both books. The governess even claims that under her guidance one of the Siamese princesses contemplated conversion. Step by step, the governess recalls, "I led her out of the shadow-land of myth into the realm of the truth as it is in Christ Jesus…and I felt that this child of smiles and tears, all unbaptized and unblessed as she was, was nearer and dearer to her Father in heaven than to her father on earth" (*Governess* 95). Like the princess, Choy, Mongkut's favorite woman, is reportedly fascinated by Christianity: "She learned in time to take pleasure in her English studies, and found comfort in the love of our Father in heaven. Without repining at her lot, hard as it was, or boasting of her knowledge, but with a loving humble heart, she read and blessed the language that brought her nearer to a compassionate Saviour" (*Romance* 144).

These are just two of many instances the author cites to illustrate her self-perceived impact on the Siamese. Considering herself a social investigator or national savior, she equates her (requested) interference with divine intervention. In *Governess*, she writes: "In case of tor-

ture, imprisonment, extortion, I tried again and again to excuse myself from interfering, but still the mothers or sisters prevailed, and I
had no choice left but to try to help them" (227). In *Romance*, she
seems rather unrestrained in pursuing social justice, even if it means
intervention and transgression on her part. Accidentally spotting
Lore, a slave woman, "chained like as wild beast," Leonowens feels
compelled to help her. "My sister," she promises to Lore, "tell me
your whole story, and I will lay it before the king" (47). As a result of
Leonowens's intervention, Lore eventually gains her freedom, is re-
united with her husband and her son's name "changed from Thook
(Sorrow) to Urbanâ (the Free)" (64).

Woman as a Voyeur

The English governess's accomplishment does not derive from
liberating the Siamese women because few of them actually benefited
from her advocacy. The images of enslaved women and an overbear-
ing king, as she presents them in both accounts, loom so large that we
tend to see Siam as a place waiting for the intervention of the West—
for rescuing, rectifying, and proselytizing. Her major achievement,
one can safely argue, rests chiefly upon the reversed gender relationship that she depicts between an English governess and a native king.
Postcolonial studies often accuse the rhetoric of colonialism of fem-
inizing non-European societies. This view has to sustain an ironic
twist in Leonowens's representation of King Mongkut and his kingdom. Perhaps Mary Louise Pratt captures the English governess's oriental discovery in her phrase "the Monarch of All I Survey." Although
Leonowens is not an explorer in a conventional sense, she does present to the home audience a sensational discovery of the Oriental
harem: an exclusive penetration into the Oriental interior. Contrary to
the male gaze at the feminized body of the non-West, *Governess* and
Harem exemplify a woman's gaze into the world of a man's
possession.

Guided by the gendered gaze of Leonowens, we enter the interior
of the Siamese court, a site not only forbidden to western men but also
closed to most Siamese people. In Nang Harm, the women's existence
centers on the absent yet domineering man, the king. "Peering into a
twilight, studiously contrived, of dimly lighted and suggestive shadows," the English governess recalls,

> we discover in the centre of the hall a long line of girls with skins of
> olive—creatures who in years and physical proportions are yet but chil-

dren, but by training developed into women and accomplished actresses. There are some twenty of them, in transparent draperies with golden girdles, their arms and bosoms, wholly nude, flashing, as they wave and heave, with barbaric ornaments of gold… (*Governess* 34)

Although inviting us to see the harem from a woman's viewpoint, this female gaze is complicated by and conflated with the gaze of the absent man. The double gaze in Leonowens's literary texts reminds us of that in Henriette Browne's[25] visual texts:

[Browne] paints from a position that had to be female, according to the prevailing ideas of artistic production, femininity and the harem, and that had to be active, according to the construction of her as the author of a text predicated on a direct viewing of an unremittingly gendered space. She thus intervenes in the dynamic of active/male and passive/female by being, and being understood to be, a female painting subject who actively looks at and represents the harem. (Lewis 164)

Analogous to Browne's dual position, Leonowens simultaneously identifies herself with and distances herself from the harem women. Leonowens's status as English governess/author requires the maintenance of difference, while her gender allows an affinity between herself and the harem women.

In her accounts of Siam, the gender reversal of voyeurism complicates—but does not entirely overthrow—the European construct (mostly sexual fantasizing) of the Orient. Though replacing the male spectator, Leonowens still sees Siam with the western masculine eye and subsequently conceptualizes Nang Harm (royal women's quarter) as the synecdoche of a feminized body waiting to be unveiled and ultimately possessed. Through the confession of Choy (King Mongkut's favorite woman), Leonowens invites her readers to peep into the sexual life of the monarch:

"'Do you know how fascinating you were this evening?' said the king. 'Older by forty years than my father,' thought I [Choy], as, dissembling still, I replied, 'Your slave does not know.' 'But you were, and I am sure you deserve to be a queen,' he added, trying to play the gallant. 'My lord is too gracious to his slave,' I murmured.

"'Why Thieng!' he said, speaking to my eldest sister; 'why have you hidden this beauty away from me so long? Let her not be called Choy any longer, but Chorm.' I would weary you if I tried to tell you how he praised and flattered me, and how before a week was over I was the proudest woman in the palace." (*Romance* 132)

Vacillating between the detached European and sympathetic woman, Leonowens directs the public attention of the West to a private sphere that has so often been perceived as an embodiment of the sensuality and barbarity of the East.

Rhetorically, the English governess may present a social-reformer's case against oriental slavery that she considers to have prevailed in the harem. Ideologically, she transcribes the Occident's conflation of sexuality and slavery onto the Orient. The erotic and exotic in the Siamese harem become the erratic in Leonowens's sensational narrative. Geographically, King Mongkut is the monarch of all Leonowens can survey, while ideologically Leonowens conceives herself as the monarch of all she surveys, thus making her the monarch of the Siamese monarch.

The voyeurism discussed thus far is by no means an individual fetish; rather, it is a western obsession with Oriental mysteries. In naming her account *Romance*, Leonowens literally plays upon the attraction of the imagined alterity of the Oriental world. Sara Mills notices this irresistible charm of difference in the discourse of discovery, but she contends that feminist discourse treats the issue of the other in a different fashion: "One of the striking features in all of the descriptions of other countries is that objects are presented only in terms of their *difference* to objects in Britain…The conventions of travel writing thus present a framework of largely masculine narratorial positions and descriptive patterns with which women writers negotiate when they construct their travel accounts" (86, original emphasis). Mills astutely notices how women writers respond variously to the discourses of difference, and in general she is right about the constraints on the reception of women's travel writing. However, constraints can sometimes become useful conventions.

In Leonowens's case, gender does not solely constitute a hindrance; it serves as a vehicle as well.[26] What *Romance* and *Governess* collectively manifest is that male and female discourses do not necessarily take opposed positions. In both accounts, the discourse of discovery features a conflation of masculinity and femininity. Though assigned to educate the women and children at the royal court, the author does not stay in the allotted sphere of femininity. Instead, she guides us in exploring the interior of the Siamese court. In her humanitarian enthusiasm for liberating women in the harem, she turns their private world into a public forum for a western abolitionist discourse, and later this private world becomes the focal point of the global theater in a continual flow of cinematic and theatrical productions.

Not many literary texts have ever reached the height of self-perpetuation, or should we say intertextuality, which *Governess* and *Romance* have, and perhaps even fewer have made such a smooth and smashing transition from literary to ocular texts. In 1944, Margaret Landon restructured both books with the author's biographical information into a single work, *Anna and the King of Siam*. In 1951, Hollywood produced the movie, *The King and I*,[27] based on Landon's book, and in the same year Broadway staged a play with the same storyline. In 1953, *Romance* was reissued under the title *Siamese Harem Life*, illustrated with sketches that featured a western fantasy of the sensuous Oriental world. These drawings conflate Chinese, Indians, and Turks in the seemingly surrealistic world of Siam.

In early 1999, Disney released a cartoon adaptation of Landon's story, also under the name of *The King and I* (though this time the film targets children as its audience). Twentieth Century Fox has recently issued *Anna and the King*, a new film starring Jodie Foster (an American actress) and Chow Yun-Fat (a Hong Kong action hero).[28] Reproductions (and re-presentations) of Leonowens's tales continue to pervade the mass media, but it is Yul Brynner's presentation that most of us associate with King Mongkut. For many of us, Brynner is the Siamese king, and his noble-savage image looms so large that it replaces what it originally meant to represent.

In 1958, in response to the Yul Brynner-and-Mongkut conflation and the wide distribution of Brynner's photographs, Prajuab Tirabutana, a Thai student at Cornell University,[29] made an interesting and insightful point: "...it was through those pictures that people all over the world would know Thailand. Of course, they would know and remember the name of our country well because they had to laugh at the queer and wild actions of their king. But the question was where did the man who told the actor to act that way get those manners from? (qtd. in Kaplan, "Getting" 47). This is truly an insightful question. How was the cinematic image of the noble savage first invented, accepted, and then so overwhelmingly perpetuated? Do these reproductions not epitomize the imagined East, as fantasized and realized by the West? Tirabutana's question reminds us of Said's remark on the self-reflexivity of Orientalism:

> That Orientalism makes sense at all depends more on the West than on the Orient, and this sense is directly indebted to various Western techniques of

representation that make the Orient visible, clear, "there" in discourse about it. And these representations rely upon institutions, traditions, conventions, agreed-upon codes of understanding for their effects, not upon a distant and amorphous Orient. (*Orientalism* 22)

The present reproduction of the Orient exemplifies a doubled self-referentiality on the part of the West. The West is both the creator and receiver of its construct of the Orient. The perpetual repetition of this construct reassures the West that it still retains the power of defining itself and the other.[30]

In her observation of Siam, Leonowens claims to capture the essence of what she deems authentically Siamese—often the radically and irreducibly exotic, erotic, and erratic. However, her endeavor to represent the Oriental other illustrates how the author's glimpses reciprocate the tourist gaze of the West. These numerous glimpses, no matter how erroneous, constitute the collective gaze of the West. Leonowens's snapshot images of Siam are immortalized in cinematic reproductions, and her individual construction of the other circumscribes the western perception of self.

Most noteworthy, though, is the actual focal point of this seemingly feminist discourse: the narrative centers more on King Mongkut than on his women.[31] Leonowens, the abolitionist *I* in her accounts, observes with an *eye* of imperialism while making feminist statements from a seat of masculine power. Siam, accordingly, is less a geographic location that an ideological *topos*; it is a site upon which Leonowens transcribes a set of preconceived cultural references. This reversal of social hierarchy between the native king and the English governess also gives us a rare sensation invoked by problematizing stereotypes of the traveling subject and the traveled object. In addition to her status as the native's English servant, Leonowens's travel distinguishes itself from the leisure-oriented travel of the Victorian bourgeoisie; residing in Siam with her son, she has to work while claiming herself a traveler. Hence, Leonowens conflates leisure with labor; similar to Trollope's account of America, her writing about Siam intermingles with diaspora writing, social critique, and travelogue.

This observation brings our discussion back to Trollope's travel and writing. At first glance, Trollope and Leonowens may seem travelers of different types. From the start, Leonowens was frank about her position in Siam while Trollope was evasive in relating her real intention in America. They are, however, alike in regard to travel and work: Both of them travel to work and work while traveling. Similar to Trollope, Leonowens reinvents herself in her writing: She empowers herself by turning the Siamese kingdom into an object of observation with herself as agent of this representation. It is precisely this combination of travel and work that blurs the generic boundaries between immigrant writing and travel writing. If work is intrinsic to travel and travel to work, as both Leonowens and Trollope show, immigrant writing (or diaspora literature) should be included in the genre of travel literature.

Most readers would agree that part of the power of Trollope's and Leonowens's work resides in the truth-value effect of the travel memoir as a realistic or autobiographical account. This correlation between a writer's empirical encounter with a foreign culture and her authority to represent that culture accordingly complicates our approach to travel writing. In Victorian women writers' travel accounts, genre and gender are two elements constantly intertwined with the issue of representative authority and textual authenticity. It is often the case that when a woman writer's textual credibility is questioned, her personal life has to sustain public scrutiny as well.

Critics who dislike *Domestic Manners* see the text as an extension of the author and thereby disparage the author as if she (often her womanhood or sexuality) is a text. In attacking the female author's personal life, critics also successfully undercut her public persona, her voice of authority. Similarly, the truth-value of *Governess* and *Romance* is discredited when critics suspect the author's integrity. They contend that if Leonowens had rearranged the facts of her life story, she was equally prone to fabricating her travel accounts. What we discover in the context of Trollope's and Leonowens's controversies is a Victorian notion of gendered authorship: The author's womanhood and her literary production are both subject to social evaluation. Also noteworthy in this context is the interplay of social (gender) propriety and geographical location. Women writers must go abroad to seek a podium that is denied to them at home. Only through writing about the foreign and speaking from abroad can they be taken seriously. The publicity they gain from voicing their views at the same time subjects them to public scrutiny; they are open like a text, available for and vulnerable to charges of transgression.

Whereas travels enable women writers to channel their thoughts and ideals, they also situate these writers on the border of gender and class impropriety. In addition, during the Victorian era, a woman's social transgression was equated with gender transgression. The equation and hence equivocation of gender, generic, and geographical encroachment is epitomized in the controversies about Trollope's and Leonowens's travel writing. Travels allow both writers to extend Britain's imaginary geography and transcend the domestic constraints of propriety. Writing about travel, Leonowens and Trollope present foreign lands to the home audience as and in texts; through writing, they also reveal themselves as a text to the reader.

Hence, Leonowens's and Trollope's transcendence of geographical boundaries simultaneously signifies an imperial expansion and a social transgression. Similarly, the textual contradiction in their accounts suggests (or derives from) the two authors' defiance of their gender role. In addition, the indeterminacy of genre both reflects and parallels the shifting borderlines between one culture and the other, between audacity and propriety, and between fiction and fact. Such generic fluidity engenders the problematics of travel discourse, in this case a gendered discourse of the other.

Another significant link between Trollope's and Leonowens's travel writing rests in both authors' alternative colonialism. While Trollope operates a political forum in a former colony of Britain, Leonowens operates hers in an informal colony. Their travel accounts imagine (or help imagine) an imperial geography, a far larger territory than the empire really possesses. Ideologically, Trollope and Leonowens apply a colonial discourse to regions beyond Britain's rule. Their travel accounts exemplify an intertextuality with other travel writings: Trollope's complies with anti-American conventions while Leonowens's reinforces the Oriental fantasy.

Travel packs multiple agendas, and it does not dwell solely upon a single cause of leisured pleasure. Every writing always entangles itself with other writings: Travel writing repeats, revises, paraphrases, and reinvents the preceding models it is modeled after. All cultures, in Said's term, are "hybrid, heterogeneous, extraordinarily differentiated, and un-monolithic" (*Culture* xxv). All individuals occupy multiple locations and assume plural identities. As Jean-François Lyotard reminds us, "[a] Self does not amount to much, but no self is an island; each exists in a fabric of relations...Young or old, man or woman, rich or poor, a person is always located at 'nodal points' of specific communication circuits, however tiny these may be. Or better: one is always located at a post through which various kinds of messages pass" (15). Lyotard is addressing the postmodern condition; but his statement applies just as well to the heterogeneity that Trollope's and Leonowens's personal lives and travel accounts epitomize.

One can readily replace the "Self" in Lyotard's passage with "genre," "culture," or "territory." A text always exists in the fabric of intertextuality: A genre often contains other genres; a territory is constantly wedged among sovereignties; a culture inherently absorbs and nurtures other cultures; genders situate themselves in between rather than at the two extremes of masculinity and femininity. As Victorian women who traveled to work and worked to travel, Trollope and Leonowens propel us to raise an array of questions regarding the nature of their travel, the genre of their writing, the meaning of their representations, and the identity of their authorship.[32] One may safely predict that these questions will continue to generate scholarly interest and vigorous discussions, for the changing and much changed nature of travel demands a timely redefining of travel literature. Through revisiting Trollope's America and Leonowens's Siam, this essay anticipates more rediscoveries of the overbeaten paths upon which Victorian travelers left their footprints.

Notes

1   See the preface by the anonymous American editor in *Domestic Manners*, ix.
2   See Helen K. Heineman's *Three Victorians in the New World*, 101.
3   For details, see Bird's *Unbeaten Tracks in Japan* and *Korea and Her Neighbors*, and Kingsley's *Travels in West Africa*.
4   This is how the *New Monthly Magazine* characterized her success in a "Memoir to Mrs. Trollope" (March 1839). Teresa Ransom borrows these words too for the title of one of her chapters in *Fanny Trollope*.
5   The relationship between Frances Trollope and the family tutor, Auguste Hervieu, generated considerable gossip and even contributed to some of the most scathing criticism of Trollope. The *Edinburgh Review*, for instance, started its review of *Domestic Manners* with direct reference to Trollope's friendship with Hervieu: "First appears her friend, a Mr. H. This is pretty good for a beginning. After that—farewell to the virtue of common sense, whatever other discretion may be retained" (qtd. in Heineman *Mrs. Trollope* 94)
6   According to Ramson, Trollope's husband quarreled with her about the disgrace that a separation would bring upon the family, but she finally persuaded him with the fact that it cost far less to live in America than to live in England (38).
7   See Helen Heineman's *Mrs. Trollope*, 79–100.
8   Informed and inspired by Thai historian Thongchai Winichakul, Benedict Anderson draws his readers' attention to the absence of borderlines in Thai maps before the 1850s. A bordered Siam came into being only between 1850 and

1920 because the country was never colonized and thereby unmapped; what later became its boundaries was determined by contending western powers. Both Winichakul and Anderson note that King Mongkut, conscious of cartography and sovereignty, modernized Thai cartography, with which he demarcated an exclusive sovereignty wedged between western powers. For details, see Anderson's *Imagined Communities*, 171.

9   From 1858 to 1861, Henri Mouhot, a French explorer sponsored by several English patrons, made four main expeditions from Bangkok into the interior of Indochina. His account of the central part of Siam, Cambodia and Laos was titled *Henri Mouhot's Diary*. Its English version was published in 1864. The account centers on Siam's landscape and exterior environment, drastically different from Leonowens's focus on internal affairs and social interaction.

10   In his recently published *Rigoberta Menchú and the Story of All Poor Guatemalans* (1999), David Stoll accuses Menchú of stretching facts in her autobiography, *I, Rigoberta Menchú* (1984). Mass media, academies, and political groups have since participated in a heated debate on Menchú's fabrication and Stoll's politicizing of the situation. This current discourse on Menchú, to a great extent, parallels that on Leonowens. Just as Menchú was the first to draw international attention to the atrocity in Guatemala, so was Leonowens the first (widely recognized) writer to bring Siam to the awareness of the West. Both authors were excessively exalted for their unprecedented positions until more inside information was revealed to contradict their contentions. Accusations against Menchú as well as Leonowens often center on their authority and authenticity of representation. The two authors are condemned for fabricating work in a genre that is supposed to be factual and objective: Menchú's genre is autobiography, while Leonowens's is a travel account.

11   To be more accurate, the United States should be considered part of the context as well, because Leonowens published both of her books first in America and apparently considered Americans part of her target readership.

12   These terms are borrowed from Deirdre David's reading of *Jane Eyre* as the governess of empire. See David's *Rule Britannia*, 78.

13   The office of royal secretary is traditionally (and almost universally) a male profession. King Mongkut still had a regular male secretary, while Leonowens assisted him in writing English letters and composing documents.

14   Had Leonowens served in an English upper-class household, her writing about an employer most likely would not have found its way to a publisher. I am also ruling out the possibility of Leonowens's working at the court of Queen Victoria because she would have been silenced before uttering a word about the queen's private life.

15   The same company, though under an older name, Field, Osgood, & Co., serialized part of *The English Governess at the Siamese Court* in 1870. James Fields, one of the partners in the publishing house, was the editor of the *Atlantic Monthly*, which featured antislavery writing. The information about Leonowens's publications is chiefly based on Morgan's introduction.

16   According to Moffat, palace ladies can resign if they no longer desire to serve His Majesty. However, while in service, they must refrain from associating with other men (*Mongkut* 150–51).

17   By the early 1870s, Leonowens had become good friends with Annie Fields (the

wife of James Fields) and Harriet Beecher Stowe (a regular contributor to the *Atlantic Monthly*). According to Morgan, a major link among the three women writers was their antislavery conviction (xxii).

18   This term is borrowed from Trinh T. Minh-ha's *Woman, Native, Other* because the book resonates with cultural hybridization, decentered realities, fragmented selves, and multiple identities.

19   Leonowens delineates a conflicted character in Mongkut, who in the public sphere is a highly revered monarch while in the private sphere a most revolting husband and kinsman: "Envious, revengeful, subtle, he was as fickle and petulant as he was suspicious and cruel" (*Governess* 205).

20   According to Moffat, King Mongkut invited into Nang Harm three wives of American missionaries in Siam in 1851. They taught English to the harem women, but the education lasted only three years. It was reported that the education ended after the king noticed that these missionary wives abused their position to proselytize for Christianity. This incident prodded him to recruit a governess from the secular world and also explained his emphatic prohibition of conversion through English education in the letter.

21   These Siamese terms respectively mean "your slave," "listen," and "bad."

22   This sentence means "Great God! What is this?"

23   These are questions one often asks when examining disciplines of social science such as anthropology, ethnography, and sociology. One often wonders how native informants are understood and how reliable their information is. What is interesting about Leonowens's accounts of Siam is that she accepts (or at least seems to accept) her translators' information and expects her translation to be accepted totally and uncritically.

24   In *Tancred*, Benjamin Disraeli notes: "The East is a career" (qtd. in Said, *Orientalism* xiii). How true it is when one thinks of Leonowens's life. She literally made a career out of the Orient or made up an Oriental world for her career.

25   A nineteenth-century French painter, Browne traveled extensively in Europe and the Middle East. She was most famous for her paintings of convents and harems. Reina Lewis's study primarily focuses on Browne's paintings of harem women.

26   According to Griswold, when the Siamese ambassador reproached Leonowens for slandering her former employer, the author excused herself by saying that readers wanted sensational stories about the Orient, and she did it to satisfy her publisher (*King* 49).

27   In 1952, Yul Brynner and Gertrude Lawrence acted in *The King and I* on Broadway. However, Landon's story of Anna and the Siamese King did not reach its international recognition until *The King and I* (1956) was adapted into a film, staring Deborah Kerr and Yul Brynner.

28   Though the gesture of including an Asian actor in this new production is laudable, I suspect this international casting will not much improve the distortion of King Mongkut. Perhaps the presence of Chow, known more for action than characterization, only reinforces the commercialization of the entire representation.

29   According to Kaplan, Tirabutana wrote "A Simple One: The Story of a Siamese Girlhood" when she was attending the Southeast Asia Studies Program of Cornell University, a program designed to teach Thai people English ("'Getting'" 47).

30 This self-reassurance through reproduction and repetition of a colonial discourse resembles Snow White's stepmother, who constantly looks at the magic mirror and demands that it assure her that she is the fairest woman of all.

31 As the focal point of Leonowens's accounts, King Mongkut becomes more and more accentuated in both literary revision and theatrical reproductions of her stories.

32 Observing the fragments and multiplicity of identity in the travel writer, their work, and its genre, I cannot help but ruminate on what Kaplan associates with travel: "leisure travel, exploration, expatriation, exile, homelessness, and immigration" (*Questions* 3).

Works Cited

Adams, Percy G. *Travelers and Travel Liar*. Berkeley: U of California P, 1962.

Anderson, Benedict. *Imagined Communities: Reflections on the Origin and Spread of Nationalism*. Rev. ed. London: Verso, 1991.

Bakhtin, M. M. *The Dialogic Imagination: Four Essays*. Ed. Michael Holoquist. Trans. Caryl Emerson and Michael Holoquist. Austin: U of Texas P, 1981.

Bird, Isabella L. *Korea and Her Neighbors: A Narrative of Travel, with an Account of the Recent Vicissitudes and Present Position of the Country*. New York: Revell, 1898.

———. *Unbeaten Tracks in Japan: An Account of Travels on Horseback in the Interior, including Visits to the Aborigines of Yezo and the Shrines of Nikk*. New York: Putnam, 1881.

Bristowe, W. S. *Louis and the King of Siam*. London: Chatto & Windus, 1976.

Brown, Susan. "Alternatives to the Missionary Position: Anna Leonowens as Victorian Travel Writer." *Feminist Studies* 21.3 (1995): 587–614.

Burton, Richard F. *Personal Narrative of a Pilgrimage to El-Medinah and Meccah*. New York: Putnam, 1856.

Calvino, Italo. *Invisible Cities*. Trans. William Weaver. New York: Harcourt, 1974.

Clemens, Samuel. *Life on the Missippi*. New York: Sagamore, 1957.

Clifford, James. "Traveling Cultures." *Cultural Studies*. Eds. Lawrence Grossberg, Cary Nelson, and Paul Treichler. New York: Routledge, 1992. 96–112.

Collins Cobuild English Dictionary. London: HarperCollins, 1995.

Cresswell, Tim. *In Place/Out of Place: Geography, Ideology, and Transgression*. Minneapolis: U of Minnesota P, 1996.

Cunliffe, Marcus. "Frances Trollope." *Abroad in America: Visitors to the New Nation 1776–1914*. Eds. Marc Pachter and Frances Stevenson Wein. Reading, MA: Addison-Wesley, 1977. 33–42.

David, Deirdre. *Rule Britannia: Women, Empire, and Victorian Writing*. Ithaca: Cornell UP, 1995.

de Tocqueville, Alexis. *Democracy in America*. Trans. Henry Reeve. Rev. ed. New York: Colonial, 1835.

Disraeli, Benjamin. *Tancred*. London: H. Colburn, 1847.

Ellis, Linda Abess. *Frances Trollope's America: Four Novels*. New York: Peter Lang, 1993.

Frawley, Maria H. *A Wider Range: Travel Writing by Women in Victorian England*. London: Associated UP, 1994.

Griswold, Alexander B. "King Mongkut in Perspective." *Journal of Siam Society* 45 (1957): 1–41.

———. *King Mongkut of Siam*. New York: Asia Society, 1961.

Hall, Basil. *Travels in North America in the Years 1827 and 1828*. Edinburgh: Cadell, 1829.

Hall, D. G. E. *A History of South-East Asia*. New York: St. Martin's, 1955.

Heineman, Helen. *Mrs. Trollope: The Triumphant Feminine in the Nineteenth Century*. Athens: Ohio State UP, 1979.

———. *Three Victorians in the New World: Interpretations of the New World in the Works of Frances Trollope, Charles Dickens, and Anthony Trollope*. New York: Peter Lang, 1990.

Houghton, Walter E. *The Victorian Frame of Mind: 1830–1870*. New Haven: Yale UP, 1957.

Kaplan, Caren. "'Getting to Know You': Travel, Gender, and the Politics of Representation in *Anna and the King of Siam* and *The King and I*." *Late Imperialism*. Eds. Román de la Campa, E. Ann Kaplan, and Michael Sprinker. New York: Verso, 1995. 33–52.

———. *Questions of Travel: Postmodern Discourse of Displacement*. Durham: Duke UP, 1996.

King and I, The. Dir. Walter Lang. Perf. Deborah Kerr and Yul Brynner. Twentieth Century Fox, 1956.

Kingsley, Mary Henrietta. *Travels in West Africa*. 2nd ed. New York: Macmillan, 1897.

Kipling, Rudyard. *Kim*. 1901. New York: Signet, 1984.

Landon, Margaret. *Anna and the King of Siam*. New York: John Day, 1943.

Leonowens, Anna. *The English Governess at the Siamese Court*. London: Arthur Barker, 1870.

———. *The Romance of the Harem*. 1873. Ed. Susan Morgan. Charlottesville: UP of Virginia, 1991.

———. *Siamese Harem Life*. 1873. New York: Dutton, 1953.

Lewis, Reina. *Gendering Orientalism: Race, Femininity and Representation*. London: Routledge, 1996.

Lyotard, Jean-François. *The Postmodern Condition: A Report on Knowledge*. Trans. Geoff Bennington and Brian Massumi. Minneapolis: U of Minnesota P, 1984.

Menchú, Rigoberta. *I, Rigoberta Menchú: An Indian Woman in Guatemala*. Ed. Elisabeth Burgos-Debray. Trans. Ann Wright. London: Verso, 1984.

Mills, Sara. *Discourses of Difference*. London: Routledge, 1991.

Minh-Ha, Trinh T. *Woman, Native, Other: Writing Postcoloniality and Feminism*. Bloomington: Indiana UP, 1989.

Moffat, Abbot Low. *Mongkut, the King of Siam*. Ithaca: Cornell UP, 1961.

Morgan, Susan. "Introduction." *The Romance of the Harem*. By Anna Leonowens. Charlottesville: UP of Virginia, 1991. ix–xxxvii.

Mouhot, Henri. *Diary: Travel in the Central Parts of Siam, Cambodia, and Laos During the Years 1858–1861*. Ed. Christopher Pym. New York: Oxford UP, 1966.

Pratt, Mary Louise. *Imperial Eyes: Travel Writing and Transculturation*. London: Routledge, 1992.

The Random House College Dictionary. Rev. ed. New York: Random, 1988.

Ransom, Teresa. *Fanny Trollope: A Remarkable Life*. New York: St. Martin's, 1995.

Said, Edward W. *Culture and Imperialism*. New York: Vintage, 1993.

———. *Orientalism*. New York: Vintage, 1978.

Stoll, David. *Rigoberta Menchú and the Story of All Poor Guatemalans*. Boulder: Westview P, 1999.

Swift, Jonathan. *Gulliver's Travels*. 1726. New York: Oxford UP, 1902.

Trollope, Frances. *Domestic Manners of the Americans*. London: Whittaker, Treacher, 1832.

Trollope, Thomas Adolphus. *What I Remember*. New York: Harper, 1888.

Zlotnick, Susan. "Jane Eyre, Anna Leonowens, and the White Woman's Burden: Governess, Missionaries, and Maternal Imperialism in Mid-Victorian Britain." *Victorians Institute Journal* 24 (1996): 27–56.

Nancy Prince and Her Gothic Odyssey
A Veiled Lady

Sarah Brusky

The attention paid to *Narrative of the Life and Travels of Mrs. Nancy Prince* (1850) is something of a paradox. Recognizing that the narrative offers one of the few opportunities to examine a black woman's writing of the pre–Civil War era, scholars have nevertheless paid it only superficial or brief attention.[1] Ronald G. Walters provides the lengthiest, though still insufficient, discussion in his introduction of a 1990 reprint of the narrative. In his attempt finally to bring this narrative to light, he claims that it is an "adventure story" of "exotic settings and remarkable happenings" that "is almost as intriguing for what lies between the lines as for what appears on the printed page. At its heart is embedded the elusive spirit of Nancy Prince herself" (ix, x). This claim of elusiveness, however, hides much of the character of Nancy Prince.[2] Indeed, gothic analysis of Prince's narrative reveals a complex, but clear, view of the "spirit of Nancy Prince." From a gothic perspective, Prince's odyssey proves metaphysical, as well as physical, as she finds voice in travels spanning almost twenty years.[3]

To begin, the phrase "gothic analysis" needs to be defined. Such proposed clarity is quite complicated in light of contemporary discourse on defining the gothic.[4] Use of two specific trends in gothic theory, however, opens Prince's narrative to a gothic reading. First, much of gothic analysis begins with lists of predominant narrative features such as ghosts, gloomy landscapes, and villains.[5] While limited in usefulness, such features, nonetheless, provide a starting point for analysis. Drawing upon such lists, identification of scenes of horror and destruction in Prince's narrative—bloody battles, natural catastrophes, and endless descriptions of death—reveals junctures of gothic and travel writing conventions at which the "spirit of Nancy Prince" becomes most visible.

A second trend in gothic theory picks up where lists leave off by providing ways in which to interpret Prince's use of gothic scenes.[6] Pushing the lists of features a step further by interrogating the existence such features appear in the text, I find that Prince's use of the gothic strategically veils and reveals various aspects of her character throughout the narrative. My approach here is to identify first the gothic scenes, then examine their connection to the "spirit of Nancy Prince," and lastly address the question of why Prince uses, or even needs, the gothic.

Prince's narrative, while short, covers her family genealogy, the trials of her childhood, and her travels in Russia, Jamaica, and the United States over the span of eighteen years. Born in 1799, Prince worked at an early age to support her thrice-widowed mother and seven siblings. In 1824, she married Nero Prince, who served the tsar of Russia, and left the United States with him for St. Petersburg, where they lived for nine years. She returned to the United States alone in 1833 for health reasons and became a widow before Nero could join her. In 1840, she went to Jamaica as a missionary, returned to the United States in 1841 to raise money, and in 1842 made a final trip to Jamaica for just a few months. In the fall of 1842, Prince returned to the United States for the last time, and her narrative ends shortly thereafter.

In writing her narrative, Prince is clearly aware of its generic implications. An extremely popular genre in the nineteenth century, travel writing was a form of literature Prince's audience knew well.[7] Indeed, they would have known immediately what to expect based solely on the title of her narrative. Farah J. Griffin and Cheryl J. Fish claim that the section in which Prince describes Russia is the most characteristic of this genre. They write, "More than in any other section of her narrative, when describing Russia Prince turns to observation in the tradition of Western travel writing" (201). Their statement, though insightful, needs to be qualified by noting the difficulty Prince seems to find in turning to observation. Characteristic of the genre, for example, Prince addresses the fashion, religion, and education of Russia (29–30). What is interesting to note, however, is the brevity with which she does it: All three areas of Russian life fall into one paragraph.

Similarly, she rushes through visits to various towns. Although Prince acknowledges her audience's expectation to find a description of her travels when she writes, "I spent some time visiting the different towns in the vicinity of St. Petersburg," she fails to give any account of these different visits (24). Rather, in the next sentence, she turns to the topic of the Emperor's and Empress's deaths, a seemingly awkward transition made more so by the fact that her visits occur in 1825 and the deaths in 1826.

Prince's interruption of the travel writing convention, e.g., skipping over the travels of an entire year to focus on the more somber topic of death, proves characteristic of her own brand of travel writing in this section on Russia. When we examine the events and customs Prince does, in fact, relate to her reader, we find an arresting number of such scenes of gothic gloom and doom. A quick overview of her observations attests to Prince's gothic tendencies. While she relates her presentation before the Emperor and Empress upon arrival in Russia, her first detailed description of life in Russia is a visit to a burying ground. The gothic scene builds as she notes the torchmen who accompany the corpse, "dressed in black garments…with lighted torches in their hands, bowing their heads as they pass along very gravely" (18–19), and the hearse "drawn by four horses, covered with black gowns down to their feet" (19). "[T]hey all move along," Prince concludes, "with great solemnity" (19).

This scene is immediately followed by another scene of gothic detail, a great flood of St. Petersburg, though, as Prince tells us, the events occurred two months apart. As the waters rose in the city, "many of the inhabitants were drowned," and as the waters ebbed, they left "a dreadful sight" (20, 21). Indeed, as Prince narrates,

> I made my way through a long yard, over the bodies of men and beasts, and when opposite their gate I sunk; I made one grasp, and the earth gave away; I grasped again, and fortunately got hold of the leg of a horse, that had been drowned. I drew myself up, covered with mire, and made my way a little further, when I was knocked down by striking against a boat…and as I had lost my lantern, I was obliged to grope my way as I could. (21)

When Prince returns to this pit the next day, she discovers a hole "large enough to hold a dozen like myself…Had not the horse been there, I should never again have seen the light of day, and no one would have known my fate" (22).

As the narrative continues, Prince demonstrates a penchant for such gothic detail. Before Prince ends the section on Russia, she notes the Decembrist Revolt of 1825, followed by two declarations of war in 1827 and 1829, and finally an outbreak of cholera with "thousands of people falling a prey" in 1831 (27). Her description of the succession crisis following Alexander's and Elizabeth's deaths in 1826 parallels that of the flood for gothic drama. She tells us that "the bodies of the killed and mangled were cast into the river, and the snow and ice were stained with the blood of human victims; as they were obliged to drive the cannon to and fro in the midst of the crowd, the bones of those wounded, who might have been cured, were crushed" (25). Nevertheless, as she concludes that "the scene was awful," one can hardly claim that Prince creates a gothic fiction (25). She does not, that is, construct a fantasy, but rather relates important historical events that are inherently gothic and that her nineteenth-century audience surely would have expected her to relay.

Conversely, the issue of whether Prince constructs a narrative is not so easily dismissed. When we look at her narration of the funeral paired with the flood, or the succession crisis of the Decembrist Revolt, the two declarations of war, and the outbreak of cholera in close narrative proximity, we are struck by large gaps in real time. Prince, in other words, does construct a gothic text in this section by selecting only those events with unusually dark and catastrophic consequences.

What could Prince have meant to accomplish, however, with such a narrative? Does she simply demonstrate, to use my own words, a penchant for gothic drama? Put too simply, yes; but what is important here is what this penchant achieves in the way of self-revelation. Prince's tendency toward gothic detail gives us insight into her psyche—precisely the insight that the few scholars of Prince's work claim to be absent. On the contrary, though, the "spirit of Nancy Prince" is quite evident, as a closer examination of the flood scene demonstrates.

Prince highlights the flood as a scene of danger and destruction, a scene whose details reveal the loneliness Prince feels during her early months in Russia. Before she describes the scene, she tells the reader that she is physically alone: "Mr. Prince went early to the palace...our children boarders were gone to school; our servant had gone of an errand" (20). Then, after the waters rise and fall, she again says that "[she] was left alone" (21). However, she makes unmistakable that there are also psychological ramifications of her physical aloneness, for "there was darkness that might be felt, such as I had never experienced before. My situation was the more painful, being alone, and not being able to speak" (21). Tellingly, Prince does not complete her sentence, or rather, completes it but not in the way we might expect. As she tells us later in the text, "I learned the languages [spoken there] in six months," but at the time of the flood she has been in Russia just under four months (31). She does not claim, however, that she cannot speak the language, but simply that she cannot speak, precluding any communication whatsoever. Through a gothic narrative construction, Prince encodes her loneliness in a particular situation; she uses the flood to make her aloneness worthy of narration. However, as her statement about her inability to speak suggests, her physical aloneness is not only psychological loneliness, but also indicative of a state more general than the particular situation of the flood.

Prince eschews the gothic in the next stage of her travels. The narration of her trip back to the United States, the subsequent trip to Jamaica in 1840, and her brief return to the United States in 1841, reveal an absence of gothic scenes and, not coincidentally, a more authoritative persona. Just as in the previous section where selections of catastrophic events illustrate a constructed gothic text, their absence in this section also indicates a careful strategy. In fact, Prince not only removes the gothic from this portion of her narrative, but also provides two counterexamples to earlier gothic constructions. In these examples, Prince draws on her earlier representation of gothic details, but simultaneously negates the drama that such details create.

The first example occurs when Prince sails for Jamaica. Initially, the scene seems reminiscent of an earlier cumulative description when she writes of a week-long storm that put the ship in "great peril" and immediately follows with a run-in with pirates. "On that day [the final day of the storm]," Prince writes, "a sail was seen at some distance making towards us, the captain judging her to be a piratical vessel, ordered the women and children below, and the men to prepare for action" (49). In contrast to previous events, however, this one stops before it starts when "the pirates were not inclined to hazard an engagement; when they saw the deck filled with armed men [sic] they left us" (49). Similarly, when she addresses slavery in Jamaica, Prince gestures toward horror, but then does not narrate it. When she is in conversation with "a respectable looking man" native to the island, she hears a story "of the wrongs he and his wife had endured while in slavery" (57). Surely this story promises something parallel to the horrors of the Decembrist Revolt, but Prince gives no details. Rather, she underscores the absence of gothic narration when she claims that this man's story is "too horrible to narrate. My heart sickens when I think of it" (57). Twice, then, Prince hints at the gothic we saw in the Russia section, but instead denies her earlier tendency to pile on the detail.

With the absence of gothic constructions to encode the psyche of her persona, Prince reveals a bolder, more authoritative, character in this section. The first stage of this transformation involves Prince's emphasis on her actions against the wrongs of slavery and racism. Upon her return to the United States, for instance, she "called a meeting of the people and laid before them [her] plan" to build shelters for poor black children (46). Moreover, after attending antislavery meetings, her mind "was bent upon going to Jamaica. A field of usefulness seemed spread out before me" (48). Similarly, in a more direct statement than we have yet encountered, Prince expresses her desire to be useful: "I hoped that I might aid, in some small degree, to raise up and encourage the emancipated inhabitants [of Jamaica], and teach the young children" (50).

Although such openness contrasts with the gothically encoded loneliness of Prince while in Russia, it is nonetheless equally constructed. The immediacy, for example, of Prince's departure from Russia and discovery of "a field of usefulness" hints at causation as Prince narrates the two events. In real time, however, Prince leaves Russia in August of 1833 and does not depart the United States for Jamaica until September of 1840. Similarly, while describing her life in Russia, Prince leaves out the fact that she assisted in the formation of an asylum for poor children in St. Petersburg. Though she reveals this later (46), its initial absence helps promote the contrast we see between the persona of Russia and that of Jamaica.

In the second stage of the transformation into a more authoritative persona, Prince emphasizes her importance to others. As she becomes active in antislavery causes—indeed, as she becomes useful—Prince repeatedly notes others' attitudes toward her. Prince appears indispensable as one missionary tries "to persuade [her] to go" to Jamaica and as the people of St. Ann Harbor "urged [her] to stay with them" rather than going on to Kingston (48, 50). Similarly, when she returns to the United States to raise money for her work in Jamaica, she meets only "with much encouragement to labor in the cause. Missionaries...all seemed to be interested in my object" (59).

While this involvement with abolition and, moreover, her intense ownership of it may not seem so bold at first blush, Prince's activities do indeed push the envelope on the issue of womanhood. Not only does she move about in such circles at a time when women's participation in abolition was suspect,[8] but also she does so alone. Although a missionary among missionaries, it is clear in the narrative that Prince moves about Jamaica solo, no small feat as the work of Mary Suzanne Schriber suggests. Schriber notes that even when the nineteenth-century woman traveler claimed to be "alone," she was most likely in the company of other women (*Telling* xxix). Thus Prince proves to be unusually independent, a remarkable quality when we remember both her social position as a black woman in the nineteenth century and how lonely she felt in Russia.

The third part of Prince's transformation to a more authoritative persona occurs as she finds herself so useful. As others rely on her and as she finds purpose in her work, her voice becomes more direct and unmistakable than in the Russia section. In fact, in comparison to the Prince we see in Russia, here she seems bold and daring. She calls slavery, for instance, "the sins of my beloved country" where earlier she only voiced her antislavery stand in a subtle negation. Earlier, when describing the classes of St. Petersburg, she writes, "The rich own the poor, but they are not suffered to separate families or sell them off the soil" (31). "[T]hey are not suffered," of course, becomes significant only to an audience that is familiar with those who do in fact suffer, but the fact that her condemnation of the United States goes unsaid is noteworthy.

Another example of Prince's boldness occurs as she describes the markets in Jamaica and defiantly attacks white American stereotypes. When she discovers the natives working these markets, she gives her white readers an unmistakable message concerning the Jamaicans. "[I]t may be hoped," Prince writes, "they are not the stupid set of beings they have been called; *here surely we see industry*; they are enterprising and quick in their perception, determined to possess themselves, and to possess property besides, and quite able to take care of themselves" (54, original emphasis). When the Jamaicans ask about her interest in them, she replies, "[W]e had heard in America that you are lazy, and that emancipation has been of no benefit to you; I wish to inform myself of the truth respecting you, and give a true account on my return" (54). Her intention to "give a true account" marks the change in Prince's persona in this section as the cautious negations accompanied by gothic selections earlier in the text become outright assertions in the absence of the gothic.

Without the gothic description surrounding her first trip to Jamaica, then, Prince's persona is direct and authoritative. It is not surprising, therefore, to find a return of the gothic element when Prince becomes disillusioned upon her return to Jamaica. After finding so much encouragement for her cause in the United States, Prince returns to Jamaica "and found every thing different from what it was when I left, the people were in a state of agitation...and the insurrection was so great that it was found necessary to increase the army to quell it" (60). This scene is no longer the "field of usefulness" that just months earlier spread before her. Rather, Jamaica now promotes in her the opposite reaction. Prince feels that "it seemed useless to attempt to establish a Manual Labor School...[I]t seemed useless to spend my time there" (63). Although she still reveals her important status—though "a movement was made to induce [her] to remain"— she is firm that she "should do no more for them" (63, 65). Not surprisingly, then, we find a narration similar to the Russia section.

The narration of this second trip to Jamaica brings a return to the mode of observation that Griffin and Fish note Prince uses in the Russia section and that is characteristic of the western tradition of travel writing. Indeed, Prince even sets off this observation with the heading "West Indies" and with the following statement: "Before giving an account of the voyage from Jamaica, it may prove interesting to some readers, to have a brief description of the country" (67). What follows over the next several pages is a catalog typical of the travel writing genre, a list, that is, of what her nineteenth-century audience would have expected upon picking up her narrative. Among other characteristics of the island, Prince mentions its climate, geography, and produce (67–71).

Again, however, as with her method of observation in the Russia section, Prince shows an inclination toward gothic detail. In giving just a two-and-a-half page history of the island, for example, she selects as the notable events of that history a 1692 earthquake, a "great fire" in 1702, "the most terrible [hurricane] on record" in 1722, and a second "dreadful hurricane" in 1780 (72–74). The randomness of her selections shows that she is not striving here to give a thorough chronological history. Moreover, her description of the earthquake

reminds us of her description of the St. Petersburg flood and the Decembrist Revolt as she tries to convey the terror of the earthquake. She
claims that she hears a story about how "the earth opened and shut
very quick in some places, and...several people [sank] down to the
middle, and others appeared with their heads just above ground, and
were choked to death" (73). Having suggested that Prince returns to
the narrative style of the Russia section, however, I would like to
make a qualification.

Before the parallel between the Russia section and this section on
Prince's second trip to Jamaica becomes too absolute, it is important
to note the subtle changes in her use of gothic description and the
travel-writing genre. First, she, in fact, combines her narrative tech-
nique of the Russia section with that of the section on her first trip to
Jamaica by connecting the gothic of the first section to her cause in the
second. Like the first section, she describes here an "awful scene" of
"terrible destruction" in which "many persons were drowned" (69).
Then, more like the second section, she takes an unequivocal stand on
the institution of slavery when she suggests that slavery is worse than
this gothic scene she is describing. Prince notes a woman saying to
her: "Not so bad now as in the time of slavery" (69). As this woman's
comment illustrates, the gothic becomes a way for Prince to make the
anti-slavery assertions we found in her first trip to Jamaica by comparing the gothic scene of the flood to slavery.

Second, Prince's use of the travel-writing genre also combines her
narrative tendencies of the first and second sections. In an artful manipulation of the relationship between sight and marker,[9] Prince combines the gothic of the first section with the issue of slavery that
becomes prevalent in the second section. As she avoids describing a
sight—"were I to tell all my eyes have seen among that people [of Ja-
maica], it would not be credited"—she in fact gives more information
about its horror than words could have accomplished (61). As a result,
however, the sight seems without any kind of marker; with a sight
beyond words, that is, Prince seemingly can draw on no explicit information to give it credibility.

Interestingly, Prince subtly reveals that the sight does have markers: her assumption of the audience's knowledge of the horrors of
slavery. She sandwiches her statement about the sight's incredibility
between two sentences that begin, oddly enough, with "it is well
known" (61). Such juxtaposition questions the supposed incredibility
of the sight. Indeed, what we discover is that Prince makes a comment

in her absence of description by avoiding direct reference to the markers: Slavery, as she sees it on the island and as her mid–nineteenth-century audience well knows, is a real gothic horror too awful even to narrate.

This combination of gothic and antislavery inclinations occurs again when Prince narrates her final return to the United States. Her trip back to the United States from Jamaica takes two months and from the start is marked by ominous tones. When the captain reveals the ship's course to Prince, she "told him it was not the case, and told the passengers that he had deceived us" (76). The problems continue as Prince's race puts her in danger when she nears the slave-holding southern states. When the ship drops anchor in Key West, for instance, the five black passengers do not go ashore with the rest because, as Prince explains, "a law had just been passed there that every free colored person coming there, should be put in custody on their going ashore" (77). Indeed, Prince reveals how dangerously close she is to slavery when her ship and "a vessel loaded with slaves, were towed down the river by the same steamer" (81). As she looks out over the sides of her ship, she sees the "awful sight" of "a drove of colored people, fettered together in pairs by the wrist; some had weights, with long chains at their ankles, men and women, young and old" (79–80).

This new type of gothic scene, a more real and immediate one, reveals a change in the kind of travel Prince does as opposed to that of her white travel-writing contemporaries. Where white travelers, as one white travel writer claims, return home with "magical spectacles which [enable]" them "the refreshing, short-lived pleasure of being able to look at [their] own land…[and] see novelty blossoming on the most commonplace and familiar stems," Prince "was made to forget [her] own condition as [she] looked with pity on the poor slaves, who were laboring and toiling…as far as could be seen with a glass" (Caesar 78, 109). The white traveler's magical spectacles become Prince's very real looking glass when gothic scenes begin to chronicle the dark reality of blacks' existence in mid–nineteenth-century America.

The difference between the white traveler's magical spectacles and Prince's real looking glass points to another aspect of travel writing. Scholars have pointed out, travel writing is a mode of self-discovery and creation. As they have examined travel writing by authors of European origin, they have found that this process of self-discovery relies heavily on the role of the Other. Schriber, for example, notes that nineteenth-century "travel, whatever else it might be, was an American exercise in 'othering' for purposes of self-definition" (*Writing* 77). This process underlies the statement about the magical spectacles, for white travelers return from abroad where they come into contact with the Other able to "look [unprejudiced] at the shell of the civilization from which [they] have emerged" (Caesar 109). That this process gives the white traveler a "refreshing, short-lived pleasure" turns attention toward the traveler.

Upon returning home, Prince, is "made to forget [her] own condition" when she looks through her glass at the gothic scenes of her native land. Thus, the process of Othering does not come into play for Prince as a black woman because the gothic scenes before her are always too dangerously close to becoming her reality. Two sets of conventions, then, one gothic and the other that of travel writing, force Prince's nineteenth-century readers into an examination of race; it forces them to take notice of those silent markers that inform Prince's sights of slavery.

One question, however, still remains: Why the gothic? Why does Prince encode her early loneliness in gothic terms, and why does the gothic drama of the early part of the narrative—the one that seems distanced from her nineteenth-century reader by time and space— finally give way to contemporary gothic, the horrors of slavery? Two interrelated concepts in gothic theory help answer this question. The first concept is what Kari Winter calls the "terror of the familiar." In her discussion of early gothic fiction, Winter writes, "[F]emale Gothic novelists uncovered the terror of the familiar: the routine brutality and injustice of the patriarchal family, conventional religion, and classist social structures" (21). Certainly this characterizes Prince as well because she exposes the terrors of her familiar: slavery.

It is also important to note here, however, that Prince does not create a gothic fiction. As Teresa A. Goddu would argue, Prince has "the difficulty of representing a gothic history through gothic conventions without collapsing the distinctions between fact and fiction, event and effect" (137). Goddu claims that Frederick Douglass negotiates this "uneasy relationship" by "both represent[ing] his history and insist[ing] that it defies narrative reconstruction" (138). As we have seen, Prince does this as well when the Jamaican man tells her stories of slavery that Prince finds "too horrible to narrate" (57). This exposure of slavery as itself a gothic scene allows Prince, in Goddu's words, to speak the "unspeakable event of slavery" (132).

Speaking the unspeakable is the second concept in gothic theory that proves useful to Prince's narrative and works on another level as well. In addition to speaking the horrors of slavery, Prince speaks the unspeakable woman. Although the large volume of literature by women in the nineteenth century attests to the existence of women's voices, the ideology of true womanhood both disapproved of women speaking and made deviations from the ideal unspeakable. As Prince shows in her preface, the true woman should at least appear as though she does not wish to deviate from the ideal: "My object is not a vain desire to appear before the public" (xxvii). As her preface also shows, however, Prince's reticence is only rhetorical, for in a preface of just five sentences, she makes seventeen references to herself (the words "I," "me," "my," and "myself"). Indeed, she has every desire "to throw" herself on the public (xxvii), and thus can be described as a "veiled lady." This veiled lady, Goddu argues, "functioned as a dominant image of womanhood" in mid–nineteenth-century America and was simultaneously "private" and "public" as a figure veiled from the public at the very moment she was on display to the public (98). Moreover, Prince is doubly veiled as woman and as black. Thus, her "display" of herself through the course of the narrative speaks the doubly unspeakable mid–nineteenth-century black woman.

The gothic helps Prince speak the doubly unspeakable. Although it may seem odd practice to use a genre whose reputation has for too long suggested flight from reality to open the writing of a genre whose reputation is the very observation and transcription of reality, gothic nonetheless proves vital to Prince's travel writing. As a way simultaneously to encode and expose, the gothic reveals the mystery behind the "elusive spirit of Nancy Prince." Indeed, over the course of the narrative, we witness the veiled lady lifting her veils.

Notes

1   To be sure, these scholars have not set out to examine the text fully. In other words, there is no substantial work on Prince. Other than Walters's introduction cited later in the paragraph, Prince receives, at best, a passing reference or a brief introduction to an excerpt in an anthology. See, for example, Dorothy Sterling, ed., *We Are Your Sisters: Black Women in the Nineteenth Century* (New York: W. W. Norton & Co., 1984); Mary G. Mason, "Travel as Metaphor and Reality in Afro-American Women's Autobiography, 1850–1972," *Black American Literature Forum* 24 (Summer 1990): 337–56; Schriber, *Telling Travels*; and Griffin and Fish.

2   Mason also finds that "there is a tone of reticence and deference in [Prince's] autobiography that suggests that self-disclosure was painful" (339). There is a development in the revelation of the personal throughout the narrative, Griffin and Fish claim that Prince's first section on her early childhood is the "most personal section of her narrative" (68).

3   I am borrowing the term *odyssey* from Walters's title of his 1990 reprint of the narrative: *A Black Woman's Odyssey through Russia and Jamaica: The Narrative of Nancy Prince* to suggest the idea of this dual travel.

4   Almost any book-length study positions itself within the conversation by chronicling the trends in defining the gothic. For recent discussions, see Goddu, and Robert K. Martin and Eric Savoy, eds., *American Gothic: New Interventions in a National Narrative* (Iowa City: U of Iowa P, 1998).

5   See, for example, Winter (19); Leonard Engel, "The Role of the Enclosure in the English and American Gothic Romance," *Essays in Arts and Sciences* 11 (September 1982): 59–68; and Eugenia C. DeLamotte, *Perils of the Night: A Feminist Study of Nineteenth-Century Gothic* (New York: Oxford UP, 1990). Essentially, such lists contain anything and everything that point toward doom and gloom.

6   This trend varies widely, but at its core assumes that the gothic does work for the author beyond thrills and chills. For example, David Mogen, Scott Sanders, and Joanne Karpinski, eds., provide a way to look at how Americans used the gothic to write about the terrors of the frontier in *Frontier Gothic: Terror and Wonder at the Frontier in American Literature* (Rutherford: Associated UP, 1993); and Elaine Showalter examines the development of women's uses of the gothic in "The American Female Gothic," *Sister's Choice: Tradition and Change in American Women's Writing* (Oxford: Clarendon P, 1991).

7   For a discussion of the genre's nineteenth-century popularity see William W. Stowe, *Going Abroad: European Travel in Nineteenth-Century American Culture* (Princeton: Princeton UP, 1994) chapter 1; Terry Caesar, *Forgiving the Boundaries: Home as Abroad in American Travel Writing* (Athens: U of Georgia P, 1995), chapter one; and Schriber, *Telling Travels*, introduction.

8   As Griffin and Fish write, Prince "left Boston for Jamaica just when the debates over women's participation in the abolition movement were heating up" (68). Prince herself notes that she attended antislavery meetings "with much pleasure, until a contention broke out among themselves" (47).

9   In the simplest terms, the sight is simply what the traveler sees, while the marker is information about a specific sight. For an interesting discussion of the transformations the relationship between sight and marker undergoes, see Dean MacCannell, *The Tourist: A New Theory of the Leisure Class* (New York: Schocken Books, 1989) chapter 6.

Works Cited

Caesar, Terry. "'Counting the Cats in Zanzibar': American Travel Abroad in American Travel Writing to 1914." *Prospects: An Annual of American Cultural Studies*. Ed. Jack Salzman. Vol. 13. New York: Cambridge UP, 1988. 95–134.

———. *Forgiving the Boundaries: Home as Abroad in American Travel Writing* Athens: U of Georgia P, 1995.

DeLamotte, Eugenia C. *Perils of the Night: A Feminist Study of Nineteenth-Century Gothic.* New York: Oxford UP, 1990.

Engel, Leonard. "The Role of the Enclosure in the English and American Gothic Romance." *Essays in Arts and Sciences* 11 (September 1982): 59–68.

Goddu, Teresa A. *Gothic America: Narrative, History, and Nation.* New York: Columbia UP, 1997.

Griffin, Farah J., and Cheryl J. Fish, eds. *A Stranger in the Village: Two Centuries of African-American Travel Writing.* Boston: Beacon P, 1998.

MacCannell, Dean. *The Tourist: A New Theory of the Leisure Class.* New York: Schocken Books, 1989.

Martin, Robert. K., and Eric Savoy, eds. *American Gothic: New Interventions in a National Narrative.* Iowa City: U of Iowa P, 1998.

Mason, Mary G. "Travel as Metaphor and Reality in Afro-American Women's Autobiography, 1850–1972." *Black American Literature Forum* 24 (Summer 1990): 337–56.

Mogen, David, Scott Sanders, and Joanne Karpinski, eds. *Frontier Gothic: Terror and Wonder at the Frontier in American Literature.* Rutherford: Associated UP, 1993.

Prince, Nancy. *Narrative of the Life and Travels of Mrs. Nancy Prince.* 1850. *A Black Woman's Odyssey through Russia and Jamaica: The Narrative of Nancy Prince.* Introd. Ronald G. Walters. Princeton: Markus Wiener Publishers, 1990.

Schriber, Mary Suzanne. *Telling Travels: Selected Writings by Nineteenth-Century American Women Abroad.* DeKalb: Northern Illinois UP, 1995.

———. *Writing Home: American Women Abroad, 1830–1920.* Charlottesville: UP of Virginia, 1997.

Showalter, Elaine. "The American Female Gothic." *Sister's Choice: Tradition and Change in American Women's Writing.* Oxford: Clarendon P, 1991.

Sterling, Dorothy, Ed. *We Are Your Sisters: Black Women in the Nineteenth Century.* New York: W. W. Norton & Co., 1984.

Stowe, William W. *Going Abroad: European Travel in Nineteenth-Century American Culture.* Princeton: Princeton UP, 1994.

Walters, Ronald G. Introduction. *A Black Woman's Odyssey through Russia and Jamaica: The Narrative of Nancy Prince.* Princeton: Markus Wiener Publishers, 1990. ix–xxiii.

Winter, Kari. *Subjects of Slavery, Agents of Change: Women and Power in Gothic Novels and Slave Narratives, 1790–1865.* Athens: U of Georgia P, 1992.

Zilpha Elaw's Serial Domesticity
An Unsentimental Journey

Rosetta R. Haynes

N ineteenth-century African American itinerant preacher, Zilpha Elaw is a radical spiritual mother, a term that I apply to the empowered subjectivity that she and other nineteenth-century African American women preachers constructed for themselves following life-transforming experiences of sanctification.[1] This new subjectivity allowed Elaw to reconceptualize power from a protofeminist perspective in the midst of a rigidly patriarchal culture, to actively participate in a public sphere that was hostile to African Americans and proscriptive to women of all races, and to claim sexual autonomy and physical freedom within a society that declared female bodies to be the property of men and which asserted "virtuous black woman" to be an oxymoron. In this essay, I will explore the ways that Elaw, as a radical spiritual mother, draws upon and revises two characteristic elements of nineteenth-century women's sentimental writing—the privileging of maternity as an important and appropriate desire for women and the assertion of home as women's proper sphere.

Radical spiritual motherhood refers to a particular pattern of behavior that draws upon and transforms the conventional roles that were assigned to women by nineteenth-century domestic ideology.[2] It is an expansive conception of maternity that extends the scope of the biological family to regard all humans as potential recipients of maternal care, both spiritual and material. This care may include spiritual sustenance such as that provided through preaching and prayer, or material support such as that given to the poor and the sick. Radical spiritual mothers were not, however, restricted to nurturing roles, but also functioned as leaders and intellectuals who actively participated in the public sphere. In addition, because they did not remarry after the deaths of their husbands, instead choosing to maintain their physical, emotional, and sexual autonomy, celibacy is an important part of this kind of maternity.

Three specific aspects of the dominant domestic ideology transformed through the adoption of radical spiritual motherhood are the designation of the private sphere as the proper domain for women, the requirement that married women cede control of their sexuality to their husbands, and the expectation that married women gain their fulfillment through biological motherhood and serving their husbands. Though the private sphere was one in which women were traditionally granted circumscribed power, radical spiritual mothers were divinely authorized to move freely between the private and the public spheres to preach the gospel. These religious leaders further capitalized on their God-given right to public intervention by using their mobility and visibility to address social and political issues such as slavery, racism, and sexism.

Radical spiritual mothers' sexual empowerment stemmed from their insistence upon the right to control their own sexual destiny by remaining single upon the deaths of their husbands and by subsequently practicing celibacy.[3] What is innovative about this decision is that they undertook it independently of any institutional mandates governing their sexuality. Catholic nuns, for example, took a vow of chastity as part of the requirements of their religious order. The radical spiritual mothers, however, took matters into their own hands and declared their bodies to be their own, to be used solely for God's work. In claiming this right they not only undermined the patriarchal prerogative of male control of the female body, but they implicitly critiqued racist assumptions about black female sexuality by insisting upon their unavailability for exploitation by white men (and black men as well).

Though radical spiritual motherhood draws upon biological motherhood for patterns of maternal nurturing, these women were not bound by the constraints of biological motherhood. For example, they sometimes left their children in the care of relatives or friends in order to fulfill their ministerial obligations. Thus, spiritual motherhood took precedence over biological motherhood if the latter interfered with the fulfillment of the preachers' itinerant missions. The kind of spiritual maternity that the radical spiritual mothers adopted resembled that adopted by a contemporary group of holy women—

antebellum Catholic nuns. According to Joseph G. Mannard, the spiritual maternity of the nuns stemmed from their identity as "brides of Christ" and from their engagement in moral reform, orphan care, teaching, and nursing (85). The spiritual maternity of the radical spiritual mothers originated, however, in the experience of sanctification, or the second blessing following conversion, which Harald Lindström defines as a kind of spiritual perfection experienced by a believer when she is wholly attuned to and governed by God's will (Lindström qtd. in Andrews 15). Though the radical spiritual mothers never declared themselves to be brides of Christ, they did dedicate themselves completely to God. In so doing, they, like the nuns, committed themselves to engaging in a life of service to the larger community. They, too, acquired extended spiritual families—the family of God.

Elaw's attitudes about maternity were no doubt shaped by the model provided by her own mother. Early in her text the author explains, "At twelve years of age I was bereaved of my mother, who died in childbirth of her twenty-second child, all of whom, with the exception of three, died in infancy."[4] The arduousness of giving birth to twenty-two children, the trauma of losing most of these children, and the ultimate horror of death resulting from this difficult cycle must surely have had a profound effect upon the author. Elaw herself had only one child, a daughter, whom she never names in her text.

Though radical spiritual mothers were free African American women, it is likely that their awareness of the degraded status of enslaved black women influenced the new identities that they sought to create for themselves as spiritual leaders. In particular, the physical and sexual abuse suffered by enslaved African American women likely played a significant role in motivating the radical spiritual mothers to seek control over their bodies and their sexuality by leading celibate lives upon the deaths of their husbands, or in the case of Rebecca Jackson, within marriage.[5] Though Elaw never identifies her mother as a former slave, the image of the breeder, forced to regularly reproduce property for her master, may have influenced the author's consciousness on some level. It is plausible that the reproduction of the image of the breeder upon her psyche may have caused her to limit her own reproduction, and may also have influenced her decision to remain unmarried and celibate after the death of her husband. For someone who witnessed the physical and psychological difficulties that could be associated with childbirth, spiritual maternity must have seemed an attractive alternative.

The decision to adopt spiritual maternity was interestingly facilitated by Elaw's own daughter. The author is careful to reproduce her child's words of encouragement to "break up housekeeping" as she grapples with the idea of pursuing the life of an itinerant minister: "'Now, mother, what is the matter?'....'If I were you, I should not mind what any person said, but I should go just as I had arranged to go, and do not think any thing about me, for I shall do very well'" (89). What better sanction could Elaw receive for an unconventional life antithetical to the constraints of domesticity? Elaw then takes her little girl and leaves her in the care of relatives so that she may begin her itinerant ministry, remaining away from her child for seven months.

Though Elaw may seek liberation from the demands and constraints of biological maternity, she is still aware of the symbolic power of motherhood and still desires to draw upon this power and the connection it can bring with her audience. There are many instances throughout her narrative where she highlights the maternal roles that she plays in connection with her ministry. For example, in describing the success she has had in ministering to people in England, she says, "I have travelled [sic] in several parts of England, and I thank God He has given me some spiritual children in every place wherein I have laboured" (141). Elaw has been fruitful in multiplying devoted followers of Christ. In this passage, she suggests the procreative role of God, who gives her spiritual children, thus displacing reproductive labor with spiritual labor. For this labor, she receives both divine and human approbation.

Ministering to the needs of the extended family of God necessarily meant traveling; it meant rejecting the confines of a single home and possessing the physical freedom to circulate broadly to meet her new family's needs. Elaw thus practices what I call serial domesticity, as she traveled from house to house and church to church (houses of God) to preach to and nurture her "children." Though Elaw appropriates the language and themes of nineteenth-century sentimental fiction, she fundamentally subverts the confining elements of sentimentality in her own quest for spiritual and physical freedom.

What empowered Elaw to travel widely to preach the gospel? Clearly, she believed that she possessed God's divine sanction to live out an unorthodox life. However, the material conditions of the lives of most nineteenth-century African American women may have influenced the spiritual practices of Elaw and other black women itinerant preachers. Specifically, the working and living patterns of black women must be considered. Dorothy Sterling explains that low paying and unstable employment for African American men made it necessary for most married women to work outside the home to supplement the family income. Whereas most women worked during the day as domestics in the homes of white families, many others lived at the residences of their employers, sometimes keeping their children with them. To further diminish the family's financial burden, it was also common for children to be bound out as indentured servants (Sterling 85, 92, 215). Elaw, for example, was placed in service at the age of twelve by her father after her mother died. Contemporary itinerant preacher, Jarena Lee, was only seven years old when she moved sixty miles from her parents in order to become a servant maid. It was, therefore, not uncommon for family members to be separated out of economic necessity. The result was a kind of elasticity of the domestic sphere that stretched the definition of the normative nuclear family structure. When some of these itinerant ministers left their children in the care of relatives or friends so that they could more freely pursue their itinerant preaching careers, it seems they were in fact drawing upon this pattern of domestic elasticity. What was initially a practice resorted to out of economic need was utilized to help transgress the rigid gender boundary that cut women off from public ministry.

Black women's work outside the home—or more accurately, outside their own homes, in the homes of others—created for them a more fluid relationship between the public and private spheres, which disrupted the demands of the dominant domestic ideology that sought to confine women to their own homes to care for their own children and their own husbands. African American women's movement between their own homes and those of their employers was another kind of serial domesticity and perhaps provided a familiar pattern for the radical spiritual mothers to draw upon when embarking upon their itinerant preaching missions.

It was a particularly daring choice for a woman, especially a black woman, to declare her intentions to pursue a life of public ministry during a time when the home was deemed the proper sphere for woman's work. When she believed herself to be divinely called to embark upon such work, Elaw already had one child, and a husband who strongly objected to her chosen course. Following her sanctification at a camp meeting, Elaw does not immediately begin traveling outside of the city in which she lives (Burlington, New Jersey) to preach the gospel. She instead engages in a five-year period of service to those in need in her community. It is a period in her life that she tellingly describes as her "family or household ministry" (71). Not only does this important work enable Elaw to transition into a full-fledged career of public ministry, but her calling this mission a "family or household ministry" seems to allow her a psychological connection to a role with which she was already intimately familiar—that of a woman in charge of her own household. Becoming a public religious leader meant fundamentally reformulating her relationship to power, and it seems that a necessary part of that reformulation meant "domesticating" that power in order to justify to herself and to others the new authority she was garnering.

Zilpha Elaw began her itinerant preaching career in Philadelphia in 1827 and worked her way throughout New York State. In 1828 she made a daring trip to the slave states, preaching in cities such as Annapolis and Baltimore, Maryland, Washington, D.C., and Alexandria, Virginia. She again visited the southern states in 1839. During this same year, Elaw met African Methodist Episcopal preacher Jarena Lee in western Pennsylvania. The two women formed a powerful preaching duo until Elaw was led to pursue a different venue of evangelism. Elaw also preached in the northeastern and middle Atlantic states, and in 1840, crossed the ocean to proselytize in London and central England. Though a member of a Methodist Episcopal Society, Elaw was never granted a license to preach, but rather relied on the promptings of her inner voice to guide her in her evangelistic pursuits. She recorded her experiences in a spiritual autobiography, published in 1846.

During her travels, as Elaw "inhabits" houses of God or private homes where prayer meetings are held, she typically describes her ability to attract large crowds and the strong impact that her messages have upon her audiences. Within these homes, she represents herself as being clearly in charge of her church family, thus subverting patriarchal expectations of authority. She explains that during services in which she presides, it was not unusual for her to have to pause in order to allow listeners who are deeply moved to express their emotions. One way that she seems to justify her authority is to suggest that within God's house, there is room for variation, including such displays of emotion. Deviations from the expected order and manner of worship are even desirable—if they demonstrate evidence of God's power:

> [H]ad it not been for some...instances, in which the Almighty displayed the wonders of his victorious grace, even though the accustomed proprieties and regularity of divine service were at the time abruptly trenched upon and suspended, there are many churches now lively and flourishing, which, notwithstanding the exactness of the order of their worship, and the beauty of their arrangements, would now be but little more than so many religious automata. (107)

In other words, it is acceptable to occasionally "shake things up" in God's house in order to breathe spiritual life into His family. Elaw perhaps envisions herself as part of this productive chaos, a part that is capable of incorporating alternative models of religious leadership within the church, specifically that of women. She thus implicitly creates a space for herself as one who possesses legitimate spiritual authority.

The houses of God that Elaw inhabits transcend the confines of church buildings to encompass camp meetings, where domesticity and publicity are symbolically linked. It is within the contexts of American camp meetings that Elaw is able to envision God's kingdom on earth: "Oh, how I should like our dear English friends to witness some of our delightful camp-meetings, which are held in the groves of the United States....[T]here all arise and sing the solemn praises of the King of majesty and glory. It is like heaven descended upon earthly soil...." (64). Perhaps for Elaw, God's heavenly kingdom represents the ultimate domestic sphere, one which is truly liberating in its promise of equality and inclusivity. She certainly would have been familiar with the Bible scripture, John 14:2, in which Jesus describes for his disciples the kingdom of heaven in domestic terms: "In my Father's house are many rooms." Not only does Elaw feel it imperative to have a place prepared for her in heaven in God's house, but she also demands exalted spaces on earth; she desires places where she is recognized and respected for her spiritual gifts, places where her leadership is validated. Camp meetings provide such venues for her, as well as enable her to reconceptualize her relationship to the earthly domestic sphere. These meetings are particularly significant for her because it is during such gatherings that she is sanctified, that she begins her public ministry, and when she witnesses her own daughter's conversion.

Camp meetings were a revivalist tool used mainly by Methodists and Baptists as a means of accomplishing religious conversions on a large scale. In particular, these denominations targeted white southern plain-folk, a term used to describe the masses of antebellum southern farmers and townspeople who were neither wealthy nor impoverished. This group made up the greatest number of antebellum southerners and provided Methodists and Baptists with their most energetic leadership (Dickson 4, 5).

At one such gathering, Elaw precipitates her own daughter's religious conversion; as Elaw addresses the crowd, her daughter is inspired by the scripture that her mother expounds: "'Oh, Lord! have mercy upon me, for I can hold out no longer. Oh, Lord! have mercy upon me'" (103). In this dramatic moment, Elaw's relationship with her daughter is transformed: Her biological daughter has now become her spiritual child, thus joining the countless other spiritual children that the preacher has acquired since redefining her identity as a religious leader. The secondary role that biological parenting has taken to spiritual parenting seems to be even further diminished by this transformation of the relationship. Indeed, Elaw does not even attend to her child during this emotional time, but instead leaves her in the hands of friends. The fact that Elaw never names her daughter in her text seems to further undermine the status of the biological mother-daughter relationship and places the girl more firmly within the ranks of the preacher's spiritual children.

As Elaw describes the conversion experience, she declares that it "occurred in the midst of listening hundreds, and it produced a most thrilling sensation upon the congregation..." (103). It is as if the author wants her readers to know that the new relationship that she has precipitated with her daughter received mass approbation by the onlooking crowd. This implied mass approval coupled with the fact that there are people willing to step in and attend to her child where it would have been appropriate for Elaw herself to care for her, would doubtless be quite affirming for a woman daring to live out such an unconventional calling.

Elaw goes on to assert that "[m]any a mother strongly felt with me on that occasion..." (103). The author thus successfully redefines maternity in a self-empowering manner, and at the same time exploits the symbolic power of biological motherhood, garnering the support of many other (conventional) women.

Zilpha Elaw and other nineteenth-century African American preaching women can all be considered a part of what Marilyn Richardson describes as "a black female tradition of activism founded on a commitment to religious faith, human rights, and women's struggles."[6] These radical spiritual mothers posited authentic, powerful alternative models of womanhood as they carried out the important work for which they had been divinely appointed. In a similar fashion as Harriet Tubman, once Elaw attained her own liberation, she heeded the calling to shepherd others along in their individual pursuits of freedom. Both Elaw and Tubman made difficult choices in following the paths along which they believed they were divinely led. Some might argue that they were merely sacralizing their desires for an unconventional way of life. To "break up housekeeping" in order to travel and preach the gospel was, to their fiercest critics, potentially threatening to the established order of patriarchal authority. However, did these women really have a choice? Fellow preacher Jarena Lee's descent into "a state of general debility" (40) when she tried to repress her spiritual gifts while she was married seems to suggest that they were truly preaching for their lives. Perhaps what these women ultimately contribute through their womanist[7] narratives of vision and empowerment is a textual witness to the indefatigability of the human spirit when charged with a sense of calling of the highest order.

Notes

1   Others such as Jarena Lee, Julia Foote, Amanda Smith, and Rebecca Jackson.

2   The domestic ideology referred to is the "cult of true womanhood." This set of ideals governing women's behavior applied, of course, specifically to middle-class white women. However, it was nonetheless the standard to which Elaw and other African American women adhered before their experiences of sanctification. According to Barbara Welter, in order to be considered a "true woman," one must manifest the four cardinal virtues of piety, purity, submissiveness, and domesticity. Ideally, a woman should be weak, timid, and clingingly dependent. To accept the roles of wife and mother was a woman's sacred duty; within these roles she was to be a source of comfort and a beacon of morality for her family and for the American culture at large. Faithfully adhering to the ideals of the cult of true womanhood supposedly assured women the respect and protection of men, as well as power within the confines of their homes. See "The Cult of True Womanhood: 1800–1860" in Welter's *Dimity Convictions: The American Woman in the Nineteenth Century* (Athens: Ohio UP, 1976) 21–41.

3   Rebecca Cox Jackson took this practice a step further by insisting upon celibacy within her marriage. See *Gifts of Power: The Writings of Rebecca Jackson, Black Visionary, Shaker Eldress.* Ed. Jean McMahon Humez (Amherst: The U of Massachusetts P, 1981), 147.

4   Zilpha Elaw, *Memoirs of the Life, Religious Experience, Ministerial Travels and Labours of Mrs. Zilpha Elaw, an American Female of Colour; Together with Some Account of the Great Religious Revivals in America [Written by Herself]* (London, 1846). Reprinted in William L. Andrews, *Sisters of the Spirit* 53. Hereafter to be cited parenthetically.

5   Of the probable influence that the condition of slavery had upon some black women's preferences for celibacy, Harryette Mullen comments, "The chastity of women like Sojourner Truth, Harriet Tubman, Jarena Lee, Zilpha Elaw, and Julia Foote often appears to be a response to the physical and sexual abuse of their and other black women's bodies in slavery or in indentured servitude, particularly because spiritual celibacy is not an indigenous tradition of pan-African cultures, which tend to honor fertility and celebrate the body's ability to create life. Nor is celibacy a component of virtually any of the Protestant religions that attracted African Americans in the eighteenth and nineteenth centuries, although Jean Humez suggests that Rebecca Cox Jackson was probably attracted to the Shaker religion in part because of its rule of celibacy as well as its emphasis on gender equality and women's leadership." See Mullen's "'Indelicate Subjects': African-American Women's Subjugated Subjectivity," *Sub/versions* (Winter 1991) 2.

6   Marilyn Richardson, "Foreword," *Sisters of the Spirit*, viii.

7   I borrow Alice Walker's term for black feminism, as defined in *In Search of Our Mother's Gardens* (San Diego: Harcourt Brace Jovanovich, 1983) xi.

Works Cited

Andrews, William, ed. *Sisters of the Spirit: Three Black Women's Autobiographies of the Nineteenth Century.* Bloomington: Indiana UP, 1986.

Dickson, Bruce D., Jr. *And They All Sang Hallelujah: Plain-Folk Camp-Meeting Religion, 1800–1845.* Knoxville: U of Tennessee P, 1974.

The Holy Bible. Revised Standard Version. Dallas: Melton Book Company, 1971.

Elaw, Zilpha. *Memoirs of the Life, Religious Experience, Ministerial Travels and Labours of Mrs. Zilpha Elaw, an American Female of Colour; Together with Some Account of the Great Religious Revivals in America [Written by Herself].* 1846. Reprinted in William L. Andrews, ed. *Sisters of the Spirit: Three Black Women's Autobiographies of the Nineteenth Century.* Bloomington: Indiana UP, 1986.

Humez, Jean McMahon. *Gilfts of Power: The Writing of Rebecca Cox Jackson, Black Visionary, Shaker Eldress.* Amherst: The U of Massachusetts P, 1981.

Lee, Jarena. *The Life and Religious Experience of Jarena Lee, a Coloured Lady, Giving an Account of Her Call to Preach the Gospel. Revised and Corrected from the Original Manuscript, Written by Herself.* 1836. Reprinted in William L. Andrews, ed. *Sisters of the Spirit: Three Black Women's Autobiographies of the Nineteenth Century.* Bloomington: Indiana UP, 1986.

Lindström, Harald. *Wesley and Sanctification.* London: Epworth, 1950.

Mannard, Joseph G. "Maternity...of Spirit: Nuns and Domesticity in Antebellum America." *History of Women in the United States: Historical Articles on Women's Lives and Activities.* Vol. 13. Ed. Nancy F. Cott. Munich: K. G. Saur, 1993. 74–93.

Mullen, Harryette. "'Indelicate Subjects': African-American Women's Subjugated Subjectivity." *Sub/versions.* Winter 1991: 1–7.

Sterling, Dorothy, ed. *We Are Your Sisters: Black Women in the Nineteenth Century.* New York: W. W. Norton, 1984.

Walker, Alice. *In Search of Our Mothers' Gardens.* San Diego: Harcourt, Brace Jovanovich, 1983.

Welter, Barbara. *Dimity Convictions: The American Woman in the Nineteenth Century.* Athens: Ohio UP, 1976.

Chapter Nine

Women's Travel Writing and the Politics of Location
Somewhere In-Between

Heidi Slettedahl Macpherson

At first our trail was intricate so that we would elude discovery, and then it was intricate because we had no particular reason to go to one town rather than another, and no particular reason to stay anywhere, or to leave.
—Marilynne Robinson, *Housekeeping*

It is no coincidence that women's fictional narratives of discovery use and reuse the metaphors of travel against stasis: *Fear of Flying, Heading West, Anywhere but Here*. While women have been cast as the ones left behind in male narratives of adventure and quest, assuming the roles of patient Penelope or, at best, the quiet muse, they have leading roles in women's narratives of discovery, travel, and escape. In women's travel narratives, men are omitted, incidental, occasionally harmful or helpful, but, almost always, secondary. In this way, women's travel narratives rework canonical formations, which inscribe the male as adventurer or quester, and the female as the one who is left behind.

It has become a cultural commonplace that women's journeys are circular, not linear; determined, like their lives, by seasons and cycles, not destinations or goals. Such a reconceptualization of women's "essential nature" is both liberating and also constricting, in that some aspects of women's lives are revalued as a result of feminist interrogations of psychoanalytic or cultural structures. The focus on a circular structure validates a form of journey that does not conform to the Oedipus complex (a pathway that equates progress and maturation with linearity), but instead exists in a preoedipal state, linked to the maternal and the feminine. At the same time, however, such essentializing places women as firmly as have other totalizing narratives. As

Mary Morris reflects, "I find it revealing that the bindings in women's corsets were called *stays*. Someone who wore stays wouldn't be going very far" (25, original emphasis). If women's clothing has historically acted as a metaphor for women's bounded behavior, it is not surprising, as Lindsey Tucker notes, that "[t]o conceive of women and mobility in the same space has been difficult in historical as well as literary terms" (1). Furthermore these overriding structures point away from cultural specificity, and do not acknowledge the matrices of race and class that inflect and infect women's lives as much as gender does.

For African American womanist authors, migration resonates strongly with slavery, escape, and the black diaspora. In Toni Morrison's *Song of Solomon*, the myth of slaves who flew to Africa informs the text at every level, and one particular flying slave, a man named either Shalimar or Solomon, provides a late narrative focus: "He had a slew of children, all over the place...he disappeared and left everybody. Wife, everybody, including some twenty-one children'" (Morrison *Song* 322). The storyteller who reveals Solomon's flight suggests that his wife, who went crazy with grief soon after his departure, was actually mourning not the loss of his love, but the loss of his help with the children.

The knowledge of flight gives the main character Milkman Dead impetus to try flight himself. He is thrilled that flight is part of his family history: "That tribe. That motherfuckin tribe. Oh man! He didn't need no airport. He just took off; got fed up. *All the way up!* No more cotton! No more bales! No more orders! No more shit! He flew, baby. Lifted his beautiful black ass up in the sky and flew on home'" (Morrison *Song* 328, original emphasis).

In Morrison's novel, the male is allowed flight—from responsibility, from family, from slavery—but the female remains bound to earth. Even the one female character who can fly in the novel remains rooted to the ground and family (though she is allowed geographical movement early on). Perhaps the message, "If you surrendered to the air, you could *ride* it" (Morrison 337, original emphasis), is easier for the male to follow. Morrison appears to confirm some representations of women as bounded; in her 1973 novel *Sula*, travel and, therefore escape, remain unnarrated in order perhaps to suggest their futility. It is staying that is narrated, return that is commented upon. Travel is associated with losing one's position, with not knowing the protocol, with being viewed, gazed at, destroyed. Despite the title of the book, the heart of the novel is not Sula, but Medallion, Sula's hometown, and the focus is not on the one who went away, but on the place from which one would attempt to flee. Novels in which women are placed and remain placed are hardly rare; they are referred to here in order to set into relief those mobile women who do travel.

Twentieth-century women's writing acts as a forum for fantastical as well as realistic depictions of women's movement, and travel writing in particular sites the feminine as a space where traversing can occur. Karen Lawrence argues that "[t]ravel writing reveals a set of alternative myths or models for women's place in society" (xi), and it is for this reason that fictional narratives of movement can be set alongside "real" travel narratives. The juxtaposition of fiction and fact—a juxtaposition that occurs in every written text—allows for an interrogation into the ways in which female movement is depicted.

Theorists endlessly debate the relationship between literature and "real life," with readings ranging from the naive "mirror of reality" position to the poststructuralist stance that meaning is endlessly deferred, and that literature is at best a self-reflexive exercise in love with its own form. Where, in this discussion, can one place fictional travel narratives? The answer—somewhere in between—mirrors the position of female protagonists in fictional journeys that do not conform to linear patterns of quest and control. Narratives of travel are ultimately linked to societal reality even as their fictional destinations resist full transcription into the real. Indeed, how could it be otherwise? To travel is to invent not only the destination, but also the traveler, as identity becomes a performance that tailors itself to whatever audience it encounters. As George Robertson argues, the desire to travel denotes "the quest for the acquisition of knowledge and a desire to return to a utopian space of freedom...Psychic desires are displaced in partial and vicarious participation in another set of relations...and the self becomes realized as the hero of its own narrative of departure and return" (Robertson et al. 5).

The self as hero, however, is a problematic metaphor that discounts the feminine and indeed envisions ultimate linearity, with return as the posited goal. However, what happens when return is impossible, when travel equates with evasion and escape? Bharati Mukherjee's variously named heroine in *Jasmine* has only one goal: "to be allowed to land; to pass through; to continue" (101), and she asserts that the "zigzag route is straightest" (101). For Jasmine, travel is less a choice than a necessity, and nonlinearity, far from being (as is often asserted) an offshoot of female psychology, is instead a political necessity. The politics of location/locating/being located are wrapped up in the problematics of border crossing: done at night, illegally, at a cost that may appear too high.

For Marilynne Robinson's protagonists in *Housekeeping*, travel is also to a certain extent a reaction to the forces of law. When transient Sylvie Fisher undertakes the fostering of her niece Ruth, she teaches the adolescent the pleasures of drifting, as well as its consequences: "So every wanderer whose presence suggested it might be as well to drift, or it could not matter much, was met with something that seemed at first sight a moral reaction, since morality is a check upon the strongest temptations" (178). Small-town society reacts badly to the pair's transience and attempts to prize them apart, necessitating a final escape that is read as . It is gender, rather than race, which determines the boundaries of legal behavior here.

For Avey Johnson, Paule Marshall's protagonist in *Praisesong for the Widow*, travel is initially a hermetically sealed experience. A cruise ship bears her toward Caribbean Islands to which she assumes no loyalty. She wraps her middle-class status about her like a cloak, fending off racial allegiances that disturb her carefully maintained distance. It is only when she is "quietly and deftly stripped" of her conditioned responses, "as if they were so many layers of winter clothing she had mistakenly put on for the excursion" (197), that Avey is able to comprehend that real travel is not a package holiday, but a spiritual experience that necessitates connection rather than distance.

What these fictional travel narratives have in common is a sense that femaleness is a condition which impinges upon—even determines—the travel experience. Each displays a postmodern sensibility, where identity is a performance, which is fluid, not fixed. This is, of course, intimately bound up in travel itself. As Trinh T. Minh-ha suggests, "If travelling perpetuates a discontinuous state of being, it also satisfies, despite the existential difficulties it entails, one's insatiable need for detours and displacements in postmodern culture" (21).

In her book *Penelope Voyages*, Karen Lawrence examines the "imaginative and conceptual appeal of movement and border crossings" while also "retain[ing] crucial distinctions within what feminist and postcolonial critics have called 'the politics of location'" (xi). Following Lawrence and other feminist critics in reworking the binaries implicit in definitions, which link women and containment, and which deny them mobility and movement, this chapter examines the fictional side of travel narratives, linking gender and location in a dialectical relationship. Travel is/acts as postmodern critique, and the discussion of fluid identity will revolve around *Housekeeping, Jasmine,* and *Praisesong for the Widow.* Of the fictional protagonists examined here only one—Avey Johnson—is a "tourist," and even she leaves behind the tourist persona, finding a falsity about the role that must be stripped bare (and so she is). Jasmine is an illegal immigrant; Ruthie and Sylvie are hoboes. All travel for different purposes, but for all, travel is or becomes a political—if not politicized—necessity. In traveling through spaces, they travel through identity, fixing on markers only temporarily, and sometimes not at all. The metaphor of space thus becomes, in Kathleen Kirby's words,

> a medium for articulating—speaking and intertwining—the many facets, or phases, of subjectivity that have interested different kinds of theory: national origin, geographic and territorial mobility (determined by class, gender, and race), bodily presence and limits, structures of consciousness, and ideological formations of belonging and exclusion." (174)

The subjectivity of the fictional female traveler necessarily alters when she is a hobo, an immigrant, or a tourist, and the space she occupies—or travels through—is infused with gendered meaning.

Hobo, Not Hero: Travel as Vagrancy

Tucker argues that women writers utilize material that suggests mobility and fluidity, because such material counteracts the stasis of Woman-as-Image (10). Nowhere is this clearer than in Marilynne Robinson's *Housekeeping,* a novel about female hoboes which invokes hoboing lore and sites the feminine as a space outside the logical and linear lines of patriarchy. The novel itself barely delineates hoboing except in narrated tales of lost women, or in the final few pages, which are left only half narrated. The majority of the book is reserved for the gentle loosening of ties to housekeeping and respectability, yet this does little to dent its status as a travel narrative, for these fictional women are traveling away from domesticity and into the unknown. In addition, what hoboing is recalled is key to the plot, and the drifting lyricism of the text mimics the drifting of the primary characters. When Ruthie and her transient aunt Sylvie finally do leave Fingerbone, there is no real surprise because they have been cast as hoboes from the start: They encounter and speak about hoboes; they find themselves pursued by dogs who mark the boundaries of enclosed domesticity; they wander in opposition to Ruthie's sister Lucille, a model of fixity and orderly stasis.

Ruthie notes that "transients wandered through Fingerbone like ghosts, terrifying as ghosts are because they were not very different from us" (178). The ghost imagery is apt, given Ruthie's eventual assumed fate of death. Indeed, it is a recurring image, for the link between ghosts and transients is firmly established throughout. At one point, Ruthie suggests that "their lives as drifters were like pacings and broodings and skirmishings among ghosts who cannot pay their way across the Styx" (179). Moreover, most of the transient women have stories of seeing ghostly, hungry children, and Sylvie herself also makes plans to encounter such children. In addition, Ruthie's own description of herself becomes spectral: "I would be a ghost, and their food would not answer to my hunger, and my hands could pass through their down quilts and tatted pillow covers and never feel them or find comfort in them. Like a soul released, I would find here only the images and simulacra of the things needed to sustain me" (183). As ghost or transient, Ruthie has no need for domesticity; she therefore becomes an unsettling force for the women of Fingerbone who have "a desire, a determination, to keep [her], so to speak, safely within doors" (183).

Feminists have long seen wandering women as transgressive characters, the choice to move signaling their resistance to structures that would limit them. In the 1981 book *Archetypal Patterns in Women's Fiction*, Annis Pratt et al, for example, argue that "Women heroes turn away from a culture hostile to their development, entering a timeless achronological world appropriate to their rejection by history, a spaceless world appropriate to rebellion against placelessness in the patriarchy" (169). Ruthie and Sylvie enter this world fully when they give up claims to housekeeping. That their success in shedding domesticity is read as death by the townspeople they have left behind is unsurprising, for they have "crossed to the other side" when they make their perilous journey across a railway bridge. They travel as nomads, hoboes, drifters, and few details accompany them. Ruthie reports that "[t]ownspeople began searching at dawn for the bodies, but we were never found, never found, and the search was at last abandoned" (Robinson 213). Seeking always containment, the townspeople desire the retrieval of dead female bodies in order to fully campaign against transience. The lake, which has putatively swallowed them (and which has dramatically swallowed other travelers in the past), remains a powerful symbol of unconscious desire and the quagmire of repressed emotions. Ruthie and Sylvie's traveling is denied because Fingerbone cannot travel, will not move outside the bounded, transcribed circles of piety and limited prosperity.

Barry Curtis and Claire Pajaczkowska contend that travelers frequently appear to take up the position of "structuralists, necessarily binarized, engaged in an outsiderly process of judgement and comparison" (201). In this fictional tale, it is the travelers themselves who are judged; they are the barriers against which the townspeople define their own respectable stasis. Afraid of the freedom of movement, the townspeople instead instill the notion that "diaspora threatened always" (Robinson 178).

Traveling outside of all conventions is impossible even fictionally, and it is ironically appropriate that when Ruthie and Sylvie do attempt temporary stasis, they "see all the movies" (Robinson 214). They consume culture, read the scripted stories, and finally remind themselves why they cannot fit the parts and must move on again. They do not travel ever westward, however, in search of some frontier space, nor do they travel across great spaces. Rather, they circle, they drift, they wander. Ellen Friedman argues that the "nomad who seeks sanctuary in the interstices of culture and replaces Oedipus as the protagonist of culture and the unconscious" is a "liberating figure" (244), and it appears that Robinson concurs. The nomad must necessarily be the opposite of the tied and domesticated woman; she fills a space in-between, for she is neither the adventurer who sets out on a quest and expects to return and share enlightenment, nor is she the heroine of a domestic novel who stays and is rewarded for her immobility with love, prosperity, and maternity. Lawrence argues that "the female traveler's particular baggage includes the historical link between female wandering and promiscuity" (16, note 18). Robinson successfully fights this connection by omitting sexuality altogether, gliding over the historical problems of women hoboes in her fictionalized account of women who wander. Robinson's fictional hobo narrative is in no way a glorified account of the peripatetic life, however. When Sylvie comments, "'It's not the worst thing, Ruthie, drifting. You'll see. You'll see'" (Robinson 210), she acknowledges the losses inherent in any unstable position; moreover, their leave-taking is as much a "casting out" as it is a chosen trajectory. Indeed, Ruthie's narrative is one in which loss is uncomfortable, but chronic, as she freely admits: "Memory is the sense of loss, and loss pulls us after it" (Robinson 194).

Lawrence asks, "Can women writers revise the various plots of wandering (in romance, adventure, exploration, and travel narratives) without succumbing to the traditional pitfalls of these plots for a female protagonist?" (17). Without providing an answer, she comments, "Such a question intersects feminist concerns about whether women will 'get caught' in their own imitation of patriarchal discourse and myth, unable to repeat with a difference" (Lawrence 17). The answer, for Robinson, is that the wandering plots can well be rewritten. The female hobo can be the heroine of a new plot which, far from replicating past patterns, asserts new ones. Robinson explores the preoedipal space of transient subjectivity, and asserts a nonlinear journey that retains value despite the cultural void it seems to suggest. Despite this optimistic assessment, however, there is a sense that the traveler must always leave someone behind. Even in Robinson's novel, the figure of the passive, waiting woman remains, if only as a fantasy projection. At the end of the novel, Ruthie comments that

> [h]owever Lucille may look, she will never find us there, or any trace or sign. We pause nowhere in Boston, even to admire a store window, and the perimeters of our wandering are nowhere. No one watching this woman smear her initials in the steam on her water glass with her first finger, or slip cellophane packets of oyster crackers into her handbag for the sea gulls, could know how her thoughts are thronged by our absence, or know how she does not watch, does not listen, does not wait, does not hope, and always for me and Sylvie. (Robinson 218–19)

Lucille, the waiting woman who may be no more than Ruthie's recollection of loss, is still inscribed in a position of passivity, reminding us, perhaps, that in any narratives of travel, there is always someone left behind.

Illegal Moves: Travel as Cultural Shift

In Bharati Mukherjee's novel *Jasmine*, deciphering who is left behind is even more complicated, because the novel consists of a series of shed identities. The narrator of *Jasmine*, alternatively named Jyoti, Jasmine, Jase, or Jane, argues that "[t]here are no harmless, compassionate ways to remake oneself. We murder who we were so we can rebirth ourselves in the images of dreams" (Mukherjee 29). The novel has been fiercely critiqued as a sop to the American Dream, and in this way, it appears initially that Lawrence's question—are women able to rewrite traditional plots like this?—can only be answered in the negative; this novel of flight depends on constructions of romance, love, the saving hero, and a westward trajectory which may or may not be ironic. Is Mukherjee able to repeat with a difference? Certainly it is a problematic novel, but to ignore Mukherjee's exploration of ethnicity and identity, because she writes a novel of assimilation, is to fall into the cultural trap whereby one can only critique what one does not ideologically oppose.

Travel, for the illegal immigrant, implies movement which is dangerous both culturally and individually: "We are the outcasts and deportees, strange pilgrims visiting outlandish shrines, landing at end of tarmacs....We are dressed in shreds of national costumes, out of season, the wilted plumage of intercontinental vagabondage. We ask only one thing: to be allowed to land; to pass through; to continue" (Mukherjee 101). Further revealing that for transients like her, "The zigzag route is straightest" (Mukherjee 101), Jasmine records the necessity, rather than the luxury, of travel.

Rockwell Gray reminds us that "[t]o travel is to move through differing geographical and cultural realms of multidetermined meaning" (36–37). Jasmine, in this sense, is the ultimate traveler, for she discards old identities as easily as past lovers, and hers is the ultimate multidetermined character. Critics have variously assigned positive or negative roles to Jasmine's "protean" nature. For critics who dislike Mukherjee's assimilation politics, *Jasmine* is nothing more than a "sort of pop multiculturalist prop" (Carter-Sanborn 575) that trades on exoticism. When Jill Roberts argues Mukherjee is commenting on the "plight of the illegal immigrant in America whose only option is to embrace the freedom of their homelessness in the absence of a safe, affirming cultural context" (92), her choice of words indicates the negative associations she carries: "plight," "absence," "only option." The immigrant has little real choice in this paradigm. Other critics disapprove of Jasmine's reliance on male intervention for identity-shifting, and Kristin Carter-Sanborn goes so far as to suggest that Jasmine is merely a passive receptacle of male violence and not an agent of change herself (580).

Alternatively, Carmen Wickramagamage contends that Jasmine alters her position, because she understands the provisionality of any subject-location and its *"man*-made" functions (174, original emphasis). Linking, as Jill Roberts does, the provisionality of identity to the tenets of Hinduism (174), Wickramagamage sees Mukherjee's aim as a positive integration of Eastern religion with western postmodern cultural critique.

The character Jasmine herself insists that "extraordinary events can jar the needle arm, jump tracks, rip across incarnations, and deposit a life into a groove that was not prepared to receive it" (Mukherjee 127). Extraordinary events do indeed determine Jasmine's trajectory and move her from rural India, to urban India, to the United States, and across the entire American landscape. Travel is at first a goal her husband Prakash has, and Jasmine assumes the role of supportive Indian wife. Asked what she thinks of America, she muses, "I didn't know what to think of America. I'd read only *Shane*, and seen only one movie. It was too big a country, too complicated a question. I said, 'If you're there, I'll manage. When you're at work in America, I'll stay inside'" (Mukherjee 81). Despite her intention to remain domesticated and indoors, Jasmine allows her husband's goal to become hers: "'If you want me to have a real life, I want it, too'" (Mukherjee 81). While she characterizes the United States as a site of the "real," her experience of America comes through others' depictions and others' desires, and even through propaganda on aerograms: "CELEBRATE AMERICA, the American postal service commanded. TRAVEL...THE PERFECT FREEDOM'" (Mukherjee 83, ellipsis in original). These aerograms can be sent by anyone (in America) to anyone (outside of America); they promote the myth of the welcoming shores precisely because they erase ethnicity; "America" as a construct can be consumed by anyone. If this America is unethnicized, other versions are explicit in inscribing ethnicity. Perusing an American university brochure for "international students," Jasmine notes, "For the first time in my life I was looking at familiar Indian faces and seeing them as strange" (Mukherjee 92); even the thought of travel changes her perceptions of her homeland.

When her husband is murdered, Jasmine decides to fulfill his dream anyway, and travels—illegally—to the United States, commenting derisively on tourists who seek migration as "adventure" (Mukherjee 102). Her aim is to commit suttee, thereby fulfilling her cultural role as Indian widow. To do so, however, would be to slip back into the role of Jyoti, her first incarnation, and Jasmine instead begins a series of reinventions in the United States; each place she travels to produces a new identity. Through this process of relocation, Jasmine comes to represent postmodern fluid identity, though she is never able to rid herself of the label of exoticism that her visible ethnic heritage engenders in the minds of her American companions. As Carter-Sanborn contends, "To act, for Jasmine, is to become entirely other" (582), suggesting that Jasmine herself embraces her Otherness. Implicitly in Carter-Sanborn's critique, as in others, becoming Other equates with loss and mutilation. It is pertinent, therefore, to examine Jasmine's perspective. The only time that she lives entirely among people from her homeland, she discovers that they are only able to teach her "about surviving as an Indian in New York" (Mukherjee 162). In fact, "They let nothing go, lest everything be lost" (Mukherjee 162). This assertion of culture as a dam against American influence is not a possible narrative for Jasmine, as it does not allow for move-ment, travel, or (in her eyes), growth. Wickramagamage argues, "If unstable heterogeneity is a fact of life, while stable identity is an illu-sion, then to perceive immigration as dislocation and loss is to sup-press the possibility of an advantageous interaction with one's new location" (189). As if to concur, the dust jacket to the 1990 British Virago edition of the novel declares, "Jasmine's passage through America, rippling with energy and daring, reflects Mukherjee's pre-occupation with the fractured lives of exiles and immigrants caught up in a painful yet exhilarating cross-cultural metamorphosis...." If Robinson's vision of America is that of stifling communities which must be resisted, and even traveled away from, Mukherjee's vision appears to embrace assimilation into these very communities, and her journey moves her ever closer to the "heartland" of America, as well as the center of familial forces.

Jasmine moves from "day mummy" of the adopted Duff in New York, to adoptive mother of a Vietnamese refugee, to mother-to-be in rural Iowa. Curtis and Pajaczkowska argue that, in opposition to the tourist who travels "backwards in time," the "immigrant, the exile and the diasporic" move "with no promise of a restored home" (202–3). Clearly Jasmine is never "restored" to home, but she does embrace "rehousement" which, for Mukherjee, is the "'re-rooting of oneself in a new culture'" (Hancock, qtd. in Wickramagamage 199). It is no co-incidence that this rooting takes place in the rural Midwest. Even when Jasmine denies the importance of location, arguing that her flight to Iowa could just as easily have been to Kansas (she chooses Iowa because that is where her young charge Duff was born), the en-visioned locale is still the Midwest, and this points to the nature of Jasmine's flight: She is midway to her goal, and even maternity will not close down her options. However, in contrast to most narratives of maternity that root and circumscribe the female, Jasmine allows mothers to leave, to flee, to travel. Jasmine is located between rooted-ness and adaptability; she uses versions of both words to describe her relationship with the various locations she occupies. More impor-tantly, she argues, "The world is divided between those who stay and those who leave" (Mukherjee 228). Jane Ripplemeyer, the significantly non-Eastern name she adopts in the Midwest, may be someone who stays; after all, she usurped the position and the name of the first Mrs. Ripplemeyer, Karin, a woman who "never got to travel" (Mukherjee 204). However, Jasmine is only Jane temporarily, and "[a]dventure, risk, transformation"—not to mention "the frontier"—call to her, "pushing indoors through uncaulked windows" (Mukherjee 240). The final lines of the novel see the traveler Jasmine taking flight again: "I am out the door and in the potholed and rutted driveway, scrambling ahead…greedy with wants and reckless from hope" (Mukherjee 241).

The last vision of Jasmine, then, is one of flight, as she and her lover head west; the frontier is invoked and challenged, as this East-ern immigrant retraces the steps of former migrants. If the traveler is, in Michael Kowalewski's words, "the reader's surrogate, a cultural outsider who moves into, through, and finally beyond the places and events encountered" (9), then it is ironically appropriate that the Americanized non-American takes center stage in this narrative of travel across the United States.

Trading in Tourism: Travel as Spiritual Reconnection

Paule Marshall's *Praisesong for the Widow*, in contrast to both novels above, is not sited in the United States except in retrospect. Avey Johnson is a tourist aboard a cruise ship to the Caribbean, and despite the fact that her intention is to leave the ship and return to the United States early, the trajectory of her travels is away from, rather than to-ward, her birthplace. *Praisesong for the Widow* is a call to home, to the country of origin, and yet for the Caribbean American protagonist, this call is multiple and shifting. When she is asked to "call her na-tion," she is not asked to identify with the United States, but with her Caribbean and African ancestors. Ethnicity is again a central factor in this novel of traveling. Avey is "hailed" as Caribbean, an identity she at first refuses to recognize: "'I'm afraid you've mistaken me for someone from around here, or from one of the other islands…who might know what you're talking about…I'm from the States. New

York...' and she repeated it, 'New York'" (Marshall 168, ellipses in original).

Avey Johnson's travel is more important spiritually than literally, as is indicated by her eventual reflections on Carriacou: "The island more a mirage rather than an actual place. Something conjured up perhaps to satisfy a longing and need" (Marshall 254). On this journey, she has an elderly man named Lebert Johnson as a guide. The name invokes the trickster Legba (Couser 110), but Avey's companion acts beneficently in urging her to reconnect with her ethnic heritage. As a tourist, Avey must insist upon and maintain distance; she is even faintly repulsed by the familiarity of the islanders, and recoils from their assumption of intimacy: "[F]rom the way they were acting she could have been simply one of them there on the wharf" (Marshall 69). As a traveler on an excursion to the island of Carriacou, however, Avey must become re-sited in her body, and allow her body the movement it has long since been denied. Curtis and Pajaczkowska argue that tourism merely confirms identity, whereas traveling involves a voyage of "metamorphosis and transformation, in which the self is changed by the experience of alterity encountered in a dialectic of difference" (206). Avey's tourist persona is shipped from one island to another, but most of her vacation is spent inside. When Avey travels to Carriacou, in contrast, she does so upon a rickety sailboat which pitches left and right with the waves, rather than cutting through them as the cruise ship did. Unsurprisingly, she is violently ill, but even this purging is metaphorically part of her journey: Until she sheds who she is, she cannot reclaim the promise of who she was.

Her journey to Carriacou is, as G. Thomas Couser argues, an "involuntarily initiated quest" (111), but its initial nature does not cancel out the rewards of the journey. Her journey is not so much circular as spiral, in that she moves back into a recognition of her historical and ethnic past, one that embraces both her African and her Caribbean heritage. Indeed, Carole Boyce Davies argues that Avey comes to represent the black diaspora (19). As a Caribbean American, Marshall draws on myths of origin different from African American women writers such as Toni Morrison or Alice Walker, while retaining a sense of connectedness to Africa, too. Eva Lennox Birch argues that the Caribbean experience includes elements of a "self-imposed economic exile from their Caribbean homeland" (88), and Marshall plays with this sense of exile in depicting Avey. As she and her husband move from relaxed and playful partners to business associates, in a sense, they subtly change their names, losing, along the way, connections to their past as they become more and more acclimated to white western capitalism. Indeed, Avey's tourist journey signifies, in Davies's eyes, "a journey into the heart of whiteness" (22). She sees it as "a frivolous journey" which make Avey nothing more than a capitalist tourist, living off her husband's wealth (22). Davies argues that for Avey to recover, she must "make the reverse journey back into the heart of blackness" (23).

This reverse journey, as many critics have commented, mimics the Middle Passage as well as, more optimistically, the "miraculous flight of the Ibos" (Couser 111). According to legend, the Ibos simply walked away from South Carolina and imposed slavery by treading across water to their homeland; Avey learns the story as a child spending summers with her Great Aunt Cuney. The spiral nature of Avey's journey is apparent when she resolves to return to the site of the Ibo Landing, in Tatem, South Carolina, where she spent her youth. Avey thus moves, initially, from the United States in a cruise ship, which is trapped in a circular and regulated pattern; she detours to Grenada, hoping for a nonstop flight back home. However, stop she does; and soon she is taking her second detour: to Carriacou. From here she moves into her past and reconnects with it, so that her proposed journey back home will lead, eventually, to a new home in the old ancestral spot of Tatem. Davies suggests that Avey's journey is "two-pronged" in that she takes one journey into the "black experience" and one into the "female experience" (21). Perhaps the most important lesson that she learns comes to her early: "'Just because we live over this side don' mean we's from this place, you know'" (Marshall 163). In learning to "call her nation," Avey learns to reconnect. Tucker argues that for African American women writers, "mobility remains potent as a metaphor that is always more collective than individual" (11). While Avey's journey is individual, it does resonate with the larger migrations—both enforced and chosen—that her Caribbean heritage implies. Her journey, unlike the journeys of Ruthie, Sylvie, and Jasmine, has an imagined endpoint: She returns. In contrast to the other protagonists' journeys, however, the shape of it depends less on canonical formations and structures than on the needs of her particular narrative.

Karen Lawrence maintains that "the trope of travel—whether in its incarnations as exile or adventure, tourism or exploration—provides a particularly fertile imaginative field for narrative representations of women's historical and personal agency" (20). It is precisely for this reason that women's narratives of travel are such rich sources for explorations of identity and representation. Fictional travel narratives, like their "real" counterparts, provide accounts of difference by exploring the politics of location while simultaneously examining localities. As cultural outsiders, these fictional travelers comment upon the society from which they spring and the societies to which they now belong. Sylvie and Ruthie shrug off conventional domesticity, exploring instead the uncertainties of transience; Jasmine shrugs off a series of identities, and fixates on assimilation, going so far as to direct her journey ever westward; Avey recognizes the need to connect and transform as the result of travel. Clearly, the protagonists in these three fictional travel narratives are positioned somewhere in-between: They resist full transcription into canonical structures while still invoking them to a certain extent; they undertake journeys determined by race and gender; they insist that movement is central to the concerns of women. In becoming wandering women, they point to the socially constructed nature of any prescribed pathway, and they demand that readers re-vision patterns of departure, exile, and return.

Works Cited

Birch, Eva Lennox. *Black American Women's Writing: A Quilt of Many Colours.* Hemel Hempstead: Harvester Wheatsheaf, 1994.

Carter-Sanborn, Kristin. "'We Murder Who We Were': *Jasmine* and the Violence of Identity." *American Literature* 66.3 (1994): 573–93.

Couser, G. Thomas. "Personal and Collective Memory in Paule Marshall's *Praisesong for the Widow* and Leslie Marmon Silko's *Ceremony.*" *Memory and Cultural Politics: New Approaches to American Ethnic Literatures.* Eds. Amritjit Singh et al. Boston: Northeastern UP, 1996. 106–20.

Curtis, Barry, and Claire Pajaczkowska."'Getting There': Travel, Time and Narrative." Eds. Robertson et al. 199–215.

Davies, Carole Boyce. "Black Woman's Journey into Self: A Womanist Reading of Paule Marshall's *Praisesong for the Widow.*" *Matatu: Journal for African Culture and Society* 1.1 (1987): 19–34.

Friedman, Ellen G. "Where Are the Missing Contents? (Post)Modernism, Gender, and the Canon." *PMLA* 108 (1993): 240–52.

Gray, Rockwell. "Travel." Kowalewski 33–50.

Kirby, Kathleen M. "Thinking through the Boundary: The Politics of Location, Subjects, and Space." *Boundary II* 20.2 (1993): 173–89.

Kowalewski, Michael. Introduction: The Modern Literature of Travel. *Temperamental Journeys: Essays on the Modern Literature of Travel* Ed. Michael Kowalewski. Athens: U of Georgia P, 1992. 1–16.

Lawrence, Karen R. *Penelope Voyages: Women and Travel in the British Literary Tradition.* Ithaca: Cornell UP, 1994.

Marshall, Paule. *Praisesong for the Widow.* 1983. London: Virago, 1989.

Minh-ha, Trinh T. "Other than myself/ my other self." Eds. Robertson et al. 9–26.

Morris, Mary. "Women and Journeys: Inner and Outer." *Temperamental Journeys: Essays on the Modern Literature of Travel* Ed. Michael Kowalewski. Athens: U of Georgia P, 1992. 25–32.

Morrison, Toni. *Song of Solomon.* 1977. London: Picador, 1989.

———. *Sula.* 1973. London: Chatto and Windus, 1980.

Mukherjee, Bharati. *Jasmine.* 1989. London: Virago, 1990.

Pratt, Annis, et al. *Archetypal Patterns in Women's Fiction.* 1981. Brighton: Harvester P, 1982.

Roberts, Jill. "Between Two Darknesses: The Adoptive Condition in *Ceremony* and *Jasmine.*" *Modern Language Studies* 25.3 (1995): 77–97.

Robertson, George, et al. *Travellers' Tales: Narratives of Home and Displacement.* London: Routledge, 1994.

Robinson, Marilynne. *Housekeeping.* 1980. London: Faber and Faber, 1991.

Tucker, Lindsey. *Textual Escap(e)ades: Mobility, Maternity, and Textuality in Contemporary Fiction by Women.* Westport: Greenwood, 1994.

Wickramagamage, Carmen. "Relocation as Positive Act: The Immigrant Experience in Bharati Mukherjee's Novels. *Diaspora: A Journal of Transnational Studies* 2.2 (1992): 171–200.

Chapter Ten

The Problem of Narrative Authority
Catherine Oddie and Kate Karko

Corinne Fowler

The study of contemporary travel narratives provides valuable insights into the current existence of imperialist discourse. Because the genre of travel writing evolved from a colonial context, it is crucial not to "depoliticise" travel writing by reading it "outside the colonial space" (Chebwera 8). While it might seem deterministic to suggest, in the manner of Foucault that "we are but the bearers of our discourses" (qtd. in Porter 11), this chapter contends that, to a significant degree, the travel-writing genre confines and prescribes the narratives of Kate Karko and Catherine Oddie. Karko produces a more self-consciously sensitive narrative figure, yet I argue that she cannot outswim the imperial current of the travel-writing genre.

Catherine Oddie is an Australian travel writer whose 1994 *Enkop Ai: My Life with the Maasai* describes her experiences of living with a group of Maasai in Kenya. The book became a bestseller in Australia following a documentary about her marriage to Robert, a Maasai warrior. British travel writer Kate Karko's marriage to a Tibetan nomad, Tsedup, also received media attention following the publication of *Namma: A Tibetan Love Story* (2000), which features a six-month stay with Tsedup's family in Tibet. Each book contains color photographs of the narrators posing with members of their new families often clothed in traditional Maasai or Tibetan dress. In her acknowledgments, Karko expresses indebtedness to Alexandra David-Néel's 1931 *With Mystics and Magicians in Tibet* for "the background on Shamanism and Buddhism" (xii), thereby perpetuating the imperial habit of privileging "the 'west' as the site of the production of...knowledge" about other cultures (McEwan 13). Similarly, Oddie's narrator aligns her gaze with that of Karen Blixen by identifying *Out of Africa* as having "rekindled [her] desire to go" (5) to Kenya, and, later on, naming Beryl Markham as a hero (48). Following the custom of their nineteenth-century predecessors, each writer prefaces her work with professions of humility. This *apologia* masks the fact that, "in literary terms" her power to represent is "absolute" (McEwan 13).

Concentrating upon ways in which Oddie's and Karko's narrators seek the discursive authority to define and explain the lifeways of those they encounter in Kenya and Tibet, I turn to a concept of contemporary relevance: Mary Louise Pratt's notion of the "anti-conquest." The anticonquest, which was a common feature of nineteenth-century travel writing, served to heighten a sense of innocent authorial intent. It was an imperialistic means of dissociating oneself from one's exploitative predecessors. The act of conquest ("invasion") produces guilt that the narrator "eternally tries to escape" and yet "eternally evokes, if only to distance himself from it once again" (57). It is perhaps for this reason that Catherine Oddie's narrator asks: "[D]id I only want an exotic black boyfriend?" (83). Ironically, the only means of stifling the question is through its evocation. By foregrounding this line of inquiry, the narrator implies that its serious consideration constitutes a superficial reading of her motives. Kate Karko's first-person protagonist engages in her own form of anticonquest when discussing her portraits of "photogenic" nomads: "In that respect I knew I was no better than these tourists. But somehow it was different. I was a part of things, and not just objectively pointing a lens at something *beautiful*. I was trying to capture *someone*...whom I respected and loved" (144). Karko's narrator shares an act of conquest (someone's "capture") with an undesirable group, "these tourists." However, in bringing her fear of exploitation to the reader's attention, she dissociates herself from it by emphasizing her personal involvement with Tibetan nomads. In order to achieve this, the narrative perpetuates what James Buzard identifies as an antitouristic binary between the *traveler* (someone genuinely interested in the lives of nomads) and the voyeuristic tourist (who is not) (*The Beaten Track*). The uniqueness of Karko and Oddie's narrative personae is predicated on confounding Paul Fussell's premise that "we are all tourists now and there is no escape" (qtd. in Kaplan 56). Their narratives are antitouristic testimonies of having gone against the grain of commodified mass tourism. Oddie and Karko participate in the scramble for authentic narratives about real, rather than inauthentic, travel experiences. Dean MacCannell identifies six stages in the progression toward authentic travel. The first is the "front region," which "tourists attempt to get behind," while the "sixth region," the "ultimate space that motivates the traveler's imaginary" is an "ideal, uncontaminated back region" (qtd. in Kaplan 60). By way of contrast with her Kenyan experience, Oddie provides an example of an inauthentic experience in Tanzania: "The tour guide lined up the Maasai so we could 'shoot' them. Out of frame, the uglier faces...stood patiently" (165). In this scene, the protagonist claims to see beyond the limits of the "frame" imposed by mass tourism, suggesting an innate ability to access the coveted "sixth region" of authentic experience that lies beyond it. By asserting that there are in fact spaces beyond tourism's reach and available to the true traveler (she writes of the "non-touristic side of Nairobi"), she claims exclusive access to the "uncontaminated back region" when advertising her own brand of "true cultural tourism" (163). She states: "our safari differed from others [because it offered] real exchanges [with the Maasai people]" (163). Karko's narrator celebrates a similar nontouristic space during a solitary ride: "I felt an overwhelming sense of exhilaration and freedom, that I was alone, that I was on this horse, that I was in Tibet. I knew that this image would be forever preserved in my imagination, like a camera shutter closing" (255). At an apparent moment of "pure travel," the narrative rudely interrupts itself with an incongruous image of photography. It is a slip of the most telling kind, an intrusion of what Caren Kaplan calls the "touristic discourse of collecting experiences" (46).

Both narrators make use of a device with which contemporary readers are only too familiar: the inverted comma. It is an established convention to deploy this device in ways that are suggestive of an ability to engage critically with, or to deconstruct, authoritative discourses. Karko frequently places inverted commas around the word *civilized,* which Oddie prefaces with "so-called" (92), and *primitives.* When used in this way, the inverted comma becomes a visual symbol of "escape from ideology" (Kaplan 63), the demonstration of one's critical reading of flawed western concepts. As mentioned above, despite her own flirtation with photography among the Maasai, Oddie's narrator manifests a concern about its exploitative aspect, e.g., "we didn't even have to get out of the bus to 'shoot' them" (165). Here the inverted commas function as a form of anticonquest, dissociating her from the excesses of mass tourism. In fact, the address of Oddie's own safari company (Safaris Unlimited) appears on the back cover under the heading "CONTACT LIST" (242). Consequently, the narrative is tugged in opposite directions: Once again, what MacCannell terms "pure travel" (qtd. in Kaplan 85) implicates itself in the touristic enterprise.

Much of the narrators' authority to describe and explain aspects of Maasai/Tibetan cultures depends upon distinguishing their experience from that of tourists. This is partly accomplished through demonstrating meaningful cross-cultural contact in the anthropological sense—a prolonged stay, an encounter in the field (Clifford). However, different from the traditional anthropologist, the travel writer is unconstrained by disciplinary taboo against going native. For Karko's and Oddie's narrators, therefore, one means of inferring profound (rather than superficial) contact is by asserting that a process of "indigenization" is taking place. Terry Goldie developed his theory of indigenization to describe white settler communities. However, I wish to extend Goldie's concept to incorporate contemporary expressions of desire, particularly the "impossible necessity of becoming indigenous" (13). Karko's first-person protagonist uses a visit by English friends to suggest increasing dislocation from her own culture:

> [Tsedup] looked at me earnestly, with a slight frown. "You Westerners are always measuring the days," he said. I hated being stereotyped...the girls' presence was making me realise a few things about myself...inside me there seemed to be some resistance to the little piece of England that they had brought with them. Things that had been part of my everyday vocabulary in London were now alien to my ear. (171)

The narrator's abhorrence of being indistinguishable among a crowd of "westerners" is clear, and she refutes the notion that she is irredeemably located in British culture by registering increasing alienation from it. Her British identity is thus represented as obsolete, some former life from which she has cast herself adrift. Both texts contain a number of moments where the narrator professes to experience the indigenization of her thoughts. Oddie's protagonist expresses a newfound distaste for writing: "My notebook felt to me like an intrusion and branded me as an outsider...I decided that anything I recorded would have to be with my heart and not my mind" (102), thereby appearing to disavow her situatedness in writing and realign herself with the oral tradition. (This sentiment is unfortunately undermined by its appearance on the printed page.) Claiming affinity with (once alien) cultural practices authorizes both narrators to establish and maintain the illusion of providing "a view from below," by speaking for and about the Maasai/Tibetan nomads (Draymond 567). Furthermore, each book has a foreign word in its title, which immediately establishes authorial supremacy. This authority derives from the writer's implied understanding of the word and the reader's contrasting ignorance. As with an ethnographical text, the narrative "accomplishes its primary strategy to create a problem"—mystification through exposure to the unfamiliar—"which the text itself will then solve" (Richards 221). Catherine Oddie reenters the stage armed with all the "tyranny" of expertise that has come to be associated with the anthropologist (McEwan 13). Indeed, the narrator borrows ethnographic authority by adopting an informative register: "Some explanation is required here about the age group system" (37).

A further expression of cultural embeddedness is what Anne McClintock calls the "voyeuristic spectacle" of cross-cultural dressing, an act highly suggestive of indigenization. However, McClintock warns against reading "theatre for reality." While acts of cultural cross-dressing may appear transgressive, they should not be taken at face value (143). Color photographs of the protagonists in Maasai or Tibetan dress operate in accordance with James Buzard's antitouristic traveler/tourist binary; these costumes are evidence of real travel. As Buzard's work suggests, we might usefully reintegrate self-appointed travelers into the category "tourist," and Kaplan points out that "all tourists search for verifiable markers of authenticity." These might include artifacts such as photographs, souvenirs (especially those that correspond to notions of cultural tradition), or evidence of having learned a language (Kaplan 60). Insofar as it is suggestive of real encounter, cross-cultural dressing operates in a similar mode. More than this, cross-cultural dressing tends to detract from the asymmetry of power relations between the travel writer and the subjects of her discourse (unless she relinquishes editorial control to those Tibetans or Maasai about whom she writes, in "literary terms," the travel writer's power to represent is "absolute"). One might even argue that acts of cross-cultural dressing come close to "mockery" (McClintock 45). The narrator, being conversant with Euro-American cultures, meets the eye of the reader (presumably dressed in non-Maasai/nomadic clothing) who—contrary to her companions in the photograph—recognizes her clothing as alien and witnesses the heroism of having boldly gone where no reader has gone before. The narrator's apparent acquisition of "double consciousness" (Gilroy 160) gains her authority not simply with the Maasai/Tibetans, but with her Euro-American audience. The depiction of Karko and Oddie's protagonists as travelers, rather than tourists, aligns them with figures of exile. According to Kaplan, the western exile figure is readily accorded a platform from which to speak, since exilic displacement "from the familiar" implies that "cultural formations" have been transcended (81). This authorizes Karko and Oddie's narrators to act as trustworthy commentators, both upon the societies they have left and the one they have joined.

A further assertion of cultural embeddedness is evident when each protagonist affixes her name to Maasai/Tibetan family trees. In one respect, her name on the family tree provides a powerful visual symbol of cultural relocation, aligning her first-person character with the Maasai/Tibetans in a way that effectively neutralizes her position as an outsider, indicating solidarity with, and knowledge of, the subjects of her discourse. However, the reverse is also true. It is an autobiographical act. Each narrator places her alien name against leagues of Amdo/Maasai names. This effectively registers her unique presence, and intervention in, their history. The family tree functions as a map might, providing visual evidence of her successful cultural infiltration of, and subsequent establishment within, the culture she has joined. Just as the eye gravitates toward incongruous geographical features, so—on this linguistic map—does an unusual name assume central place. She is therefore not merely an *us* but an *I*, an outsider with the capacity to "stand back" from Tibetan or Maasai cultures. There are anthropological resonances here. Traditional anthropological strictures against *going native* are there for a reason. Like the anthropologist, by venturing too far into other mind-sets, Karko and Oddie risk appearing to lose their objectivity. Therefore each protagonist retains a sense of bicultural agility. The back cover of Oddie's book celebrates her ability to "WALK IN TWO WORLDS" (240). The statement, in capitals as though to emphasize the significance of a cultural achievement, is supplemented with pictorial evidence. In the first photograph, she stands alongside her husband in traditional Maasai clothes. In the second, she sits typing at an Apple Macintosh computer.

It is through the deployment of authority-gathering strategies that Oddie, in particular, is able to position herself in traditional colonial roles: as Interpreter, e.g., "I stayed with the group [of tourists] to interpret and explain" (166), Health Worker, e.g., "to inform Kenyans about Aids prevention" (141), and Educational Advisor, e.g., "Maasai history should be taught in all its glory to Maasai children" (127). In addition, the book contains her own maps of the locale, hand drawn as though to suggest intimate personal knowledge of the region. In a gesture of anticonquest, she denounces colonial mapping strategies, asserting colonial guilt in a way that implies the innocence of her own cartography. The maps' inclusion positions her as an agent of recovery; she "puts the Maasai on the map" in a way that is consistent with the benevolent anthropological tradition of salvaging dying forms of cultural life (Clifford 118). Karko's narrator implies that she, too, is an agent of recovery, bringing nomadic lifeways into the public eye: "for the people of Machu....This book is my way of giving back to them" (v).

As Sara Mills has pointed out, nineteenth-century women who wrote about their travels were often belittled or disbelieved (125). As Oddie's protagonist discovers, this tendency persists. She dedicates one chapter to the resistance of male stereotyping ("Don't Call Me Memsahib" 53): "Tony suggested that the 'Memsahib' should sit in the front....'Don't call me memsahib' I muttered through gritted teeth as we drove off" (60). The label *memsahib* bears their female predecessors' memory of colonial patriarchy, recalling the attempt to position white women in India as the stumbling block of empire. In a double gesture of resistance, Oddie's character defies the attempt to deny women's historical contribution to travel (and, by extension, to the colonial enterprise) while also rejecting the trivialization of her own travel experience. However, as Elinettie Chebwera suggests, having subverted "their positions within masculinist discourses," women travel writers often proceed to "engage in similar discursive practices and strategies, exploiting their location to create a space" for the emergence of a unique first-person persona (iii).

Travel books stand at what Rob Nixon calls the "[g]eneric crossroads" of ethnography and autobiography (166). I have alluded briefly to the importance of ethnography to the problem of narrative authority. Autobiography is equally important. Partly because of its traditional association with enlightenment notions of selfhood, which, as John Sturrock points out, charges autobiography with "turning life into Life" (2). Each protagonist, and to an extent, each husband, is portrayed as a unique individual. Among other things, this representation enables the portrayal of each marriage as the marriage of two exceptional characters. However, both narratives have built-in tensions between the delineation of Tsedup (Karko) and Robert (Oddie) as autonomous selves and their depiction as essentially Tibetan or Maasai. This is exemplified in Oddie's mini-biography of Robert, which denies him a sense of kinship with the Maasai: "I tried to imagine Robert as a snotty-nosed Maasai kid with flies drinking from his eyes...but it was impossible. I can think of him as nothing but a...young warrior." She notes: "[H]e was the first of his generation to be circumcised," being "of the strongest character, for he will be a leader for the rest of his generation" (86). There follows a "second significant episode"—"significant" in relation to the invention of Robert's character as uniquely different—in which Robert kills a lion and we are told that his "bravery and strength came together spectacularly" (87) showing his "marked individualism" (60). Tsedup is constructed in similar ways, declared singular in his "desire to be educated" (Karko 117) and being "not entirely the nomad he resembled" (90). The underlying suggestion is that, like her, he has a capacity to transcend Tibetan cultures. However, the individualism of the husbands tends to be subordinate to the individualism of the *I* narrator. Elsewhere in the narrative Tsedup is relocated within a group of nomads: "[H]is face that morning was the face of a nomad...wind-whipped and wild" (87). When Tsedup behaves in ways with which Karko's first-person narrator disagrees, she suggests that he is to be seen "in context" (268). To borrow Said's phrase, Tsedup is Tibetan first, an individual second (11): "he was an Amdo man. According to his culture, his behaviour was appropriate" but, "[i]t seemed cruel" (268). At moments such as these, Tsedup's character is irredeemably located in Tibetan lifeways, unable to achieve the variety of universalized understanding to which the protagonist aspires.

A similar strategy can be seen at work in Oddie's narrative. When the protagonist's husband, Robert, watches the film *Cry Freedom*, the narrative becomes inflected with prelapsarian notions of good and evil: "Robert turned to ask me a question I could not answer, 'Why did they shoot the children?' I felt almost guilty because I had shown him many evils that he did not know existed before" (135). Robert is constructed as childlike, a shielded being suddenly thrust into a knowledge of evil. He appeals to the narrator to explain it to him. The narrator does not renounce the position of knowledge that the scene bestows on her. Rather her profession of guilt (that she has "shown him many evils") is an acceptance of her role as the agent of his corruption. Thus, she adopts an educative role in relation to her unworldly husband. Her role as educator does not stop there. She appropriates the spiritual purity of Robert's perspective: "[W]atching these videos with Robert was like seeing them clearly for the first time" (139). The apparent indigenization of her thoughts authorizes her to assume the role of moral teacher to the west. Thus, she achieves double supremacy: over Robert and over the reader.

As Oddie's *memsahib* example illustrates, women who travel from the west continue to transgress certain assignments of gender. However, as Sidonie Smith and Julia Watson imply, these transgressions do not inevitably lead to the relinquishment of narrative authority (420). Both Oddie and Karko consistently overlook how frequently race, rather than gender, determines relations of power. In such "unexamined relations of privilege" (Pratt 220), ignorance is power. Karko notes that "as foreign women we were able to enjoy similar freedom to the men, which set us apart from the nomad women" (164). By adopting a "symbolic masculinity" that is "predicated on her whiteness" (McEwan 34), she breaks a strict nomadic taboo by climbing a holy mountain. She views this accomplishment as a pioneering achievement: "We continued up to the craggy heights of the mountain top....We were making history. No woman had ever before set foot on Amnye Kula" (166). She fully inhabits the "craggy heights" of her authority, savoring the god's-eye view afforded from the top:

> The view from the summit took our breath away. Below us was the great grassy desert of our home. Beyond, the Machu river snaked between the flatland and the undulating mountains, which receded into an azure horizon. The tribe's tents formed a circle in the middle of the scene, smoke drifting from each tiny roof and the black and white dots of yaks and sheep formed pointillist brush marks on the canvas. (116)

In an attempt to immortalize what she terms an historical moment, the landscape is transformed into a "scene" painted on a "canvas." She thereby adopts nineteenth-century explorer discourse through the use of the picturesque, producing what Simon Ryan calls "a frame which makes a text of the landscape so that it may be compared to the ideal" (53). It is an act of "framing" in two senses. First, it is self-portraiture. The scene radiates downwards and outwards from her first-person narrator, capturing a woman making history in the footsteps of her nineteenth-century antecedents. Her "ideal," or model, is autobiographical (ostensibly feminist) individualism. The "frame," positioned so as to feature her protagonist as the key historical figure in "the scene," confirms that it is she, rather than Tibetan nomads, who forms the focal point of the narrative. She, unlike the nomad women, has managed to access the "inaccessible" (166). The nomadic tents and "great grassy desert" provide an auspicious backdrop for the staging of her uniqueness, converting her "life" into a "Life" (Sturrock 2). In addition, it is an act of "taming" (81), an attempt to conceal certain complexities from view, fading "into an azure horizon" her ambivalent relationship with the nomadic women. Potential objections to her violation of the taboo are edited out of the frame. The "tribe's tents," which are subjugated far below, acquiesce, sanctioning her violation by "forming a circle in the middle." By these means, a potentially threatening landscape is converted into a marketable product in the metropolitan center (the portrayal of her experience in a travel book), which enables her to celebrate the "triumphant portability" (Ryan 60) of her experience with the nomads. However, the narrative curbs its own expression of dominance. As Mary Louise Pratt points out, it is "only through a guilty act of conquest (invasion)" that "the innocent act of anti-conquest (seeing) can be carried out" (66). It is a final irony, then, that the narrator, having violated a taboo in order to perform the innocent act of seeing, pulls back from the threshold of absolute power, by registering a "deep sense of humility" (Karko 166). This profession neutralizes the impression of dominance by appealing to the reader's sense of her "sympathetic subjectivity" (Richards 225), her "great respect for" nomadic beliefs (130).

In a similar moment of honorary manhood, Oddie's first-person character is "led…away into the forest [to] attend [a] site of slaughter" (98), something the narrator knows is "not permitted" (98) for Maasai women. However, the act of "invasion" is excused by a profession of innocence; she was "led" into wrongdoing rather than actively taking herself there. The guilt therefore lies with the tribesman who *mis*led her when he "insisted" that she see "'everything for Maasai culture'" (98). It is worth considering exactly *whose* ignorance the text is dealing with. The broken English of the tribesman disadvantages him, situating him in a position of "ignorance" of the narrator's language (rather than her ignorance of his) that facilitates a sense of general ignorance: that of his own culture. While her ignorance is temporary, his endures. The incident serves to measure her character's subsequent growth into the customs of Maasai society: "(These days I would rather die than walk into a male gathering such as this one, however, my ignorance protected me and I walked blithely in)" (98). Thus, the narrator achieves distance from a previous self who, like an unaware tourist, disregards the taboo, simply because she does not belong. Behind this lies a sinister logic; the tribesman, being intellectually static, is relegated to the status of tourist in his own culture (Richards 1994). She, by contrast, develops knowledge of its taboos. However, the mere presence of this passage disrupts the narrative's self-righteous rhetoric because the paragraph proceeds to detail that which she professes shame at having seen. Once again, the scientific right to see "everything for Maasai culture" is asserted over and above the sacredness of the taboo. The taboo is thus violated twice over; not only does she go and see, but she tells us what she saw. The reader might easily become complicit in this act of conquest because, if she or he forgives it, he or she very likely does so for two reasons. First, because providing vicarious access to the "inaccessible" (Karko 166) is practically a contractual obligation for travel writers. Second, because it is assumed that the reader shares an unspoken belief that taboos are binding only for the irredeemably local, those unable to transcend their locatedness.

As with early explorer narratives, it remains naïve to interpret descriptions of flora and fauna as being for their own sake. Rather, as Ryan argues, it has often to do with prospect of future wealth (71). Oddie's company (Safaris Unlimited) is dedicated to the promotion of what she terms "cultural tourism" (163). In describing the setting for her touristic enterprise, the narrator aligns her exploitative gaze with that of her nineteenth-century predecessors: "The Naimina Enkaiyio Forest is one of the last pristine forests left in Kenya. It covers hundreds of kilometers of ancient, undisturbed trees and is rich in plant and animal life. The forest harbours almost all species found in Southern Kenya, including elephants" (210). The reader might be forgiven for confusing this passage with a tourist brochure. The forest contains the promise of a truly "rich" game-viewing experience, it is a pretouristic Eden—an "undisturbed," "pristine" (even virginal) space offering itself up for possession as though for the first time. In a similar gesture, Karko's narrator donates the entire landscape to her unborn child: "I scanned the vast panorama of my Tibetan home: the mountains, the grassland, the tribe. 'All this is for you, our son,' I said, 'All this is for you'" (296). As Mills has pointed out, it remains the case that she who dwells on a panoramic view "aggregates to herself the power of the colonial position" (79). Utilizing the spiritually innocent premise of an unborn child, together with an emotional repetition of the act of donation and inheritance, the narrator undermines the arrogance of the gesture.

Karko and Oddie's books clearly illustrate the problem of narrative authority associated with the travel-writing genre. Moreover, the emergence of women travel writers such as Karko and Oddie is problematically associated with a tendency to reinvent nineteenth-century colonial women as proto-feminist heroes while celebrating contemporary writers who follow in their footsteps (McEwan 5). Celebrating women's travel writing (past and present) as emblematic of transgressive feminist individualism risks overlooking cross-cultural acts of conquest. Anthropology has been criticized as "ethnocentrism thinking itself as anti-ethnocentrism" (Richards 231), and a similar criticism may be leveled at Karko and Oddie's travel writing. Regardless of gender, no writer can step in and out of her culture as easily as she can step off a plane into Maasai or Tibetan clothes.

The establishment of narrative authority is greatly facilitated by the readership back home, as opposed to a Tibetan or Maasai one. In an untypical passage, Karko's narrator considers how Tibetans perceive her when she wears nomadic dress. They see through her disguise in a way that makes her feel "uncomfortable" (148). Momentarily disorientated within her own narrative, she considers placing her text "under [a Tibetan] microscope" (148). To reimagine her audience as Tibetan would render visible her cultural biases and errors of interpretation, thereby stripping the text of inappropriate narrative authority. Whether or not the text could withstand such unbearable scrutiny remains to be seen.

Note

1   The apparent possession of insider knowledge commonly acts as an authorizing
     strategy. As the blurb of Mary Taylor Simeti's *On Persephone's Island. A Sicilian
     Journal* suggests, Taylor Simeti's marriage to a Sicilian provides her with "both a
     native's intimacy and the impartial eye of an outsider."

Works Cited

Blixen, Karen. *Out of Africa* and *Shadows on the Grass*. New York: Penguin, 1984.
Buzard, James. *The Beaten Track. European Tourism, Literature and the Ways to "Culture,"*
     1800–1918. Oxford: Clarendon Press, 1993.
Chebwera, Elinettie. "Colonialism and the Construction of the Individual White Female Subject in Kenya." Master's thesis. La Trobe University, Victoria, Australia, 1994.

Clifford, James. *Routes: Travel and Translation in the Late Twentieth Century.* Cambridge: Harvard UP, 1997.

David-Néel, Alexandra. *With Mystics and Magicians in Tibet.* London: John Lane, 1931.

Draymond, Margaret. "Class in Sindiwe Magona's Autobiography and Fiction." *Journal of Southern African Studies* 1995. 21–24.

Gilroy, Paul. *Small Acts: Thoughts on the Politics of Black Cultures.* London and New York: Serpent's Tail, 1993.

Goldie, Terry. *Fear and Temptation: The Image of the Indigene in Canadian, Australian, and Canadian Literatures.* London: McGill Queen's UP, 1989.

Kaplan, Caren. *Questions of Travel: Postmodern Discourses of Displacement.* London: Duke UP, 1996.

Karko, Kate. *Namma: A Tibetan Love Story.* London: Hodder and Stoughton, 2000.

Markham, Beryl. *West with the Night.* London: Penguin Books, 1988.

McClintock, Anne. *Imperial Leather: Race, Gender and Sexuality in the Colonial Conquest.* London: Routledge, 1995.

McEwan, Cheryl. *Gender, Geography and Empire: Victorian Women Travellers in West Africa.* Aldershot: Ashgate, 2000.

Mills, Sara. *Discourses of Difference: An Analysis of Women's Travel Writing and Colonialism.* London: Routledge, 1991.

Nixon, Rob. *London Calling: V.S. Naipaul: Postcolonial Mandarin.* Oxford: Oxford UP, 1992.

Oddie, Catherine. *Enkop Ai (My Country): My Life with the Maasai.* East Roseville, NSW: Simon and Schuster Australia, 1994.

Porter, Denis. *Haunted Journeys: Desire and Transgression in European Travel Writing.* Princeton: Princeton UP, 1991.

Pratt, Mary Louise. *Imperial Eyes: Travel Writing and Transculturation.* London: Routledge, 1992.

Richards, David. *Masks of Difference: Cultural Representations in Literature, Anthropology and Art.* Cambridge: Cambridge UP, 1994.

Ryan, Simon. *The Cartographic Eye: How Explorers Saw Australia.* Cambridge: Cambridge UP, 1996.

Said, Edward, W. *Orientalism. Western Conceptions of the Orient.* London: Routledge and Kegan Paul, 1978.

Simeti, Mary Taylor. *On Persephone's Island: A Sicilian Journal.* London: Bantam Books, 2001.

Smith, Sidonie, and Watson, Julia, eds. *De/colonizing the Subject: The Politics of Gender in Women's Autobiography.* Minneapolis: U of Minnesota P, 1992.

Sturrock, John. *The Language of Autobiography: Studies in the First Person Singular.* Cambridge: Cambridge UP, 1993.

Part Three

Identity

Chapter Eleven

A Protestant Critique of Catholicism
Frances Calderón de la Barca in Nineteenth-Century Mexico

Linda Ledford-Miller

Frances Calderón de la Barca's *Life in Mexico during a Residence of Two Years in That Country*, based on a series of letters home from 1839 to 1842, was published in 1843 to general acclaim in the United States and Britain. In Mexico, however, Calderón's work gave rise to concerns that her ambassador husband, who may have had access to state secrets, may have provided information or otherwise assisted his wife. The first four letters were published in Spanish over a period of four weeks in the *Siglo Diez y Nueve* [*The Nineteenth Century*] newspaper. The fourth letter, somewhat critical of Veracruz, elicited complaints that, combined with the contents of the fifth letter, which touched on General Santa Ana, then president and *de facto* dictator of Mexico, put an end to the planned serialization of her letters. Not until 1920 was a complete Spanish translation published.[1] In this century *La vida en México* (*Life in Mexico*) was considered "el mejor libro sobre México que haya escrito un extranjero" ("the best book on Mexico written by a foreigner") (Appendini 8; this and subsequent translations are mine).

Calderón's letters describe her travels to and within Mexico, giving many details of her daily life and the lives of those around her, especially women. She witnesses two small uprisings, the chaos of the copper monetary crisis, and a change of president, among other momentous events. However, it is her deep interest in women, convents, churches, and religious practice that we will investigate in this essay, focusing particularly on Calderón's outsider (Protestant) observations of insider (Catholic) religious practice, and her critique of such practices as instances of a desire for social justice for Mexican women.

Frances Calderón de la Barca was the Scottish-born American wife of Angel Calderón de la Barca, Spain's first envoy to Mexico after it had won its independence from Spain in 1821. Frances Erskine Inglis was born in Edinburgh in 1804, but she moved to Boston with her mother and sisters in 1831, where they established a school for girls. They relocated to Staten Island in 1835 and opened another girls' school. It was in New York that she met her future husband. Fifteen years her senior, Calderón was born in 1790 in Buenos Aires, then a colony of Spain.

He was educated in England, had been a prisoner of war of the French, had served diplomatic missions in Germany and Russia, and was the Spanish minister to the United States under President Martin Van Buren when he and Fanny met. She was a confirmed Protestant; he was Catholic. They were married in the Church of the Transfiguration in New York by Father Felix Varela y Morales, a Cuban-born Catholic priest (Wood 47; Fisher and Fisher xxv). Molly Marie Wood notes that

> Upon marrying Calderón, Fanny was educated in Catholic doctrine, perhaps by Father Varela himself. She knew the terminology, memorized the prayers and attended Catholic mass in the United States. In preparation for her journey to Mexico, she read the history of the Church in Latin America and saw pictures of the splendid cathedrals. After all, she knew that she would be expected to "act Catholic" for diplomatic reasons...No amount of preparation, however, could transform her naive, romantic and aesthetic view of the Church into the real Church she encountered in Mexico. (48)

Indeed Calderón does "act Catholic": She attends many masses, chats with many priests, bishops, and even the Archbishop; she witnesses many processions, participates in the *posadas* and, due to her status as wife of the Spanish ambassador, and her condition as outsider, visits monasteries and convents closed to most Mexicans. Indeed, in a letter to William Hickling Prescott, Calderón comments that, because her husband is not considered a foreigner, she is "intimate" with Mexican society and has received permission from the Archbishop to visit convents, "which is never permitted" (Prescott letter from Calderón dated June 5, 1840, 128–29).

While at mass, her commentaries on churches and cathedrals tend to focus on two main topics: the beauty and wealth of the church and its images—whether the color and richness of statues of saints or the vivid purple robes of priests in procession; and the class or status of those worshipers in attendance. For example, Calderón recounts her visit to the cathedral of Our Lady of Guadalupe, contrasting the colonial church with the Temple of Tonantzin, the mild goddess of earth and corn worshipped by the Aztecs, upon which the cathedral was superimposed (85). She marvels at the quantity of silver in the rich edifice, and the quantity of beggars, unwashed lepers who beg by appealing to religious or domestic sentiment, or perhaps to superstition, calling on potential benefactors "por el amor de la Santisima Virgin!" ("for the love of the Most Sacred Virgin"). They appeal to men "by the life of the Señorita," to women "by the life of the little child!" and to children "by the life of your mother!" (87).

At New Year's mass in the church of San Francisco, one of the cleanest in Mexico and "most frequented by the better classes," she again comments on the presence of lepers and beggars, as well as Indians (306). Though in the San Francisco you may find yourself between two well-to-do women, you might also find yourself next to "a beggar with a blanket," or an Indian woman with her baby in tow and a basket of vegetables on her head (306–7). As a result of the excessive dirtiness of the Mexican churches and the constant presence of the lepers and other (unclean) beggars who frequent them, "the principal families" frequently have their own private oratorios and contract the services of a priest for private masses at home (308).

Calderón's preoccupation with the uncleanliness of Mexican churches may elicit our sympathy when we discover that "men may sit on chairs or benches in church, but women must kneel or sit on the ground. Why? *Quien sabe* (who knows) is all the satisfaction I have ever obtained on that point" (147, original emphasis). During the very special ceremony confirming an Archbishop, Calderón complains that she "had the pleasure of kneeling beside these illustrious persons for the space of three or four hours," because no seating was provided for the wives of cabinet members or diplomats (190). Blessed by gender, the men sit comfortably; undone by gender, the women kneel at their men's feet.

During the period of *desagravios*, or public penance in which all Mexicans participate, according to Calderón, she observes the women at their morning penitence. It is 6 a.m., and no men are allowed to enter the church; in contrast, Calderón sees women doing their penance by kneeling with their arms extended in front of them in the shape of a cross, groaning with discomfort after about ten minutes of maintaining the uncomfortable pose (275).

However, the men's penitence is a much more peculiar scene, and one Calderón is able to witness due only to admission having been arranged "by certain means, *private but powerful*," probably referring to the Archbishop (275, original emphasis). She and an anonymous female companion cloak themselves completely and go after dark to the church of San Agustin, where they look down upon about one hundred fifty men similarly cloaked and made anonymous. After the priest's homily on the torments of hell awaiting unrepentant sinners, the church suddenly goes dark and a voice calls out, "My brothers! When Christ was fastened to the pillar by the Jews, he was *scourged!*" (276, original emphasis). To Calderón's horror, she then hears "the sound of hundreds of scourges descending upon the bare flesh...Before ten minutes had passed, the sound became *splashing*, from the blood that was flowing" (276, original emphasis). The scourging, sometimes done with scourges of iron designed with sharp points to pierce the flesh, continues for half an hour. Calderón finds it "sickening" and says, "had I not been able to take hold of the Señora ————'s hand, and feel something human beside me, I could have fancied myself transported into a congregation of evil spirits" (276). Thus, the very act designed to drive out evil, an act of penance and repentance for one's sins, seems to her evil. We might notice as well that, although Calderón seldom names names in her text, she usually follows the convention of supplying the first and last letter of the surname. Here, however, her companion has only gender to identify her, which suggests the need for the utmost secrecy and discretion due to the improper nature of their visit.

Though laywomen did not scourge themselves, Calderón discovers that the nuns of Santa Teresa do. On a visit to that convent she sees a crown of thorns worn on certain days by one among the nuns. Similarly to the scourges she witnessed at St. Agustin, this crown is made of iron with sharp points directed toward the head, causing the wearer to suffer cuts and bleeding from the wounds made by wearing the crown (285). In the individual cells she notices instruments designed for self-inflicted torture, such as an iron band with sharpened points to wear around the waist, a cross with iron nails to enter the flesh, and a scourge like those of St. Agustin, covered with iron nails designed to wound the flesh (286). She notes that most of the nuns look happy enough, if pale, but closes with this telling comment: "[I]f any human being can ever leave this world without a feeling of regret, it must be a nun of Santa Teresa" (287).

We find a less gruesome critique of Catholic practice in Calderón's reflections after attending the *honras* of the daughter of the Marquis de S—a, or the mass for the repose of her soul, for which every possible expense was lavished.

> If this Catholic doctrine be firmly believed, and...the prayers of the Church are indeed availing to shorten the sufferings of those who have gone before us; to relieve those whom we love from thousands of years of torture, it is astonishing how the rich do not become poor, and the poor beggars, in furtherance of this object, and...if the idea be purely human, it showed a wonderful knowledge of human nature, on the part of the inventor, as what source of profit could be more sure? (110–11)

Such comments represent a typically Protestant view of purgatory and the practice of paying for prayers and masses to shorten the stay, or of "buying" God's influence, from the Protestant perspective. However, Calderón goes on to describe the elegance and richness of the ceremony, demonstrating once again her own divided reactions to the mysteries of Mexican Catholicism.

Her inner conflict is manifest to some extent even among her harshest and most direct criticisms of insider religious practice. She visits a number of convents and admires them for their fine gardens and the art they contain. (In fact, convents and monasteries were often the repositories of great works of art, particularly of paintings.) She develops a close friendship with a woman who is happily a nun. In a letter to Prescott she describes the ignorance of Mexican women as "*total*," and suggests that sheer boredom may lead them to the convent. "They are very amiable and good natured, but I do not wonder that so many become nuns, as I think they amuse themselves quite as well in a convent as at home" (Prescott, letter from Calderón dated June 5, 1840, 128). Nevertheless, Calderón is frankly appalled by what she considers the sacrifice of young girls to the convent veil.

The convent Encarnación she says is the richest and finest in Mexico, with the possible exception of the Concepción (151). In fact, it is "a palace" where each nun has at least one servant, and some have more, for the Encarnación is not as strict as some of the other orders (153). She adds that each novice pays five thousand dollars to the convent when she enters, a fantastic sum in those years, and that pride seems to be the prevailing sin of Encarnación's wealthy nuns (153). Even here, in the gilded cage, her sympathies lie with the nov-

ices, whom she calls "poor little entrapped things!" who falsely believe that they can leave the convent at the end of the year if they
should tire of the convent life. However, Calderón intimates that the
novices will never be allowed to tire, never be permitted to leave
(153).

Calderón witnesses the taking of the veil by three different nuns-
to-be, and considers it "next to death...the saddest event that can occur in this nether sphere" (199). Indeed, her descriptions everywhere
suggest death. One young woman embraces the nuns of her order,
whom Calderón calls "dark phantoms" who "seem like the dead welcoming a new arrival to the shades" (204). At another convent entry,
the young girl is "consigned...to a living tomb" upon entering the
convent under the influence of her confessor and with her father's
consent, but against her mother's will, and we recognize the powerlessness of the mother, of women, in the face of male power.

Though Calderón makes much of the strength and depth of family bonds among Mexicans, she reveals that these bonds are torn
asunder when families give their daughters to convents, for they will
never see them again, nor embrace them, nor will the nuns ever leave
the convent, even for the death of a mother. Nevertheless, she says,
"the frequency of these human sacrifices here is not so strange as
might first appear" (199). Of course "here" is the foreign and Catholic
Mexico, not, by implication, the "there" of sensible Protestant homes
in the United States.

Why are such sacrifices so common, we wonder? Calderón believes that religion and romanticism, in combination with the status of
women and girls, make the convent an attractive option. According to
Calderón's observations, young Mexican girls of the upper class have
little instruction beyond piano and embroidery lessons. They must
remain at home, without the freedom to walk alone or even with others of their age and station, with little to occupy or interest them. The
Mexican girl who "from childhood is under the dominion of her confessor, and who firmly believes that by entering a convent she becomes sure of heaven" and who, furthermore, finds the pageantry of
the ceremony irresistible, with its costumes, dresses, and candles, and
knows the attention of the world will focus on her, may indeed decide
to take such a momentous step. Further, once taken, there is no going
back. The actress cannot abandon the stage in mid-act, after all. In
fact, Calderón does suggest the church-as-theater, as the guests take
their seats and "the *second act* begins" (204, original emphasis). Fur-

thermore, the girls hold it as an essential point of propriety and honor to demonstrate cheerfulness and gaiety,

> demonstrating the same feeling...which induces the gallant highwayman to jest in the presence of the multitude when the hangman's cord is within an inch of his neck...which makes the gallant general whose life is forfeited, command his men to fire on him; the same which makes the Hindoo [sic—meaning "Hindu"] widow mount the funeral pile without a tear in her eye, or a sigh on her lips. If the robber were to be strangled in a corner of his dungeon; if the general were to be put to death privately in his own apartment; if the widow were to be burnt quietly on her own hearth; if the nun were to be secretly smuggled in the convent gate like a bale of contraband goods,—we might hear another tale. (203)

Once again, metaphors of death and imprisonment abound. Calderón is clearly opposed to getting the daughters of Mexico to a nunnery. She just as clearly finds their education inadequate and their socialization insufficient, as we noted above. Although she describes the pomp and circumstance of the ceremonies with a journalist's lively eye, she sees no justice for women in the events and influences that lead them to take the veil.

In fact, Calderón's deep interest in convents and nuns may stem from the "loss" of her sister Jane, who converted to Catholicism and herself took the veil of a nun, living in a convent in France (Fisher 713, note 6). Jane was only fourteen months Fanny's senior, so Jane's "defection" from a solidly Scottish Protestant family must have marked Calderón deeply (Wood 49). Nevertheless, her ambivalence about the Church in Mexico is evident in the back-and-forth of criticism and praise throughout her letters. Although she critiques the Archbishop for the comfort in which he lives, she compliments the kindness of the parish priest. She expresses horror at the "sacrifice" of young girls to the convent veil, while maintaining a close friendship with a nun in the convent of Santa Teresa, the very convent whose masochistic practices so horrify her (Calderón 199). Though she observes Catholic religious practices as an outsider, she acts out the rituals of the Church, genuflecting and making the sign of the cross alongside her Mexican colleagues (Fisher 121). Moreover, she does comment on the beauty and mystery of the Church as a force for the subordination of the people (Wood 86), but also as a source of community. Indeed, perhaps the ambiguity of her responses, or the divided self manifest in them, is the first indication of the transformation she must have been slowly undergoing. The divided self became one, the outsider became the insider, when Calderón herself converted to Catholicism on May 10, 1847, at the Holy Trinity Church in Georgetown, Washington, D.C. There is some evidence that Calderón wished to alter, or at least temper, some of the criticisms in her letters. In a visit to her family in 1848, she apparently made marginal notes in an edition of the *Letters* at the family home, softening her earlier harsh words. Her younger sister Lydia, who also converted to Catholicism and, like her sister Fanny, later settled in Spain, wished to bring out a new, softened edition after her sister's death (Wood 90–91). That edition was never released, so we do not know how Calderón's outsider (Protestant) observations of insider (Catholic) religious practice might have been altered as a consequence of her conversion to Catholicism and, thus, to the belated, or retroactive, insider status. Nonetheless, we must agree with Prescott's comment that "none but a Spaniard or the wife of a Spaniard could have had such opportunities for observation, and no one less acquainted with the language of the country could have so well profited by them" (Prescott, Letter to Charles Dickens dated December 1842, 329).

Unlike most women's travel narratives of the period, which tend to focus on picturesque descriptions of peoples and landscapes and the details of domestic life, particularly in relation to a dominant male figure of husband or father (Helen Sanborn's *A Winter in Central America and Mexico*, 1886, for example), Calderón's *Life in Mexico* transgresses the boundaries of women's writing. Not content to receive Mexican society women in her home on calling days, or to sit quietly doing needlepoint, Calderón plays a quasi-masculine role as an adventurer. Though her husband's diplomatic status and the Mexican view of him as not really a foreigner may have provided the needed entrée to proscribed areas, it is Fanny Calderón who enters and describes those areas. Fanny Calderón's *Life in Mexico* blends the male perspective of public life with the female perspective of domestic, or private life (Leask 187). Her convent visits fuse the private lives of nuns with the public practice of the Catholic religion, concomitantly demonstrating the private (female) price that women and girls pay to satisfy public (male) expectations.

Note

1   For a history of the book's publication and reception in the United States, Britain, and Mexico, see Ledford-Miller, "Fanny Calderón de la Barca" and "First

Appearance of *Life in Mexico*; Early Comments; Subsequent History," in Fisher and Fisher 629–36. Though Fisher and Fisher's 1966 edition of *Life in Mexico* presents the letters with "new material from the author's private journals," and offers extensive endnotes and annotations, for purposes of this essay we use the 1982 Berkeley edition, which is essentially a facsimile of the original 1843 edition.

Works Cited

Calderón de la Barca, Frances. *Life in Mexico*. Berkeley, CA: U of California P, 1982.

———. *Life in Mexico during a residence of two years in that country*. London: Chapman and Hall, 1843.

Fisher, Howard T., and Marion Hall Fisher. Introduction and "First Appearance of Life in Mexico; Early Comments; Subsequent History." *Life in Mexico: The Letters of Fanny Calderón de la Barca*. Garden City, NY: Doubleday, 1966. xxi–xxix, 629–36.

Leask, Nigel. "'The Ghost in Chapultepec': Fanny Calderón de la Barca, William Prescott and Nineteenth-Century Mexican Travel Accounts." *Voyages and Visions: Towards a Cultural History of Travel*. Eds. Jás Elsner and Joan-Pau Rubiés. London: Reaktion Books, 1999. 184–209.

Ledford-Miller, Linda. "Fanny Calderón de la Barca." *Dictionary of Literary Biography*. *American Travel Writers, 1777–1864*. Detroit: Bruccoli Clark Layman, 1997. 43–47.

Prescott, William Hickling. *The Correspondence of William Hickling Prescott, 1833–1847*. Transcribed and edited by Roger Wolcott. Boston and New York: Houghton Mifflin Co., 1925.

Sanborn, Helen. *A Winter in Central America and Mexico*. Boston: Lee and Shepherd, 1886.

Wood, Molly Marie. *A Search for Identity: Frances Calderón de la Barca and "Life in Mexico."* Master's Thesis, U of Richmond, 1992.

Identity in Rosamond Lawrence's *Indian Embers*
"I cannot somehow find myself"

Terri A. Hasseler

A recently married woman in British colonial India of 1914, Rosamond Lawrence faced the uneasy prospect of holding several entirely new roles: "wife" to Henry Lawrence, a widower previously married to her sister, Louise; "burra-memsahib" of Belgaum's Anglo-Indian community; "helpmate" to an empire builder; and "supporter" of the imperialist "white man's burden." Rosamond Lawrence articulates her anxiety by identifying a sense of estrangement from her "self": "Coming to a new country, living an entirely different life, seeing not one living soul one has ever met before, and putting on each day new and unfamiliar clothes, I cannot somehow find myself" (45). Lawrence identifies a form of colonial dissociation—an alienation from the environment, an uncertainty concerning what is appropriate conduct and a depersonalization or bewilderment over a misplaced "self." However, she quickly brushes aside her uneasiness by reconnecting with a former, more familiar, self in England:

> But to-day there was heavy rain after a thunderstorm. I put on a thin coat and skirt I had worn at home, as the temperature had dropped appreciably. That coat and skirt enabled me to find myself. I slipped back into Rosamond Napier, and I began to walk feet on the ground instead of floating along. I even inadvertently signed a cheque Rosamond Napier. I should always advise a bride to include some of her old clothes in her trousseau. (45)

Several features of this passage strikingly illustrate the anxiety Lawrence feels in this new environment. First, after the passing storm, she feels the need for her dress to reflect her former life in England. The significance of the "heavy rain" is not missed either; rain is a frequently used metaphor in the writings of memsahibs, signaling the washing away of the "dust" of India and, for a moment, providing a "respite" from its alienness. This passage also reveals a return to embodiment that is lacking in the first; Lawrence's dissociated self "slips back," like a spirit, into her body, the very weight of corporeality forcing her to follow the rules of gravity as she must now "walk on the ground" rather than float along. Another striking feature is her use of her maiden name in the commercial process of signing a check— signifying, perhaps, a degree of economic autonomy. Each of these actions seems to move her further away from Anglo-India and marriage and closer to England and autonomy. Most significantly, however, Lawrence identifies her key dissociation when she returns to her maiden name, Napier, in an attempt to be tied more comfortably to home. Her unconscious rejection of the "Lawrence" name is significant because that name is thoroughly entangled in the history of British rule in India. The Lawrence family has a lengthy connection with British imperialism in India. Sir George St. Patrick Lawrence, grandfather of Rosamond's husband, was the ruler of the Frontier Province and of Rajputna. He also survived the First Afghan War. Sir Henry Lawrence, a former ruler of the British Punjab, was killed at Lucknow, during the Indian "Mutiny" of 1857. John Lawrence was named Viceroy of British colonial India, holding the post from 1864 to 1869.

Rosamond Lawrence's movement from Lawrence to Napier might be read as an attempt to both distance herself from her marriage and from the colonial implication of the Lawrence name. However, the Napier name allies her even more profoundly with British colonial rule in India, and Lawrence is deeply aware of the significance of her maiden name. Her introduction to her autobiographical text, *Indian Embers*, serves as a genealogy of imperialist Napiers; in particular, she focuses on Sir Charles Napier and his conquering of Sind. In attempting to dissociate herself from Anglo-India and India, Lawrence becomes more deeply embroiled in them. She attempts to be *in* and *not in* India in the single gesture of writing the Napier name. The fact that she is the agent of that embroilment is particularly significant, for it reveals her ambivalence within her role. In the last sentence, she appears to acknowledge and embrace the colonial connection by taking on the "burra-memsahib" role of giving advice to young wives. By the end of the second passage, she has made the uneasy, disjointed movement between dissociation and association.

Literary critics of colonial western women's autobiographical writings have commented upon the uneasiness and anxiety evident in their journals and diaries. Mills argues that women were not able to "adopt the imperialist voice with the ease with which male writers did. The writing which they produced tended to be more tentative than male writing, less able to assert the 'truths' of British rule without qualification" (3). Similarly, Paxton argues that women's autobiographical works often express "more ambivalence about the colonial project, ambivalence that was more systematically silenced in texts by men who were their contemporaries" (388). The ambivalence of these positions comes from their ability to use, as Mills claims, "the dominant discourse formations and yet being excluded from full adoption of them because of their position within the discourse of the 'feminine'" (22). Being unable to use the discourse of colonialism in the same manner as men (Mills 23), western women are compelled to write from a unique position that carries elements of the dominant pattern in conflict with their own marginality as women in a patriarchal system. Kroller labels this practice "speak[ing] with multiple voices" (98). Julia Watson and Sidonie Smith state, however, that this multiple positionality allows the western woman writer to write "with a difference. She thus exposes their gaps and incongruities, wrenches their meanings, calls their authority into question, for 'illegitimate' speakers have a way of exposing the instability of forms" (xx), developing a form of autobiographical practice that "go[es] against the grain" (xix). Alternatively, as Mills states, illegitimate speakers are able to use a pattern of critique whose "constraints enable a form of writing whose contours both disclose the nature of the dominant discourses and constitute a critique from its margins" (23).

These critics pose the key dilemma for western women writing about their experiences with and in empire—that their inclusion in empire is limited and that this limitation gives rise to an unstable position from which to speak. Their speech is often multiply designated—at once seeming in accordance with empire and at other times in strange conflict with it. What remains unique about Rosamond Lawrence's journal is her attempts to speak via her ancestral connections. In this way, she negotiates her position in India through her spiritual connection to former ancestors that ruled and lived in India.

Genealogies: Situating Rosamond Lawrence
in British Colonial India

Rosamond Lawrence's journal, *Indian Embers,* reveals a disjointed association with a series of colonial ancestors that help her find a place in India. Indeed, this journal demands a particularly attentive reader especially because the text offers a strange juxtaposition of time periods, forming a collage of conversations between Lawrence and the journals of her ancestors. On the surface, her journal appears to be a narrative held to the confines of a chronological autobiography; however, the text is complicated by her recursive movement backward and forward through time, making it particularly self-conscious. Therefore, the reader must read different time periods against each other as Lawrence shuttles between British colonial India from 1914 to 1920 (the point of her stay and of her "original" diaries) and colonial India of the mid-1840s (the time period of her ancestor, Sir Charles Napier in British colonial India). Similarly, the reader must take into account that significant portions of the text, including the introduction and various dated commentaries throughout the journal, reveal a heavily revised draft—a revision process that appears to have occurred during the mid-to late-1940s, sometime just previous to and immediately after her husband's death in 1949—only two years after India achieved independence from British rule.

In order to manage the disorder created by the juxtaposition of multiple time periods, Lawrence begins her journal with a detailed genealogy: "Napiers and Lawrences." This introduction, written roughly thirty years after she left India, is a cacophony of voices— selections from countless Napier and Lawrence journals—forming a text that is heteroglot (and male and female) from beginning to end. This genealogy also appears to be a mechanism she uses to locate herself firmly in British India, and more significantly, in her marriage to Henry Lawrence. This position as the wife of her deceased sister's husband makes her role as wife particularly unstable. In 1835, Lord Lyndhurst's bill made a man's marriage to his deceased wife's sister invalid. Until 1907, such marriages were considered incestuous. Lawrence married Henry Lawrence in 1914, seven years after the change in the laws of consanguinity and affinity; however, Lawrence, herself, reflects on the problems still associated with being the deceased wife's sister: "Owen is to be christened by the Scotch Padre from Poona. We did not care to have the Padre here, and indeed the Bishop of Bombay might have objected. But we were married in the Scotch church, and they, of course, have no feeling against the marriage of deceased wife's sister" (193). In choosing a place to get married or have her child christened, Lawrence had to exercise more caution in case of objection.

Lawrence shows the appropriateness of her marriage by arguing that it was a love match. She illustrates this by cataloging a long list of love matches on either side of the family—both Henry's and her own. "For in both families there had been wonderful lovers" (13) and "Then too on my side love matches were famous..." (14). The genealogy justifies the marriage: "Yes. Napiers and Lawrences had snarled at each other in India and at home, but both families had bred grand lovers. Henry and I risked it...and now, after thirty-five years can say we have never regretted it" (15). Therefore, she averts attention away from the risk evident in her suspect marriage to her brother-in-law, by making the greater risk the quarreling families and by underscoring their extraordinary love. This emphasis is especially important as only seven years earlier her marriage would have been a crime against the laws of consanguinity and affinity. Not only does she highlight the romance of the match, but also she stresses its suitability by emphasizing the merging of two remarkable "Indian" families, Lawrence and Napier. Lawrence suggests that this merging is unprecedented: "When I first became engaged many were the remarks, 'How suitable! The two famous Indian families. A Napier marrying a Lawrence'" (13). On one level, she uses this quote to illustrate that she belongs in India and, particularly, that her marriage is "suitable" and appropriate to "many." By placing her marriage in the pattern of grand romances and in describing it in the language of suitability, she implicates herself in those particular patterns, allaying potential criticism.

In addition to authenticating her marriage, Lawrence uses the genealogy in order to justify her own specific presence in India. Her long list of ancestors—father, brothers, and so forth—proves the unquestioned reasonableness of her presence in India: "When in 1914 I first went out it did not seem going to a strange country, for the forbears of both my husband and myself had been servants of India—Ma-Bap—for close on one hundred and twenty years in military, political or forest spheres" (11). Lawrence identifies a one hundred twenty–year connection between India and her family as its "servants." This terminology is, of course, in strange contrast with the Ma-Bap or Mother-Father justification for British presence in India. In this analogy, Indian people become children of the benevolent mother-father figure of the British Raj. Coming from a long line of mother-fathers, Lawrence, then, is implicated in this "benevolent" imperialism. However, more specifically, the genealogy does not simply justify but situates her in the place of British India and in the category of Anglo-Indian: "My first station was Belgaum, in the Province of Bombay. My father had been there as a young cavalry officer shortly after the Mutiny, and one of my brothers followed him as Forest Officer fifty years later. In 1916 my husband and myself left Belgaum to take up life at Government House, Karachi, which had been built by Sir Charles Napier, and bears a plaque upon its walls to say so" (11). Lawrence emphasizes her connection to India, in particular, by placing herself in the position of servant of empire: "My first station." In *Plain Tales from the Raj*, Charles Allen defines "station" as the "place where officials of district live" (239). The station included not only the offices of civil and military forces but also the social gathering space, such as the club. Women held no formal position in either the club or the military and civil establishments of the station. Charles Allen writes that the club provided a place for women to gather "even though they had no official standing and their names did not appear on its list of members" (99).

Comparable to Lawrence, Monica Martin, in her journal *Out in the Mid-Day Sun*, similarly appropriates the term "station," entitling one of her chapters, "My First 'Station." Martin writes, "This word 'station' was universally used, and I quickly fell into line. It meant any place, other than a large town, where people lived who were responsible for administration" (15). Martin illustrates her uneasy appropriation of the term, "station," by enclosing it in quotation marks, thereby stressing her uncertain incorporation into her husband's work, and the manner in which that incorporation was universalized. Rosamond Lawrence's use of the phrase "my first station" is even more politicized than Martin's as she uses this term in immediate connection with the military and political actions of her ancestors. Women, then, used the term *station* as routinely as their male counterparts, but their connection to the term and its implications was attenuated. Lawrence's language reveals her full incorporation[1] into the organization of empire, collapsing the difference between her husband's role and identity and her own. The statement also reveals a degree of agency over the definition of herself in Anglo-India. As a senior lady or burra-memsahib of her station, Lawrence might feel she has a greater claim on the authoritative connection to the station. Even so, despite her authority, her connection is at best tenuous. Her commands could just as easily be ignored as followed. Thus, at the same time her words carry a tacit connection to policy, for many imperialists her comment would be absurd—a woman cross-dressing as an imperial figure. This absurdity is heightened by the long list of male predecessors—father, brother, Sir Charles Napier. Against their history of service and actions, the imperialist would find her presumptive and impertinent.

In addition to locating Lawrence in her marriage and in Anglo-India, the introduction illustrates her long connection to aristocracy—dating as far back as Henry IV, King of France, and Charles I and II, Kings of England. In particular, she is interested in Lady Sarah Lennox, the mother of Sir Charles Napier, her favorite colonial ancestor: "Sarah, in particular, was provokingly attractive and beautiful. As a little girl she was petted and teased by George II, and later George III fell passionately in love with her and proposed marriage" (12). Through this genealogy, Lawrence announces her connection to England and Home as well as to British India, in many ways, making her position in either place unstable. For to be an aristocrat in India is to be always in exile, whereas to be in England is to be separated from her birthright of leadership in India.

Her genealogy, then, attempts to offer a specific template for her readers:

1. Because of my families' history of love matches, it is appropriate that I am married to Henry Lawrence.
2. Because of my ancestors' connection to India, it is appropriate that I am a part of British colonial society.
3. Because I am an aristocrat, it is appropriate that I represent England in British Indian society.

Lawrence appears to be actively situating herself very firmly as wife, imperialist, and aristocrat; however, in her act, she reveals the instability present in those associations. Thus, she is moving in a strange dance between association and dissociation, trying to find a spiritual partner whose presence will completely locate and stabilize her. The identity found in connection with an Other is a frequently highlighted feature of women's autobiographical practices, a feature Mary G. Mason calls "alterity-equality" (41): "An alter ego...with and through whom she might identify herself" (32). Bella Brodzki and Celeste Schenck argue that "Being *between two covers* with somebody else ultimately replaces singularity with alterity" (11, original emphasis). For Lawrence, however, each attempt at an association with an Other in the colonial order results in a complicated dissociation. In reading her need to associate herself, it is very interesting to consider which ancestors she mentions in passing, on whom she focuses, and whom she ignores—as these choices reveal the distinct feelings she has about her connection to India and Anglo-India.

Honoria Lawrence: Rejecting the Platonic Memsahib

In her introduction, Lawrence only mentions in passing her connection with Honoria Lawrence, the wife of Sir Henry Lawrence of Lucknow: "Sir Henry had waited nine years for his Honoria, and their absorbed devotion never faltered" (13). Sir Henry Lawrence of Lucknow was Rosamond Lawrence's husband's great-uncle, who governed in the Punjab and is most famous for serving and dying at the siege of Lucknow in 1857. The similarity between Honoria Lawrence and Rosamond Lawrence could not have escaped Lawrence, however. An avid reader of the journals of all the Napiers and Lawrences, she would probably have been very conscious of the connection between Honoria and herself—both having married men named Henry Lawrence who claimed a deep affection for the western regions of India, both having been older than other women when they were married, both playing secondary roles to their husbands' work, and both dreadfully obsessed with illness and death. Rosamond Lawrence is also mentioned in the preface of Maud Diver's biography on Honoria Lawrence: "I have to thank the India office and my friend Mrs. Henry Lawrence for the loan of many books on the period" (*Honoria* 11).

However, Lawrence chooses not to claim an "alter ego" in Honoria Lawrence. Indeed, Honoria Lawrence represents a level of memsahib perfection that Lawrence seems incapable of achieving. In writing about exceptional memsahibs, colonial writers often employed a rhetoric of oddity: These women were "remarkable," out of the ordinary, never to be seen again in empire. In *Ladies in the Sun*, a work on memsahibs during the early years of the East India Company, J. K. Stanford employs this strategy. However, in speaking of the memsahibs, he generally glosses over large groups of women until his attention is drawn to the exceptional woman: "Maria Hastings must have been a remarkable woman" (14). In the mid-seventeenth century, rumors swirled through Bengal that the Governor-General Hastings had been killed. Stanford states that Maria Hastings "saved the day" through her "firmness and address." He argues, however, that she is an oddity, a deviation from the norm: "Not again in India history shall we find any similar case of a Governor-General, aided and abetted by his wife, acting in this resolute way" (14). An even more striking example comes from Philip Mason's introduction to Charles Allen's *Plain Tales from the Raj*:

> I recall for instance one formidable old lady—she seemed old in those days—who after her morning ride and her inspection of the stables and the garden, the cook-house and the cook, would then be off to her maternity centre and child welfare clinic in the city and would fit in a purdah party for Indian ladies before her dinner party for the brigadier. *She* told the cook exactly what to do; she saw that his pans were properly scoured and the kitchen table scrubbed; she inspected the dishcloths. She told me that when the camping season began, the first thing to start was the cold weather stock-pot...and she must see it simmer, just as she saw the water boiled and the cow milked. She had done twenty-five Hot Weathers in the plains—and I silently resolved that my still problematical wife should not! She really was the platonic idea of a memsahib. (17)

Here Mason provides the platonic memsahib as a foil against which other memsahibs are measured: The platonic memsahib capably entertains the empire-builder and Indian women; she can do all domestic work and inspect all domestic workers. Unlike the problematical wife, the platonic memsahib focuses on her "feminine" duty as a member of the imperial structure, and she reveals that these enormous duties can be accomplished with grace and style. As Mason's comment suggests, the exceptional woman is, of course, the exception that proved the rule.

Honoria, however, is embraced by the image of the platonic memsahib. Saunders Abbot, assistant to Sir Henry Lawrence, describes Honoria in that image:

> In such roughings this admirable wife delighted to share; and at other times she would lighten his labour by reading books he wished to consult, or making notes and extracts for his literary work. She was one in a thousand. A woman, highly gifted in mind, of a most cheerful disposition, she fell into his ways of unbounded hospitality with no attempt at luxury or refinement...No man devoted himself so entirely to what he considered duty...and none had a better help-mate than he had in his wife. (qtd. in Diver, *Honoria* 102–3)

Using the rhetoric of oddity, Abbot defines Honoria as the perfect "help-mate" to the colonial worker. She does not distract her husband from his duties by her "waywardness" but lightens his labor, fulfilling her duty as platonic memsahib by being, first and foremost, a good wife.

Honoria also holds a special position as a sentimentalized heroine. Pat Barr emphasizes her ability to efface herself before the importance of Sir Henry Lawrence's work: "It was her first experience of the fact that duty and ambition overruled his life; even she had to take second place" (*Memsahibs* 38). Honoria reflects those self-abnegating characteristics that make her a worthy emblem of the feminine memsahib—again, the good wife. Moreover, Honoria dies in her duty to her husband and empire:

> But her small store of strength was ebbing, like an outgoing tide. About midnight she simply and frankly told her heart-broken husband that in twelve hours' time she would be gone from him.
> Before midday her spirit passes—and he was left alone… (Diver, *Honoria* 447)

In true sentimentalist fashion, Honoria must die in order to be elevated to the point of perfection.

Although Lawrence might see a connection between Honoria and herself, she does not employ her as her partner in her journal. Honoria sets a specific standard of perfection that Lawrence must measure herself against. In the *Incorporated Wife*, Callan and Ardener argue that "propaganda directed to wives, often by other wives, may clothe the organization in an exaggerated glamour or sense of mission which may call on idealized images of an earlier period. Thus any failure of reality to measure up is easily seen as personal failure" (22). This sense of apprehension about her performance runs throughout Lawrence's journal as she attempts to define herself and her role: "How am I ever to become a Bara Memsahib?" (34). In this sense, Honoria too perfectly establishes a standard of memsahib greatness that Lawrence does not wish to and/or cannot seem to duplicate in the pages of her text.

Lawrence's feelings of inadequacy are complicated by feelings of superiority born of her aristocratic background. In many ways, Lawrence's class privilege puts her in a position to disparage colonial, "middle-class" society. In one incident, she tells a hospital matron not to send a thank you note each time she sends flowers to the hospital.

This interchange comes to the attention of a wife of a senior Indian Civil Service (I.C.S.) member who writes to criticize Lawrence's slip of etiquette. Lawrence comments, "She reproves me in her exquisite writing for 'lowering the prestige of the Commissioner in Sind' by permitting flowers to be received without written acknowledgement...I force myself to remember that this respect for position in the I.C.S. is genuine. It is impossible not to laugh—not to feel superior..." (207).

As a member of the aristocratic class, Lawrence can laugh at her flaunting of precedence. Another memsahib, like the wife of the I.C.S. member, who is not placed in as high a class position in England, would be less likely to flaunt the rules of precedence as her social prestige would be bound up in the world of Anglo-India. That memsahib's disregard would be more dangerous as she would not have England and gentility to fall back on. Similarly, Rosamond Lawrence tends to place herself above the Lawrences, and particularly, Honoria Lawrence, who was raised in an evangelical, middle-class family. Quoting her father, Lawrence writes, "Lawrences and Napiers quarrelled like hell. The Lawrences were always a d[amned] psalm-singing lot..." (13).

However, Lawrence's laughter is short-lived as her position as wife to the Commissioner in Sind presses her into acknowledging her duty to the rules of precedence. She acknowledges that connection by conceding to the civilizing mission of the Raj—a mission greater than herself and intimately connected with her husband's work. For Lawrence, as *wife* to the Commissioner in Sind, her laughter at precedence would have devastating implications for Henry's position in the I.C.S. Thus, as a woman learning to become a memsahib, she expresses a sense of inadequacy. However, as a person of an aristocratic class, she expresses a sense of superiority over the very system in which she feels inadequate. Still as a wife, she is compelled into service to that system. A connection with Honoria would demand that Lawrence disown her stronger connection to her class and would ask her to embrace the conflicted space of the platonic memsahib. That adoption would also demand an uncomplicated recognition of her role as wife, a similarly conflicted one due to her status as a deceased wife's sister.

Sir Charles Napier: Colonial Cross-Dressing

With whom, then, does Lawrence choose to share her text? With whom does she choose to be "between two covers"? Throughout her journal, Lawrence shows a fascination with her kinship to Sir Charles

Napier, her distant cousin. Lawrence directly descends from her great-great-grandfather, William, the seventh Lord Napier, who was brother to Colonel George Napier. Colonel George Napier and Lady Sarah Lennox were parents to Sir Charles Napier. Napier was the British conqueror of Sind, who lived from 1782 to 1853. In her discussion of women's autobiographical practices, Mason has identified a "duo" rather than a "dual" association in autobiographies as a strategy of not subordinating the autobiographer to her alter-ego's image but of identifying herself "most sharply when she is identifying him too" (23). Indeed, Lawrence's journal proceeds in this fashion. Often excerpting major portions of Napier's text as a means to locate herself more solidly in India and Anglo-India, she situates herself in her inter/textual relationship with Napier. In Napier, Lawrence finds an unmediated connection to India, unlike the tentative association found in Honoria's Evangelical femininity. Moreover, she associates with an aristocrat-in-India, someone matching her in social class and worldview.

In her deeply intimate inter/textual relationship with Sir Charles, Lawrence evidences a form of agency in her colonial cross-dressing—an attempt to locate a colonial identity through desiring to unite with the masculine features of colonialism. When Lawrence's husband, Henry, is transferred from Belgaum to Sind, she expresses delight at being closer to her kinsman Napier: "...I confess I like living in the Government House built for my kinsman. I like to see his lighthouse winking at me each night as I lie in bed...I like, too, to think of our horses stamping and eating where his beloved charges tossed their heads. Red Rover, whom he had to lie down in his own tent to shelter him from the desert sun. Red Rover, brought to his bedside as he lay dying in England. Perhaps my Leviathan stands in Red Rover's stall?" (206). Lawrence locates a potential integrated personality in her colonial association with Napier, both their horses sharing a similar stall. The ease of this passage differs significantly from the colonial uneasiness in her phrase in Belgaum: "I cannot somehow find myself." Rather quickly, her colonial association with Sind raises Sir Charles Napier to a position of co-equal in the story of her life, a duo approach where her identity is revealed in her description of his: "Of his work in Sind I have already seen something of myself. I determine now to learn more of this 'benevolent despot.' I shall read his journals, for whether a man wish it or not most surely does he betray his real self in his diary" (228). In contrast to her unsure self-as-bride in

Belgaum, now Lawrence begins to see aspects of herself reflected back at her in Napier's writings and life experiences. Consequently, Napier's journals serve as a guidebook for her own search for colonial stability and identity.

One particularly striking incident in *Indian Embers* sets up a distinct connection between Rosamond Lawrence and Napier. Lawrence receives an Indian guest who wishes to acknowledge the "great works" of her ancestor, Sir Charles Napier. Joe, Henry's assistant, serves as translator for her conversation with the Sirdar:

Joe:	"The Sirdar wishes to thank you in person for your help in civilising [sic] his kinsmen."
R:	"I?"
J:	(*Smoothly*). "Yes. Your kinsman, Sir Charles Napier, ordered the Sirdar's ancestor to be blown from the mouth of a gun."
R:	*Inarticulate murmurs.*
J:	"Sir Charles accused him of having stolen two hundred camels, but far from having stolen the camels, he was the means of finding and punishing the man who had really done so. Therefore Sir Charles, instead of blowing him from the mouth of a gun, paid him 300 rupees and granted him lands and a pension. The village was called Napierabad, and now the Sirdar has come to thank you for having civilized his people." (225–26)

Joe's translation of the Sirdar's words, "your help," illustrates the coalescing of the two identities; Sir Charles's help is equated with Lawrence. This passage sounds quite similar to a passage from Rudyard Kipling's *Kim*, where a former sepoy castigates his own people for their uncivilized behavior during the Indian "Mutiny" of 1857. In Lawrence's journal, the Sirdar castigates his own ancestor as being "uncivilized." Edward Said in his critique of *Kim* argues that placing the critique of "natives" in the mouth of the "native" eliminates "any chance of conflict," altering the actual historical event in a manner where "we have left the world of history and entered the world of imperialist polemic, in which the native is naturally a delinquent, the white man a stern but moral parent and judge" (26).

In the passage above, Napier serves as a Solomonic figure, an analogy that Sir Charles would have no doubt liked, dishing out justice in a manner that is full of wisdom and elevates and civilizes the people. Nevertheless, the above passage practices an exscription of Sir Charles's horrible and bloody murders of thousands of Sindis on the battlefield at Miani—leaving behind the "world of history." In *A New History of India,* Stanley Wolpert gives an historical overview of Sir Charles's character:

> In September 1842, General Sir Charles Napier disembarked at Karachi to take formal command of all British Indian troops in Sind and Baluchistan. Fashioned in the mold of Clive, Napier was determined to use Sind as a launching pad for his dreams of glory, and he bullied, goaded, and berated the *amirs* of Sind before taking to the fields to destroy them. Napier's sadism was matched only by the mystic fervor of his religious zeal, for he believed himself to be a divinity incarnate. (221–22)

In speaking of the particularly ruthless and bloody battle at Miani, Wolpert writes, "Leading his men on forced marches across the desert, Napier proceeded in January 1843 to blow up the unresisting Iman Garh fortress. The following month, he stalked his prey to Miani, attacking on the morning of February 17, 1843. Five thousand Sindis were butchered, and he lost 256 of his own troops, but Napier won Sind for Britain and himself, becoming the region's first British governor when it was formally annexed that June" (222). Wolpert's description of the battle at Miani greatly contrasts with Lawrence's brief comment about the battle in her biography of Napier: "Why paint the lily? For this writer to describe the battle of Miani would be to offer a milk pudding to one who can feast on caviare" (123). In this way, Lawrence can avoid detailing the battle, which would force her to address the devastating death toll, by putting the battle in the mouths of other historians—in particular, the sympathetic historian, William Napier, brother of Sir Charles. In this light, to name the town "Napierabad" would be the height of absurdity.

In looking at this incident of Napierabad, we must question why this is presented as an actual event in the life of Lawrence. Aside from serving as an "imperial polemic" and situating her firmly within British rule in India, what other purpose does it serve? In one way, the text shows that at the height of a public acknowledgment of her integration with Sir Charles and British India, is a recognition of the absurd side of her colonial cross-dressing. For instance, Lawrence "detect[s] humour in that shy smile of Joe's" (225), as he comes to introduce the Sirdar. The situation becomes potentially more comic as she is unable, as most memsahibs were, to communicate directly with the man: "It is a little difficult to think of appropriate remarks, but no doubt Joe makes them!" (226). Lawrence and the Sirdar carry on a diffused conversation mediated by the more appropriate representative of empire, Henry's assistant, Joe. Joe appears to be willing to play at this colonial gag as long as it is humorous. Lawrence is again outside of the colonial dialogue, even though this incident might seem to root her firmly within empire. By juxtaposing her visit with the kind of official visits Henry receives just prior to this section of her journal, her "humorous" visit moves from the comic to the ridiculous. Where Henry's visits are serious and affect the future of empire, her visits leave her dissociated and unable to communicate, further highlighting her inadequacy.

Lawrence eventually compiled her commentaries and reflections on Sir Charles present in *Indian Embers* and placed them in a biography on Napier published in 1952. This biography represents perhaps the height of her colonial cross-dressing. For if Napier's journals serve as the template for her journal, then her biography of Napier serves, on several levels, as the imagined autobiography of her life. In the biography *Charles Napier: Friend and Fighter*, Lawrence writes, "but the reader of these pages will realise that a factual narrative has never been their aim. It is not so much what happened as what was in the mind of the man who caused these happenings. Otherwise it would be to consider this book as an inanimate affair of cloth, print and paper, ignoring the meaning it attempts to give" (150–51). Through the breadth of her own editorializing, Lawrence transforms fragments of the biography into her imagined autobiography, where Lawrence can envision herself as the general fighting for empire. She defines Napier strictly in the language of the heroic, established by Thomas Carlyle, a contemporary of Sir Charles, in *On Heroes and Hero-Worship* and *Past and Present*: "Many can remember the days of Hero-Worship, when from the indistinguishable mass certain beings stood like caryatids bearing the world upon their head. But to youth of to-day such Hero-Worship seems unknown..." (Lawrence, *Napier* ix). Thomas Carlyle wrote of Sir Charles Napier, "A fiery lynx-eyed man with the spirit of an old knight in him more than in any modern I have met" (quoted in Lawrence, *Napier* x).

A caryatid as emblematic of the heroic is an interesting metaphor for Lawrence to use. Here, the feminine figure of the caryatid stands in for the heroic figure, and one could argue that Lawrence is attempting to collapse the difference between Sir Charles's heroic position and her own. She similarly uses Napier's life to lend "respectability" to her marriage. The biography helps Lawrence to measure her own marriage, to her deceased sister's husband, against Napier's similarly unconventional marriages to two women considerably older than himself. Lawrence equates his choice of marriage partners with his love for his mother, Lady Sarah Lennox: "With the yawning gap left in his life by the death of Lady Sarah it would be natural for Charles to turn to some older person" (76). In her biography of Napier, Lawrence finds her own marriage, which, in many minds, was still labeled incestuous, mirrored in Sir Charles's incestuous fascination in women as old as his mother. However, Lawrence, in contrast with Napier's and her contemporaries, defines his actions as "natural." Through her biography of Napier, Lawrence is able to confer on her life a naturalness and authority that is missing in her own autobiography.

In her colonial cross-dressing, Lawrence reveals an ability to align herself with a distinctive, but vicious and odd man. To position herself as a distinctive but vicious and odd woman would have been disastrous: "For women...rebellious pursuit is potentially catastrophic. To call attention to her distinctiveness is to become 'unfeminine.' To take a voice and to authorize a public life are to risk loss of reputation" (Smith *Poetics* 9–10). In her connection with Napier, then, she can revel in his eccentricity without drawing excessive attention to her own difference. She can use him in order to more firmly root herself in India; however, she must do so through a process of strongly identifying herself with her ancestor Napier and allowing her life to be defined most clearly when she is defining his. Thus, her agency in her imperial setting is routed through another imperial time (1840s) and figure (Sir Charles), thereby revealing a depersonalized connection to her particular colonial time and order.

Louise Lawrence: Confronting the Specter of the Deceased Sister

In her introductory genealogy, Lawrence consciously fails to mention her sister, Louise. Rather, she chooses to present her genealogy as if the merging of the Lawrences and the Napiers was something that had never happened before—an unprecedented alliance. However, as we read her journal, we discover that Henry had been previously married to her sister, Louise, who gave birth to three children. In this sense, Lawrence is merely the substitute in the unprecedented alliance; she is not the first nor necessarily the better. Her need to consciously overlook this fact reveals an extreme instability of position in colonial Indian society and in her marriage, an instability that is at odds with the colonial cross-dressing she performs with Sir Charles

Napier and the superiority she calls upon in her relationship with Honoria Lawrence. Lawrence's attempts to overlook Louise are unsuccessful as the specter of the sister haunts the text, compelling her to address her own instability and anxiety. She is forced into an intense intimacy with her sister as the story of her own life is profoundly connected with her sister's. Similarly, she is forced to acknowledge that her marriage to Henry is measured against her sister's marriage to Henry.

Unlike the empowering inter/textual relationship with Sir Charles, the textual connection with her sister betrays her lack of confidence. Sections of her journal reveal a distinct sense of uneasiness with herself in comparison with Louise's strength of character and purpose: "The welfare of Indian women had been of special interest to Louise. She had laboured to alleviate their sufferings, and now Henry would like me to carry on her work. This worries me" (144). In Louise, we see the "discourse of philanthropy" that was evident in middle- and upper-class women in the nineteenth century (Mills 96). By the twentieth century, this discourse had been appropriated by feminists and transformed into the "white woman's burden"—a concept manifested in the sentimental rhetoric of Maud Diver. Barbara Ramusack defines these women as "maternal imperialists," seeking to help younger/lesser sisters or daughters achieve "adult rights and responsibilities" (120): "They were frequently referred to as mothers or saw themselves as mothering India and Indians (133). In Lawrence's text, Indian men and women frequently refer to Louise as "mother." However, Lawrence presents Louise as a much more complicated character than the straightforwardly benevolent, maternal imperialist; Louise also seems to be a "feminist ally" of Indian women (Ramusack 120)—exhibiting an ability to cooperate as an "equal" across race lines. Lawrence writes, "Mrs. Ranade is the most dignified and gracious woman. She shows me round with pride, and with genuine feeling and affection speaks of Louise as 'my sister Mrs. Lawrence who persuaded me to do this work.' She is now a leader of the advanced school of politicians and she tells me again how it was Louise who encouraged her in this" (157). According to Lawrence, Louise appears able to form multiple relationships with Indian women, relationships that Lawrence never attempts to form or to continue beyond a few meetings. Indian women are points of oddity in her journal; there are a few brief encounters, most often instigated by Henry's urging Lawrence to renew a relationship with a former friend of Louise's. As is the case in many memsahibs' journals, "Indian women disappear entirely" (Paxton 391).

In strange contrast to Louise's surety of performance is Lawrence's uncertainty and uneasiness: "This worries me." This apprehension about her performance runs throughout the journal as she attempts to define herself and her role: "This prospect of dinner parties, garden parties, and buying food and furniture for months in camp stunned me. I was next to tears in my ignorance and perplexity…How am I ever to become a Bara Memsahib?" (34). Despite the fact that her genealogy confirms an association with the Ma-Bap imperial ethic, Lawrence acknowledges a troubling dissociation from that life: "After a mere seven months, interested as I am, I still feel rather outside this Ma-bap life" (79). Similarly, in responding to her husband's request that she take up Louise's focus on Indian women, she expresses fear that she is still too inexperienced: "I've been out here a year, but my ignorance is still great. It is all very well for the young wife of a junior Assistant Collector. She begins at the bottom, climbs slowly up taking a little more responsibility as she climbs…but here am I inexperienced, starting away at the top!" (144). Her comments address what she feels is an inequitable comparison between her sister and herself. Louise had the opportunity to begin on the bottom of the ladder with Henry as he moved slowly up. Lawrence, however, had to start at the top without the years of preparation. Confronted by her worries, she chooses to revert to a role in which she feels more comfortable: "…but without deliberately reasoning it out, I have decided, in spite of Mr. Couch and Mrs. Brown, that my job is not to take an active part in this sort of thing, but to keep Henry happy, amused and untrammelled, so that he can do *his* work, his most exacting work…" (228, original emphasis). Lawrence embraces the purely domestic aspect of her memsahib role; she becomes a wife, sounding much like Honoria Lawrence and, in the process, looking distinctly different from her sister.

However, the reader learns from her journal that each role—wife and burra-memsahib—has been flawlessly performed by her sister. Furthermore, we know that any appropriation of the wifely role remains in tension with her position as the deceased wife's sister. Indeed, Lawrence's text suggests that Louise was the platonic memsahib. Unlike Lawrence, Louise was comfortable speaking in public and taking on the burra-memsahib role; she enjoyed shooting panthers; she felt no anxiety in working to shoulder the "white woman's burden." Louise responded to India like an "adult," whereas Lawrence often adopts a childish persona when confronted by the "excitement" of India: "And the naked babies carrying their stomachs in front of them like pregnant women. They had silver anklets and painted eyes. 'Oh I must have a tea party for them all,' I cried with memories of school treats at home I suppose running in my head" (25). Where Louise would see a call to her "maternal" imperialist duty, Lawrence sees a party, and Henry looks "astonished" but says "nothing" (25). In her journal, India and Indian people are merely forms of entertainment, so exciting that she does not want to sleep: "I feel like a child with too many Christmas presents. I don't know which to play with. Thoughts turn restlessly from one thing to another" (28). Louise, however, inspired "intense admiration" in those who met her—English and Indian alike; the admiration of these people resulted in the building of the Louise Lawrence Institute in order to continue her work in training Indian women as midwives for the mofussil districts (210). The respect and admiration Louise inspired would help further Henry's career in a manner that Lawrence's more timid and childish appropriation of the domestic role would not. Louise does seem the more perfect partner for Henry—matched in age, sentiment, and duty. Lawrence, however, frequently mentions a feeling of inconsistency between Henry and her, a slight discord that would perhaps not be evident in the more fitting relationship between Louise and Henry: "I begin to recognise that though there is less than ten years between Henry and myself there are certain phases through which he has passed already, and done with, and that I yet have to find my way through" (42). These discrepancies set up a more unequal relationship.

Lawrence's anxiety concerning her relationship with her sister is best illustrated in her dread about embodiment—both in the forceful image of her sister's decaying body and in the presence of her own physical deterioration. The female body plays a major role in western women's journals in India especially present in fears of dying suddenly or in childbirth and of physically coming apart too soon. Medical texts enjoined women to not stay too long in India: In a *Medical Guide for Anglo-Indians,* R. S. Mair states, "A lady's health is almost invariably so affected by the climate of India, after six or eight years' unbroken residence, that she is compelled to seek that change in her native land which alone can restore her" (216). This aspect of India was frightening to memsahibs—and each addresses this fear in some manner in her journal. Particularly striking are those journals that personify India as a murderer: Quoting Mary Curzon, Fowler writes, "Some day though, the bell will go and I shall not appear, as India, I know, slowly but surely murders women" (281).

Suleri's critique of the feminine picturesque identifies a form of "colonial panic" (82) experienced by memsahibs who read "the Indian as a body out of control, swelling with an internal evil or wearing evil on its skin in a hideous reminder of the grotesquery encoded within the colonial will to aestheticize" (89). However, the attempt to "quarantine" the infection to India and Indians is subverted by the ways in which India seems to threaten the bodies of western women in India (90). Suleri argues that the suffocation women feel from the heat or the fear they experience with the insects and the spiders provided western women's writings "one safe way of recording colonial claustrophobia without transgressing onto the overtly political terrain of the male Anglo-Indian" (90). Confined to the body, her "colonial dejection" does not "spill over into the psychic or political realms" (90).

Although Suleri rightly argues that the Otherness of India and, in particular, Indian women's bodies helped sustain the narrative of confinement, I would argue that being so forcefully confined to the physical often inspired memsahibs to find that claustrophobia mirrored, not entirely in the body of the Other, but more fully in other western women's bodies. The fact that most memsahibs witnessed countless deaths of friends who seemed healthy one day and were dead the next made them very conscious of their own mortality. However, many record a sense of depersonalization and corporeal dissociation. In colonialist discourse, it tends to be memsahibs' physicality, most often as a sexual presence, which seems to place them in the most dangerous positions. Moreover, we can see how memsahibs might not see themselves in control of their own bodies—as empire controls the manner in which they are employed. We can see why memsahibs would choose to dissociate themselves from their materiality. However, Sidonie Smith, in part quoting Frances Baker, states, "...the body itself as a mere object is dissociated from our conscious being and situated elsewhere: 'Neither wholly present, nor wholly absent, the body is confined, ignored, exscribed from discourse, and yet remains at the edge of visibility, troubling the space from which it has been banished'" (*Subjectivity* 6). Although memsahibs may deny their bodies on one level, these bodies are always prodding their owners. Memsahibs' fear, then, is not only the realization that India is a body out of control, but, that they are bodies out of control. Memsa-hibs are implicated in the terror, and they see that bodily deteriora-tion most evidently in the physical death and disease of other western women in India.

Lawrence responds to this fear of the body. In a section of her journal entitled "The Bride," she maps the passing of a young bride newly arrived in India. This bride hates everything Indian. "She is horrified at the huge pot-bellied figure of Ganpati with his elephant head at the gate, always kept freshly painted in pink gold and scarlet. 'An idol,' she exclaims" (63). Within a short period of time, the bride dies: "Day before yesterday Dr. Fisher told me she had dysentery. Yesterday that she was dead. To-day she is to be buried. Hating and fearing India as she did it seems a pitiful thing she should be buried out here" (63). This observation closely matches Lawrence's initial reaction to India: "...there was a freshly daubed Ganpati with his ele-phant head, and wrinkled belly. A woman was laying a little bunch of marigolds before him. 'Idols!' I thought, astonished, I don't know why" (25). Lawrence is drawn throughout her journal to the image of a bride coming apart, transposing her own sense of dissociation and fear of the alienness of India onto the body of the young bride. As readers, we must also remember that Lawrence herself is a "young bride" newly arrived in India. The leap of comparison would not have been very great for Lawrence. Moreover, vexed by her own sense of inadequacy as a wife and the unconventiality of her mar-riage, Lawrence's emphasis on the bride becomes doubly significant, revealing the fear of her materiality in the reflection of her marriage.

Lawrence is also continually plagued by the untimely deaths of female friends. In addition, she experiences a great deal of physical pain, both at the birth of her child and when a later serious illness forces her to consider the possibility of dying from a hemorrhage: "They press me gently back on to my pillows, telling me I may bring on a haemorrhage by getting so excited...and all the while hovering behind is the picture of 'Blood.' Would it ooze out of my mouth, or come spurting out as from Blanco's leg? Would it be warm and taste salty?" (327). These fears and her physical collapse are mirrored in her comments on the illness of a friend:

> An urgent message comes from some friends in upper Sind. Can we put
> them up for a night? I have always liked her. She looks ill and harassed.
> She shows me a hard, dreadful lump on her breast; she is to see a doctor
> this afternoon.

> She is to have an operation here in this house tomorrow morning.
>   It is over. She is out of her anaesthetic. She is very sick. They have taken off her breast. We were both married the same year. We were both so happy...and here she is maimed with a shadow darkening her future, and me motionless in bed with a shadow darkening mine. (329)

Lawrence, again, reflects on the illness in correspondence with marriage, recalling, at the end of her journal, her much earlier reference to the young bride. In this passage, Lawrence calls upon the nostalgic memory of being a bride, which implies freshness and wholeness, both in body and spirit. Thus the bride image is paradoxically linked with innocent beginnings and forbidding deaths, creating for Lawrence the pervasive image of the dying/decaying bride. The terror memsahibs feel when India threatens their bodies is complicated by Lawrence who feels her panic most alarmingly when the bodies of other European women (the bride, her friend) rupture her text, compelling her to acknowledge her own materiality.

Most notable, however, is Lawrence's feelings of affinity with Louise's death. Indeed, Lawrence almost dies in the same manner as Louise: "At the time I had felt no fear (does one ever at the time?). The one thought 'My poor Henry; first Louise killed by a horse. Now me. And before his eyes,' ...but it has left me unnerved" (164). No doubt the near fatal riding accident unnerves her, but so does the almost exact replication of her sister's death, once again forcing Lawrence to evoke the specter of the sister. Louise, like the platonic memsahib, reaches mythic proportions in her death. Perhaps the most striking passage in Lawrence's journal is her reflection on Louise's memorial tomb in the desert of Sind. In her first recorded visit to the tomb, Lawrence goes with Henry; it cannot be lost on her that Henry's visit to the tomb is to a former wife, who was mother to three of his children and was his companion as he rose up the ranks of the I.C.S. Lawrence writes of the myths that have developed surrounding Louise's life and death:

> It is recorded that a Baluchi shikari said:
>   'Sahib, when I learned of the death of the Memsahib, then was afflicted with great grief. In all the country of Sind there was not such another Memsahib.' 'Throughout the Province she was the People's Physician, a name synonymous with healing. She alone has been called Sister by Mussulman ladies, Mother by the women of the people everywhere. She won the affection of wild men and hostile women, of Mussulman men and of Brahmin women, whom the Hills called Mother and the Plains Sister.'
>   So the record goes. (211)

The Baluchi shikari's observations read like a paean where the appellations of the goddess are chanted in celebration. Lawrence remarks on this appropriation of Louise's body by the Indian people: "Already the Mussulmans are making of the tomb a holy place. Little chiraghs, that is, wicks floating in oil, are placed on the plinth at night, their tiny flames guttering and blowing in the wind" (211). Putting the myths in the mouth of a Baluchi shikari and the act of worship in the hands of the Muslims raises Louise to a position rivaling the Indianization of Mrs. Moore in E. M. Forster's *A Passage to India*: "The tumult increased, the invocation of Mrs. Moore continued, and people who did not know what the syllables meant repeated them like a charm. They became Indianized into Esmiss Esmoor, they were taken up in the street outside" (218). Mrs. Moore's son, of course, finds this transformation a "revolting" travesty as the imperialist loses control over the naming process (219). We see a similar imperialist loss of control over the significance of Louise's name as the Baluchi shikari invokes "Indianized" titles. Similar to Mrs. Moore, the specificity of Louise's life is lost as she becomes appropriated and reinscribed in an altered colonialist discursive system.

Particularly interesting is how this argument suggests that Indians are uninterested in origins. According to Forster, those Indians who do not know "what the syllables meant" (218) are essentially uninterested in knowing; rather, they appropriate the language for their present use, in this case the freeing of Aziz. Lawrence implies a similar Indian lack of concern for origins in her discussion of Louise's tomb: "I suppose in years to come, when the stones split and gape and crumble as in those other tombs one sometimes passes, the origin of the lamps will be lost though still they may be lit" (211). In this passage, as in the one on Mrs. Moore, origins, quite literally originating in the bodies of these two memsahibs, are rendered immaterial. Even so, Lawrence's "Indianization" of Louise employs the Orientalist focus on India's timelessness; we see this in the mingling of her sister's decaying body with Indian religions. Perhaps, more than anything, this event terrifies Lawrence, as she sees India consuming the body of her sister. This process is similar to Mrs. Moore's body's transformation into something specifically tied to India: "[H]er body was lowered into yet another India—the Indian Ocean" (249). Although Mrs. Moore's ghost is said to follow the ship, that ghost is unable to enter the West: "Somewhere about Suez there is always a social change: the arrangements of Asia weaken and those of Europe begin to be felt,

and during the transition Mrs. Moore was shaken off" (249). This colonialist discourse makes India and Indian people, not the British, responsible for the annihilation of the origin (the body of the
memsahib).

This exscription of the body of the western woman creates a
sense of terror for the memsahib who needs to know, wants to know,
must know and remember the origin. However, as in the case of Lawrence, to remember the origin is to uncover the specter of the sister.
Lawrence voices this terror in her second recorded visit to Louise's
tomb. This visit serves as a metaphor for her dissociation: "Leaving
the car Umar and the dogs and I plough through loose sand up to
Louise's tomb lifted pale and solemn against the dark sky. For once
the wind has dropped. Not a dry thread on me. An ugly evening, an
uninspiring evening. I am defeated before I begin" (270). Her expression of defeat at the foot of her sister's tomb figuratively stands as her
ultimate failure. Because her sister has been raised to mythical proportions as the platonic memsahib and as an "Indianized" goddess,
Lawrence is predestined to fail. In the midst of her defeat, she becomes caught in a storm that instantly whips up, beating her physically, and seemingly metaphorically as well.

> Unexpectedly I am all at once TERRIFIED. Snatching up my things I begin
> floundering and running down hill through the loose sand, fast as I can.
> The heat, the stillness is frightful. Something is going to happen...an ap-
> palling noise. I'm on the ground. I can't breathe...I can't get up...Every-
> thing is quite black...I'm choking, I'm being beaten...I gasp...I try to get
> on my knees...I am forced down. What is it? WHAT IS IT? Is it the end of
> the world? (271)

In the chaos of the storm, Lawrence has an overwhelming sense of
annihilating terror and claustrophobia, typified in her inability to
breathe and in her choking and gasping. It is fitting that this terror
occurs at the place of her sister's decaying body and that Lawrence's
body takes an intense physical beating because, in confronting the
specter of the sister, Lawrence appears to be completely unable to assert any agency ("I am forced down"). Moreover, she is physically
obliterated, which is most evident in her cry, "Is it the end of the
world?"

Despite the fact that her body continues to prod her, this moment
at her sister's tomb serves as her rite of passage into the world of the
memsahib. After her metaphorical physical destruction, she locates
her greatest colonial association in her role as silent wife during a

moment of colonial revolt. The last pages of Lawrence's journal are devoted to the Punjab "uprisings" of April 1919. These incidents, beginning with Indian reaction against the repressive Rowlatt Acts, reawakened memories of the "Mutiny" for the British when a white woman, Miss Sherwood, was attacked by a group of Indian people. Major-General Dyer instituted the "crawling order," forcing all Indians to crawl on the street where Miss Sherwood had been attacked. The Punjab "uprisings" culminated in Dyer's horrific murders of hundreds at Jallianwalla Bagh. Lawrence, glossing over Dyer's action, situates the Punjab "uprisings" in a rhetoric of English women's bravery. "Horrible, most horrible murders. Police beaten, kerosene poured over them and set light to while they are still alive...I think how brave English women were, with their children, in the Afghan war, in the Mutiny; but I am afraid, though Henry does not guess it (388). Lawrence evokes the images of mutilated British women from the Indian Mutiny and thereby implicates herself in a rhetoric of narrative revolt.

However, Louise, who has become, surely a mythic figure, is unable to invoke the intensified discourse of a "native" revolt. In this way, Lawrence can supersede her sister by becoming the emblematic representation of all that is good and wholesome in empire. Lawrence, then, is most associated with empire when she exerts no agency and subjectivity. Henry makes this apparent when he sends Lawrence a poem, "To the Wife Silent in War-time," which praises the wife, "Who keeps safe locked within her breast....What things her soldier lord hath told" (qtd. in Lawrence 390). The paradox is that her greatest incorporation into empire comes at the price of her own individual identity. Lawrence is "honoured" for her "silence." The more she removes herself from view and binds herself to the will of her lord, the more she as an individual becomes nonexistent, the greater the honor. Therefore, her value to empire is achieved in her transformation into a nameless, "silent," disembodied figure. In fact, Lawrence tells us, "I was never more proud of anything in all my life" (391).

Lawrence's text reveals a disjointed movement between association and dissociation with India and Anglo-Indian society. In her attempt to locate a "misplaced identity," she calls up the alter egos of her spiritual ancestors for guidance. Some, like Sir Charles Napier, she manipulates to situate herself firmly in her new environment, but, at the same time, this association reveals her incomplete incorporation into the colonial project; as a woman, she can only vicariously experience the "masculine glories" of empire. Others, like Honoria Lawrence's association with the platonic memsahib, she seems to reject. Still others, like Louise Lawrence, she attempts to deny, but her body compels her to an acknowledgment. Always, however, attendant upon this process of association with and *in* India and Anglo-India is the slippage between herself and her alterego—the point where the metaphoric connection breaks down, revealing her uncertain and diffused perception of her role as a memsahib and allowing her readers to see how she designates herself and is designated multiply in colonial discourse.

Note

1   I use the term *incorporation* in the manner that Hillary Callan and Shirley Ardener do in their text, *The Incorporated Wife*. In the "Introduction," Callan states that incorporation explores "the condition of *wifehood*...where the social character ascribed to a woman is an intimate function of her husband's occupational identity and culture" (1).

Works Cited

Allen, Charles. *Plain Tales from the Raj: Images of British India in the Twentieth-Century.* New York: St. Martin's, 1975.

Barr, Pat. *The Memsahibs: The Women of Victorian England.* London: Secker and Warburg, 1976.

Brodzki, Bella, and Celeste Schenck, eds. *Life/Lines: Theorizing Women's Autobiography.* Ithaca, NY: Cornell UP, 1988.

Callan, Hilary, and Shirley Ardener, eds. *The Incorporated Wife.* London: Croom Helm, 1984.

Diver, Maud. *Honoria Lawrence: A Fragment of Indian History.* London: John Murray, 1936.

Forster, E. M. *A Passage to India.* San Diego: Harcourt Brace Jovanovich, 1984.

Fowler, Marion. *Below the Peacock Fan: First Ladies of the Raj.* Markham, Ontario: Viking, 1987.

Kroller, Eva-Marie. "First Impressions: Rhetorical Strategies in Travel Writing by Victorian Women." *Ariel* 21.4 (October 1990): 87–100.

Lawrence, John, and Audrey Woodiwiss, eds. *The Journals of Honoria Lawrence: India Observed, 1837–1854.* London: Hodder and Stoughton, 1980.

Lawrence, Rosamond. *Charles Napier: Friend and Fighter, 1782–1853.* London: John Murray, 1952.

———. *Indian Embers.* Oxford: George Ronald.

Mair, R. S. *A Medical Guide for Anglo-Indians.* Addendum to *The European in India; Or, Anglo-Indian's Vade-Mecum.* Ed. Edmund C. P. Hull. London: Henry S. King and Company, 1872.

Martin, Monica. *Out in the Mid-Day Sun.* Boston: Little, Brown and Company, 1949.

Mason, Mary G. "The Other Voice: Autobiographies of Women Writers." *Life/Lines: Theorizing Women's Autobiography.* Eds. Bella Brodzki and Celeste Schenck. Ithaca, NY: Cornell UP, 1988.

Mills, Sara. *Discourses of Difference: An Analysis of Women's Travel Writing and Colonialism.* New York: Routledge, 1991.

Paxton, Nancy. "Disembodied Subjects: English Women's Autobiography under the Raj." *De/Colonizing the Subject: The Politics of Gender in Women's Autobiography.* Eds. Sidonie Smith and Julia Watson. Minneapolis: U of Minnesota P, 1992. 387–409.

Ramusack, Barbara N. "Cultural Missionaries, Maternal Imperialists, Feminist Allies: British Women Activists in India, 1865–1945." *Western Women and Imperialism: Complicity and Resistance.* Eds. Nupur Chaudhuri and Margaret Strobel. Bloomington: Indiana UP, 1992. 119–36.

Said, Edward. Introduction. *Kim.* By Rudyard Kipling. New York: Penguin, 1987.

Smith, Sidonie. *A Poetics of Women's Autobiography: Marginality and the Fictions of Self-Representation.* Bloomington: Indiana UP, 1987.

———. *Subjectivity, Identity and the Body: Women's Autobiographical Practices in the Twentieth Century.* Bloomington: Indiana UP, 1993.

Smith, Sidonie, and Julia Watson, eds. *De/Colonizing the Subject: The Politics of Gender in Women's Autobiography.* Minneapolis: Minnesota UP, 1992.

Stanford, J. K. *Ladies in the Sun: The Memsahibs' India, 1790–1860.* London: Galley, 1962.

Suleri, Sara. *The Rhetoric of English India.* Chicago: U of Chicago P, 1992.

Wolpert, Stanley. *A New History of India.* 3rd ed. New York: Oxford UP, 1989.

American National Identity Abroad
The Travels of Nancy Prince

Kristin Fitzpatrick

Ships at a distance have every man's wish on board. For some they come in with the tide. For others they sail forever on the horizon, never landing until the Watcher turns his eyes away in resignation, his dreams mocked to death by Time. That is the life of man.

Now, women forget all those things they don't want to remember, and remember everything they don't want to forget. The dream is the truth. Then they act and do things accordingly.

—Zora Neale Hurston, *Their Eyes Were Watching God*

Travel literature has traditionally been the domain of every man's wish, its texts freighted with promise moving across distant horizons. The opening lines of *Their Eyes Were Watching God* rewrite Frederick Douglass's *Narrative of the Life of Frederick Douglass, an American Slave,* where he stands on the shores of the Chesapeake Bay and longs to flee on the white-winged ships thronging the horizon (Gates 3). Zora Neale Hurston uses the horizon to reconfigure the relations between home and abroad, men and women (1). By writing in reference to an already established African American tradition of letters, Hurston complicates the whiteness of American national identity and situates at its heart what Toni Morrison calls an "unsettled and unsettling population" against which American literature and nationality define themselves (6). In speaking of her project to explore Americanness, Morrison opens with metaphors of travel and charting the New World "without the mandate for conquest" (3). Her writing, like Hurston's, has a topographical dimension that carries encoded within it movement across the middle passage and the conceptualization of identity as lost and rewoven in the movement shuttling between points, with the beyond, both a threat and a promise.

She and Hurston cast the relationship between national and personal identity as one of individual to horizon, and, indeed, America has historically been formed at the crossroads of traveling cultures, many of them moving in order to escape oppression. The country is a nation of travelers, willing and unwilling, who unsettle American conceptions of self. However, most tales of travel handed down to us are the accounts predominantly of Anglo-American men. Gender and travel intersect in Hurston's rewriting of Douglass, where women and men's different relationships to the horizon throw "home" and traditional gender roles into question.

Travel literature makes a project of difference. Nations, as well as individuals, define themselves comparatively against that which they are not. If countries are, as Benedict Anderson has proposed, imagined communities, then they need to tell themselves and the international community coherent tales about themselves. Travelogues thus reaffirm or question the integrity of national identity. In nineteenth-century America, the spate of publications by women about overseas voyages allowed women to engage issues of nationalism indirectly. However, women—particularly women of color—often betrayed ambivalence toward their country, which did not grant them full access to all rights of citizenship. African American women in particular were painfully aware of these inequities at home. Considerable attention has focused on writings by Anglo-American and European women abroad, mainly because few women of color had the financial resources—or the physical liberty—to travel and publish. However, while we have access to few travel narratives by women of color, we need to explore them for the ways in which they can unsettle established conventions of travel literature and our understanding of American nationalism then and now.

Nancy Gardner Prince, one of the best traveled American women of her time, wrote the first travel narrative by an African American woman. On April 14, 1824, Prince left the United States for Russia, where she lived for nine years, married to a footman in the court of the Czar. Seven years later, inspired by the British Assembly's emancipation of former slaves in the West Indies, she traveled to Jamaica, where she witnessed the jubilation and turmoil in the aftermath of colonialism. Prince lectured on and published her travels in order to raise consciousness about racism and to support herself. On March 8, 1839, the antislavery newspaper *Liberator* carried a small notice announcing a lecture by her on Russia. She later wrote a pamphlet on

Jamaica (1841) and finally combined her accounts of Russia and Jamaica in *Narrative of the Life and Travels, of Mrs. Nancy Prince,* which was first published in 1850, followed by an expanded edition in 1852, and released in a third and final edition in 1856. The edition cited here was published as *A Black Woman's Odyssey through Russia and Jamaica* (1990) with an introduction by Ronald G. Walters.

Prince's narrative raises the challenges African American women faced when writing themselves as American subjects in the predominantly white, male genre of travel. Travel literature requires the American national abroad to anchor the narrative with a clear sense of his or her own identity as an American. This proved to be doubly complicated for black women travelers writing within a genre largely dominated by white, male writers. How to claim the narrative "I," when it wasn't clear who the "I" was in terms of a nationality predicated on masculinity and whiteness? How to write within a genre that essentially demanded allegiance to these women's oppressors?

Without female literary antecedents in the field of travel, Prince drew on two particular genres, the spiritual narrative and slave narrative that allowed black, self-educated women to claim the traditionally male prerogatives of literacy and movement. Nineteenth-century women were not expected to articulate themselves publicly, much less raise voice to criticize their circumstances. They suffered a lack of authorial legitimacy, and black women doubly so. However, as critics such as Frances Smith Foster (*Written by Herself*), Hazel Carby ("Hear My Voice, Ye Careless Daughters"), and Joanne Braxton (*Black Women Writing Autobiography*) argue, slave narratives provided black women with an already established genre devoted to explicating and condemning exploitation. As William Andrews (*Sisters of the Spirit*), Joanne Braxton, and Joycelyn Moody ("On the Road with God") point out, first-person spiritual narratives, often written by itinerant women preachers, validated the mobile female voice and justified women claiming authority for themselves. Critics have generally discussed Prince's *Narrative* in the context of these genres because she draws very strongly on them to criticize slavery and colonialism. However, in doing so, critics have focused on only part of Prince's work, the sections on Jamaica and the United States, while ignoring the opening in Russia. Prince's stay in Russia indeed appears remarkably unremarkable and reads like any other nineteenth-century travelogue. Including Russia, however, and tracing the whole trajectory of the *Narrative* through Russia, Jamaica, and the United States allows us to investi-

gate Prince as a writer at the roots of African American travel literature, one whose writing had consequences for later travelogues by
black Americans.

Travel allowed black writers like Prince to create an international
standpoint from which to criticize the United States. Extensive travel
urged readers to see the black writer as "truly a world citizen whose
knowledge extends beyond American scenes of poverty, beyond
America and beyond Europe" (Martin 64). Such a writer tried "to establish credibility for the international black mind, important not
for its color, but for its sensitivity and reach" (64). By portraying
themselves as "world citizens," black American travelers like Prince
challenged nineteenth-century America's refusal to accord them citizenship. African Americans who found respect on the other side of
the Atlantic put the United States in the unsavory position of supporting an internationally condemned institution, which is the strategy
Prince subtly follows by contrasting the equitable treatment she receives in Russia and the West Indies with continued slavery in the
States.

Her return to the United States by way of the South is often seen
by critics simply as extending her criticism of slavery to the United
States; what is striking, however, is the sense in the conclusion that
she is not returning home but entering another foreign country more
hostile than any other she has visited. With legal actions like the Fugitive Slave Act (1850) and the Dred Scott Case (1857), the United States
effectively framed all black residents as, at best, legal aliens, and we
sense that in Prince's homecoming, which really highlights the absence of a home for black Americans at this time. However, this
meaning only becomes apparent by recasting Prince's writing as a
travel narrative and tracing the tensions that arise between home and
horizon in her narrative. As Prince shuttles between the United States
and abroad, she uses geography to triangulate who she is as a black
American, woman, and American. By looking at the tensions among
these identities in her narrative, we can develop some understanding
of how gender, ethnicity, and nationality mesh to form a national
identity.

Prince's narrative falls in three parts, moving through Russia,
Jamaica, and back to the United States. Before beginning with Russia,
however, it is worth exploring her motive for leaving the United
States in the first place and how she frames her departure, because
these things reveal the strategies she uses to establish authorial le-

gitimacy vital to the narrative. Prince's foremost concern is to establish authorial legitimacy as a black American and as a woman. As a black American, she initially subordinates her skin color to nationality by detailing her family's long historical roots in the United States and expressing her deep loyalty to her country. This opening genealogy, while standard for autobiographical narratives, also documents her family's American nationality and secures her audience's trust in her as an American. Thus, her hardships cannot be brushed off as individual but rather become national difficulties. Consequently, when Prince finally does admit that she decided to leave the United States, because seven years of providing for her siblings and fighting racial prejudice had worn her out, her departure obliquely criticizes the nation and makes racial prejudice a national rather than a personal burden.

Prince's desire to leave is not only motivated by discrimination, but, she says, by a determination to do something for herself. However, it is not until her marriage to Nero Prince, one of twenty black foreigners serving in Alexander's court, that she leaves the United States. Her relationship with "Mr. Prince," as she insists on calling him throughout, seems simply to fill the narrative function of lending propriety to her movements abroad. Mr. Prince is never referred to outside his capacity as a husband, and the marriage is conflated with Nancy's desire to leave and subsequent departure. Her most intimate remarks on the subject are merely that "after seven years of anxiety and toil, I made up my mind to leave my country. September 1st, 1823, Mr. Prince arrived from Russia. February 15th, 1824, we were married. April 14th, we embarked on board the Romulus, captain Epes Sargent commander, bound for Russia" (15). We hear little more about Nero Prince, except that he was born in Marlborough, met Nancy at her mother's in-between trips in 1810 and 1812 to St. Petersburg (16), served Princess Purtossof in the Czar's court (17), and died before he could follow her back to the United States (45). Curiously, she doesn't tell us that he was also a prominent citizen in the United States, where he was elected the second grand master of the African Grand Lodge of the Masons, which he had organized and helped found in 1791 (Blakely 15). While Prince's reticence about their relationship is not unusual by nineteenth-century standards, the way in which she articulates her marriage is clearly a perfunctory nod to conventions demanding that women not travel alone. The marriage, along with her conversion to Christianity at age sixteen, and insistent propriety (she doesn't drink, dance, or gamble, even at the Russian court), set her up as a decent Christian woman whose veracity—and, by extension, that of her narrative—can be trusted.

Most importantly for narrative credibility, where the reader might expect a self-educated black woman to have limited powers of perception or stock of cultural knowledge, Prince commands a cultural mastery that rivals any other nineteenth-century traveler. While in Russia, Prince learns Sclavonian and Polish, languages of the common Russians, as well as modern Greek and French, languages of the nobility—all in the space of six months, she tells us. She writes extensive histories of the areas she visits, not only giving factual information but using the past to explain present developments. In St. Petersburg, she traces the origins of the 1825 Decembrist Revolt back to 1814, when German and Russian nobility united in the hopes of establishing a republican government, details Russia's wars with Turkey and Poland, and explains the origins of the 1831 cholera epidemic. In Jamaica and the West Indies, she shows how extant political chaos, corruption, and racial tensions were the legacy of colonialism and slavery, not proof of blacks' inherent inability to govern themselves, as many tried to argue in the United States. By working her great command of history, languages, and politics into the narrative, Prince proves her intellectual equality and demands membership in Europe and America as an equal. Due to the limited number of publications by black female contemporaries, Prince must have been aware that anything she wrote could have been seen as representative of black American women in their entirety. If, as Edward Said theorizes, cultural access also provides entrance to political communities, then literacy becomes a passport to citizenship, and Prince was literally writing herself and others into the American citizenship still denied them at that time.

The rhetorical strategies Prince uses to legitimize her narrative are set up in the section on Russia, a country seemingly free of racism. Critics have generally passed over Prince's writing on Russia because it makes little direct mention of racism, but this issue needs to be addressed precisely because the quiet acceptance Prince encounters in Russia contrasts strongly with the racially charged atmosphere in the United States and Jamaica, where such normative relations are impossible. Russia functions as an exemplar of racial tolerance in Prince's text: By the time she arrived, slavery had been outlawed in Russia since the previous century, and there were many blacks who had obtained high social and professional status, both inside the court and in Russian society at large. Along with her husband, Prince was invited to court social gatherings, accepted orders from the Empress and ladies of the court for her needlework and children's clothing, and was active in a local church. She writes that upon arrival, Emperor Alexander and Empress Elizabeth presented her with a watch and other gifts. There "was no prejudice against color; there were all casts, and the people of all nations, each in their place" (17–18). Her strategic comment on the lack of prejudice in Russia's highest institution implies that a country's racial divisiveness or tolerance flows from its highest governing seats. She insinuates that American racism is effectively condoned by its government, for if czarist Russia is enlightened enough to accept all colors, casts, and nations, surely the republican, democratic United States can do the same. As Hazel Carby notes, Prince continues to criticize the United States throughout her narrative by using indirect international parallels (60). This tactic proves particularly effective, because it avoids directly undermining the American nationalism that she draws upon to enlist her reader's empathy and trust, and yet it does shame the United States through comparison with other countries.

This international perspective also allows Prince to analyze the mechanics of oppression and theorize ways in which power operates across national, ethnic, and gender lines. Prince was one of the first black Americans to use international analysis to criticize imperialism in Jamaica and, by extension, the United States, which Prince showed as an imperial power with oppression at its foundation. While the United States tried to cast slavery as a purely internal matter, Prince's international analysis of colonialism argues otherwise. Her analysis begins, oddly enough, in Russia, where she criticizes slavery by comparing it with exploitation of the serfs: "This class of people till the land, most of them are slaves and are very degraded. The rich own the poor, but they are not suffered to separate families or sell them off the soil" (30). Her international comparison reminds readers that exploitation is not limited to a particular country. The comparison also denies biological essentialism as the grounds for American slavery: The serfs are suffering due to an imbalance of power, not to the color of their skins. Shared race does not undermine Prince's critique, as initially might seem to be the case, but becomes central to it by de-essentializing American slavery. This example foreshadows Prince's much more direct attack on slavery in the next section on Jamaica, where she analyzes the wages of colonialism in the aftermath of British rule.

Prince returned home from Russia in 1833 due to failing health, unable to tolerate another Russian winter. Her husband planned to follow after a couple years but died before returning to the United States. Prince involved herself in social work and the Anti-Slavery Society, and later that year, inspired by British manumission freeing the slaves in the West Indies, she resolved to go to Jamaica. Her purpose was to aid the black community in its transition to self-government, but when she arrived in Jamaica after a harrowing voyage plagued by storms and pirates, she was appalled at the extent of colonialism's legacy. Whites still controlled the government and resources, missionaries exhorted money where they could, and sharecropping kept black Jamaicans in perpetual slavery. Racial tension was extremely high, with former slave owners destroying relinquished property and putting down celebrations with force, and blacks paying back white cruelty in turn. For example, Prince relates that the Maroons, former slaves who arrived from Sierra Leone in 1841 and now controlled Jamaica's mountainous areas, trapped whites crossing the passes. The Maroons killed their prisoners or returned in kind the cruelty they had suffered as slaves (60). Ironically, in the years following Prince's visit, the Maroons were hired by whites to hunt down black Jamaicans.

Prince traces all problems back to colonialism and concludes: "It is not surprising that this people are full of deceit and lies, this is the fruits of slavery, it makes master and slaves knaves" (65). In the process of analyzing the lasting scars of slavery and British rule, she lays out the dynamics of colonialism and extends them to the United States by connecting her stay in Jamaica with her subsequent return to the United States by way of the South. Comparison with the foreign allows for an indirect critique of home that avoids openly implicating or accusing white abolitionists in Prince's audience, yet her intention of countering American arguments for slavery is very clear.

Her principal strategy for undermining slavery is to dispel stereotypes about blacks that were used by slave owners to justify slavery's ostensible necessity. One argument slave owners regularly fronted was that African Americans were inherently lazy and therefore needed a firm hand to discipline and provide for them. Prince proves this idea as specious, noting that the farmers' markets in Jamaica are all built and run by black Jamaicans:

> Thus it may be hoped they are not the stupid set of beings they have been called; here surely we see industry; they are enterprising and quick in their perceptions, determined to possess themselves, and to possess property besides, and quite able to take care of themselves. They wished to know why I was so inquisitive about them. I told them that we had heard in America that you are lazy, and that emancipation has been of no benefit to you; I wish to inform myself of the truth respecting you, and give a true account on my return. (54)

The Jamaicans' work ethic and self-sufficiency challenge racist portrayals of American blacks and throw into question the logic of arguing inherent superiority based on skin color. Prince's insistence on the veracity of her words and theirs harkens to narratives by escaped slaves, who were in the position of convincing skeptical white audiences of the horrors they had fled. In her travels throughout Jamaica and the West Indies, Prince quotes a great number of former slaves, whose firsthand accounts lend credence to her arguments. The international context of her critique renders it even more effective because she can confront the United States with evidence of a black community's successful transition from forced dependence to freedom, and Britain's recognition of black rights across national boundaries further sanctions her critique. Manumission in countries so close to American borders added impetus to the abolition movement and left the United States with the shameful international reputation of defending slavery.

The section on Jamaica is targeted at black as well as white members of Prince's readership. Prince writes to disillusion, effectively writing an immigrant guide warning the black members of her audience who might go seeking new freedom in Jamaica. She notes that many blacks arrive in Jamaica under the impression that their passage was free: Instead, they are jailed upon landing and generally end up back on plantations, ostensibly working until they can pay back their passage (55). Even those who are free, she says, face many of the same obstacles present under slavery; given the challenges of sharecropping, opportunist merchants, and racial prejudice, whites take blacks' money as fast as they can earn it. Some have such difficulty earning a living that they return to work for their former masters, who then, one man notes bitterly, proclaim that free blacks do not know how to work. Looking at the aftermath of British rule in postcolonial Jamaica, Prince identifies violence, economic exploitation, and prejudice as strategies employed by a dominant group to maintain power. With these methods of control perpetuating white dominance even under the guise of freedom, the end of slavery does not automatically establish an egalitarian society. Through comparison, Prince warns African Americans not only against false assumptions about Jamaica but about the United States. As free blacks like Prince already knew too well, life in the North was not free from racial prejudice, and abolishing slavery would not immediately end attempts by whites to control and subjugate black Americans. Despite this grim picture, Prince leaves her audience with some hope and little doubt about the moral imperative of abolishing slavery. During a brief visit to the liberated West Indies, she quotes an older woman who, despite her poverty, says: "'Now not bad now as in the time of slavery; then God spoke very loud to Bucker (the white people,) to let us go.'" Prince amends, "May these words be engraved on the post of every door in this land of New England. God speaks very loud..." (69).

Casting slavery as an abomination in terms of Christian morality was a common rhetorical practice in abolitionist texts. Many slave narratives found powerful sanction in the very religion that was also used to justify slavery. Nineteenth-century America strongly identified itself as Christian, with Christian morality forming the backbone of the nation. By arguing slavery's immorality on these religious grounds, abolitionists cast slavery as not only un-Christian but un-American. Writers like Prince used their faith to break convention conservatively, in the name of maintaining a Christian morality fundamental to American national identity. Thus, although this *Narrative* risked losing readers' sympathy by denouncing America's racism and sexism, the appeal to God as a final authority ultimately made her criticism patriotic and reinforced the status of blacks and women as American citizens.

While white women travelers could draw on male narratives and class privilege for validation, these avenues were generally closed to black women on the road, who chose to see racial and sexual differences as secondary in the eyes of God. Prince does use the form of a traditional travel narrative in describing Russia, but in writing about Jamaica and the West Indies she chooses a narrative form better designed to legitimate her authorial position vis-à-vis the highly charged topic of slavery. There is no need to invoke a higher power when describing the Frozen Market of St. Petersburg or Greek Orthodox funeral rites she observed in Russia because these hardly challenge America's self-image. Slavery, however, was the cleft in national identity at this time, and if Prince was going to argue not only against slavery, but against the myth of racial equality in the North, she needed to reach for the most powerful validation possible.

One of the institutions Prince criticizes most strongly for exploiting blacks in Jamaica and the United States is, ironically enough, the church. The extent to which white missionaries take advantage of the people tremendously discourages her in Jamaica. Prince reports being threatened by local missionaries after they discover her giving, rather than selling, Bibles to the poor. Churches actively recruit blacks to raise membership and donations, because "colored people give more readily, and are less suspicious of imposition, if one from themselves recommends the measure; this the missionaries understand very well, and know how to take advantage of it" (49). Black Jamaicans are such a profitable source of income for the church that many of the missionaries joke about becoming "macroon" hunters (49). This exploitation is not limited to Jamaica, however. Prince also has little good to say about white Christians in the United States. As a child, she recounts, she worked for a "religious family." Her days with them often began at two in the morning and ran until late in the night. After three months, she left them, exclaiming, "They had family prayers, morning and evening. Oh! yes, they were sanctimonious!" (7).

The church, it seems, is simply yet another colonialist institution in both Jamaica and the United States that hedges white privilege and takes little interest in blacks aside from their potential as a financial resource. Prince concludes that "man has disobeyed his Maker....God has in all ages of the world punished every nation and people for their sins. The sins of my beloved country are not hid from his notice" (47–48). Even men and nations are subject to divine authority, a particularly effective rhetorical strategy given that a large part of Prince's audience is Christian and will feel itself called to account. Despite her call to judgment, however, she still asserts her loyalty to the "beloved country" of her audience, thus situating the abolitionist position as truly patriotic.

However, Prince's return to the United States is not an occasion for patriotism. While her first voyage home from Jamaica is uneventful, like that from Russia, and is simply noted as "successful," her final return in 1841 was perilous in the extreme. The ship sailed through several storms, and the captain made unannounced stops in New Orleans and Key West, where Prince and the other passengers bound for New York were forced to change ships before reaching relative safety in the North. The black passengers were in great danger the moment they left the ships: As soon as their feet touched American soil, they could be taken into so-called "custody" and sold into slavery. At each stop in the South, Prince writes, "[E]very inducement was made to persuade me to go ashore, or set my feet on the wharf. A law had just been passed there that every free colored person coming there, should be put in custody on their going ashore" (77). Due to this law, Prince and the other five African Americans on board did not dare stir from the ship, at each stop spending three or four days tied up in dock, unable to go ashore for dry clothes, fresh food, or water. This second voyage meandering back through the South contrasts the freedom of black Jamaicans with the sharply proscribed freedom of ostensibly "free" African Americans like Prince. Whereas the racial egalitarianism she experienced in Europe now extends even to Jamaica and the West Indies, slavery still thrives in the United States, the single site of virulent racism and inequality in her worldly narrative. The transition in the Caribbean from colonial rule to equality is undeniably rough: The power inequities that are colonialism's legacy will, it seems, continue to distort relations between people of color and whites for years to come. However, the process has begun, whereas in the United States, colonialism continues in full force. By detailing her experiences on this final return to the United States, Prince carries over the dynamics of colonialism to home and brings the critique, subtly begun in Russia, full circle to the United States.

When the ship docks in New Orleans, it becomes clear that white Americans do not view Prince as an American citizen returning home but as a ruled subject again under their jurisdiction. The southerners demand to see her protection, saying they have heard that it is under the Russian government. She counters their demands for national identification with a biblical passage foretelling the fall of Babylon, a city grown wealthy from the slave trade: "I pointed them to the 18th chapter of Revelations and 15th verse: 'The merchants of these things which were made rich by her, shall stand afar off, for the fear of her torment, weeping and wailing. For strong is the Lord God who judgeth her.' They made no answer, but asked the Captain how soon he should get away" (81). By speaking of Babylon's fall due to slavery, Prince condemns the slave owners taunting her from the docks and the captain of her ship, who stops just short of physically putting her off board into their hands. Whether Prince's listeners realize it or not, she is prophesying the fall of at least the South, if not the entire

United States, grown rich from slavery. However, Prince's listeners need not be intimately acquainted with the Bible to read the threat in this passage. As a black woman, she is without recourse to American citizenship or its attendant legal rights, but by reframing a debate about nationality, where she necessarily loses, into one of morality, she appropriates the religion of her oppressors and holds them accountable to their own beliefs. With her "citizenship" Christianity and her "protection" God, Prince has ingeniously given an answer to which there can be no objection that does not challenge the overriding authority of God. By denying the divine authority behind Prince's passage, her interlocutors, even if less than devout Christians, run the risk of proving American morality a sham, so Prince gambles on the southerners' allegiance to God and country, and she wins.

The ship becomes a contested space, which Prince defends verbally against the men cajoling and threatening her from the shore and docks. She uses "sass" to talk them down and hold them back from the ship. "I found it necessary to be stern with them," she writes; "they were very rude; if I had not been so, I know not what would have been the consequences" (80). As long as Prince and the other African Americans remain on board, they are on neutral ground outside the reach of southern law, and as long as the Southerners remain reluctant to physically assert their intentions, the fragile line of demarcation holds. Interestingly, the men outside are nearly as afraid of Prince as she is of them. They insist they do not want to harm her, but "'we do not want you here...' said they; 'we shall watch you like the d— until you go away; you must not say any thing to these negros whilst you are here.' 'Why, then, do you talk to me, if you do not want me to say any thing to you? If you will let me alone, I will you'" (80–81). As the Southerners' nervousness attests, Prince is dangerous. Her freedom of speech and movement defy their equation of blackness with slavery and could incite other blacks to demand the same liberties she possesses. Her very existence testifies to the possibility of black literacy, self-determination, and potential racial and gender equality.

Prince's extensive use of dialogue in this section is noteworthy as well. William Andrews explains that black nineteenth-century writers often included dialogue in their narratives to counter abolitionist and southern images of women as passive. Black women's voices were often left out of print at this time, and this silence abetted objectification and abuse. Prince writes herself as a speaking subject into the text and, by documenting her exchange with the southerners, she gives lie to their power and black women's presupposed helplessness. Prince's oratory skills essentially create a free space on board the ship: Biblical literacy and oration prove to be the currency of freedom. They hold back the Southerners and allow Prince to articulate herself as a subject demanding equal consideration in the eyes of her opponents. This is the only time Prince ever includes extensive direct dialogue in her *Narrative*: In Russia, she writes descriptively, and in Jamaica and the West Indies, she records the voices of manumitted blacks. Here, however, her status as a human being is threatened as nowhere else in her travels. By recording her exchanges with the men about her status as a sentient, self-possessed human being, Prince documents her humanity and makes a powerful argument for black Americans' rights to citizenship.

Prince seems to be aware at some level that, as a traveler crossing national and ideological boundaries, she represents a certain potential for transgression. The comparative perspectives Prince develops allowed her to survey home and herself from various angles and to question American presumptions about America's place in the world, while the need for authorial legitimacy also keeps her tethered to certain conservative ideologies of propriety and femininity. The multiplicity of cultural and national practices she encounters relativizes American ideals and leaves readers forced to take stock of their own participation in the inequities she experiences at home. Europe afforded Prince some degree of latitude regarding her status as a black American: Repatriation therefore necessitates making a series of difficult decisions about which national ideologies to challenge upon return, with what strategy, and at what price.

Nineteenth-century women travelers usually finished their narratives by emphasizing their happy satisfaction at coming home, thus reassuring their readers that their ultimate allegiance lay with American ideologies. Freedoms enjoyed abroad can thus be recast as adventurous flirtations with foreign ways, now set aside as souvenirs— literally memories, in the French sense of the word—separate from the fabric of daily life, with no threatening implications for American ways. However, these conclusions often sound strained, suggesting that returning stateside meant giving up the freedom of movement and sometimes greater social latitude many American women reported enjoying abroad.

Prince's *Narrative* presents a startling contrast and reminds us that race has been elided in discussions of nineteenth-century travel narratives by predominantly white women. Happiness is markedly absent from Prince's return. The last words of her narrative are, rather than a move toward closure, an appeal for continued protection. She closes with a poem titled "The Hiding Place," thanking God for safe passage and continuing to provide a haven from the dangers of the world:

> ...I'm in a wilderness below,
> Lord, guide me all my journey through,
> Plainly let me thy footsteps trace,
> Which lead to heaven, my hiding place.
> Should dangers thick impede my course,
> O let my soul sustain no loss;
> Help me to run the Christian race,
> And enter safe my hiding place.
>
> Then with enlarged powers,
> I'll triumph in redeeming love,
> Eternal ages will I praise,
> My Lord for such a hiding place. (90–91)

While the poem's content is continuous with the faith running through her account, the way each verse concludes with the words "hiding place" coincides very uneasily with this, the end of her journey. Who or what is she hiding from if she is truly home? History gives us a clear answer, and the American nation is implicitly condemned: God, not America, is her refuge and the highest authority to which she can appeal. The freedom she experiences as an American citizen abroad melts away upon reentry, an irony not lost on Prince or her readers. Freedom at home is at best a conditional, uncertain state. As an African American, she is suspended in the hyphen in-between identities, with neither promising stability nor protection. "The Hiding Place" leaves us with the uneasy sense that the country Prince repatriates to is not, and has never been, her own. Rather than a returning citizen, she is a fugitive in her own land, where the journey out is less perilous than the journey home.

Works Cited

Andrews, William L., ed. *Sisters of the Spirit: Three Black Women's Autobiographies of the Nineteenth Century*. Bloomington: Indiana UP, 1986.

Blakely, Allison. *Russia and the Negro: Blacks in Russian History and Thought*. Washington, DC: Howard UP. 1986.

Braxton, Joanne. *Black Women Writing Autobiography: A Tradition within a Tradition*. Philadelphia: Temple UP, 1989.

Carby, Hazel. "'Hear My Voice Ye Careless Daughters': Narratives of Slave and Free Women before Emancipation." *African American Autobiography*. Ed. William Andrews. Englewood Cliffs, NJ: Prentice Hall. 1993. 59–76.

Foster, Frances Smith. *Written by Herself: Literary Production by African American Women, 1746–1892*. Bloomington: Indiana UP, 1993.

Gates, Jr., Henry Louis. "*Their Eyes Were Watching God*: Hurston and the Speakerly Text." *Zora Neale Hurston: Critical Perspectives Past and Present*. Ed. Henry Louis Gates Jr. and K. A. Appiah. New York: Amistad Press, 1993. 154–203.

Hurston, Zora Neale. *Their Eyes Were Watching God*. New York: Harper & Row, 1990.

Martin, Charles. "Coloring Books: Black Writing on Europe." *Mosaic: A Journal for the Interdisciplinary Study of Literature* 26.4 (1993): 53–67.

Moody, Joycelyn. "On the Road with God." *Religion and Literature* 27.1 (1995): 35–50.

Morrison, Toni. *Playing in the Dark: Whiteness and the Literary Imagination*. Cambridge: Harvard UP, 1992.

Prince, Nancy Gardner. *Narrative of the Life and Travels, of Mrs. Nancy Prince*. In *A Black Woman's Odyssey Through Russia and Jamaica*. Ed. Ronald G. Walters. 1850. New York: Markus Wiener Publishing, 1990.

Said, Edward. *Culture and Imperialism*. New York: Vintage Books, 1994.

Walters, Ronald G. Introduction. *A Black Woman's Odyssey Through Russia and Jamaica*. Ed. Ronald Walters. New York: Markus Wiener Publishing, 1990. 9–23.

Chapter Fourteen

Alexandra David-Néel's Home in the Himalayas
Where the Heart Lies

Margaret McColley

lexandra David-Néel (1868–1969), traveler, writer, scholar, and anarchist, became a figure of international renown as the first western woman to cross the forbidden border of Lhasa in 1924. Disguised as a beggar, draped in dark clothing, and with her face painted in dark brown paint, David-Néel stealthily crossed this border by night with her Sikkimese traveling companion Aphur Yongden. Her disguise as a native Tibetan pilgrim was perhaps her most literal form of assimilation throughout her travels in the East. Her overall mission, however, was to learn about eastern religions and philosophy through serious linguistic and cultural immersion, in the hopes of bringing a more vibrant aspect to what she believed was the unnecessarily dry and lifeless erudition of the French orientalists of her era (*Correspondence* 84).

David-Néel's narrative account of her rebellious border crossing, *My Journey to Lhasa*, was published simultaneously in Paris, New York, and London in 1927. In her introduction to the English edition, she addresses the English who made her a guest during her Asian travels, thanking them "for so many hearty welcomes in so many houses where kind ladies have endeavored to make me feel as if I were in my real home" (xxxix). Prior to her travels in India and Tibet, David-Néel had spent time in England studying the English language in order to facilitate her communication with speakers of English during her travels. By addressing English women in this way, she builds a linguistic bridge of thanks in the closing lines of an introduction in which she also criticizes Britain's colonial presence in Asia, stating: "[T]he Asiatic who sees his country enslaved is...justified in lacking friendly feelings toward the people who have robbed him of his possessions" (xxxvi). Interestingly and perhaps ironically, she thanks British women for taking her into their colonial homes at a time in her life when she has abandoned the building of a traditional western home for a nomadic life on the trail.

The present discussion of home is primarily drawn from David-Néel's voluminous collection of letters to her husband, Philip Néel, a railroad magistrate whose residence was in Tunis (*Correspondance* 11). This two-volume collection was written during her remarkable thirty-five years of travel in Asia, and published for the first time in 1975 as her *Journal de Voyage: Lettres à son Mari*. In 2000 it appeared in a new edition as *Correspondance avec son mari: 1904–1941*.

Although David-Néel's *Correspondance* is written almost entirely in French, she employs the English word *home* throughout. The word *home* thus rings like a kind of mantra throughout her letters, standing out from the otherwise French context in a semantically noteworthy way, as when, shortly after her marriage to Philip at the Tunisian consulate in 1904, she writes to him from Paris, saying: "Nous nous ferions un home confortable...et je me plongerais jusqu'au cou dans mes études d'orientalisme...." ["We would make a comfortable home... and I would plunge myself up to the neck in my Orientalist studies"] (44). Although David-Néel expresses a desire for home building with her husband in this letter, it was written at the beginning of a correspondence that would eventually become the main tie she keeps to him after her departure in 1911 for Asia from the Tunisian address they shared.

We can decipher within the early stages of the correspondence that the domestic space Alexandra shares with Philip has already been troubled by what appear to be confessions of infidelity on the part of Philip. Significantly, Alexandra calls this infidelity "les erre-ments," or, "strayings," as when she expresses her wish to rebuild a home with her husband "sans chercher à introduire...les errements de ménages commencés sous de tout autres auspices" ["without seeking to introduce...strayings from the home which began under completely different auspices"] (47). Alexandra's use of the word *errements* is particularly interesting in consideration of her own wanderings from Tunis to France so soon after her marriage, for her first departure from the home she shares with Philip provides her with the distance necessary to envision (and to articulate) ideas about a more perfect home. Thus, she writes to Philip from Paris on September 27, 1904, wishing for a more peaceful place to return to, and beckoning Philip to help her create this space: "travaille avec joie à notre nouveau home qui sera un asile de repos et de paix pour tous deux" ["work joyfully on our new home which will be a sanctuary of rest and peace for both of us"] (26). What we do not know at this point in the correspondence is that Alexandra will find this place of peace on her own on a high mountain slope in the Himalayas.

While further considering David-Néel's frequent use of the word *home* in her correspondence with Philip, the *Oxford English Language Dictionary* was consulted in an effort to measure its significance in an otherwise French context. It revealed a chosen hierarchy of meaning covering several pages, telling of how Anglophones have come to view home and its linguistic parameters.

The entry for *at home* reads:

   a. At one's own house, or place of abode,
   b. In one's own neighborhood, town, country, etc.; in one's native land. (Opp. To abroad.) In the mother-country, in England.
   c. At one's ease, as if in one's home; in one's element; [...] familiar or conversant in. ("Home", def. 11)

This last, interiorized, concept most closely resembles *home* as Alexandra understood and lived it. Home was a place that she carried inside of herself, a spiritual place that called for few material accoutrements. By carrying her sense of home within, especially at a time when the word *home* had evolved to mean "the mother country" of England and the homes the English made for themselves abroad, she breaks down the traditional walls of this concept. Furthermore, her choice to live on a path of mobility can be read as a resistance to adhering to widely accepted constructions of home that had sprung from nineteenth-century bourgeois values in England, Belgium, and France. For by actively seeking displacement from a domestic life that threatened to keep her immobilized, David-Néel embarks upon a long journey within the early stages of her marriage to Philip, thereby actualizing her desire for permanent and unhampered mobility. Then, by attempting to maintain communication with her husband as his wife, she asks him to meet her on intellectual and spiritual ground, and to help build what she calls "un rapprochement de nos esprits," a bringing together of souls crossing continental divides (55).

In her introduction to *Home and Its Dislocations in Nineteenth-Century France,* Suzanne Nash artfully points to how the notion of *home* (and even more significantly, the *lack* of home) plays a fundamental role in our understanding of modern history and artistic representation, saying that "Twentieth-century theorists of modernity have frequently chosen metaphors of homelessness to describe the aesthetic repercussions of cultural change" (1). In what might seem to represent a paradox, material *homelessness* was at the very core of Alexandra David-Néel's sense of home, for she adopted two personal devices which, when read together, reflect how her notion of Self is linked to *homelessness* and the desire for movement. First, she borrowed from *Ecclesiastes* (XII: 1) in adopting: "Walk where your heart leads you and where your eyes take you" (455). Then, drawing together Hebrew and Hindu verse, she also adopted the essential call to "find everything within the self" from the Upanishads (478). Thus, her philosophical path reflects a marriage of traditions shaping Eastern and Western thinking that is at the very core of her outward gaze as a travel writer (Désiré-Marchand 5). The union of these two ideas also suggests that forward movement necessarily fuels her need for inner reflection; it is both the very foundation for building a sense of wholeness and the nourishment that feeds the flow of her pen.

The desire for travel was a seed firmly planted in the heart and mind of Alexandra during her childhood. The young Alexandra was raised an only child in a bourgeois home in late nineteenth-century Belgium, characterized by what she describes in her letters as an atmosphere of suffocation. She was the daughter of Louis David, a journalist of Huguenot descent who sought exile in Belgium with his friend Victor Hugo after the coup d'état of 1852 (39). Her mother, Alexandra, was a devout woman of Catholic faith who showed very little affection toward her daughter and namesake (36). In one description of her life as a child within her parents' house, she tells of a museum-like setting in which her mother and father resembled statues facing one another for fifty years, as much strangers to one another at the end of their marriage as at the beginning: "Mon ami, si tu savais la terreur que j'ai d'une existence comme celle de mes parents: deux statues qui sont restées plus de cinquante ans en face l'une de l'autre aussi étrangères maintenant que le premier jour de leur rencontre" ["My friend, if you knew the terror that I have of an existence like that of my parents: two statues who stayed more than fifty years facing each other as estranged from one another as the first day they met"] (45). Through her early letters to her husband Philip we also learn that the severe climate of her childhood home was one that fostered feelings of alienation and loneliness within her. These feelings appear to have been at the very origin of her love for *fugue*, or, for straying away from a home that seemed to be a place of utter immobility. In her retrospective writing about her childhood home, David-Néel seems particularly haunted by the absence of a spiritual and intellectual tie between her parents, for through her correspondence we learn that she feels a similar emptiness within her marriage to Philip. Hence, we see in her letters that her aim is to give life to a more fulfilling dialogue with her husband in a mode that does not build boundaries to communication and offers more limitless self-expression (except when she practices epistolary discretion to protect herself from border-control authorities and the boundaries they regulate).

Furthermore, while drawing a detailed psychological portrait of her home-life as a child in the *Journal de Voyage*, David-Néel also describes her way of escaping the feelings of desolation that she experienced as a child, confiding that pride was her only true refuge (36). This "refuge," which David-Néel remembers seeking out during her lonely years as an only child, could be seen as a kind of blueprint for the nomadic home(s) she creates for herself, both literally and figuratively, during her Asian travels.

In another letter to her husband about her childhood home, she describes the suffering she endured while being raised in a bourgeois household, proclaiming that her soul is unlike that of her bourgeois parents (62). Together, these thoughts reflect a strong desire not to repeat, during her life as a married adult, the kind of home building that she was exposed to as a child.

It would be a mistake to think that while rebelling against traditional bourgeois values, David-Néel allowed her husband to finance her travels. We know from her letters that when she embarked upon her travels in Asia, she left savings with Philip in Tunis, which he sent to her in increments at her written request. Part of her ability to fund her travels was due to an accumulation of inheritances that she acquires both before and during her travels (14). She did not marry Philip until the age of thirty-six, and prior to her marriage she had earned a living in ways that also prepared her in her path to becoming a travel writer later in life. First, she had a short but noteworthy career as a soprano for a traveling lyric opera, traveling as far as Hanoi to appear on stage. She also worked as a journalist, publishing articles in several Parisian magazines, including *la Fronde*, and learning several aspects of the trade that would later prove very useful to her in her career as writer (11).

If David-Néel believed that her soul was not bourgeois, she also felt deeply that it was not French. In fact, she traces her lineage to a distant Asian relative, seeing her Asian ancestry as the source of her deep-seated calling to become an orientalist scholar of eastern religions. In a letter from Tibet, for instance, she describes a reawakening of her Asian sense of self just as she is starting to reach the apex of her goal, geographically and culturally, toward assimilating within her Tibetan surroundings. Similarly, in her narrative description of finally arriving at the end of her pilgrimage to Lhasa, David-Néel proclaims that she felt "as if I had come home…" (*My Journey to Lhasa* xxxiii).

Furthermore, while insisting upon the utmost importance of her incognito in order to succeed in her goal of attaining the forbidden city and the Dalai Lama's palace, she describes how her Tibetan "disguise" actually makes her feel closer to her roots, declaring, "I am one of the Genghis Khan race who, by mistake and perhaps for her sins, was born in the Occident" (*My Journey to Lhasa* 61). As her narrative voice explains, she feels misplaced in the west and discontent in "civilized" places; it was her deeply instilled desire for a more profound sense of place that pulled her eastward. It is interesting to note that while a comprehensive critical comparison of David-Néel's narrative and epistolary styles reveals that her epistolary voice is markedly different from her narrative voice, these two voices similarly project this overwhelming feeling of finally coming *home*.

In 1915, Alexandra David-Néel went into spiritual retreat in the high Himalayas at nearly four thousand meters (13,000 feet) of altitude. David-Néel had developed an important relationship with the head lama of a nearby monastery, the *Gompchen* of Lachen, who asked her to join him near his own mountain retreat. This Tibetan holy man helped to oversee the construction of a shelter built into the face of a mountain for meditation and study. In this remote, makeshift hermitage, she exchanged English for Tibetan language instruction with her spiritual mentor, and learned many of the secrets of Buddhist Tantric Practice from him. She would name this retreat *Dechen Ashram*, "the hermitage of peace" (377), her Himalayan realization of an "asile de repos."

From this mountain retreat not far from the very highest point of elevation in the world, Alexandra drafted letters to Philip in which she made many observations about human nature, both East and West. Her desire to gain perspective by seeking out a change of place in order to resituate and reassimilate the Self points to Edward Said's eloquent words concerning the richness in perspective to be gained by departure from one's familiar understanding of home: "The more one is able to leave one's cultural home, the more easily one is able to judge it, and the whole world as well, with the spiritual detachment and generosity necessary for true vision..." (259). Within this context, David-Néel's "cultural home" is not only the country in which she was born but the traditions and ideologies that she espouses, both consciously and subconsciously, as a result of having been born in a European country. By actively seeking linguistic and cultural assimilation while on the high Himalayan trail, she shows an eagerness to leave her cultural home behind, both intellectually and spiritually, in favor of a new, eastern one.

When addressing the universal desire for home in her letters to Philip from her Himalayan retreat, David-Néel decries the attachment to material constructions of home found in western countries. She openly challenges the fixed notion of what home should be through an eastern lens, calling upon westerners to shake off their instinctive impulse to lay down roots. Furthermore, she digs at the very foundation of the western instinct to home build ("cet instinct du home"), pointing to the negative repercussions of having an attachment to home, both materially and ideologically (397). Thus, from her temporary mountain retreat, her nomad's eye is particularly sensitive to the idea that home is a construction of the western imagination just as much as the notion of "civilization" is.

David-Néel's concept of home very clearly reflects Buddhist notions of impermanence. It follows from this awareness of the impermanence of all things that we must not overdo our emotional attachments to anything, be it a material object, or something as intangible as a sense of place. Likewise, she understood that if our notion of home comes from within ourselves it is only as ephemeral as we are.

David-Néel's spiritual retreat coincided with the early stages of the first world war, offering her a dizzying contemplation of two radically opposed worlds of uprootedness: East and West. In July of 1915, for example, she writes to Philip from her ashram, describing the out-of-body phenomenon of feeling removed to France as she reads about wartime destruction in the newspapers he sends to her: "je me trouve transportée en France parmi la fièvre de ces heures tragiques" ["I feel myself being transported to France amidst the fever of these tragic hours"] (394).

In the same vivid stream of thought, she accentuates the linguistic displacement from Self she feels hearing herself speak the sonorous tones of the Tibetan language while all at once surprised by the surrounding Himalayas, her sense of solitude, and the perception that she is dreaming: "[L]es hautes montagnes, la solitude, tout ce décor himalayen me semble un rêve et la sonorité étrangère des mots tibétains m'étonne à l'entendre sortir de ma bouche..." ["the high mountains, the solitude, all of this Himalayan décor seems like a dream to me and the strange sonority of Tibetan words surprises me as I hear it leaving my mouth"] (394). Within this *eerie* moment she oscillates back and forth between feeling alienated by the familiar (her former home) and the new (her mountain retreat). Then, she is all at once displaced from her (French) Self and surprised by a new, and linguistically assimilated, (Tibetan) Self.

By elaborating upon this uncanny experience, David-Néel records an important moment in the shaping of her own identity as a travel writer: The sensation of being displaced to her original home momentarily, while all at once realizing that she has become linguistically assimilated, and thus *at home*, within her surroundings. In effect, this is the merging of her eastern and western identities, an evolution in her selfhood in which she is neither there nor here but in both places at once. Thus, from her highest vantage point on the Himalayan trail, David-Néel is overtaken by what Susan Morgan calls the "slipperiness" of identity and the shifting ground of its association to place (2).

Occasionally David-Néel's western voice slips into her correspondence from the east, such as when she writes to Philip from the newly constructed Dechen Ashram in August of 1915, exuberantly announcing that she has become a landlord in the Himalayas (344). In this rare outburst of enthusiasm, she applies a concept of ownership well rooted in her European upbringing. However, from the material descriptions of Dechen Ashram, which she draws in her letters, describing little else but a shack with a bed, a stool, and a yak-skin on the floor, we are reminded that less is ultimately more for her (342).

At her home in the high Himalayas, David-Néel's sense of time slowed down enough that she often lost track of time as we know and regulate it with watches and clocks. Sunrise and sunset would become the two most significant markers of the passage of time here. In fact, several of her letters have only the year and the place from which she wrote marked in the upper right-hand corner of the Chinese or

Tibetan paper on which she wrote them. The day of the month would often be replaced by a simple question mark. One letter, for example, reads, "Fin août ou début septembre 1915????" ["End of August or beginning of September 1915????"] (346). As David-Néel's notion of time became reoriented to a new Himalayan concept of time, the map of the world would radically alter through two world wars.

When Alexandra David-Néel projects the imaginary space she would share with Philip upon her return from her travels in Asia, it is clear that a place for quiet study and writing is what she envisions. She makes a preliminary sketch to Philip outlining the most essential aspect of the home she hopes, one day, to return to, underscoring the importance that it include a room in which she would write about her Asian travels. This projected desire echoes her earliest thoughts from the correspondence about the home they would one day share; it would be a place where she could plunge herself wholeheartedly into writing about her extraordinary experiences.

In a world in which the passage of time was measured more by the depth of her cultural and linguistic immersion than her readiness to leave Asia, lengthiness of stay would become the very proof of where David-Néel truly felt most at home. For she was not to make her final return to France until 1946, after the second world war, and five years after the death of Philip Néel (9).

David-Néel's evolved sense of place would manifest itself in the material aspect of the house in Digne, Haute Provence, that would become her final home upon her return. She was originally enchanted by this small house because its location allowed for a spectacular view of the surrounding Alps of Haute Provence. Most importantly, the structure included a second-floor terrace where David-Néel could sleep outside on a blanket underneath the night sky. She would ultimately build onto the original house that she purchased, adding a quadrangular tower and roofing closely designed to resemble a Tibetan chapel. She would christen her new home *Samten Dzong*: "The Fortress of Meditation" (11).

The room in which David-Néel would spend nearly all of her time during the last twenty-three years of her life had, in imitation of her home on the Himalayan trail, little more than a desk and a chair in it with a bed nearby. It was the "room of her own," which she had envisioned from the trail and in which she would write about her travels prolifically until the end of her life.

Philip Néel ultimately played the role of an epistolary audience to David-Néel, for if he wrote few letters in comparison to the number his wife wrote to him, he did read, safeguard, and catalogue them for her, thereby participating in the recording of her life story. He was, for all intents and purposes, the guardian of her mobile *journal intime*. We can also think of Philip as an epistolary sounding board; for he plays the role of silent audience to David-Néel as she articulates her philosophical thoughts, political beliefs, and travel writer's ambitions from Asia. In this analysis of Philip's role as epistolary audience, we find that he is another "other" in her fascinating world of alterity. Alexandra depicts the wilds of this world, and the mountains which meet her eye there with panoramic embrace, acknowledging that in order to see them, one must know how to see them: "[L]es Himalayas, sans doute, constituent un cadre grandiose et pour qui *sait* voir leur majestueuse beauté" ["The Himalayas, without a doubt, constitute a grandiose environment for those who know how to see their majestic beauty"] (397).

It is David-Néel's perseverance at Dechen Ashram, even as the Himalayan snows block her inside of her hut, that give her this knowing, for as she explains: "[La nature] exige de nous un long temps de probation avant de nous initier à sa vie spéciale, de nous admettre dans son intimité" ["Nature requires a long period of probation from us before initiating us to her special world, and admitting us into her intimacy"] (376). She also accentuates the alterity of her Tibetan life by alerting Philip to the hardship she endures on the mountain and by contrasting her world with that of traveling luxury-seekers: "Ce n'est pas là terre à l'usage des sybarites. Le climat est âpre, le confort impossible et le régime alimentaire d'un ascetisme peu encourageant" ["It isn't a land to be exploited by sybarites. The climate is harsh, comfort is impossible and the diet is of an asceticism which is hardly encouraging"] (380). In fact, she sketches her surroundings in such a way as to deter Philip from having any preconceived notions about her life in Tibet coming from his own experiences in colonial Africa. To this effect she draws the following contrast to places with more "civilized" (to be read: "artificial") characteristics: "Tu imagines bien que nos montagnes ne sont pas des montagnes civilisées, avec des sentiers tracés et des poteaux indicateurs du Touring Club" ["You imagine correctly that our mountains aren't civilized mountains, with marked paths and sign posts from the Touring Club"] (415). Underscoring the wilder aspect of her own experience, she points to the very real dangers of her solitary walks through mountain passes, some of which take her close to death on more than one occasion: "ici, deux ou trois fois, dans mes courses solitaires...je me suis trouvée en situation critique...la mort presque certaine" ["here, two or three times, in my solitary walks, I found myself in critical situations...death almost certainly before me"] (419). We are drawn more deeply into a world of alterity when she switches tongues while writing, such as in this description of the endless Tibetan winter: "'Tada goumgka tchoung-tchoung doug! Jougla gounka tchempo yong inkiam dirou goungka nomgyun'....Cela veut dire: 'Maintenant c'est le petit hiver, plus tard sera le grand hiver, ici c'est toujours l'hiver!'" ["This means 'Now it is little Winter, later the big Winter will come, here it is always Winter!'"] (385). In this manner she elucidates her evolving linguistic selfhood while keeping Philip abreast of her progress in Tibetan.

David-Néel is at her most sublime when describing the snow-capped peaks that climb even higher than her camp, such as her description of the mountains rising under a full moon: "Le spectacle des monts géants, tous vêtus de blanc, a été inimaginablement grandiose lors de la dernière pleine lune. Avec cela un silence extraordinaire...." ["The spectacle of the giant mountains, all robed in white, was unimaginable during the last Full moon. With that an extraordinary silence..."] (409). She would often climb higher than her camp in order to meditate even closer to these peaks, which promised to envelope her in silence. Later, when writing from Japan, she would express homesickness for these mountains, their eternal snows, and the silence surrounding them, all covered by the wide Himalayan sky: "A vrai dire, j'ai le mal de pays pour un pays qui n'est pas le mien. Les steppes, les solitudes, les neiges éternelles et le grand ciel clair de 'là-haut' me hantent!" ["To tell the truth, I'm homesick for a country which is not mine. The steppes, the solitudes, the eternal snows and the great clear sky found 'up there' haunt me!"] (438). In one of her earliest letters to Philip dated August 1904, David-Néel offers some insight into her marriage and why it was ultimately one characterized by separation. Here, Alexandra alludes to the aforementioned marital struggles in the early stages of their marriage and suggests that they married more out of thoughtlessness than tenderness (38). Even so, her marital uncertainties can only be part of the reason why Alexandra decided to enact a different kind of fidelity through her pen while she was physically and geographically separated from Philip. In pointing to these uncertainties, I mean to cast light on the intricacies of the textual fibers of David-Néel's life story rather than to draw unequivocal conclusions as to how they relate to its weaving. For in the complicated mesh of yearning that took many different forms in David-Néel's life on the trail, her desire for mobility and passion for the firsthand study of ancient philosophical and religious texts were the two most powerful forces that compelled her to stay in Asia for so many years.

The sheer wealth of letters that David-Néel wrote during her travels in Asia deserves special emphasis. Her steadfast commitment to recording her own life story in her letters from the trail can be tangibly measured by carefully considering the lengths she took to write at high altitude: In order to document her steps under extraordinary conditions for a letter-writer, she would stretch her ink with Himalayan snow when her supply became dangerously low. She also maintained a rather miraculous faith in the postal system of her era and geographical place, and was not hindered from mailing her correspondence, even though her letters took an average of six weeks to reach her husband from the remote stations where she posted them in the Himalayas. One very difficult reminder of the lengthy amount of time it took for letters to reach David-Néel came when, at the end of her stay in the Himalayas, she received written notification of her mother's death in Belgium one full year after the event (491). If there is an undeniable sadness inherent in this lapse of time between her mother's death and her daughter's awareness of it, its symbolism is no less rich given that the news comes when she is at the high summit of her path as a travel writer, living the antithesis of the life her mother knew. In acknowledging her commitment to epistolary expression then, one might argue that Alexandra was committed to writing her letters because they allowed such a unique forum for reflections on the self and their resonance over time and space.

We learn within this forum that Alexandra strongly believed she had within herself the capacity to love someone in a relationship of mutual respect and understanding: "[J]'aurais pu aimér quelqu'un grandement qui m'en aurait paru digne, qui m'aurait aimeé de même" ["I could have loved someone who seemed worthy of it to me, who would have loved me equally"] (48). Her choice to make a town with the name of Digne the place for the building of her home away from Asia is richly significant in this light. Furthermore, if there is one thing that Alexandra learned in her many years of travel, it was that, unlike all things impermanent such as house, husband, and finally, self, the Himalayas (and later the Alps of Provence) were the most likely to maintain a sense of lasting and unchanging dignity. This is ultimately why her heart would remain in the Himalayas, her spiritual home, until the end of her life.

Works Cited

David-Néel, Alexandra. *Correspondance avec son mari: 1904–1941*. Paris: Plon, 2000.
———. *Journal de Voyage: Lettres à son Mari*. 2 vols. Paris: Plon, 1975.
———. *My Journey to Lhasa*. Boston: Beacon P, 1993.
Désiré-Marchand, Joelle. *Les Itinéraires d'Alexandra David-Néel*. Paris: Arthaud, 1996.
"Home." Def. 11. *The Oxford English Dictionary*. 2nd ed. 1989.
Morgan, Susan. *Place Matters*. New Brunswick: Rutgers UP, 1996.
Nash, Suzanne. *Home and Its Dislocations in Nineteenth-Century France*. Albany: State U of New York P, 1993.
Said, Edward. *Orientalism*. London: Penguin Books, 1995.

A Feminist Lens for Binx Bolling's Journey in *The Moviegoer*
Traveling Toward Wholeness

Kathleen Scullin

W alker Percy spent his life trying to disentangle himself from the effects of Cartesian thought. He argued that, in sundering mind from body, Descartes fundamentally distorted our understanding of human nature and shaped culture in disastrous ways (Descartes, "Meditation VI" 160–175).[1] In seeking a new model for human existence, he was traveling, unbeknownst, with feminists. Differences in language, aims, and emphases obscure the significant points of convergence between Percy and many feminists in their critiques of Cartesian thought and culture and their vision of alternative paradigms. Feminists emphasize that the "self" is discovered not through isolated reflection but through the experience of "identity-in-relation" (Cooey 37). Further, human existence is not revealed through disembodied thought; to be human is to be embedded in history and the individual body. Percy similarly emphasized that a sense of self must be grounded in relationship. However, his critique of Descartes does not directly emphasize the embodiment issue—though he rejects the mind-body split and argues that the human being is incarnate, meaning that body and spirit are fundamentally inseparable. In his novels, Percy worked out his philosophical vision by situating his protagonists on a journey in search of self that begins as a solo search for self-knowledge (a mythic archetype with Cartesian overtones), but typically culminates as a journey in the company of others, without whom they cannot come to a sense of themselves.

This essay explores how the feminist emphasis on grounding oneself in the body illuminates Percy's complex handling of life as a journey in *The Moviegoer*. In that novel, the protagonist Binx Bolling undertakes what he calls "the search" for a way to live his life, to connect with his authentic self and avoid falling prey to "the malaise" that he sees all around him: people sunk into "everydayness," trapped within roles, caught on a treadmill of consumerism, social climbing, self-improvement—all swallowed up and "dead, dead, dead" (228). Genuinely in pursuit of a way to inhabit his own being, he is "onto" some clues about the direction to take. He is a close observer of details; he is given to pondering "the wonder" of life; most of all, he loves movies. Movies are typically about people on some sort of journey, in a particular time and place.

However, as long as he cannot ground himself in his own body, as long as he searches for a way out of "everydayness" as a role-player, analyzer, and distanced observer, he continues to sabotage his "search." Disembodiedness is the heart of Binx's problem; his search cannot become fruitful until he finds a way to live out a principle implicit in Percy's thinking but explicit in feminist thought: that "individuality"—that is, the self—cannot be experienced as distinct from a specific body. Conversely, in Margaret Atwood's comic formulation in *Surfacing*, "*The trouble is all in the knob at the top of our bodies*. I'm not against the body or the head either: only the neck, which creates the illusion that they are separate" (89, original emphasis). Percy portrays in Binx a man who keeps his head separate from his body, and his own body at a remove from others' through role-playing, analyzing others, and overrelying on sight, the one sensory organ that functions (in the Cartesian paradigm at least) by distancing rather than by merging. In order to claim selfhood, Binx must turn from this abstracted existence and choose to "stick himself," embodied, into his life and thereby connect with others on their life's journeys.

Binx is both literally and metaphorically a moviegoer. Moviegoing is perhaps the most obvious sign of his need for some meaningful shape and direction in his life. Even so, by relying on movies to provide roles, he lives a life outside his own concrete existence. He frequents movies that play out, in cinematic form, versions of myths that perpetuate what Alicia Ostriker calls the "ascents and conquests of male heroism" ("Thieves" 72). In these, the code requires that women be objects, of rescue or desire: woman, in other words, as perceived through "collective male fantasy" (73; see also Gledhill 817–20). Writers, such as Margaret Atwood, deconstruct such myths to show their depersonalizing effects on persons. In the poem that concludes her "Circe/Mud Poems," for instance, she sketches life on a generic "island" of heroic myth, where *"the events run themselves through/almost without us"* (*Selected Poems* 222, original emphasis).

It is precisely this absence of the "I" that characterizes the Binx who role-plays his way through events in his life—particularly the would-be romantic episodes. When he sets about to maneuver Sharon, his secretary, into her intended role of lover, asking her to work after hours on a project he has invented for the purpose, he adopts a series of roles, all of them cool and fatally charming to many a movie secretary: Now he is Dana Andrews, loosening his collar and rubbing his neck, and now Rory Calhoun, hands outstretched to Sharon's desk, head down between arms, ready to dictate a letter: "All right. Take it this way" (106). Binx here employs his body as someone else's movie body—only to escape his own body, which can, after all, spoil everything: by trembling, sweating, breaking out in hives. The body gets in the way of myth.

In this and other scenes with Sharon, Percy comically and incisively deconstructs even as he constructs the moviegoer Binx as both character and concept, living out the heroic ethos. In his mind, Binx has scripted not only his own but Sharon's part. However, Sharon gives herself a role that both resists Binx's role for her and at the same time allows her to play his game to the extent that she chooses, looking back at him "ironically and with lights in her eyes" (106). The deconstructive hint is there: She might just turn out not to be the passive-woman-as-erotic-object. A few days later, as the two are driving to the ocean and a car hits them on the driver's side, Sharon, checking to see if he is hurt, discovers scar tissue on his shoulder and asks in disbelief whether the accident caused it, giving Binx a chance to say it is a war wound. She steps into his myth, glorifying the wound with her sympathy and, he presumes, her admiration. Binx's silent response is, "O Tony [Curtis]. O Rory. You never had it so good with direction. Not even you Bill Holden, my noble Will" (127). That Binx here speaks not to Sharon, not even to himself, but to Tony, Rory, and Bill in their roles tellingly points to the heroic-romantic conquest as an enterprise removed from any individual's identity. Although it would seem that Binx's obsession with desire, with making his secretaries his lovers, indicates that he is all too much "in the body"; his desire, severed from genuine relationship, only dislocates

him. His sobering line as he returns Sharon to her apartment one af-
ternoon underscores the point: "I go home as the old Gable, asweat
and with no thought for her and sick to death with desire" (96). We
see here the depersonalizing effect of myth: He is the victim of desire,
and she the idea that disappears altogether.

Binx needs movies not only to place himself in relation to others
but to locate himself in place and time, another indication that he is
disembodied. Whenever he goes to a movie, he strikes up a conversation with the ticket taker or manager—not because he wants to be
friendly but because if he does not, he would be "lost, cut loose meta-
physically speaking" (75). Seeing a film that could be shown "anywhere and at any time," he is in danger of "slipping clean out of space
and time" (75). No place, in fact, seems fully real to him until he sees
it filmed in a movie, and thus "certified" (63).

Moviegoing also serves as a metaphor for Binx's stance in many
encounters. Despite his knack for noticing the minutest details about
the other's body language—a gift that could open him to compassionate insight—his gaze typically functions like the lens of an impersonal
camera. In this mode, he becomes the Cartesian knower, the observing subject removed from the object of knowledge. As Evelyn Fox
Keller and Christine R. Grontkowski demonstrate, sight, in the Cartesian model, becomes not only the vehicle for knowing but at the same
time the instrument for distancing from the corporeal (215).[2] In Ursula
LeGuin's words, "The essential gesture of [Cartesian thought and
language] is…distancing—making a gap, a space, between the subject
or self and the object or other…It goes one way. No answer is expected, or heard" (qtd. in Sellers 1107). Binx's clinical observation
widens the gap between himself and others, and in so doing, casts
him further from himself.

Moreover, just as a camera focuses attention on the image it cap-
·tures and diverts attention from itself as the vantage point for capturing the image, so the Cartesian observer, analyzing what is seen,
disappears from notice as the perspective that shapes the analysis.
Binx's description of Eddie Lovell (a successful estate lawyer) in the
following passage perfectly exemplifies this process:

> As he talks…his eye watches me and at the same time sweeps the terrain
> behind me…A green truck turns down Bourbon Street; the eye sizes it
> up….A businessman turns in at the Maison Blanche building, the eye
> knows him….He understands everything out there and everything out
> there is something to be understood. (18–19)

In this account, the focus on Eddie Lovell's "eye," one that sees and assesses, obscures Binx's own role as an "eye" that is doing essentially the same thing. In summing up Eddie as a type, Binx appropriates his otherness as being somehow less whole, less complex, than he himself is. Binx remains the unknowable knower while Eddie becomes the object known.

As Percy and a number of feminists would agree, the theoretical split between observer and observed fails to account for the dynamic of actual human relationships. The human being is not, fundamentally, a camera. The Eddie Lovell encounter exemplifies what often happens when Binx seems, through analyzing, to distance himself from others: He is drawn into a mirror relationship with the other, thus underscoring that relationships are grounded in connectedness. Percy argued that relationship is the condition of any kind of knowing—rather than separateness, as Cartesian thought would have it (*Message* 274). Evelyn Fox Keller would agree with Percy, noting that modern physics challenges the traditional model of knowledge-by-separation by revealing "transitional phenomena" in which the observer cannot clearly be distinguished from the observed ("Gender" 195–96).

Throughout the novel, Percy leaves signs that Binx is not only subject to relationship with others even in the act of objectifying them, but that he is also capable of entering into a relationship that arises from the core of himself—particularly with Lonnie his half brother and Kate, his aunt's stepdaughter. Perhaps it is significant that both Lonnie and Kate suffer an affliction that ties them to their own bodies, Lonnie a crippling physical disease and Kate an emotional illness that manifests itself by self-wounding: shredding the flesh of her fingers, overdosing on alcohol and pills. They bear out Alicia Ostriker's insight that "for some, the dominant expression of life in the flesh is suffering" (*Stealing* 119).

Binx's relationship with Kate is not romantic in the idealized, conventional mode of his flirtations with secretaries.[3] He is not, however, unaware of, or indifferent to, her good looks or her body. He speaks of her in one passage as "frail as a ten year old, except in her thighs. Sometimes she speaks of her derrière, sticks it out Beale Street style and gives it a slap and this makes me blush because it is a very good one, marvelously ample and mysterious and nothing to joke about" (42). However, they relate to each other as friends and confidantes. He knows how to help her get through her scariest episodes by allowing her to pretend that she is a small boy tagging along, to whom he needs not pay much attention. Here, role-playing serves an entirely different purpose than with Sharon. Binx and Kate mutually choose their roles as a form of play. Play is a form of intimacy, which allows Binx to help her, and her to accept help, without falling into patterns of dominance or manipulation.

Kate, though, is privy to Binx's search, and just by having the freedom to speak of it can help him to recognize the downright absurdity of his abstract and schematic approach to "the search," in which he undertakes "rotations" and "repetitions" and alternates between the "vertical" and the "horizontal" search.[4] One time when she questions him about the "vertical" search, he suddenly recognizes that he has become as eccentric as a girl Kate knows called BoBo, who, Kate once told him, located and named every iron deer in Westchester County, making monthly rounds to visit them. Irritated, he admits to himself that he does "sound like BoBo and her goddamn iron deer (82). The parallel is wonderfully revealing. What could be more unnatural in itself than an iron deer, the antithesis of a natural deer—a soft, gentle, fluid creature—and then to make a fetish of collecting and naming them! BoBo's obsession becomes a perfect objective correlative of Binx's search, which denatures both him and the mystery of the human journey. Also in this scene, Kate openly challenges him, knowing that the scientifically oriented search takes him away from himself, into a bodiless, "nowhere" existence. (Descartes attempted to reach truth through a mathematical "view from nowhere," *Discourse* 40–44). To Binx's explanation of why he loves the search for "the big one, the new key, the secret leverage point," she replies, "And it doesn't matter where you are or who you are...And the danger is of becoming no one nowhere." He is, as she says, "a cold one...Cold as the grave" (82–83).

The struggle to avoid becoming "no one nowhere" is one Kate herself knows well; it is part of her illness. Several times, Binx notes that her eyes have gone blank as disks. She felt most alive, she tells Binx, when she and her fiancé Lyell had the car accident in which he died and she felt not horror but exaltation. People are only "real" in times of personal tragedy, she tells Binx (81). Two people who both have trouble inhabiting their bodies and lives would hardly seem likely to help each other. Nevertheless, they are connected in fundamental ways. Each needs to find a way to live authentically, beyond conventional prescriptions, and each recognizes the signal importance of near-death experiences, death being the most elemental of bodily experiences. Binx was wounded in the Korean war and conceived the idea for his "search" upon regaining consciousness; Kate safeguards the possibility of committing suicide as the only thing that keeps her alive. Most importantly, the relationship itself is full of potential for mutuality. With Kate, Binx is free from the endless role-playing, known and valued for who he is, able to minister to her in her illness. With Binx, Kate can carry on despite her illness, help Binx break out of abstractedness, and take charge of practical tasks, which she is better at than he.

Their journey toward finding "identity in relationship"—where flesh and spirit, self and other, move in tandem—reaches its turning point on a literal journey, a train ride to Chicago. Binx is sent there to attend a convention, much to his dismay because the city's "genie soul" (202) empties out his fragile sense of well-being. Kate demands to accompany him, sunk in the grip of her own malaise. Determined to have a purely physical "fling" as an escape from the everlasting demands of the spirit, Kate commandeers Binx's services, warning him, "Just don't speak to me of love, bucko" (198). She has, in effect, summoned him to sex in a Cartesian mode (Poteat 64). Their inability to carry it off well arises from the fundamental integrity of this relationship, which cuts off Binx's usual escape route—into a movie role that perpetuates the mind-body split. He can neither tuck her in bed and virtuously sleep elsewhere, nor give her as "merry a time" as she could wish for. Instead, he laments that, despite his labors, they did "very badly and almost did not do at all," having tried to force "poor flesh" (200) to bear the burden of the spirit's needs. With Kate, Binx cannot—as with secretaries in the past—simply use the body as a means to an end, which is the antithesis of "living in the body." However, he also cannot resort to a familiar movie role. Retreats to past behavior are doomed to fail now that he and Kate are poised on the verge of breakthrough to a new mode of living.

In a nice reversal of the mythic pattern, Kate rescues Binx at the end of the novel from yet one more relapse into role-playing and impersonal desire. He waits for her on a playground, his spirit defeated by the virulence of his aunt's tirade of moral outrage over his recent behavior and even more by the existential distance between her world and his. Fearing that Kate, too, has abandoned him, he picks up the phone to "find a girl"—any girl—and finds himself yet again inhabiting Rory Calhoun and Marlon Brando. When Kate drives up, he sees her, not as the distanced other, but rather the other who helps him discover himself: "[S]he could be I myself, sooty eyed and nowhere" (231). They talk and agree to marry, a commitment that roots Binx as a person in relationship. He can now express concretely the form his "search" will take in answer to Kate's question, "What do you plan to do?" Although she only means to ask what occupation he will choose, his reply expresses a newfound recognition that choosing an occupation is secondary to undertaking his journey as a human being: "There is only one thing I can do: listen to people, see how they stick themselves into the world, hand them along a ways in their dark journey and be handed along, and for good and selfish reasons" (233). Binx is talking from the body here: He will "listen to people" and "hand them along," and in this reciprocal handing along, he will stick himself into the world—no longer an "anyone, anywhere." He has found, in the words of Annie Leclerc, "a new nexus of relations no longer [privileging] sight, since it is that faculty that distances us from others."[5] The language that Binx speaks arises from "those faculties which—instead of marking our limits from others—function to create the relation: the 'consciousness' of ears, nostrils, tongue, fingers and skin" (qtd. in Sellers 30).

Fingers and skin literally end this scene between them as Kate, frightened by such a commitment, begins to shred the flesh around her thumbnail. In a gesture rooted deeply in the body and the relationship that can arise out of embodiedness, Binx takes her hand, kisses the blood, and gently urges, "try not to hurt yourself so much" (234).

The main action of the novel does not quite end here, because locating himself within the boundaries of his own existence opens Binx to mysteries that go beyond the body, and thus Binx is ready to discover that grace, like love, spills over the boundaries. While talking with Kate, he has also been watching in the rearview mirror a black man who seems the quintessence of the upwardly mobile businessman get out of the car behind them, enter a church, and leave a few minutes later. Recalling that it is Ash Wednesday, Binx speculates that the man may have gone into the church to receive ashes and reflects on this assumption in what at first seems to be his old manner, wondering why the man is here. Is publicly coming for ashes a way of getting ahead in Catholic New Orleans? Does he actually believe that God is present at this intersection, "the corner of Elysian Fields and Bons Enfants" (235)? However, Binx is now opened to new understanding, not confined to the dualistic separation of world from spirit. Could it be true, he wonders, that "through some dim dazzling trick of grace," the man could come for a worldly benefit and even so, receive a divine blessing? Is this "God's own importunate bonus"? (235). The binaries dissolve. Reality is a "both-and" that transcends the bounds of any paradigm, beyond any possibility of analysis: "It is impossible to say," he concludes (235).

Very likely, Binx's own recent experience has opened him to this insight. He has, after all, just received his own "importunate bonus": being rescued by Kate amid the regression of phoning Sharon is comparable to being given the gift of grace while attempting to enhance one's social standing. In this moment, Binx looks upon the stranger who has just emerged from church not through distancing analysis but through the experience of "identity in relation": as someone else on a journey wrapped in mystery, someone who, in Binx's recent phrase, "could be I myself."

The epilogue, narrated over a year later, allows the reader to glimpse the life Binx has undertaken with Kate. The change in him, though undramatic, is radical. He accepts human finitude and our "inescapable physical locatedness in time and space," which "shapes" and "limits," but at the same time "empowers" us (Bordo 181–82). Binx now lives out Moira Gatens's model of how mind relates to body (a model inspired by Spinoza): "[T]he body is not part of passive nature ruled over by an active mind but rather the body is the ground of human action...[R]eason is active and embodied precisely because it is the affirmation of a *particular* bodily existence" (57, original emphasis).

Binx's language throughout the epilogue arises from his "particular bodily existence." No longer does he speak of his search in the abstracted, impersonal voice he used earlier, as in these passages: "The search is what anyone would undertake if he were not sunk in the everydayness of his own life" (13); and "when a man awakes to the possibility of the search..." (89). Now he speaks in first-person pronouns (Kobre 114) and has stopped intellectualizing: "As for my search, I have not the inclination to say much on the subject" (237). The language in this passage is personal, yet oblique—and necessarily so. He can no longer speak of his search analytically because it no longer is something external to himself. Moreover, he knows that the journey into oneself cannot yield some prescription with which to "edify" others. Thus, what must be said can only be hinted at.

In the epilogue, Binx turns from a flight from death to a confrontation with it—death being the most powerful reminder of human finitude. His intellectualizing itself has constituted a form of escapism: the classic Cartesian "transcendence" of the body's limits. However, he has also turned more overtly from personal confrontations with death. Although awakened to "the search" during the Korean War as he "came to [himself]," lying flat on the ground after being wounded (10), he later avoided the intense immediacy of that ordeal by turning "the search" into a scientific pursuit. Moreover, though Binx sought information about his father, who died when Binx was a child, he failed to probe the personal meaning of what he learned. Clearly, his father had a death wish. Twice in his life, he stopped eating; the second time, nothing could persuade him to eat until he needed to regain enough weight to enlist in the war, where he died the kind of death he would have romanticized: in the "wine dark sea" of Crete (25). However, instead of asking how the early loss of his father has shaped his own life, or whether that love of death was somehow manifest in himself as well, Binx had contented himself with studying his father's ironic look in a photograph taken during World War II, shortly before his death (25).

The epilogue, by contrast, shows Binx in close relationship with his half-brother Lonnie, who is dying, and with family members who need comforting over this death. When Kate and Binx emerge from the hospital, she is traumatized by seeing Lonnie so wasted and jaundiced looking. He calmly and lovingly talks her through the shock—though Kate for once misunderstands, accusing him of being "cold-blooded" in his matter-of-factness. Because Lonnie is the only person in the novel to whom Binx can say aloud, "I love you" (162, 165), he could hardly be taking this death unfeelingly. Rather, both his tone—no longer coolly distant but quietly present—and his behavior throughout the scene hint that he now accepts death as an integral part of life. As Binx tells Kate two things Lonnie whispered to him—that he has finally "conquered an habitual disposition" (toward envying his brother, after a long spiritual battle), and that Kate is "a very good-looking girl"—the reader suspects that, like Lonnie, Binx now moves seamlessly between the worlds of spirit and flesh (239). Kissing Kate's scalp where her hair parts, he tells her that she is indeed very good looking that day. He has indeed turned from the "transcendence of mind" that masks a flight from nature, which subjects all bodies to death (Ruether 80), to enter "forms of understanding in which the body plays a part…[and] in which limitation by nature, death, and finitude are accepted" (Christ 130).

Accepting our finitude, as Susan Bordo points out, "empowers," even as it "limits" (182). The epilogue shows Binx no longer existentially stranded but firmly planted in the community of his immediate and extended family. He takes charge of Lonnie's younger siblings for the day, helping them to deal with their brother's death by answering their questions straightforwardly. Significantly, he no longer keeps them at a linguistic distance by calling them "my half-brothers and sisters." Here, he calls them "the children" and, finally, "my brothers and sisters" (239, 242). He is also now attuned to the sacramental power within nature to bond us with what is beyond ourselves, transcending sheer materiality. Binx asks Kate to do an errand for him by streetcar, having assured her that she can do this alone despite her fear. Then, in a gesture that grasps the potency within things, he picks a cape jasmine and gives it to her to hold on the trip—through which he will hold her in support and love. The last sentence of the novel poignantly shows how, in an embodied life, "spiritual insight [is realized] in social reality" (Christ 130): "I watch her [Kate] walk toward St. Charles, cape jasmine held against her cheek, until my brothers and sisters call out behind me" (242).

For Percy, to "live a life" meant recovering the sense of life as relational, as sacramental. In this vision, he accords with a great number of feminists who envision both a new language and a new way of life that would transform the relationships between self and other, spirit and flesh. In *The Moviegoer,* however, Percy adds one more dimension to this picture. Binx no longer mentions movies or adopts movie roles, a change that points to a deeper shift: His life now constitutes his own narrative myth. The mythology of the movies, derivative (though often in diluted forms) of classic quest and rebirth mythology, offers, as Binx has always known, an inadequate model for his own journey. Early in the novel, he lamented that "[t]he movies are onto the search, but they screw it up" (13).

Despite this insight, he has tried, in vain, to escape the mire of "everydayness" through inhabiting movie roles. Now, though, having "stuck" himself into everyday life, he is paradoxically freed from the fear of being overwhelmed by the malaise. His Aunt Emily accepts him as, he says, "not one of her heroes but a very ordinary fellow" (237), an image that mirrors his own acceptance of life grounded in the here-and-now.

Living out his own particular story opens the possibility of creating his own forms of quest and rebirth. Near the end of the novel's main action, Binx mentions two images that suggest what forms his own "myths" will take. The context of the first one partly accounts for its sober tone; in near despair before Kate arrives, he calls his life "my dark pilgrimage on this earth" (228). A pilgrimage, in contrast to a quest, transforms not by journeying to encounter something outside oneself but through participating in the journey itself; not by individual endeavor but in the company of others headed for the same destination; and not by heroic action but by conversion of spirit. Whereas the quester seeks self-transcendence in the conquest of evil, the pilgrim seeks right relationships with self and others, and comes to terms with the complex interrelationship between good and evil—both within and without. A pilgrimage is the journey of the embodied human being, who will, in Binx's words, "listen to people, see how they stick themselves into the world, hand them along a ways in their dark journey and be handed along, and for good and selfish reasons" (233).

The second image, one of rebirth, comes to Binx as he sees, in Kate's arrival, the possibility of rescue from despair:

> Is it possible that—For a long time I have secretly hoped for the end of the world and believed with Kate...and many other people that only after the end could the few who survive creep out of their holes and discover themselves to be themselves and live as merrily as children among the viny ruins. Is it possible that—it is not too late? (231)

The keys here are survival, coming home to self, and living together. The emphasis is not on escape from the ordinary but on living fully each day in one's own skin. Taken together, these two images "embrace an idea of self-acceptance and relationship quite different from the traditional ideals of self-transcendence and attainment." The journey Binx is on, the epilogue shows us, is one in which "it becomes admirable to go through experience without going forward or getting anywhere....The challenge of this kind of 'journey' is simply to 'Be Alive'" (Lauter 77–78).[6]

In *The Moviegoer*, Percy dramatizes his sense of what a journey out of Cartesian estrangement from self, toward wholeness, might look like. Seen through a feminist lens, the novel also shows his unconscious recognition that living "in the body" is intrinsic to this journey. He did, however, intentionally dramatize a view he shared with many feminists: that western culture, still permeated by Cartesian principles, distorts our understanding of human existence and sabotages the journey toward human wholeness; but radical change cannot come through intellectual arguments alone. What is ultimately needed is a new stance, a new way of undertaking the journey of life, one that takes into account how we human beings really come to authentic selfhood: grounded in the particularity of our own existence, in relation with others, and freed to move beyond the boundaries ascribed to gender by culture and myth.

Notes

1   The reference to Descartes' is also amplied by the many quotes from Walker Percy in Lawson's *More Conversations* (e.g., 64). For an overview of Percy's critique of Cartesian scientism, see Walker Percy, *Signposts*, 271–91, and J. Gerald Kennedy, "The Sundered Self in the Riven World: *Love in the Ruins*." For an extended analysis, see Patricia Lewis Poteat, *Walker Percy and the Old Modern Age*.

2   Keller and Grontkowski trace the philosophical evolution by which sight has become designated as the conduit for knowledge, beginning with Plato, for whom the "eye is likened to the intellect, the 'eye of the mind'" (210). When Descartes declared, however, that "It is the soul that sees [with inner sight], not the body" (215), the body was dismissed as a source of knowledge and the knower severed from the objects of perception (215).

3   In an earlier draft of *The Moviegoer*, Binx and Kate disrupt conventional categories in speaking of each other. She says, "We were good friends like boys are friends and then we wanted each other, didn't we?" He describes her, in a photograph taken at age fourteen, as "smart, but not the way girls are smart; she carries her head shyly, a little tucked down, in a way that is like a little girl and yet like a man a scientist or professor who knows a lot but is shy about what he knows" (Percy, "Confessions" 49). The published novel drops this passage but still communicates a sense that the relationship stretches gendered boundaries.

4   "Rotation" and "repetition" are borrowed from Kierkegaard, the philosophical mentor whose thought provided Percy with a framework for writing about the complexities of the human journey, as he attests in many interviews (e.g., Lawson and Kramer, *Conversations*, 67, 75, 82, 108–115). "Rotation" and "repetition" characterize the "aesthetic" stage, the first of Kierkegaard's "stages on life's way." Rotation is the pursuit of new experiences; repetition is a retreat into the nostalgic past. Both forms of escape lead to despair. In the "ethical" stage, one seeks validation through faithfulness to internalized moral codes. In the "religious" stage, one abandons all to faith, finding no earthly source to satisfy infinite longing—and, paradoxically, this leap returns one to oneself, able to savor the goodness of everyday living. In *The Moviegoer*, Percy says, Binx "jumps from the aesthetic...to the religious," bypassing the ethical (Lawson and Kramer, *Conversations* 66).

5   Percy and Keller/Grontkowski would partially disagree. Both argue that although sight can be a vehicle for distancing (i.e., in a Cartesian mode), seeing

can open one to a sense of communion. Both cite the example of gazing into the eyes of the other as a primal means of communion. See Percy, *Message*, 285; Keller and Grontkowski, "The Mind's Eye," 220.

6   The quoted passages summarize what Estella Lauter believes Margaret Atwood attempts to do in her "Circe/Mud Poems"; that is, to contribute to the slow cultural process by which we transform quest mythology, opening new possibilities for selfhood and relationship. I believe that Walker Percy tries to do something similar in *The Moviegoer*.

Works Cited

Atwood, Margaret. *Surfacing*. New York: Fawcett, 1972.

———. *Selected Poems 1965–1975*. Boston: Houghton Mifflin, 1976.

Bordo, Susan. "Bringing the Body to Theory." *Twilight Zones: The Hidden Life of Cultural Images from Plato to O. J*. Berkeley: U of California P, 1997. 173–91.

Christ, Carol P. *Diving Deep and Surfacing: Women Writers on Spiritual Quest*. 3d ed. Boston: Beacon Press, 1995.

Cooey, Paula M. *Religious Imagination and the Body: A Feminist Analysis*. New York: Oxford UP, 1994..

Descartes, René. *Discourse on Method and the Meditations*. Trans. F. E. Sutcliffe. New York: Penguin, 1975.

———. "Meditation VI." *Meditation on the First Philosophy*. Trans John Veitch. *The Rationalists: Descartes, Spinoza, Leibnitz*. New York: Dolphin Books, 1960. 160–75.

Gatens, Moira. *Imaginary Bodies: Ethics, Power and Corporeality*. London: Routledge, 1996.

Gledhill, Christine. "Recent Developments in Feminist Criticism." *Film Theory and Criticism*. 3d ed. Gerald Mast and Marshall Cohen. New York: Oxford UP, 1985. 817–45.

Keller, Evelyn Fox. "Gender and Science." *Discovering Reality: Feminist Perspectives on Epistemology, Metaphysics, Methodology, and Philosophy of Science*. Ed. Sandra Harding and Merrill B. Hintikka. Boston: D. Reidel Publishing Company, 1983. 187–205.

Keller, Evelyn Fox, and Christine R. Grontkowski. "The Mind's Eye." *Discovering Reality: Feminist Perspectives on Epistemology, Metaphysics, Methodology, and Philosophy of Science*. Ed. Sandra Harding and Merrill B. Hintikka. Boston: D. Reidel Publishing Company, 1983. 207–24.

Kennedy, J. Gerald. "The Sundered Self in the Riven World: *Love in the Ruins*." *The Art of Walker Percy*. Ed. Panthea Reid Broughton. Baton Rouge: Louisiana State UP, 1979. 115–36.

Kobre, Michael J. "'A Quality of Consciousness': Walker Percy's Dialogic Art." Diss. Ohio University, 1992.

Lauter, Estella. *Women as Mythmakers: Poetry and Visual Art by Twentieth-Century Women*. Bloomington: Indiana UP, 1984.

Lawson, Lewis A., and Victor A. Kramer, eds. *Conversations with Walker Percy*. Jackson: UP of Mississippi, 1985.

———. *More Conversations with Walker Percy*. Jackson: UP of Mississippi, 1993.

Ostriker, Alicia Suskin. *Stealing the Language: The Emergence of Women's Poetry in Amer-ica*. Boston: Beacon Press, 1986.

———. "The Thieves of Language: Women Poets and Revisionist Mythmaking." *Signs: Journal of Women in Culture and Society* 8.1 (Autumn 1992): 68–90.

Percy, Walker. "Confessions of a Moviegoer." Typed Ms. Folder A.3.1, Series I (Cata-logue #4294). University of North Carolina-Chapel Hill (received 1981).

———. *The Message in the Bottle: How Queer Man Is, How Queer Language Is, and What One Has to Do with the Other*. New York: Farrar, Straus and Giroux, 1980.

———. *The Moviegoer*. New York: Alfred A. Knopf, 1980.

———. *Signposts in a Strange Land*. Ed. Patrick Samway. New York: Farrar, Straus and Giroux, 1991.

Poteat, Patricia Lewis. *Walker Percy and the Old Modern Age*. Baton Rouge: Louisiana State UP, 1985.

Ruether, Rosemary Radford. *Sexism and God-Talk: Toward a Feminist Theology*. Boston: Beacon Press, 1983.

Sellers, Susan. *Language and Sexual Difference: Feminist Writing in France*. New York: St. Martin's Press, 1991.

℘ Contributors

SUKANYA BANERJEE is Assistant Professor in the Department of English, University of Wisconsin-Milwaukee. Also affiliated with the Women's Studies program, her teaching and research interests include Postcolonial Studies, Victorian Literature and Culture, and Studies of Transnationalism and Diaspora. Currently, she is working on a book that examines notions of citizenship and national identity within the diasporic framework of the late nineteenth-century British Empire.

SARAH BRUSKY is completing a Ph.D. in English at the University of Florida. Her current study explores representations of African American women's bodies in turn-of-the-century America. She has published articles on nineteenth-century black and white women's literature.

CHU-CHUEH CHENG is Associate Professor of English at National Chung-hsing University in Taiwan. She earned her doctoral degree from Texas Christian University in 2000. Her previous publications include journal articles on Shakespearean drama and Victorian novels. She is currently working on a study of Kazuo Ishiguro's rhetorical strategies.

JESSICA ENEVOLD received her Ph.D. in English at Göteborg University and Blekinge Institute of Technology in Sweden. Her thesis "Women on the Road: Regendering Narratives of Mobility" investigates the entrance of women into narratives of the road, looking specifically at the relationship between women's subjectivity and mobility. Her current interests include representations of mobile women in popular culture and expressions of contemporary feminist movements. She also works with other scholars on the symbolic and actual place of women's mobility in transport policy, national and international, and its concrete manifestations.

KRISTIN FITZPATRICK is currently in charge of localization training at Microsoft. Prior to that, she was an Assistant Professor of English at Tunghai University in Taichung, Taiwan. She has had "Disillusioning Eve: Caroline Kirkland's Gendering of America" (University of Minnesota, 1997) and "What is the Place of Literary Studies in Taiwan?" (Tunghai University, 1999) published as part of conference proceedings. "The Travels of Nancy Prince" is drawn from her dissertation, *Broads Abroad*, which she further researched and revised while on a grant at the Huntington Library.

CORINNE FOWLER is currently writing her Ph.D. thesis on contemporary travel writing about Afghanistan. She has a special interest in the relationship between travel writing and ethnography and, in addition, between travel writing and imperialism. She has co-edited the forthcoming issue of *Journeys*, which focuses on those ethical dilemmas that narratives of travel invariably raise. In her spare time, Corinne makes radio documentaries, which strive to put into practice some recent ethnographic theories regarding equitable cross-cultural representation.

TERRI A. HASSELER is Chair and Associate Professor in the Department of English and Cultural Studies at Bryant College, Smithfield, Rhode Island. She is the V.P. of the Northeast Victorian Studies Association. She has published various articles on postcolonial studies, Victorian literature of empire, and feminism. She is currently working with Sue Lonoff on an MLA *Approaches to Teaching Wuthering Heights* edition.

ROSETTA R. HAYNES is Associate Professor of English and Women's Studies at Indiana State University in Terre Haute, Indiana. She has published articles on African American and Multicultural American women's autobiographical writing.

RUTH Y. JENKINS is Professor of English at California State University, Fresno. She has published *Reclaiming Myths of Power: The Victorian Spiritual Crisis and Women Writers* as well as numerous articles on nineteenth-century British writers and feminist, cultural, and writing theory.

RACHEL JENNINGS has a Ph.D. from the University of Warwick, United Kingdom, on contemporary British travel writing. She teaches composition and literature at Antelope Valley College, Lancaster, California, and has published articles on the U.S. road trip and women's travel.

LINDA LEDFORD-MILLER earned her doctorate in Comparative Literature from the University of Texas at Austin in 1988. She is Professor of Spanish, Portuguese, and Women's Studies at the University of

Scranton in Scranton, Pennsylvania. She received three Fulbrights (Brazil, 1979; Guatemala, 1990; and Mozambique, 2000) and has published many articles on travel writing, literature of the Americas, and minority writers of the United States.

HEIDI SLETTEDAHL MACPHERSON is Reader in North American Literature at the University of Central Lancashire in Preston, England. She is the author of *Women's Movement: Escape as Transgression in North American Feminist Fiction* and the co-editor of *Transatlantic Studies* and *New Perspectives in Transatlantic Studies*. She is a co-director of the Maastricht Center for Transatlantic Studies and has published widely in the fields of women's writing, transatlanticism, and contemporary literature.

MARGARET McCOLLEY holds a Ph.D. in French language and literature from the University of Virginia (and has recently taught at the University of Provence, Aix-Marseille). She has published widely in journals on the subject of women's travel and identity.

KATHLEEN SCULLIN is Professor of English at Mount Mary College in Milwaukee, Wisconsin. She has published several articles on philosophical and cultural themes in the fiction of Walker Percy and Flannery O'Connor. At present, she is completing a book on the intersections of feminist thought and Walker Percy's fiction.

KRISTI SIEGEL is Associate Professor of English and Division Chair of Languages, Literature, and Communication at Mount Mary College in Milwaukee, Wisconsin. She published *Women's Autobiographies, Culture, Feminism* (Peter Lang, 1999, 2001), edited another collection of essays about travel writing, *Issues in Travel Writing: Empire, Spectacle, and Displacement* (Peter Lang, 2002), serves as General Editor for the book series, *Travel Writing Across the Disciplines* (Peter Lang), and has published various articles on postmodern, feminist, cultural, and autobiographical theory.

⅌ Index

A

abolition, and Leonowens, Anna , 142, 144, 145, 146, 155, 157; Prince, Nancy , 173, 179, 270–272, 273, 275

advertising (advertisers, commercials), 105, 211

Africa, 1, 4, 6, 18, 33, 50, 205, 210; Bird, Isabella, 127; David-Néel, Alexandra, 288; Dixie, Lady Florence, 24–25, 28; Kingsley, Mary, 144; Marshall, Paule, 204, 205; Morrison, Toni, 194

African American, 6, 181–190, 194, 205, 206, 263–278

African American women preachers, 6, 181–190

alterity, 20, 155, 205, 241, 242, 288–289

America, 4, 6, 8, 64, 65, 84–86, 88, 92n21, Mukherjee, Bharati, 201–204; Prince, Nancy, 173, 176, 178, 263–277; Trollope, Frances, 133–139; 144–160

American culture, 5, 8, 65; critiqued by Trollope, Frances, 126–133; and road genre, 74–76, 84, 86, 88, 98–99, 103–105, 108–109; Mukherjee, Bharati, 200–203; Prince, Nancy, 173, 177, 263–278

America Day by Day, 75, 86, 91

American dream, 103, 117n6, 200

anarchist (David-Néel, Alexandra), 279

anonymity, 98, 114

anticonquest, 210–211, 215

antitouristic, 210, 213

ashram, 284, 285, 286, 288

Asia, 32, 33, 39, 123, 127; Leonowens, Anna, 139, 140, 144, 145, 150, 162n28; David-Néel, Alexandra, 279–280, 284–285, 287–288, 290

Atwood, Margaret, 294, 295, 306n6

Austria, 34, 41, 43, 47

authenticity, 134, 136, 142, 158, 161n10, 213

authority, 37, 58, 125, 126, 141, 144, 150, 158, 186–187, 189, 237, 250; narrative authority, 209–221; Prince, Nancy, 265, 272, 273, 275, 277

autobiographical, 10n2, 15, 28n5, 89, 123, 158, 214, 217, 236–237, 241, 246, 267

autobiography, 5, 6, 7, 10n2, 123, 186, 215, 230, 249, 250; and Victorian women's travel writing, 134, 138, 139, 161n10

B

Beauvoir, Simone de, 75, 76, 80, 81, 87, 91n7

Belgium, 135, 281, 282, 290

Bhabha, Homi, 15, 16, 20

Bible, 187, 273, 275

Birch, Eva Lennox, 205

black diaspora, 194, 205

Blixen, Karen, 210

Blunt, Alison, 15

body, women's, 10n1, 80–81, 115, 153, 294; Lawrence, Rosamond, 253–260; and medical analysis, 60–62

body/embodiment, 9, 105, 236, 253, 293–307

border crossing, 196, 279

bourgeois, 8, 15, 27n1, 44; David-Néel, Alexandra, 281–284; Trollope, Frances, 126, 127, 130, 133

Buddhist, 284, 285

Burton, Antoinette M., 27n1

Buss, Helen M., 7, 10

C

Calderón de la Barca, Frances, 7, 225–233

camp meetings, 187–188
car guy, 109, 111, 114, 115, 116
Carter, Angela, 57, 70
Carter-Sanborn, Kristin, 201, 203
Cartesian thought, 9, 293–307
Catholic, 7, 131, 282, 300; Calderón de
    la Barca, Frances, 225–233;
    Montagu, Lady Mary, 36–39
Catholic Europe, 37
Catholicism, 7, 36, 37, 38, 39, 225–233;
    Elaw, Zilpha, 182, 183
celibacy, 182, 190n3, 190n5
Christianity, 32, 38, 152, 162n20, 275
church, 184, 186, 187, 225, 273
Ciolkowski, Laura, 17, 19, 28
citizenship, 37, 264, 266, 268, 275, 276
civilized, 211, 247, 284, 288
class, 1, 2, 5, 8, 194; Calderón de la
    Barca, Frances, 227, 230;
    Lawrence, Rosamond, 244, 246,
    251; Leonowens, Anna, 142, 144,
    146, 156; Montagu, Lady Mary,
    31, 32, 45, 46; Prince, Nancy, 173,
    269, 270; road genre, 102, 103;
    Trollope, Frances, 128, 130, 133;
    and women travelers, 15, 20; and
    women traveling alone, 55, 60–
    61, 65, 66, 68, 69
Cohen, Patricia Cline, 60, 70
colonial, 3, 7, 31, 209, 215, 220; David-
    Néel, Alexandra, 279, 280, 288;
    Lawrence, Rosamond, 235–261;
    Leonowens, Anna, 139, 151, 153;
    Leonowens and Trollope, 159,
    163n30; Prince, Nancy, 265, 268,
    270, 273, 274; and Victorian
    women travelers, 15–29
colonial gaze, 16
colonialism, 2, 153, 158, 237, 246;
    Prince, Nancy, 265, 268–270, 274
conquest, 4, 9n1, 81, 210, 218, 219, 220,
    294, 295, 304
Constantinople, 32, 43, 48, 49, 51n2
contact zones, 19, 21
contact zones, internalized, 19, 21
conversion, 149, 152, 162n20, 232, 267,
    304; Elaw, Zilpha, 183, 187, 188

Coombes, Annie E., 16, 28
cosmopolitanism, 48
Couser, G. Thomas , 205, 206, 207
cross-cultural dressing, 213
cross-dressing, 53, 103, 213, 241;
    Lawrence, Rosamond, 241, 245,
    246, 248, 249, 250
culture, 3, 5, 7, 61, 123, 132, 136, 160,
    203, 214, 264; Maasai/Tibetan,
    212, 213, 216, 218, 219, 220;
    Montagu, Lady Mary, 32, 36, 44,
    48, 51n4; patriarchal, 181, 189n2,
    198, 199, 305; popular, 102, 112,
    115, 118, 119; postmodern, 196;
    Trollope and Leonowens, 132,
    143, 158, 159; perceptions of
    Victorian women travelers, 15,
    16, 22–27; western/Cartesian,
    293, 304
cultural home, 285
Curtis, Barry, 199, 203, 205, 207
customizers (cars), 107, 109

D
Daly, Margo, 76, 93, 94
David-Néel, Alexandra, 8, 209, 221,
    279–291
Davidson, Robyn, 68, 70
Davies, Carole Boyce, 205, 206, 207
death, 107; Calderón de la Barca,
    Frances, 230, 231; David-Néel,
    Alexandra, 288, 290; Elaw,
    Zilpha, 183; Lawrence,
    Rosamond, 242, 248, 250, 254,
    255, 256; *Moviegoer, The* (Binx
    Bolling), 299, 203, 303; Prince,
    Nancy, 167, 169, 170, 175;
    Robinson, Marilynne, 196, 198
deceased sister, 238, 249, 250
Dechen Ashram, 284, 286, 288
Derrida, Jacques, 73, 93
Descartes, René, 293, 298, 305n2, 306
de-scripting, 84, 85, 88, 90
desire, 212; Elaw, Zilpha, 181, 184,
    187, 189; male, 294, 295, 296, 299;
    to travel, 195, 198, 199, 281, 282,
    283, 284, 290; of Victorian

women travelers, 16, 17, 19, 20, 22, 23, 25, 26, 29

diaspora, 124, 157, 158, 194, 199, 205, 208

Digne, 287, 290

displacement, 123, 164, 196, 214, 221, 281, 286

Dixie, Lady Florence, 3, 16, 17, 19, 21, 24–27, 28

Doane, Mary Ann, 26, 28

domestic ideology, 181, 182, 185, 189n2

Domestic Manners of the Americans, 6, 11, 126–129, 133, 134, 135–139, 142, 144, 158, 160n1, 160n5, 165

domesticity, 37, 77, 98, 114, 115, 129, 130; Elaw, Zilpha, 181–190; Robinson, Marilynne, 197, 198, 207

double-consciousness, 23, 26

double-voiced, 26

Douglas, Susan J., 64, 66, 58, 70n4, 70

Dubinsky, Karen, 20, 28

E

Easy Rider, 76, 85, 88, 93

eccentric female, 17, 27

Ecclesiastes, 282

Edwards, Amelia, 3, 16–27, 28, 29

Elaw, Zilpha, 6, 181–191

England, 15, 19, 124, 212, 235, 236, 241, 245, 246, 281; Leonowens, Anna, 143, 146, 150, 151; Montagu, Lady Mary, 32, 38, 40, 41, 43, 45, 50; Trollope, Frances, 130, 131, 132, 134, 137, 160n6

English Governess at the Siamese Court, The, 6, 10, 139, 142, 157, 161n15, 164

environment, 110, 111, 161n9, 235, 259, 258

escape, 17, 76, 77, 114, 115, 193, 196; *Moviegoer, The* (Binx Bolling), 295, 299, 303, 304, 305n4

essentialism, 113, 269

ethnicity, 8, 201, 202, 204, 266

ethnocentrism, 220

Europe, 4, 16, 25, 144, 146–156, 162n5; Lawrence, Rosamond, 256, 257; Montagu, Lady Mary, 31–54; Prince, Nancy, 268, 274, 276

European, 2, 256; David-Néel, Alexandra, 285, 286; Grand Tour, 15, 57; interpretations of Eastern culture, 3, 21, 31, 41, 48; Leonowens, Anna, 139, 144, 146, 147, 152, 154, 155; sensibilities applied to other cultures, 46, 49, 50, 52n9, 146; Trollope, Frances, 127, 135, 136

existentialism, 76, 87

exotic, 40, 90, 124, 125, 202, 210; Leonowens, Anna, 142, 144, 149, 151, 155, 157

F

fabrication, 132, 142, 147, 161n10

feminine picturesque, 254

feminine/masculine, constructions of, 66, 80, 81, 83, 92n17, 102, 109, 110, 112, 116, 237; Lawrence, Rosamond, 243, 244, 249, 250, 254; of Victorian women travelers, 18, 21, 22, 24, 25, 26, 125; women's travel, 195, 197

feminism, 27n1, 44, 77–78, 82, 85, 87

feminist(s), 3, 9, 56, 74, 76, 78, 80, 85, 87, 89, 92n18, 141; in relation to African-American women, 181; Karko, Kate, 217; Percy, Walker, 293–307; and "politics of location," 186; psychoanalytic, 193; Robinson, Marilynne, 200; and stereotypes of women's travel, 220

fetish/fetishism, 20, 155, 298; cars, 100, 104–111

Flaming Iguanas, 81, 82, 85, 88, 90, 94, 113, 118

Foucault, Michel, 209

France, 241; David-Néel, Alexandra, 280, 281, 285, 287; Trollope, Frances, 131, 135

Frank, Katherine, 18, 29

Friedman, Ellen, 199, 207
fugue, 282
Fuller, Margaret, 59, 70
Fussell, Paul, 210

G

Gatens, Moira, 301, 306
gaze, androcentric, 3, 15–29, 115, 153,
 194, 296; female, 153, 154;
 western, 142, 157, 210, 219, 282
gender, 1–11, 21; and black women,
 185, 190n5, 194, 196, 266, 269,
 275; and genre, 73, 75, 76, 79, 83,
 86, 88, 89, 90, 158, 159
 Leonowens, Anna, 142, 143, 144,
 146, 153–155; and location, 196,
 197, 207; Montagu, Lady Mary,
 31–32, 35, 36, 37, 41, 43–45, 47–
 50; and narrative authority, 217,
 220; and road trip genre, 98, 100–
 103, 105–110, 114–116;
 theorizations of, 80, 81, 117n1,
 160, 264, 305, 305n3; Trollope,
 Frances, 127, 130; Victorian
 women's perceptions of, 16, 17,
 20, 24, 26, 158
gendered critique, 44
generic boundaries, 131, 158
Genghis Khan, 284
genre, 1, 4, 5–7, 9, 19, 27; gothic, 167–
 180; road literature, 74–76, 79,
 80, 81, 83, 84, 86, 90, 168, 174,
 175, 178, 209, 220, 265; spiritual
 narrative/slave narrative, 265;
 women's travel writing, 31, 125,
 132–139; *see also* gender, and
 genre
Gikandi, Simon, 27, 29
Gilbert, Sandra M., 27n2, 29, 60, 70, 72
Gilligan, Carol, 23, 29
going native, 212, 214
Gordon, Lady Lucie Austin Duff, 3,
 16–21, 25–26, 28n4, 29
gothic narration, 172
gothic theory, 167, 168, 177, 178
governess, 139–147, 148, 160, 161n12
Grand Tour, 15, 57

Gray, Rockwell, 201, 207
Gregory, Derek, 79–80, 82, 91n16, 93
Grewal, Inderpal, 57, 58, 70
Gubar, Susan, *see* Gilbert

H

Hanoi, 292
harem, 41, 43–44, 46–47, 51n6, 140–
 147, 151–156, 162n20, 162n25
Hatem, Mervat, 21, 25, 28n4, 29
Haute Provence, 287
Hayward, Susan, 20, 29
Heat-Moon, William Least, 75, 94, 99,
 118
Hennessy, Rosemary, 20, 29
Himalayas, 279, 282, 284, 288, 290, 291
Hindu, 202, 231, 282
Hollywood, 64, 65, 66, 67, 68, 156
home, 5, 8, 126, 129, 130, 133, 158, 176,
 204, 206, 241, 263, 264; and black
 women, 185, 266, 270, 274, 276,
 277; David-Néel, Alexandra,
 279–291; as women's proper
 place, 6, 62, 63, 65, 66, 97, 127,
 181, 185, 230, 232
honorary manhood, 218
horror, 17, 18, 21, 26; in gothic, 167,
 171, 172, 175, 176, 177, 178
Housekeeping, 193, 196–198, 208
Hugo, Victor, 282
Huguenot, 282
hybridity, 148
hysteric, 22

I

ideal, of womanhood, 19, 37, 158, 244;
 Turkey as, 45
identity, 1, 6, 7–9, 15, 23, 26, 196, 197,
 201–205, 207, 212, 293, 295, 299,
 301; David-Néel, Alexandra,
 279–291; Elaw, Zilpha, 188;
 Lawrence, Rosamond, 235–261;
 Montagu, Lady Mary, 36–37, 41,
 48, 51n4; Prince, Nancy, 261–278;
 and travel, 20, 195, 197
imperialism, 8, 142, 157, 236, 240, 269

Incorporated Wife, 244, 260n1, 260
India, 7, 8, 21, 150, 202, 215, 235–261, 279
Indian "Mutiny", 236, 247
indigenization, 212–213, 217
intertextuality, 126, 156, 159, 160
Islam, 32, 38–39

J

Jamaica, 8, 168, 171–178, 264–266, 268, 274, 276, 278
Japan, 127, 289
Jasmine, 195, 197, 200–204, 206, 207
Jong, Erica, 97, 92n22, 92n23, 94
journey, 9, 15, 74, 124, 126, 193, 200, 203, 205, 206–207, 293, 299, 300, 301, 304, 305

K

Kaplan, Caren, 29, 57, 58, 71, 146, 156, 164, 210, 211, 213, 214, 221
Kaplan, E. Ann, 20, 21, 29
Karko, Kate, 7, 209–221
Keller, Evelyn Fox, 296, 297, 305n2, 305n5
Kerouac, Jack, 4, 10, 75, 76, 82, 83, 94, 78, 118
Kierkegaard, Søren, 305n4
King Mongkut, 139, 140, 148, 151, 153, 154, 155, 156, 157, 160n8, 161n13, 162n20, 162n28, 163n31
Kingsley, Mary, 17–19, 23, 26, 29, 127, 144, 160n3
Kirby, Kathleen, 197, 207
Kowalewski, Michael, 204, 207
Kristeva, Julia, 22, 27, 29

L

Lackey, Kris, 74, 94, 98, 102, 104, 110, 118
Lawrence, Henry, 235, 286, 241, 242, 243, 244
Lawrence, Honoria, 242, 245, 251, 252
Lawrence, Karen, 9n1, 10, 97, 111, 118, 195, 199, 200, 201, 206, 208
Lawrence, Louisa , 250–260

Lawrence, Rosamond, 235–261
Leclerc, Annie, 300
Lee, Jarena, 185, 186, 189, 190n5
Leonowens, Anna, 5, 6, 10, 123, 139–146, 147–160, 161n9, 161n19, 162n23, 162n24, 162n26, 162n31
letters, 3, 4, 7, 15, 19, 31, 32, 33, 35, 36, 37, 40, 40, 44, 45, 47, 49, 50, 129; Calderón de la Barca, Frances, 225, 231, 232, 232n1; David-Néel, Alexandra, 8, 280, 282, 283, 284, 285, 286, 287, 289, 290
Levine, Philippa, 15, 16, 29
Lhasa, 279, 284, 291
Life in Mexico, 225, 232, 233
literacy, 265, 268, 275, 276
"Little Red Riding Hood", 4, 55–57, 65, 70, 71
Lopez, Erika, 85–87, 92n23, 94, 113, 117

M

Maasai, 7, 209, 211, 213, 214, 216, 218, 219, 220
MacCannell, Dean, 179n9, 180, 211, 212
mantra, 65, 280
manumission, 270
marketing, 80, 90, 111, 112, 114, 117n8
Markham, Beryl, 1, 10, 28n5, 30, 210, 221
Marshall, Paule, 6, 196, 204–208
Martin, Emily, 61–62, 71
masculine/feminine, *see* feminine/masculine
mass tourism, 210, 211
Memsahib, 8, 215, 217, 235, 236, 240–245, 252, 253–258, 260
Mexico, 7, 225–233
Middleton, Dorothy, 15
Mills, Sara, 1, 10, 16, 26, 98, 113, 117n1, 119, 155, 164, 215, 219, 221, 237, 251, 261
Minh-ha, Trinh T., 20, 162n18, 196, 208
missionaries, 147, 148, 162n20, 183, 270, 273
Mohan, Rajeswari, 20, 29

Moi, Toril, 80–81, 92n17, 92n18, 92n19, 94
Montagu, Lady Mary, 3, 31–54
morality, 4, 44, 55, 57, 61, 66, 69, 138, 189n2, 196, 272, 275
Morris, Mary, 2, 10n1, 11, 194, 208
Morrison, Toni, 194, 205, 208, 263, 278
movies/moviegoing, 64, 65, 66, 77, 78, 98, 100, 103, 294, 296, 303
Mukherjee, Bharati, 6, 195, 200–205, 208
Mulvey, Laura, 20, 27n3, 29, 66, 71
myth/mythic, 55, 89, 194, 200, 202, 205, 256, 257, 258, 259, 293, 294, 296, 299, 303, 304, 305, 306n6

N

Nang Harm, 141, 145, 146, 153, 154, 162n20
Napier, Sir Charles, 236, 238, 239, 240, 241, 245–250, 251, 259
narrative authority, 215, 217, 220
national identity, 8, 27, 100, 263, 264, 266, 272
Néel, Philippe, 280, 287
new women, 17, 93
nomadic, 213, 215, 217, 218, 220, 280, 283
nomads, 198, 210, 213, 216, 217, 218

O

Oddie, Catherine, 7, 11, 209–221
Oedipus complex, 193, 199
oedipal, 193, 200
Orientalism, 46, 47, 50, 156
Orientalness, 147, 148, 151
Ostriker, Alicia, 294, 297, 307
Other (racial/ethnic), 20, 21, 26, 27, 203, 242
Ottoman Empire, 3, 9, 31–53

P

Pajaczkowska, Claire, 199, 203, 205, 207
paradox, 129, 131
Parisian, 283

Paxton, Nancy L., 21, 29, 237, 252, 261
Penelope Pitstop, 5, 97, 98, 102, 110, 114–116, 117n5, 119
Percy, Walker, 9, 11, 293–307
performance, 6, 78, 89, 98, 105, 118; and identity, 195, 196; as a woman, 244, 252
Phenomenon, 15, 16, 21, 22, 23, 24, 26, 27, 147
pilgrimage, 18, 99, 105, 109, 149, 284, 304
place, 5, 8, 26, 43, 62, 124, 125, 152, 195, 205, 240, 276, 281, 283, 284, 287, 294, 296
platonic memsahib, 242–245, 256, 258, 260
postmodernism, 88, 90
Praisesong for the Widow, 196, 197, 204, 207, 208
Pratt, Annis, 198, 208
Pratt, Mary Louise, 16, 19, 29, 45, 53, 146, 153, 164, 210, 217, 218, 221
pretouristic, 219
Primeau, Ronald, 74, 94
Prince, Nancy Gardner, 6, 8, 11, 70, 167–180, 263–278
private sphere, 5, 125, 155, 162n19, 182, 185
Protestant, 7, 34, 37, 39, 131, 148, 190, 225–233
psychology and gothic narration, 167, 168, 169, 170, 171, 172, 177, 178
public sphere, 5, 6, 47, 140, 181, 182

Q

quest, 9n1, 111, 184, 193, 195, 199, 205, 303, 304, 306

R

race, 1, 5, 16, 20, 60, 69, 207; and black women writers, 194, 196; Leonowens, Anna, 142, 146; and Turkey, 49, 50, 52n7; Prince, Nancy, 176, 177, 269, 277; and power, 217
racism, 172, 182, 264, 268, 269, 272, 274

radical spiritual motherhood, 181, 182
readership (of women's travel
      writing), 108, 113, 135, 141, 144,
      145, 161n11, 271,
Reform Bill, the, 137
remapping, 35,
repatriation, 276
representation, of America, 127; of the
      "boundaries" of Europe, 40, 46,
      50; of men, 106, 108, 109; of
      women, 78, 97, 111, 112, 113, 114,
      115, 116, 194, 207
rhetoric, 4, 16, 33, 39, 84, 88, 101; of
      class and race, 45, 46, 47, 49, 57;
      of home, 281; of imperialism,
      143, 219, 242; Leonowens, Anna,
      on Southeast Asia, 145, 146, 151,
      152, 153, 155; of medicine, 61, 62,
      63, 64; Prince, Nancy, 268, 272,
      273; of travel, 124, 128, 130, 135,
      136; about women, 57
rhetoric of peril, 4, 55, 61, 62, 63, 66,
      68, 69
road genre, 74, 76, 80, 81, 84, 87, 90,
      92n20, 99
road movie, 66, 76, 92n20, 98, 108
road trip, 4, 5, 64, 76, 83, 84, 86, 97, 98,
      99, 102, 103, 104, 105, 106, 108,
      109, 112, 114, 115, 116, 188
Roberts, Jill, 201, 208
Robertson, George, 195, 207
Robinson, Jane, 10n1, 11, 58, 59, 71
Robinson, Marilynne, 6, 193, 196, 197,
      198, 199–200, 203, 208
Romance of the Harem, The, 6, 10, 139,
      141, 142, 164
Roy, Violet, 18, 29
Russia, 6, 8, 168, 169, 170, 175, 264,
      265–270, 272, 273, 274, 276
Rycaut, Paul, 28, 38, 39, 51, 53

S

Said, Edward, 16, 29, 32, 47, 50n1,
      92n16, 151, 156, 159, 162n24, 216,
      247, 261, 268, 284
sanctification, 181, 183, 186, 189n2
scripting, 79, 84, 92n16

search, 247, 293, 294, 298, 299, 300,
      301, 302, 303
self/selfhood, 215, 286, 289, 294, 305,
      306n6
semiotic, 22, 24
sentimentalized heroine, 244
serial domesticity, 184–185
ship, travel on, 18, 19, 171, 176, 196,
      204, 205, 206, 273, 274, 275, 276
Siam, 6, 123, 139, 140–147, 148, 149,
      150, 152, 153, 154, 156, 157, 160,
      160n8, 161n9, 161n10, 162n20,
      162n23
Sikkimese, 279
slavery, 124, 126, 134, 144, 145, 147,
      155, 171, 172, 173, 175, 178, 182,
      194, 206, 265, 266, 268, 275
Smith, Sidonie, 21, 28n5, 29, 217, 237,
      250, 254
social critique, 123, 132, 139, 157
Song of Solomon, 194, 208
South (United States), 206, 266, 270,
      274, 275, 276
spectacle, 3, 17, 21, 26, 98, 112, 115,
      124, 142, 147, 176, 177, 213
spectator, 17, 19, 20, 26, 28n3, 77, 98,
      154
spiritual maternity, 182, 183, 184
spirituality, 60, 107
Steinbeck, John, 75, 91n2, 94, 105, 111,
      116, 119
stereotype, 132, 147, 150, 157, 173, 270;
      of gender, 78, 80, 81
subject, 4, 5, 74, 296; black women as,
      265, 274, 275, 276; colonizing, 32,
      35, 37, 46, 146, 157; Victorian, 19,
      26, 28n3; woman as, 88, 90, 115,
      201
Sula, 194, 208
symbolic, 22, 24, 184, 188
symbolic masculinity, 217

T

taboo, 5, 212, 217, 218, 219
Thailand, 6, 139, 140, 141, 156
Thelma & Louise, 4, 11, 64, 72, 76–88,
      91n13, 97, 114, 115, 119

Tibet, 8, 124, 209, 210, 211, 212, 213, 214, 216, 217, 219, 220; David-Néel, Alexandra, 279, 284, 286, 287, 288, 289
tourist, 88, 134, 135, 137, 157, 197, 202, 203, 204, 205, 206, 210–214, 219
transgression, 37, 44, 73, 125, 127, 143, 153, 158, 159, 217, 276
transience, 123, 125, 196, 198, 207
translocation, 21
transvestism, 16, 26, 28n5
travel, men vs. women, 1, 3, 4, 6, 9, 17, 21, 89, 97, 98, 113, 265
travel writing, 2; and autobiography, 7, 9, 139, 176; and fiction, 6, 36, 132, 141, 178; genre, 19, 73, 74, 79, 88, 89, 123, 124, 125; imperialism in, 142, 148, 158, 210; stereotypes of women's travel writing, 3, 4, 5, 155; tradition of male travel writing, 36, 37, 74, 79, 98, 124, 155, 168, 174, 209; Victorian women's, 26, 125; women's travel writing, 9, 31, 76, 98, 103, 113, 114, 117n1, 169, 195, 220
travel writing, genre, *see* travel writing, genre
travel writing, men's vs. women's, 5, 9, 26, 89, 98, 103, 113, 114, 155, 220
trespass, 123, 125, 144
Trollope, Frances, 5, 6, 11, 123, 126–139, 142, 144, 157, 158, 159, 160, 160n5, 160n6
Tucker, Lindsey, 197, 206, 208
Tunis, 49, 280, 283
Turkey, 31, 32–35, 38, 43–45, 47–50, 51n1, 51n10, 268
Tuttle, Cameron, 5, 110, 111, 114, 115, 116, 119

U
United States, travel in, 8, 75, 83, 84, 85, 137, 142, 168, 171, 172, 176, 202, 204, 266, 267, 268, 270, 271, 273, 274, 275

Upanishads, 282
upper- vs. lower-class women travelers, 2, 31, 32, 58, 59, 60–61

V
veiled lady, 167, 178
voyeur, 142, 153, 154, 155, 213

W
Wacky Races (Dastardly and Muttley, Arkansas Chugabug, Peter Perfect), 5, 97, 101, 102, 103, 104, 115, 117n5, 119
West Indies, 174, 264, 266, 268, 270, 271, 272, 274, 276
Where the Boys Are, 66–68, 70n3, 72
whiteness, as a race, 8, 206, 217, 263, 265, 278
Wickramagamage, Carmen, 201, 202, 203
woman writer, 158, 237
womanhood, Elaw, Zilpha, 189, 189n2; Prince, Nancy, 173, 178; Turkish, 40, 45; Victorian, 17, 19, 129, 130, 138, 146
women, traveling alone, 4, 55–71, 98, 103, 116, 173, 211, 276
Women's Autobiographies, Culture, Feminism, 10n2, 11, 70n2, 71
women's sentimental writing, 6, 181
women's suffrage, 144

Z
Zeppa, Jamie, 1, 11